\\\\\ *Singin' in the Rain*

Singin' in the Rain

THE MAKING OF AN

AMERICAN MASTERPIECE

///

EARL J. HESS AND

PRATIBHA A. DABHOLKAR

University Press of Kansas

Excerpts from the film
Singin' in the Rain
granted courtesy of
Turner Entertainment Co.

© 2009 by the University
Press of Kansas

Published by the
University Press of Kansas
(Lawrence, Kansas 66045),
which was organized by the
Kansas Board of Regents and
is operated and funded by
Emporia State University,
Fort Hays State University,
Kansas State University,
Pittsburg State University,
the University of Kansas, and
Wichita State University

Library of Congress
Cataloging-in-Publication Data

Hess, Earl J.
Singin' in the rain : the making of an American
Masterpiece / Earl J. Hess and Pratibha A.
Dabholkar.
    p.   cm.
Includes bibliographical references and index.
ISBN 978-0-7006-1656-5 (cloth : alk. paper)
1. Singin' in the rain (Motion picture)
I. Dabholkar, Pratibha A. II. Title.
PN1997.S5133H47 2009
791.43′72—dc22   2008054898

British Library Cataloguing-in-Publication Data
is available.

Printed in the United States of America

10 9 8 7 6 5 4 3 2 1

The paper used in this publication is recycled
and contains 30 percent postconsumer
waste. It is acid free and meets the minimum
requirements of the American National
Standard for Permanence of Paper for Printed
Library Materials z39.48-1992.

*For all the beautiful spirits who
inspired and guided this book.*

\\\\\ *Contents*

A photograph section follows page 106

When M-G-M released *Singin' in the Rain* in the spring of 1952, the golden era of the Hollywood musical was reaching its peak. Soon after, a number of developments contributed to the decline of the movie musical, including the divestment of the major studios from ownership of theaters, the rapid expansion of the television industry, and the increasing cost of producing lavish Technicolor films that mixed dancing with music, singing, and character development. None of the 237 creative people involved in making *Singin' in the Rain* could predict the demise of a genre that had enthralled millions of viewers since the advent of sound pictures in the late 1920s, although many of them sensed that important changes were just around the corner.

M-G-M was a moviemaking factory, and the actors, producers, directors, technicians, bit players, and musicians sandwiched their work on *Singin'* between equally hard work on other projects. They sensed that this movie was special, due to the collection of talent assembled for it, but no one thought it would become the classic of all movie musicals.

That exalted status developed over time. *Singin'* was a commercially and critically successful film from the time it was released, but its elevation to classic status began with repeated viewings. The picture appealed to succeeding generations, indicating that its qualities were timeless, until fans and critics began attaching accolades to it that set the movie apart from many other successful musicals.

Singin' in the Rain reached its exalted status in the 1970s with reflective analysis by film scholars and popular writers. Termed "probably the most popular of all Hollywood musicals, and a favorite subject for film students," it also was called "an American classic" and a "Hollywood hymn to itself." More recently, movie critic Pauline Kael called it "probably the most enjoyable of all American movie musicals." "Only a curmudgeonly wet blanket couldn't love *Singin' in the Rain*," as Judy Gerstel has written. She considered it "the pinnacle of the American movie musical." Or, as a newspaper reviewer wrote in 1997, "Watching it, you forget other movies exist."[1]

Those men and women who made the picture, of course, felt immense pride in their achievement. Even M-G-M employees who did not work on the project, like art director Jack Martin Smith, admired it immensely. "Pictures like *Singin' in the Rain* . . . you couldn't put more charm into a picture. I didn't do it. I wish I had, but it was a lovely thing."[2]

Despite its enormous popularity and the general feeling that *Singin'* represents something unusual among the outpouring of Hollywood film musicals, no one has written a full-scale history of the movie. A transcription of the release print, written as a screenplay, was published by the original scriptwriters Betty Comden and Adolph Green in 1972. John Mariani wrote a groundbreaking article on the picture in 1978, trumpeting its significance and including many quotes from interviews with participants. The only book-length study of *Singin' in the Rain* was authored by film scholar Peter Wollen. Published in 1992 as part of the British Film Institute's series of short studies, intended mostly for reading in university film classes, Wollen's book largely covers technical aspects of the movie.

None of the previous work on *Singin'* delves deeply into the many memoirs and recorded interviews of its participants, nor does it explore the rich storehouse of archival material that details the behind-the-scenes activity during its making. Moreover, no previous work has examined the marketing aspects of the movie, issues regarding its release, or why and how it evolved into a classic over the half century since it was first seen by appreciative audiences.

The rich literature on the history of movies tends to be bifurcated into two opposing camps that rarely mix. On the one hand, the majority of articles and books on movie history tend to be written by nonprofessional historians, and all too often they are based on slim research or a scanning of previously published secondary works. This type of literature is repetitive and geared for the widest possible reading audience. It is often marked by a concentration on colorful and sometimes unsubstantiated stories of the personalities involved.

At the other extreme is a small but growing collection of articles and books written by academics and geared toward serious students of the movie industry. Film scholars tend to focus on the finished product. They analyze the staging, choreography, camera movement, and other aspects of filmmaking from the standpoint of what one sees on the screen. History and biography sometimes make their way into this literature, but it is usually of secondary importance compared to film theory and cultural meaning.

Our book does not fall into either of these two categories. We agree that both traditions have an important role to play. The general histories entertain millions of people and help to create an expansive audience for film history. The film scholars rigorously focus on the central art of filmmaking and explicate it in detail for a small, thoughtful audience. But neither tradition makes full use of the rich storehouse of archival and published primary material that has always been available to writers, and neither tradition reaches a sizeable middle audience, the individual who desires more depth than the general histories provide and more breadth than the scholarly studies offer. Our book is an attempt to fill that broad middle ground between the two divergent traditions in the literature on movie history, and we hope that it appeals to readers at both extremes as well.

There is both an interesting and an important story to be told in the making of *Singin' in the Rain*. Such a story takes the history of this picture beyond the brief accounts normally found in newspaper retrospectives and commercial publishing ventures that stress the colorful stories behind moviemaking. Our purpose is to present a well-rounded history of the film, detailing its genesis, creation, production, marketing, and reception. Its legacy is an important part of the story as well, as are the biographies of people, large and small, who participated in making it the best film musical ever produced.

We cast our research net as widely as possible, making extensive use of unpublished letters, memos, production records, difficult to find magazine and newspaper stories, published interviews and memoirs, and unpublished oral histories. In addition, we have incorporated the assessments of film scholars, published in a variety of articles and books, and added our own insights to round out the full history of this film and its extended appeal to generations of students and viewers. Finally, many websites contain information about the movie and the people who made it, and we have carefully sifted through that material for reliable information not found elsewhere. In particular, the Internet Movie Database (IMDB) reliably provides basic factual information on thousands of people and movies, while much of the interpretative information it contains is questionable. As with our other sources, including interviews, books, and scholarly articles, we have taken what seems reliable from IMDB and left the rest behind, or discussed it in our endnotes.

We hope that our book will allow readers of all orientations to fully appreciate the rich history of *Singin' in the Rain* and the work of all the participants, from Gene Kelly down to the most obscure bit player, who contributed in their own way to making this American masterpiece. This book tells their story.

\\\\\ *Acknowledgments*

We wish to thank all the staff members at the libraries and archives we visited to gather material for this book. They played a key role in making rich material available to us, without which this study would not have been possible. Barbara Hall and the staff at the Margaret Herrick Library, Ned Comstock at the University of Southern California, and Ryan Hendrickson at Boston University deserve special commendation for their efforts in helping us.

We thank the Turner Entertainment Company for permission to use excerpts from the various scripts of *Singin' in the Rain* and the DeGolyer Library, Southern Methodist University, for permission to quote from the Ronald L. Davis Oral History Collection. We also thank the Columbia University Oral History Research Office and the Academy of Motion Picture Arts and Sciences for permission to quote from their oral history collections.

Our research was partially underwritten by a Jean Ritchie Fellowship from the Appalachian College Association in the summer of 2006. Lincoln Memorial University also supported the research for this study through its award of an Institutional Mini-Grant in 2007. Our thanks go to the folks at both the ACA and LMU for their help and encouragement in this endeavor.

We are especially grateful to Michael J. Briggs, editor in chief, for his enthusiastic support in making the manuscript into a book. His appreciation of the topic as well as of our writing offered us great encouragement. Our thanks to Susan Schott for her help and positive outlook and to the rest of the staff at the University Press of Kansas for their support. We also appreciated the help of the two manuscript reviewers, Rick Altman at the University of Iowa and John Tibbetts at the University of Kansas. Both offered high praise for our research and writing, strong support for publishing the manuscript, and ideas for improving it as well.

1

All We Were Told Was to Write a Movie

Betty Comden and Adolph Green changed their busy schedules in New York on the basis of a brief, but urgent, message. They had worked with producer Arthur Freed before, most notably on the highly successful film *On the Town,* and felt comfortable as adjunct members of the famed Freed Unit at Metro-Goldwyn-Mayer (M-G-M), the premier maker of Hollywood musicals. They knew only that Freed wanted them to write the screenplay and lyrics for a new picture—no details, but the Freed Unit was on a roll with one blockbuster after the other. If Arthur wanted them to make another musical, they were ready.[1]

The two writers arrived in Los Angeles on Monday, May 29, 1950, but no one had informed them that the employees of M-G-M would be gone for a longer than usual weekend to celebrate Memorial Day. They found offices empty and phones unanswered. Freed had left the pair "to grind our teeth to the eyeballs in frustration, and run up six days of epic phone bills calling our loved ones back East." It seemed an inauspicious beginning for the new project.[2]

When M-G-M opened for business again, Freed seemed more diffident than usual. He hesitated all morning to tell Comden and Green his ideas before finally exclaiming, "C'mon, kids, let's have some lunch." The writers were used to this; they knew Freed was not very articulate and liked to refer to his writers and actors as "kids" because he was almost a quarter-century older than most of them. He continued to put Comden and Green off during lunch and for most of the afternoon as well. It seemed as if the writers might end their seventh day in Hollywood with no more awareness of what they were expected to do than when they arrived. Freed finally broke down about 4 p.m. and said, "with a proud but shy chuckle," that he wanted them to choose songs from the Freed-Brown catalogue for the new movie. The title of the picture would be *Singin' in the Rain,* one of the songs Freed and Brown had written.[3]

Comden and Green knew Freed's history. He had given up his first show business career as a song plugger in the early 1920s to partner with the composer Nacio Herb Brown, and together they produced a number of popular song hits. With the coming of sound to the movies, the team quickly moved their wares into motion pictures. Here they enjoyed unusual success, placing their songs in many M-G-M musicals in the early days of sound pictures. Legendary films such as *The Broadway Melody* (1929) and *The Hollywood Revue of 1929* were filled with their tunes and lyrics. While Brown eventually dropped out of show business, Freed went on to become a major producer with M-G-M by the late 1930s, carefully crafting his own unit within the corporate structure and dedicating it to making musicals. He had not been shy about sprinkling his songs throughout his own movies, and now he wanted to relive the old days when entire films featured nothing but Freed-Brown tunes. Freed was just then making *An American in Paris,* which featured the songs of George and Ira Gershwin, so he felt there was a precedent for his scheme that would make the new project seem part of a logical sequence rather than an exercise in egotism.[4]

Ironically, Comden and Green were less than enthusiastic about Freed's idea at first, perhaps because they had been waiting a week and expected something more to do than recycle old tunes. They had also reached a pinnacle in their careers by the early 1950s, with the enormously successful stage production of *On the Town* and other theater musicals to their credit. Comden and Green refused to work on the new movie. They cited a clause in their M-G-M contract to argue that unless the lyrics were written by one of the three top names in musicals—Irving Berlin, Cole Porter, or Richard Rodgers—they were to write the lyrics themselves. Freed replied that he knew of no such clause, but the two insisted on it and left the office that evening adamant in their refusal to work on the new project.[5]

Over the next two weeks, Comden and Green continued to refuse every time Freed brought up the idea, until finally they thought about checking the contract. Much to their chagrin, the clause was a figment of their imagination. Apparently the two had discussed such a restriction while negotiating their contract but had forgotten, if they had ever bothered to check, that M-G-M never included it. With that issue settled, the two had little choice but to roll up their sleeves and start to work.[6]

The man who created the Freed unit and brought the Hollywood musical to its artistic and commercial peak was born September 9, 1894, in Charleston, South Carolina. His parents were members of the small but vibrant Jewish community of that port city, but the family later moved to Seattle. Arthur Freed attended Phillips Exeter Academy in New Hampshire. He became head of the household in his family when his father, an art dealer, died at a relatively early age. Freed later married Renee Klein, a Californian of Alsatian heritage. Their daughter Barbara was their only child.[7]

Freed eked out a living in the early 1920s plugging songs for a music publisher, playing the piano to move the merchandise, and performing a bit in vaudeville as well. He met his future partner Brown in 1921. Born Ignacio Herb Brown in Deming, New Mexico, on February 22, 1896, the composer grew up in Los Angeles where his father served as sheriff of the county. He attended the Musical Arts High School and the University of California, but dropped out of college to play the piano in vaudeville. Brown later operated a "custom-tailoring business" that catered to silent movie stars and invested in Hollywood real estate, writing songs as a sideline. He and Freed formed a partnership by the mid-1920s, writing tunes for stage musical revues.[8]

Sound technology offered huge opportunities for adding music to films, and all the major studios rushed to take advantage of it. Irving Thalberg, the major creative force at M-G-M, hired Freed and Brown to write songs for the studio's first all-sound musical film, *The Broadway Melody*, in 1929. The pair wrote six songs for the picture, three of which became major hits and were later included in *Singin' in the Rain*—"You Were Meant for Me," "The Broadway Melody," and "The Wedding of the Painted Doll." Brown played the piano for the recording of these songs, even though he received no screen credit, and he also served as musical director for the picture. *The Broadway Melody* was a resounding success that also set up the movie career of the song-writing team. Freed and Brown appeared as themselves in *The Song Writers' Revue* (1930), where Freed sang "The Wedding of the Painted Doll."[9]

Freed and Brown continued to collaborate throughout the 1930s until their day in the Hollywood sun began to fade. Louis B. Mayer, the boss at M-G-M, moved Freed from songwriter to producer in 1939, "specifically to develop musical properties." Hugh Fordin mentions that Brown left "to try his hand at serious composing," but exactly why the composer gave up entertainment and resumed his previous business pursuits is unclear. An executive at M-G-M named Robert Vogel later remembered him with ambivalence. Vogel said that Brown was "the real moving spirit of that team," and Freed "had just been the rear wheel on the cart." But Vogel also recalled that Nacio Herb Brown was widely known as "Nasty Old" Herb Brown at M-G-M.[10]

M-G-M AND MUSICALS: HOW IT ALL STARTED

Of all the studios that produced musicals, none came to shine more brightly than M-G-M. Formed by a merger of three companies in 1924, the studio engaged in the business of making musicals with a lavish expenditure of resources. The three companies which formed M-G-M included Metro Pictures, organized in 1915 and purchased by a distributing company headed by Marcus Loew five years later. Loew's strategy was to acquire production companies to ensure a steady flow of movies into his string of theaters. Another Loew acquisition was Goldwyn Pictures, organized in 1916 by independent producer Samuel Goldwyn. The company leased Triangle Studio in Culver City, six miles southwest of Hollywood, in 1918. New York advertising executive Howard Dietz (who later worked for M-G-M) came up with the slogan Ars Gratia Artis (Art for Art's Sake), as well as with the "roaring lion as a company trademark" for Goldwyn in 1921. Goldwyn left the company in 1922 and Marcus Loew acquired it two years later. He based his Goldwyn and Metro operations at the Culver City studio's six sound stages.[11]

Louis B. Mayer Productions became the third and final production company to form Loew's M-G-M. A small company created by Louis Burt Mayer, it nevertheless brought two important executives, Mayer and Irving Thalberg, into the Loew's operation. Mayer was born as Lazer Meir in 1885 in Dymer, Russia, twenty-five miles from Kiev. His birthdate was not recorded, so Mayer decided to make it the Fourth of July. The family immigrated to England in 1886 and to Canada after six years. Mayer later moved to Boston and engaged in the scrap metal business which his father had established in 1902. He indulged his interest in the entertainment industry by buying theaters to offer stage and film productions, and created his own film production company in 1914. When Loew acquired that company in late 1924, Mayer became vice-president in charge of production at M-G-M. Thalberg, one of Mayer's employees, became a major producer with the new corporation.[12]

Marcus Loew, the man who created all this, passed away in 1927, but Nicholas Schenck replaced him as president of M-G-M. With Thalberg managing the talent and setting high production standards, and Mayer handling the finances allowed him by Loew's and Schenck's New York–based headquarters, M-G-M acquired prestige and profit with a number of dramatic films in the 1920s.[13]

Sound prompted all the major studios to produce musicals. At first, they concentrated merely on adding talk to their output. While 70 percent of Paramount's releases in 1929 were talkies, and Fox released *all* talking pictures in the same year, less than half of M-G-M's 1929 movies were adapted to the new technology. Mayer wanted to catch up with his competition quickly and pinned his hopes on *The Broadway Melody,* an all-sound movie that also would become the first real film musical. Although it was packed with Freed-Brown songs and shot mostly at night to obtain quieter conditions, Mayer also decided to film a silent version to hedge his bets. The storyline set the pace for dozens of future musicals. Two sisters (played by Bessie Love and Anita Page) break up their act as a result of a love triangle with a budding songwriter, but the plot works to a happy ending. The actors put a great deal of heart into their performances and the movie offers viewers a backstage perspective on the interactions involved in producing a stage show called "The Broadway Melody."[14]

The Broadway Melody involved many innovations that became standard in musical films. It was "the first musical film with a completely original score," and witnessed the first dubbing in movie history. Thalberg was dissatisfied with the filming of "The Wedding of the Painted Doll," and insisted on a second, expensive shooting. Soundman Douglas Shearer realized the sound recording was fine and proposed reusing it to save money. Director Harry Beaumont agreed to film the number again, using a playback of the recording. This method solved a serious problem, for it was difficult to do everything at once in making a movie that not only talked but sang and danced. Compartmentalizing the various aspects of filming song and dance into manageable segments worked so well that it spread throughout the industry. "The Wedding of the Painted Doll" also was the first number filmed in color, a two-strip version of Technicolor.[15]

After only twenty-six days of filming, *The Broadway Melody* premiered on February 1, 1929, at Grauman's Chinese Theatre, following a performance of George Gershwin's *Rhapsody in Blue*. It opened in New York City a week later. Marketed as an "all-talking, all-singing, all-dancing" picture, *The Broadway Melody* took audiences by storm. The movie grossed $4,366,000, but $1,558,000 of that income was due to foreign distribution. It won an Oscar for best picture in April 1930, only the second Oscar given for that category, and was the first musical film to win the award.[16]

Harry Beaumont spoke to the premiere audience at Grauman's Theatre on opening night, thoughtfully pointing out that *The Broadway Melody* held the potential to shape the development of movie musicals. He called on other moviemakers to integrate the storyline and songs within their films, to avoid the revue format where songs and dances were assembled with little regard to their relevance to each other or to the movie as a whole. "I look upon real human interest stories with a natural musical setting as the most fertile field for progress here," Beaumont continued. "The direction of talking pictures demands much closer attention to detail than the silent film. A sound picture is virtually 'made' before its scenes are photographed, for every sequence must be rehearsed until it is perfect before the filming begins."[17]

Mayer and Thalberg apparently paid little attention to Beaumont's idea, for the other major movie which featured Freed-Brown songs in this era was a revue film exactly like the kind Beaumont wanted to avoid. The revue format offered a quick and easy way to make musicals. Jack Benny made his film debut as one of the two hosts of *The Hollywood Revue of 1929*, and the movie included virtually every star on the M-G-M payroll. The highlight of the picture was an elaborate Technicolor staging of the new Freed and Brown song "Singin' in the Rain," with Cliff Edwards ("Ukulele Ike") singing the song. The number was filmed on a large sound stage, with Noah's Ark as a background and dozens of chorines dressed in raincoats and hats. Among the stars participating in this number were Joan Crawford, Marion Davies, and Buster Keaton. The movie took in $2,421,000 and led to full-time contracts for Freed and Brown with M-G-M. Color sequences became the rage; *The Broadway Melody* and *The Hollywood Revue of 1929* were among sixty feature films which included color in 1929.[18]

Although the Depression began late that year, the studios issued fifty-two musical pictures in 1929, and the number rose to sixty-seven the next year. But then the market began to collapse; only seventeen musical films were released in 1931. The year of Franklin D. Roosevelt's first election to the presidency witnessed the low point in public interest in film musicals, but the release of *42nd Street* in 1933 marked a rebirth of the market. It was the first successful picture to carry on the ideas Beaumont had enunciated at the premiere of *The Broadway Melody* in 1929. It focused on characters and plot, revealing the backstage perspective on producing a Broadway musical comedy.[19]

42nd Street was a huge moneymaker for Warner Brothers, reviving an interest in film musicals among producers at the major studios. But the studios had to relearn some of the filming techniques pioneered in *The Broadway Melody*. In his first four films at RKO, Fred Astaire danced mostly to a live orchestra while trying to film his numbers. It did not work well, as the technical people at M-G-M could have told their counterparts at RKO. As Astaire later put it, the fifty-member orchestra was placed on the "extreme opposite side of the stage about a block away" from the camera so the technicians could "control the sound properly when picked up 'live' on the set." Astaire and everyone else involved in the burgeoning business of film musicals during the 1930s learned to pre-record music and songs and dub while filming.[20]

The Broadway Melody (1929) and *42nd Street* (1933) served as the starting points of the film musical, attempting to combine character, story, song, and dance into a single complicated package. M-G-M tried to duplicate its historic contribution with several "spin-offs," including *The Broadway Melody of 1936*, followed by another in 1938 and one in 1940. A fourth spin-off was planned for 1943 with Eleanor Powell and Gene Kelly, but it was dropped before production began when Kelly was loaned to Columbia for *Cover Girl* (1944).[21]

THE FREED UNIT

Irving Thalberg dominated production standards at M-G-M, but when he died in 1936, M-G-M could not replace him. This helped to open the door for Arthur Freed, who had worked as a songwriter at the studio throughout the decade. Freed became a full-time producer in 1939 with primary responsibility for handling musical projects.[22]

The production unit that Freed began to assemble over the years played a huge role in modernizing and improving the film musical. While drama and comedy had a long, sustained history from the beginning of motion pictures, musicals became possible only with the creation of sound technology. Compared to the film musicals of the 1940s and 1950s, the early efforts seen in *The Broadway Melody, The Hollywood Revue of 1929*, and even *42nd Street* seem crude. The singing is not necessarily of the highest order and the dancing often is the least enjoyable aspect of those movies, which are not as strong in their art or craft as the better dramas and comedies of their era.

Fred Astaire almost single-handedly improved both the dancing and the filming of dance numbers in his popular movies with Ginger Rogers during the 1930s, insisting that he be photographed in full figure with minimal cuts and no extraneous shots of the audience interwoven into the routine. Yet Astaire rarely tried to develop the characters he portrayed through his dance numbers. Arthur Freed and the unit he created at M-G-M built on Astaire's work at RKO and took the film musical to a new level, creating what many believe was a golden age of the Hollywood musical.[23]

Ironically, Nacio Herb Brown was not part of the Freed Unit. He returned to his real estate business and even moved to Mexico for a time. Brown continued to write songs for the movies now and then, but essentially retired from the entertainment business by the late 1940s.[24]

Freed's great strength lay in his ability to recognize talent and acquire it for his unit. "I brought in a whole new crowd of people," he later recalled. "I wanted a fresh start from what had been before, a combination of the new ideas that had been happening on the stage and what could be done with film. The early musicals were novelties, but few of them were *real* musicals."[25]

A key figure in the unit was Roger Edens. Born November 9, 1905, in Hillsboro, Texas, Edens came to Freed's attention in 1934 when he accompanied a singer-performer named Patricia Ellis at the piano during her audition. Freed recommended the studio hire Edens rather than Ellis, and the Texan eventually became his right-hand man. Many members of the Freed Unit could not pinpoint the exact role Edens played because he did so many things in a quiet, unassuming way. Comden and Green described him well: "Assisting in all departments, as musical supervisor, sometimes script shepherd, arranger, associate producer, general coordinator of production—sometimes one or all of these." The most visible, and perhaps the most important, task taken on by Edens was orchestrating movie scores, mostly from tunes composed by others, but often based on his original compositions as well. He was partly responsible for the lush sound of M-G-M musicals, along with M-G-M musical director Johnny Green (who conducted the studio orchestra in the recording hall) and several other gifted orchestrators such as Conrad Salinger.[26]

All the major studios organized around the unit concept, each unit headed by a producer and answerable to the studio chief. The units specialized in genres and often employed the same team of actors, directors, and technicians. A particular unit was responsible for the long run of Tarzan movies at M-G-M, for example. Freed eventually had to share the musical genre at the studio with two other producers, Joe Pasternak and Jack Cummings. Even though Cummings was Mayer's nephew, Freed received the lion's share of support and produced a greater number and higher quality of films compared to the other two. He concentrated on quality although his movies consistently made lots of money for Mayer. There existed an "unspoken competition," as director Vincente Minnelli put it, between Freed, Pasternak, and Cummings, but he agreed with Gene Kelly that the real competition existed between the musical units and those that produced dramatic films. As Minnelli explained, drama "could be made at half the cost of a musical and grossed twice as much."[27] This was an important financial consideration in the making of movie musicals. They were much more expensive than drama and comedy because they were more complex productions, involving a wide mixture of creative elements that had to harmonize (at least to some degree) for effect.

Freed initially concentrated on so-called barnyard musicals—simple stories about young people putting on a show in a barn. Films like *Babes in Arms* (1939) were popular and made money mostly because of the charisma between stars Judy Garland and Mickey Rooney, not because of particularly high levels of dancing, singing, or choreography. At a cost of three-quarters of a million dollars each, these films were relatively expensive compared to drama and comedy.[28]

But the Golden Age of the Hollywood musical would not have occurred if Freed had been satisfied with this level of attainment. Beginning with *Meet Me in St. Louis* (1944), the Freed Unit began to set an entirely new standard. Although he was not part of the project, Gene Kelly later said that *Meet Me in St. Louis* "was probably the first all-round Freed Unit picture on which Arthur found the level we should be working on."[29] Much of this came about because of Minnelli, who directed his first important success with this picture. Minnelli brought to his job a keen eye for color and set décor and knew exactly what he wanted from his actors, even though he found it hard to articulate his ideas to them. He also had a strong desire to meld good characterization and story development with top-notch singing. Judy Garland set the pace for the latter, and the film proved to be enormously popular with audiences.

By 1948, "the Freed Unit took on a different complexion," as Fordin notes, and a "more realistic, contemporary approach and style emerged, greatly influenced by the New York stage." This direction was engineered by a number of people Freed brought in from Broadway, including Comden and Green, Gene Kelly, and other stage actors and choreographers. Freed surrounded himself with young, sterling talent, and gave them the resources to practice their art. Peter Hay characterizes the Freed Unit as a "Broadway-Hollywood connection"; credits Freed, Edens, and Kelly with creating it; and says *Singin' in the Rain* was the "apotheosis, its major celebration of both the Broadway connection and MGM itself."[30]

Along with a higher level of artistic endeavor, movies produced by the Freed Unit strove to express character in the dances and songs, deepening the emotional significance of the numbers within the context of plot development. It also led to the insertion of complex dance numbers, bereft of songs, that came to be referred to as movie "ballets," inspired initially by the dream ballet in the stage version of *Oklahoma!* (1943). The Golden Age of the Hollywood musical came to rest mostly on the work of two inspired geniuses, Fred Astaire and Gene Kelly, both of whom did their best work for Freed at M-G-M.

With the increasing artistic complexity involved in making the Golden Age musicals came increasing demands for more money to make these films. While movies like *Babes in Arms* cost about $750,000, the Golden Age product demanded more than three times the amount

—nearly $3,000,000. Such a risky expenditure was possible only if results justified the risk, and Freed's best movies came through with huge profits, 250 percent according to some estimates. The total output of the Freed Unit brought in $14 million to M-G-M in 1948–1949 alone. Audience willingness to pay a higher admission price for these films compared to other movies played a huge role in creating the Golden Age of the Hollywood musical.[31]

The economics of producing movies in general began to alter right after World War II. Wartime emotions and studio ownership of theaters led to the highest output of movies in history during the early 1940s. But in May 1948, the federal courts decided that the studios had to divest themselves from theater ownership, cutting a key link between production and distribution. The separation would go into effect several years later, but it meant that independent theater owners could pick and choose which films to show. No longer was there an assured outlet for pictures, regardless of their quality, and the development portended leaner times for the movie industry. Coupled with a rise in production costs, the number of films released by M-G-M declined from an average of fifty-two during the war years to only twenty-three in 1948.[32]

Also, Louis B. Mayer seemed, according to some observers, to become more interested in his race horses than in moviemaking during the immediate postwar years. He brought in Dore Schary as vice-president in charge of production in July 1948. Described as a "liberal Democrat," Schary immediately clashed with Mayer's conservative political and social views. Born Isidore Schary on August 31, 1905, in Newark, New Jersey, the new vice-president had entered the entertainment industry as a screenwriter, winning an Oscar in 1938 for his script of *Boys' Town*. He had briefly worked as an executive producer at M-G-M in 1942 but left to work for independent producer David Selznick, who was Mayer's son-in-law, and later for RKO. Schary clashed with Mayer over many issues, including the activities of the House Un-American Activities Committee, which had stirred up and divided Hollywood with its Red-hunting investigations in 1947. When the two clashed over projects and funding, Schary sometimes went over Mayer's head to appeal to Nicholas Schenck in New York, knowing that Mayer and Schenck often fought over many issues.[33]

The divestment problem, which loomed as a monster on the horizon, and the in-fighting between Mayer and Schary in the M-G-M boardroom, did not affect the Freed Unit immediately. The actors, dancers, singers, choreographers, directors, and technicians continued to "put on a show" every time the money flowed in from New York, gleeful at the opportunity to ply their art in a supportive atmosphere. Living almost in a dream world, the members of the Freed Unit created an interesting blend of art and fantasy for the enjoyment of millions of viewers. As Jeanine Basinger has put it, they "worked together to re-shape the concept of the musical film. . . . With this new style of musical, the dances and songs moved the story along, while still expressing an emotion or an attitude. They not only set character, but developed environment or locale, and advanced the action."[34]

Nearly everyone who worked with Arthur Freed praised him as a producer and as a person. The overwhelming testimony of all who have gone on record is that he was a considerate man who understood talent and went out of his way to support his people. Andre Previn worked on the music for eight Freed pictures and recalled the producer as "tough and occasionally ruthless, but if you had done good work for him, he was forever loyal and would hire you time and time again." Previn admitted that Freed had an annoying foible, he "simply could not admit to not having seen something, not having heard something, not having been someplace." Along with his usual inarticulateness and his irritating habit of jingling change in his pants pocket, these seem relatively unimportant weaknesses.[35]

Gene Kelly always remembered Freed with gratitude and respect. "He knew talent and how to use it, what projects were best to do and which people were best to work on them. He was a nonpareil, and when I think back about all the people I had the good fortune to work with under his gentle command, I'm amazed." The Freed Unit was, for Kelly, "one great confraternity. We liked each other professionally as well as socially. We understood each other's temperaments and talents, so that when we came to work together on a project, there was usually a most wonderful blending of ideas. . . . It was no accident that M-G-M musicals were the best in the world."[36]

It is possible Freed came to worry that his career as a producer would overshadow his career as a songwriter, and he wanted new recognition for his earlier accomplishments. He had produced at least forty musicals from 1939 to 1951. But he also had five of the ten bestselling songs in the country in 1929 and, together with Brown, received $500,000 in royalties that year. M-G-M certainly valued Freed's songs, and in 1950 the studio paid him $25,000 for the right to use them in movies without having to pay him royalties. But Freed continued to hold the copyright to his songs and kept looking for ways to offer a new generation of moviegoers the opportunity to discover the Freed-Brown magic.[37]

INITIAL IDEAS

Freed began thinking about a project based on his songs as early as 1949, with every intention of calling the movie *Singin' in the Rain*. It was scheduled for the 1949–1950 season, and Freed planned not only to use old songs but to write new ones as well, and to film it in color. Freed ordered a story outline based on a silent movie called *Excess Baggage* which M-G-M had released in 1928. That film, based on a stage play by John McGowan, was a typical backstage story about a vaudeville acrobat who marries a dancer. The couple splits when the dancing wife becomes a film star, but the plot ends in a predictably happy ending with their reunion. Dan Dailey had already starred in a Twentieth Century–Fox movie with many of the same plot elements, released as *You're My Everything* in 1949.[38]

The story outline, written by Ben Feiner Jr. and dated January 28, 1949, bears no resemblance to the movie Comden and Green would write for Freed. The producer continued to think about the project for five months, announcing that Ann Miller would star in it. Howard Strickling, the M-G-M publicity director on the West Coast, spread the word to Howard Dietz, the M-G-M director of advertising and publicity in New York. But Freed assigned no scriptwriters because he decided to scrap the idea of basing his new movie on *Excess Baggage* by mid-June. He now wanted "an entirely original story," but still meant to title the movie *Singin' in the Rain*. And, of course, he still intended to fill the film with his own songs. In a draft of a speech Freed later gave about the making of the movie, he linked the origin of *Singin' in the Rain* with the other hit movies based on popular music that preceded it, including *Till the Clouds Roll By* (1946), *Easter Parade* (1948), and *An American in Paris* (1951). "Having had a bit of luck with these," Freed said, "I timidly decided to use some of my own songs which eventually grew into the movie Singing in the rain."[39]

Having given up the idea of using a preexisting storyline, Freed wanted to weave the plot out of the atmosphere in which his songs had been composed. He admitted that "none of the words or music suggested an actual story—to me they represented moods and memories." Still, Freed had no ideas to offer Comden and Green when he finally called them to California in May 1950. If he had developed anything more than a vague idea that the movie ought to reflect the early sound days of Hollywood, he does not seem to have told anyone about it at the time. After the success of the film that Comden and Green wrote, Freed suggested that he had in general thought about basing the plot within the movie industry of 1928 all along, even though there is no evidence to support this contention.[40]

Given the fact that *Singin' in the Rain* would consist almost entirely of his own songs, the movie probably was "the most autobiographical" of Freed's films.[41] Ironically, it would be an "autobiography" written by others, for Freed had never written a plot line or dialogue. He needed help to enable his songs to once again take wing and support a feature-length movie as they had done in *The Broadway Melody* and *The Hollywood Revue of 1929*.

COMDEN AND GREEN

Freed could not have entrusted his new project to a writing team that was better equipped to make a movie out of a catalogue of old, disparate songs. Comden and Green were in the flush of their success, busy with successive movie and stage projects. They were based in the Broadway milieu of New York but fit themselves into the Hollywood scene anytime Freed had an assignment for them.[42] They reached their screenwriting peak with *Singin' in the Rain*.

Elizabeth Cohen was born in Brooklyn on May 3, 1919, to Russian immigrant parents. She graduated from New York University with a Bachelor of Science degree but acted with the Washington Square Players while in college. Forsaking science, she struggled with a career in the performing arts, changing her name to Betty Comden in 1936. Comden married Siegfried Schutzman in 1942, but her husband later changed his name to Steven Kyle, claiming it was closer to the original Russian name of his ancestors.[43]

Adolph Green was born in the Bronx on December 2, 1914, of immigrant parents from Hungary. He also attended New York University and acted with the Washington Square Players, where he met Comden. Green married Allyn Ann McLerie in 1945.[44]

Comden and Green both pinned their hopes for a successful career as performers in a group called The Revuers. Formed in 1938 with Judy Holliday, John Frank, Alvin Hammer, and Comden and Green, they opened at the Village Vanguard in Greenwich Village the following year. Leonard Bernstein sometimes played the piano for the group. He had met Green in 1937 when the two spent their college break as counselors in a summer camp. The Revuers moved to the Blue Angel, a club owned by Max Gordon, who also owned the Village Vanguard. As their name implied, the group wrote and performed a series of skits based on a variety of current topics. No one stood out in the group more than Judy Holliday, and Twentieth Century–Fox offered her a contract. She insisted the studio executives take the entire team and they reluctantly agreed. In the end, Twentieth Century–Fox deleted everything the others did, retaining only Judy's scenes for *Greenwich Village* (1944).[45]

Disappointed and frustrated, Comden and Green returned to the Blue Angel in New York. Bernstein asked them to help make a full-blown stage musical out of a short ballet called *Fancy Free*, which had been created by choreographer Jerome Robbins and set to Bernstein's score. It was a seminal, modern piece of popular ballet that had inherent potential for becoming a musical comedy, and Comden and Green threw themselves into the project. They called the show *On the Town* and opened it on Broadway in December 1944. Comden and Green wrote huge parts for themselves, for they loved performing more than writing. Viewers of the 1949 movie version of *On the Town* might well be surprised to discover that anthropologist Claire de Loon (played by Comden) and sailor Ozzie (played by Green) are the main characters of the stage show rather than dancer Ivy Smith (Vera-Ellen) and sailor Gabey (Gene Kelly), as in the movie. The stage musical was an enormous success due to the clever plot, witty dialogue, and the vibrant, often bittersweet music of Bernstein. Comden and Green quickly wrote another stage musical, *Billion Dollar Baby* (1945), and were working on a third, *Two on the Aisle* (1951), neither of which proved to be commercial successes.[46]

Yet their reputation on Broadway was made by *On the Town*. Ironically, that reputation was based on their writing, not their acting, and this offered them another try at Hollywood. Freed brought them out to write the screenplay for *Good News* (1947), a mildly successful film based on a popular stage musical. Comden and Green achieved more marked success with the script for *The Barkleys of Broadway* (1949), starring Fred Astaire and Ginger Rogers. In writing the script for the film version of *On the Town* (1949) they could not hope to duplicate their acting roles and instead reworked the characters so that Ivy and Gabey were in the forefront for Vera-Ellen and Gene Kelly. It was an enormous commercial success that also influenced many filmmakers with its innovative editing and the electrifying effect of filming the introduction to the movie on the streets of New York City. "The picture retained a kind of vitality and gaiety and rightness and fun that the show had," Comden later recalled, "and also some of the poignance." But she admitted that the street scenes at the movie's opening were the key. "That really made the picture, that opening." Those compelling sequences on the streets were primarily the work of Gene Kelly, who not only starred in *On the Town* but co-directed it with his assistant, Stanley Donen.[47]

Many people assumed Comden and Green were wife and husband, but the pair told interviewers later in their career that they never considered marriage, even though they had met while both were single. "The fact that I worked with a man caused confusion and questions," Comden recalled in her memoirs, "but to . . . us, everything was perfectly clear." She and Green had inextricable ties: their early struggles to gain recognition as performers (which ultimately failed), their enormous success as writers, and their sharing of many interests, including a fascination with film history. All of these things bound them together professionally and personally.[48]

Their closeness was, if anything, cemented by their personality differences. Andre Previn described Comden as "calm, soft-spoken, and beautiful. Adolph is hyperactive, a born clown, and looks as if he has been exploded onto the earth." Green's interest in and knowledge of music was "encyclopedic. He can identify absolutely any fragment of a theme, no matter how arcane or how tunelessly demonstrated, seems to own every classical record ever made, and hasn't missed an interesting concert in decades." Previn probably focused on Green's love of music because of his own involvement in that profession, but Green had a wide-ranging interest in nearly everything from politics to history, poring through the major daily newspapers with as much avidity as he listened to classical recordings or watched old silent movies. He and Comden were united in their "great sense of humor," which "ricochets off all four walls."[49]

It is possible, as Green's Internet biographer Richard Severo puts it, that the two writers were "incomplete" without each other. "They both knew it and acknowledged it frequently." Green admitted to the *New York Herald Tribune* in 1961 that Betty was far more organized and responsible. Jule Styne, a popular composer who often worked with the team, described Comden as "realistic" and Green as "dreamistic," and that seems an appropriate way to describe their personality differences. Yet the two worked very closely and cooperatively. "Adolph and I have lots of old, outdated references and phrases we have mutually piled up over the years," Comden wrote in 1995. "There is a kind of radar between us, knowing what the other is thinking based on stuff we have both read or heard or shared."[50]

Their long working relationship, from the Washington Square Players through the Revuers and several Broadway and film hits, had developed the most successful writing team in popular entertainment. "Comden and Green were beyond adjectives," Severo has written, "they were in a category that only they occupied. There was no other team that could match both their quality and productivity over so many years."[51]

WORKING ON THE SCRIPT

And yet, when given this particular assignment by Freed, Comden and Green faced the toughest writing project they had yet encountered. The storyline had to evolve from the songs, and the Freed-Brown catalog, although rich with commercial successes and catchy tunes, had no thematic coherence.

"All we were told was to write a movie," Comden recalled in 1989, "and to get twenty or as many as you could of these wonderful songs into a story." These catalog movies, films inspired by and incorporating the life's work of a popular songwriter, were among the toughest to write. "There's nothing more difficult," Green admitted. "It's like higher mathematics." Leslie Caron recalled that Comden and Green came to Gene Kelly's house on weekends and complained that they couldn't think of anything to write for this movie. She quoted them as saying, "I mean 'singin' in the rain.' What can we do with that?"[52]

The writers decided to rent a house in Beverly Hills to work the script into shape. The house was number 527 on North Camden Drive, a short distance south of its intersection with Sunset Boulevard. Gene Kelly's house was number 725 on North Rodeo Drive, three blocks from their rented house, and the same distance from the intersection of Camden and Sunset. As an inside joke, "Camden and Sunset" found its way into the screenplay of *Singin' in the Rain* as the vicinity of Don Lockwood's Spanish colonial–style home.[53]

The house that Comden and Green rented had been owned by a silent screen star named Marie Prevost. They claimed to have taken the house "with mixed laughter and shudders because the price was right." It seemed an appropriate venue for writing a screenplay using songs of the silent and early sound era. "The place screamed, in its tattered elegance, of high times in the twenties, with its glory suddenly extinguished." The pool behind the house was filled with leaves and shadowed by nearby trees, while "torn strips of faded awning flapped mournfully against the terrace windows." The interior was filled with "peeling gilt and needlepoint pieces," and there was a massive "concert grand player piano, its piano roll stuck from there to eternity somewhere in the middle of 'Fascinatin' Rhythm.'"[54]

Working at the house and at the Culver City studio, Comden and Green tackled their first problem, deciding which songs of the many in the Freed-Brown catalog to use. Roger Edens played and sang many for the writers as they slowly became inspired. "Many of them were famous songs, standards," Comden and Green recalled, "bristling with vitality and part of the nation's collective unconscious." They knew that the title song of the movie, "an irresistible ode to optimism which no one can possibly sing without acting out the line 'There's a smile on my face,'" had to be prominently featured. As students of film history, Comden and Green knew the silent era and the shift to sound very well, and early on decided to set the new movie in that period. "We knew one thing about the story. There would have to be some scene where there would be rain, and the leading man (Howard Keel? Van Johnson? Fred Astaire? Gene Kelly?) would be singin' in it."[55]

When working at the studio, Comden and Green began to view a number of old movies of the era to find ideas. Stanley Donen joined them, and later recalled that everyone thought of basing the new project on a preexisting film such as Jean Harlow's *Platinum Blonde* (1931) or *Bombshell* (1933), or Red Skelton's *Merton of the Movies* (1947). According to Donen, Comden and Green rejected that concept after seeing "literally dozens" of movies, saying they had "this other idea." Donen spent hours with the pair in this initial phase of the project, thus he was "*in* on the genesis, in that sense," recalled Comden and Green, "worrying along with us both, as friends, and hopefully as a future co-director with Gene of whatever evolved."[56]

But, whether Gene Kelly or someone else would star in the new project was uncertain. Comden and Green heard a rumor that Howard Keel would star in the picture. Without consulting Freed on this critical issue, they "made a few dispirited stabs at a yarn about a minor Western actor in silents who makes it big with the advent of sound as a singing cowboy." This line of advance did not capture their imagination, and it soon gave way to a deep-rooted interest in creating a movie about a silent star who was tripped up by the transition to sound but caught his balance in time to adjust and become a talking star. The writers were greatly interested in the story of John Gilbert, who had risen to the heights of stardom during the silent era only to fall to the depths because his melodramatic acting appeared silly with the addition of sound. Comden and Green's hero would overcome that problem.[57]

With this scenario in mind, they realized that Howard Keel and a musical western would not work. The plot needed to accommodate "a lighthearted satirical comedy that featured fifteen or twenty Freed-Brown songs." The character of the star had to be believable as a song and dance man if they wanted this plot to work, and that kind of "character felt more to us like Gene Kelly than Howard Keel."[58]

A number of people have argued that the idea for *Singin' in the Rain* derived from a sketch Comden and Green had done with The Revuers at the Village Vanguard, with Judy Holliday, or that it had originated within another movie, such as *Once in a Lifetime*. That film, appearing in 1932, had been adapted from a Moss Hart and George S. Kaufman play. It is easy enough to make connections between *Singin' in the Rain* and any play, skit, or movie that also deals with the transition from silent to sound screen technology, for there is no shortage of fictional treatments of that interesting period. But mere similarity of subject does not mean that one project inspired another. Kelly said neither he nor Comden and Green had seen *Once in a Lifetime* before making *Singin'*. Although some scenes in *Singin' in the Rain* did have tie-ins to skits that Comden and Green did as The Revuers, their ideas for the plot of the movie were original, and based more on their knowledge of historic events and real people than on any fictional treatment of the era.[59]

Comden and Green started work on the project about June 19, 1950, three weeks after coming to California. It took them about a month to view films, work out the ideas they wanted to deal with, and block out the screenplay with a basic plot. Their first roadblock appeared in the often troublesome area of finding a proper start for the movie. They devised three possibilities—beginning the film with the premiere of a silent movie in New York City; a magazine interview in Hollywood with the star character who lies about his past; or a sequence from a silent movie in which the star meets the girl in New York City, loses her, and goes back to Hollywood. All three avenues seemed promising, and the pair could not agree on which to choose. In fact, they later admitted to feeling a bit depressed by their inability to resolve "this seemingly insoluble mess, in which the story never seemed to get started."[60]

About this time, in mid-July, Betty's husband came out to California with their young daughter Susanna for a visit. Comden and Green explained their problem to Kyle, and he offered a common sense solution—integrate aspects of all three scenarios. Brainstorming led to a conclusion that he was right, and that setting the premiere in Hollywood instead of New York City would work. Kyle had broken the logjam. "From here on, the gates were open and the writing of the screenplay gushed in a relatively exuberant flow," wrote Comden and Green. "We tapped the roots of our memories and experiences without editing ourselves when our ideas got wild, satirical, and extravagantly nonsensical." Edens and Freed instantly liked the ideas, situations, and characterizations as Comden and Green revealed them. A year and a half after word of the new movie was first announced, it finally was taking shape.[61]

In the middle of their most creative work on *Singin' in the Rain,* Kyle and Comden suffered a terrible shock. They celebrated Susanna's first birthday in late July with a simple gathering. Susanna was just beginning to walk and unexpectedly stood up, grabbed the table, and upset everything on it. A cup of hot coffee spilled all over her. She screamed and cried; her mother tried to get her clothes off but the fabric stuck to her skin. They summoned a doctor who found the child burned from her neck to her legs. Susanna stayed for several days in a nearby hospital and recovered well, but developed a noticeable scar which increased her self-consciousness at a tender age. The incident delayed her willingness to walk, and for another year she preferred to crawl rather than risk standing and braving what the world had to offer.[62]

THE FIRST SCREENPLAY

The first complete screenplay for *Singin' in the Rain* was finished by August 10, 1950. Comden and Green revised it a bit and produced new versions dated September 14 and October 5. Several small changes were incorporated into the next draft of the script, dated October 14, with slight revisions made for the next draft dated October 20. Comden and Green returned to New York City some time after the last-named date to continue working on their current stage production, *Two on the Aisle,* having left behind five slightly different versions of the screenplay.[63]

Fans of the finished product may be surprised to discover that the original draft of *Singin' in the Rain* consisted of a solid core that was retained throughout the entire revision process, but at the same time many changes were inserted fairly late during the preparation that led up to filming. The solid core consisted of the basic plot and its major elements. The story remained set in the changeover from silent to sound movies, involving a silent screen star named Don Lockwood who fumbles the transition to talkies but recovers with the idea to make his latest picture sing as well as talk. Joined by his lifelong friend and colleague, Cosmo Cosgrove (whose last name was later changed to Brown, possibly for Nacio Herb Brown), and the as yet undiscovered starlet, Kathy Summers (whose last name was later changed to Selden), the team has to contend with Lina Lamont, the other half of Don's silent screen duo. Working against Lina's romantic jealousy, and dubbing her voice (which sounds like fingernails scratching across a blackboard), Kathy, Don, and Cosmo produce a hit musical with the happy pairing of Don and Kathy to follow. Many of the songs Comden and Green suggested for inclusion in the original draft remained throughout the revision phase, although their placement was completely changed. However, no details of the dances were included in the first draft—that was to be worked out by the choreographer and star, Gene Kelly.[64]

One of the most prominent differences between the original screenplay and the finished film consisted of both a change in performer and situation. Comden and Green knew that Arthur Freed wanted Oscar

Levant to co-star as Cosmo. A droll pianist with undeniable gifts for interpreting classical pieces as well as the music of George Gershwin, Levant also was widely noted for his sharp, sardonic wit. Also, he had just played Kelly's sidekick in *An American in Paris*. But he could not sing or dance, and his acting abilities were restricted to playing characters who happened to be similar to his real-life persona.

Comden and Green envisioned a number entitled "Piano Playing Pioneer" for Oscar Levant as Cosmo. Studio chief R. F. Simpson worries about finding enough good popular songs for the musical version of the studio's first talkie, *The Duelling Cavalier*. Cosmo assures him, "R. F., I know I could do it, but I don't want to be a pig about this. I know a couple of wonderful song writers out here. Arthur Freed and Nacio Herb Brown—I'll bring them in to see you." He then suggests to Simpson that the studio's next musical picture be titled *The Piano Playing Pioneer*, with none other than Cosmo Cosgrove as the star. Cosmo pitches his idea as follows: a pioneer wagon train moving across the frontier is suddenly attacked by Indians. They perform "a threatening dance around a small covered-wagon train. In the center stands Cosmo in a Daniel Boone outfit, complete with coon-skin cap, one hand on a rifle, and the other around a frightened girl." When the men run out of ammunition, "Cosmo and a few other men drag a huge grand piano out of the covered wagon. Cosmo sits down and starts to play a famous piano concerto. The other pioneers grab musical instruments and quickly form an orchestra to accompany him. As they play, the Indians stop in their tracks and listen spellbound. After a while we see tears trickling down their war paint as the piece draws to a close, over the hill we SEE the U. S. Cavalry coming to the rescue. The pioneers cheer Cosmo and the Indians are routed."[65]

"The Piano Playing Pioneer," of course, was not a Freed-Brown song but a title dreamed up by Comden and Green with the assumption that Levant would select an appropriate classical piece. Comden and Green fully realized how ludicrous all this sounded, and made fun of it in the script. After the scenario is played out for the viewer, the cameras were to dissolve back to the projection room where Don, Cosmo, and Kathy were pitching their ideas for the musical version of *The Duelling Cavalier* to Simpson. Everyone except Cosmo dissolves into uncontrollable laughter as Simpson finally recovers enough to say no to his idea, but yes to the remake of the flawed talkie.[66] The idea of using Oscar Levant was dropped well before *Singin' in the Rain* went into production.

A number of minor details appear in the initial script that were changed or dropped later. The venue for all premieres is the Egyptian Theatre, rather than Grauman's Chinese, as in the movie. The list of stunts suggested in the flashback of Don's career early in the movie is different than the stunts that were eventually used in the final film. So is the list of down-and-out circumstances experienced by Don and Cosmo as they struggle in their early career. Don rides in his own chauffeured car to the post-premiere party for *The Royal Rascal* at Simpson's house, while in the finished film he and Cosmo ride in Cosmo's car.[67]

Other minor differences between the original script and the finished film include the name of R. F. Simpson's movie studio. Comden and Green initially called it Imperial rather than Monumental Pictures as in the movie. They referred to the first talkie as *Mammy's Boy*, which was later changed to *The Jazz Singer*. The dialogue remained more or the less the same throughout subsequent revisions, but in the original script, when Cosmo demonstrates how dubbing could work, encouraging Don to "Watch my Mouth!," Don says, "Enchanting. What are you doing later?" This line later raised the eyebrows of the censors.[68]

Other differences between the original script and the final film product are also striking. Kathy and the other girls were to sing "You Are My Lucky Star" instead of "All I Do Is Dream of You" at the party. The latter works much better, with its peppy tune, to introduce Kathy's talents and charm to Don (and more importantly, to better present Reynolds to the film audience). Also, originally, Comden and Green did not include a segment where Cosmo cheers up Don after the latter realizes he likes Kathy but cannot find her, and so there was no "Make 'Em Laugh" number. There was no montage sequence depicting the changeover from silent to sound movies such as we now see in the "Beautiful Girl" number. Instead of finding Kathy again during the filming of this number, Don and Cosmo discover her on the studio grounds, bully her into getting into their car, then drive her to the casting office to secure a role for her in Zelda's new picture, none of which would have made their characters appealing to movie audiences. Instead of Don Lockwood singing "You Were Meant for Me" to Kathy on an empty sound stage, as in the film, Comden and Green envisioned the pivotal love duet and dance taking place on a back lot composed of a variety of sets. The two would move from one set to another, Don providing "a kind of travelogue spiel." Comden and Green suggested a medley of Freed-Brown songs including "Would You?," "Chant of the Jungle," and "Broadway Melody" for this sequence. As in the final version, Phoebe Dinsmore appears in a vain attempt to help Lina with her lines. "Now remember, Miss Lamont, watch out for those dentalized 'd's' and 't's' and those flat 'a's'." However, she is the only diction coach in the original screenplay. Consequently, there was no "Moses Supposes" number.[69]

The penultimate number of the movie, its title song, was to be performed after Don, Kathy, and Cosmo decide to make the failed sound picture into a musical. They meet in a restaurant called the Pink Fedora, rather than at Don's house as in the finished film. After developing the idea, all three leave the restaurant and perform "Singin' in the Rain" on a street. Comden and Green might have been inspired by the well-known "Make Way for Tomorrow" number from *Cover Girl* (1944), in which Gene Kelly, Rita Hayworth, and Phil Silvers perform a joyous dance of hope and camaraderie on a New York street set. Also in the original script, Kathy helps Don and Cosmo pitch the new idea to R. F. Simpson. In the scene where Kathy is shown dubbing for Lina, Comden and Green suggested "All I Do Is Dream of You" instead of "Would You?," as in the final version of the movie. Also, they at first envisioned a longer sequence to demonstrate the dubbing of the new musical version of *The Duelling Cavalier*. At the end of the sequence, Don and Kathy were to perform "You Were Meant for Me," and as they kiss, Lina comes in and finds them. In contrast to the final version, she realizes what she is up against without Zelda's help.[70]

In the original script, Lina Lamont's downfall (the revelation that her voice and singing were dubbed in the new movie) takes place at Don's home rather than in front of the premiere audience. Comden and Green initially built a lot more tension into the "third act" crisis of the movie. After the successful premiere of *The Dancing Cavalier,* Don kisses Lina in a moment of excitement. Kathy becomes angry at this, and even angrier when Don tells her she must continue to dub Lina for the sake of the team. Kathy tells Don, "You're not in love with anybody but yourself. You use anything and anyone you can as long as it suits your purpose." "I fell for it!" she interrupts his protestation, "I thought when you were faced with failure you had become a real person at last.

I wanted to help you and I did. That was all that mattered to me, but now! With the very first sniff of success you're exactly what you always were—I won't be taken in again—I'm through!" Don is stunned and afraid she will leave him. "Don't worry little man," she continues, "The Lockwood-Lamont career is safe. I've got a contract and it pays well and I'm not going to walk out on it. (her feelings mounting) I'll go right on being her double and you can have one smash after another. And you can have Lina too! She may be a cross between a toad-stool and a rattle-snake but I still think she is a little too good for you."[71] Fortunately, all of this rancor was dropped and Don's character also became much more likable.

Comden and Green's original draft had Cosmo sympathizing with Kathy in this major problem, but the two go to the post-premiere party at Don's house anyway. When Don asks Cosmo for help, telling him he loves Kathy, Cosmo retorts, "You sure showed it tonight. . . . You offered her the dazzling career of complete oblivion." Don admits that "nothing means anything to me without Kathy." When columnist Dora Beagle (whose last name was later changed to Bailey) gushes over Lina's singing voice at the party and asks her to sing, Lina panics, just as in the final movie. But here, both Don and Cosmo come up with the idea to expose Lina by having Kathy dub her voice from behind a curtain—lifting the veil on the truth and paving the way for Don and Kathy's reconciliation at the same time. Also, in the original draft, when Cosmo's voice replaces Kathy's as the curtain rises, Don has his hand over Kathy's mouth, and Lina faints. Dora stares with her mouth open as Don and Kathy kiss, and there is no movie audience laughing raucously at the denouement as in the movie.[72]

Finally, Comden and Green ended their initial screenplay with a joke rather than the romantic sweetness that ended the film. Don and Kathy marry before the premiere of another picture, entitled *Broadway Rhythm,* starring the pair. More surprisingly, Cosmo and Lina also marry. Dora Beagle, who is covering the premiere once again held at the Egyptian Theater, remarks, "Here come Mr. and Mrs. Lockwood," and the crowd gushes over them as they had at the beginning of the film over Don and Lina. Then, as Cosmo and Lina arrive, Dora announces that in her latest film, *The Jungle Princess,* Lina "doesn't say a word—just grunts!" Comden and Green laconically indicate that the movie would end with a "big musical number finale."[73] What exactly they had in mind is unclear, for the final version of the movie does not end with a big musical number. "The Broadway Ballet" was later inserted as Don's effort to explain to R. F. Simpson what yet needed to be filmed for *The Dancing Cavalier.*

Yet, despite all these important changes, the initial draft of *Singin' in the Rain* had the fundamental elements right. The basic storyline remained intact and the basic characterizations, with the exception of Cosmo, also remained intact. However, Kathy was a more combative character initially than in the final version, and her crisis of romance and career with Don was more pronounced, portraying Don as a self-serving heel rather than the hero he became in the film. Yet, the initial draft has the same spirit of sarcastic fun mixed with genuine feeling for the subject, the characters, and the era that audiences would come to love in the final movie. Although the changes wrought in the next few months, mainly by Kelly and Donen, were indeed significant, Comden and Green had already conceptualized the basis for a classic with their first draft.

2

The Reason We Had Such Good Musicals

Betty Comden and Adolph Green insisted that Arthur Freed had not decided who would star in *Singin'* for some time after they started working on the movie, but Stanley Donen believed that Freed wanted Gene Kelly all along. Personally, Comden and Green also wanted Kelly to play the leading role and asked him at one point while they were working on the first draft of the script. Kelly put them off by saying he intended to carefully pick his next project and did not want to know what they were working on so he could choose objectively. The writers understood. "Gene was now, deservedly, at that happy moment when everyone wanted him for everything," they later wrote, "and had he expressed the desire to film Kafka's 'Metamorphosis' featuring the 'Million-Legged Cockroach Ballet,' the studio would have considered it a smart commercial move, and gone all the way with him."[1]

It is possible, of course, that both Donen and Comden-Green are at least partially right in their conflicting views. Freed most likely wanted Kelly but hesitated to push the issue because Kelly was heavily involved with *An American in Paris* at the time. Comden and Green certainly had no assurance that the star of this next movie would be Kelly, which is why they tried some ideas about a singing cowboy. But as they crafted a plot centered around a silent star caught in the transition to sound, they knew Kelly would be perfect for the role. This explains why even the first draft of the screenplay seems so well suited for Kelly as the star. The writers also hoped, although they had no assurance of it, that Kelly and Donen would co-direct the movie.[2]

Kelly finished filming *An American in Paris* on January 8, 1951, and soon afterward Freed suggested that Comden and Green show him their new screenplay. The writers returned to Culver City when their lease on the Prevost house was about to expire and "geared ourselves for a friendly refusal" from the star. Much to their relief, Kelly and Donen met them in the M-G-M commissary the next day, excited and "filled with ideas" about the new movie. The four immediately formed a close partnership. "We started meeting with them instantly for final changes and rewrites," Comden and Green recalled, "going over the script shot by shot." All four were good friends, which helped the collaboration a great deal. They could "use many ideas and visual details that might have seemed irrelevant or a total mystery to anyone else."[3]

GENE KELLY

The star who so enthusiastically signed onto the Comden-Green project became a driving force to make *Singin' in the Rain* the preeminent movie musical. In fact, Gene Kelly was nearing the peak of his impressive career as a dancer, leading man, choreographer, and director. He was a multitalented superstar in a class only with Fred Astaire when it came to dancing, and in a class all by himself when it came to dabbling successfully in a variety of roles as a moviemaker.

Born Eugene Curran Kelly on August 23, 1912, in the Highland Park District of Pittsburgh, the new leading man of *Singin' in the Rain* grew up in tough working-class neighborhoods of this industrial city. His father, James Kelly, was a second-generation Irishman from Ontario who had migrated to the United States to become a successful phonograph salesman. Although James was a devoted father, Kelly's mother, Harriet Curran Kelly, was primarily responsible for Gene's upbringing and that of his four siblings. With James traveling most of the time to conduct his business, Harriet raised the kids and taught them values of hard work, high aspirations, and controlled, economical ways of living. For Gene, growing up in Pittsburgh meant learning how to take care of himself on the streets as well. "Because I was so small," he later admitted, "I felt that I always had to prove myself, and the best way to do this was with my fists." Between fights, Gene also tended to be accident prone. At age six, he fell head-first off his tricycle and cut his left cheek on "an exposed piece of cast iron." After a local doctor sewed it up, the wound created a "small, half-moon scar" on his cheek visible in all his movies. True to his values, Kelly insisted that makeup artists leave the scar alone.[4]

Part of Harriet's plan for her three sons and two daughters (Gene was the third born) was to expose them to as much culture as possible. She took them to all the shows in Pittsburgh and forced them to learn to play a musical instrument. When Gene was seven, she insisted that all three boys take dancing lessons. Gene's younger brother Fred was a natural-born dancer who loved the opportunity, but Gene hated the idea. Stung by the accusation that he was a sissy, he fought neighborhood kids who taunted the boys on their way to the lessons. Harriet then began to send them to the dance studio by taxi, but Gene eventually persuaded his mother to drop the whole idea. Ironically, despite Gene's distaste for dancing as a young boy, his teachers recognized his dancing talent and "beautiful high-tenor voice" and put him in school shows and concerts, where his performances were "vigorously applauded by parents and teachers." But Gene himself was far more interested in sports. He excelled at all physical activities, especially gymnastics and ice hockey. He became a superb skater at a very young age when his father flooded their backyard in winter to create a crude skating rink and then took the children to a huge frozen lake nearby to perfect their skills.[5]

Kelly's love of dance blossomed in high school. He later joked that it was because he realized the girls were more interested in him when they found out he could dance, but it was also due to his own innate interest and the financial needs of his family. Kelly's biographer writes that even as a teenager Gene danced, whether around the table as he dished out mashed potatoes or when walking with his friend Jules Steinberg. But it was financial need that made Gene work at dancing seriously. The Depression broke James Kelly's career; he lost his job and stayed at home for many years without work. Gene and Fred began to supplement the family income by performing in clubs around town. They were excellent tap dancers and built several routines that included acrobatics and roller-skating as well. Many of the clubs, however, provided such a crude venue for their talents that Gene came to call them "cloops," a term he concocted to combine "club" and "chicken coop."[6]

Harriet got involved in a local dance studio as a business manager, and took over the studio when its owner could not make a success of the enterprise. With a solid sense of personal responsibility for his family, Gene became the chief dance instructor of the new school while still a senior in high school. His brother Fred and sisters Louise and Jay also helped. "I loved it," Kelly later recalled, "I loved teaching children."

With his family pitching in to help, Gene adopted costumes inspired by those worn in *42nd Street,* developed a comprehensive dance curriculum gradated according to the age of each class of pupils, and turned on the charm to become a sort of Pied Piper of dance in the suburbs of Pittsburgh. The family later opened a branch studio in Johnstown, sixty-five miles away, and named it the Gene Kelly Studio of the Dance. At the time, Gene was only twenty years old. The studio was an impressive financial and pedagogical success, due to hard work and dedication by the whole family. But Gene's talent for dancing, his charismatic way of dealing with children, and his dedication as a teacher were the keys. He staged annual shows with his young pupils that did extremely well, and many of his students went on to build careers in show business.[7]

Kelly entered Penn State in 1929 but returned to Pittsburgh after only one year, enrolling instead at the University of Pittsburgh so he could help out with the family's finances. In addition to instructing at the two dance studios, he taught dancing at a YMCA camp at Lake Erie, where his self-appointed mission was to teach boys that dancing was not effeminate. Starting in 1931, Kelly also worked for the Beth Shalom Synagogue in Pittsburgh for seven years, organizing an annual show to raise money for the synagogue. Years later, people associated with Beth Shalom recalled Kelly's "incredible magnetism," and how he made even children with little talent "shine under his guidance." In addition to teaching dance to children in these different venues, Kelly worked at a variety of odd jobs to pay for his tuition and living expenses, and graduated from the University of Pittsburgh in 1933 with a Bachelor of Arts degree in economics.[8]

Harriet planned a career in law for the graduate; she had always viewed Fred, not Gene, as the promising dancer in the family. But after a few weeks of law school, Gene dropped out to devote himself full time to his varied jobs in show business. In addition to teaching at his two studios and at Beth Shalom, Kelly also arranged many successful Cap and Gown shows for the University of Pittsburgh and starred in them too. At the same time, he developed a deep interest in classical ballet and took lessons several summers in a row in Chicago. When Robert Alton, a successful Broadway choreographer, arrived in Pittsburgh to do a show, Gene brought his students to help fill the stage. Alton was so impressed that he urged Gene to come to New York as a performer or as his assistant, but Kelly hesitated some time before he realized that Pittsburgh could no longer offer opportunities for his artistic growth.[9]

Kelly went to New York in 1938, expecting to get a job as a Broadway choreographer. But no one was impressed by the choreography he had done in Pittsburgh, so Kelly had to take a job performing on stage. His first appearance was in *Leave It to Me* (1938), as one of six Eskimos accompanying Mary Martin in her rendition of "My Heart Belongs to Daddy," the showstopper that started Martin's career. The next year, Katharine Cornell suggested he take diction lessons to tame his "flat Pittsburgh accent." The instructor "would ask me to say 'water' and I'd say 'wadder,'" he recalled. "Or she'd ask me to say 'orange' and I'd say 'ooringe'—just like the Jean Hagen character in *Singin' in the Rain*."[10]

But soon enough Gene secured jobs choreographing shows, including *Green Grow the Lilacs* (in summer stock) and an all-black performance of *The Emperor Jones*. The former show was later turned into the hugely successful musical *Oklahoma!* (1943). While choreographing Billy Rose's *Diamond Horseshoe* in 1939, Gene met dancer Betsy Blair, who became his wife two years later. But the first show that truly started Kelly's career was William Saroyan's *The Time of Your Life* (1939), where he played Harry the Hoofer, a down-and-out dancer who ties together many of the themes of the play. Kelly's performance as Harry "stopped the show." Gene, for the first time, realized he could develop a character through movement on the stage in addition to dialogue.[11]

It was during the twenty-two-week run of *The Time of Your Life* that Arthur Freed first saw Kelly, and visited the dancer backstage one night. "He came into my dressing-room," Gene later recalled, "and for a moment just stood there—this imposing man with his kind face and blue eyes—and smiled. I didn't know what he was thinking, but I liked him immediately." But Kelly thought he was not ready yet to go to Hollywood.[12]

The success of Saroyan's play provided the springboard for Kelly's second great role on Broadway in *Pal Joey* (1940). Gene created the lead role of Joey Evans, a heel who took advantage of the women in his nightclub but who remained a strangely likable character. It was a tough job making Joey real and vulnerable, but Gene succeeded admirably. His performance matched the sardonic, bittersweet story, lyrics, and music of this Rodgers and Hart success, starting a new trend in more realistic characterizations in Broadway musicals. Gene worked a variety of dance styles into his numbers, encouraged by Bob Alton who urged him to explore and develop his own combination of styles. Described as "amoral rather than immoral," Joey Evans became a likable, or at least a tolerable, heel in Kelly's hands. While there was no improvement in Joey's morals during the course of *Pal Joey*, Gene would develop this highly successful character type into a redeemable heel in his movie career. Act One closed with a dream ballet, a concept that Kelly would continue in many of his films, including *Singin' in the Rain*.[13]

Pal Joey was a perfect springboard to Hollywood. Freed talked Mayer into offering Kelly an M-G-M contract, but Gene refused to undergo a screen test in New York, and Mayer agreed because he had seen Gene perform on stage. But later, Freed mistakenly thought Gene was being tested in New York for a part in the new movie *Strike Up the Band*, and telegraphed Al Altman for still photos of the test to be sent to him at Culver City. Altman asked Gene to come in for a screen test without explaining that this had nothing to do with signing the contract, which led Kelly to assume Mayer had gone back on his word. He refused to be tested and wrote an angry letter to Mayer, calling him a liar. Two months later, independent producer David O. Selznick also saw *Pal Joey* and talked Gene into signing a seven-year contract with no screen test. Kelly married Betsy Blair on September 24, 1941. In early November, the newlyweds drove out to California, where their daughter Kerry was born on October 16, 1942.[14]

Kelly never made a movie for Selznick. Uninterested in musicals and banking on utilizing Kelly's acting ability, the producer could not find a suitable project for the Broadway dancer. Freed soon convinced M-G-M to listen to Judy Garland, who had met Gene months before in New York, and now wanted him as her leading man in *For Me and My Gal*. Directed by Busby Berkeley, the picture centered around the relationship between Harry Palmer, a vaudeville entertainer, and the girl Harry loses when he deliberately injures his hand to avoid the draft in World War I. He eventually redeems himself and wins the girl again, making *For Me and My Gal* an effective movie for the early months of World War II. Kelly played a Joey-like character in Harry, except for the happy ending. It was both a commercial and a critical success, starting Gene's movie career off on the right foot.[15]

But Kelly was shocked when he saw himself on the screen for the first time. "In my first picture I knew I was doing everything wrong," he later confided. The problem lay in trying to transfer what he had learned on the stage to a two-dimensional screen that was bigger than life. "I was flabbergasted at how *flat* everything looked. The fact that I didn't jump out of the screen the way that I did on the stage." Kelly continued to dance his character, and to segue in a plausible way from dialogue to dance through song. He also learned to shorten his dance routines by as much as two-thirds, for the camera seemed to have a shorter attention span than theater audiences. But he needed more time to wrestle with the greatest problem, how to get the most out of his dances on the screen. He knew that there was a certain kinetic effect when viewers watched a dancer in real life on a stage that was completely lacking on film. *For Me and My Gal* not only started Kelly's screen career, it set him on a crusade to figure out how to compensate for that lack of kinetic effect. He worked this issue out in successive movies by experimenting with camera placement and movement, revising his choreography, and searching for effects possible on the screen that were impossible on the stage. "You have to construct a dance so that it can be cut and edited, and do it in a way that won't disturb the viewer. You learn to use the camera as part of the choreography." Kelly initially viewed film dancing as a problem, but soon became aware of its potential as well.[16]

For Me and My Gal did not automatically lead to other good movie projects. Kelly tried to hone his acting in a handful of dramatic roles within unsuccessful movies, such as *Pilot No. 5* (1943) and *The Cross of Lorraine* (1943). He did well in minor musicals such as *Thousands Cheer* (1943), where he demonstrated his creativity by devising a dance with a mop and several other props. He provided the only dance entertainment in *DuBarry Was a Lady* (1943). Not until M-G-M loaned him to Columbia to make *Cover Girl* (1944) did Kelly begin to hit his stride in a role whose stature foreshadowed the best of his coming musicals. In *Cover Girl*, Kelly flexed his muscles and created not only his own but also Rita Hayworth's dances. He even brought nondancing funny man Phil Silvers into the scene with a rousing number, "Make Way for Tomorrow," in which the three characters dance with joyous abandon down a New York street set. The most impressive technical achievement of *Cover Girl* was the famous "Alter Ego" number in which Kelly danced with himself. It was the earliest fulfillment of his strong desire to push the envelope of film dancing. Stanley Donen provided important help in this achievement as Kelly's assistant. Today the "Alter Ego" dance may not look like a technical achievement compared to modern computerized filmmaking, but at that time, given the crude technology available, it was not only a painstaking endeavor but also a revolutionary step in creating "cine-dance," a term that came into vogue to denote a kind of dance that could only be created in the medium of film. In fact, *Cover Girl* itself broke new ground in the evolution of the movie musical with its brooding, bittersweet themes and the quality of its dancing. Kelly excelled not only in his performance, both dancing and acting, but in his singing as well. Jerome Kern's "Long Ago and Far Away" was rangy and difficult, but Kelly sang it so well for Kern that the composer said, according to Phil Silvers, "If you want to make an old man happy, please sing it again." Kelly also became involved in all aspects of production, from editing to directing, to crafting steps suited for each participant in his numbers.[17]

Cover Girl was a clear sign of what was to come, and Louis B. Mayer resolved not to let Kelly work for another studio again, refusing all of Harry Cohn's offers for Gene. Kelly's next major appearance was with the reigning film dancer of the time, Fred Astaire. The two teamed up in a sketch entitled "The Babbitt and the Bromide" for *The Ziegfeld Follies,* a celebration of M-G-M's twentieth anniversary. Mostly filmed in 1944, the movie was not released until two years later. "The Babbitt and the Bromide" proved to be the only time that Astaire and Kelly danced together until three decades later, long after their major dance careers had ended. Thirteen years younger than Astaire, Kelly comes across as the brash newcomer, for effect, but the different dancing styles both employed in their careers melded well on screen. Off screen, they were friends who respected each other personally and professionally.[18]

Anchors Aweigh (1945) took Kelly's career to its first peak. It was the first of several times he would portray a sailor, and the first pairing with Frank Sinatra, whose phenomenal singing career had not yet been translated into a successful acting career in the movies. Kelly taught Sinatra how to dance well enough to get by, and crafted a varied number of routines to enliven the one-dimensional plot of the film. The highlight of *Anchors Aweigh* was another technical breakthrough as Kelly, with the important assistance of Donen, devised a way to dance with an animated character, Jerry the Mouse. Using M-G-M's own cartoon department, this was the first of several times Kelly relied on William Hanna and Joseph Barbera to fulfill his ongoing dream of creating cine-dance. "The Worry Song," as the dance number with Jerry came to be called, combined a technical achievement superior to the "Alter Ego" dance. Moreover, its cheery, sweet nature captivated audiences, unlike the brooding introspection of the "Alter Ego" number. *Anchors Aweigh* was nominated for best picture, with Kelly for best actor in the next round of Academy Awards, but failed in both categories. Enormous popular success was its consolation.[19]

Kelly joined the Navy soon after finishing *Anchors Aweigh,* having felt uneasy about staying in Hollywood while so many actors were serving in the war. He made movies in the United States dealing with naval affairs, honing his knowledge of editing and directing, and returned to Hollywood in May 1946. His first postwar movie was *Living in a Big Way* (1947), which was intended to feature him in a straight acting role about the problems veterans faced while readjusting to civilian life. But at the last minute, Gene was asked to work up a few dance routines to enliven the film. The most impressive was a number in which his character dances with children and then cavorts alone on a partially constructed building for the children's amusement, giving Kelly the opportunity to show off his athletic skills.[20]

The next project got Kelly back on his career track. He was teamed once again with Judy Garland in *The Pirate* (1948), and Kelly and director Vincente Minnelli collaborated to turn it into a minor classic among film musical comedies. Playing the role of an actor, pretending to be a blood-thirsty pirate to win his love, Kelly indulged in his tendency to overact melodramatically, but always with a touch of sardonic knowledge that what he is doing could easily go beyond the pale. Minnelli and Kelly *intended* to create this effect, peopling the movie with wonderful character actors, brilliant costumes, and absurd but believable situations. Kelly also performed amazing stunts and acrobatic, athletic dancing. The result is a marvelous movie filled with humor and astonishing dance routines, which nevertheless flopped at the box office because middle-class audiences of the day did not understand its tongue-in-cheek quality.[21]

M-G-M planned to keep Kelly and Garland together for the next project, *Easter Parade,* but Gene broke his ankle while playing a particularly vigorous game of volleyball during one of the famous weekend parties at his house on North Rodeo Drive. At Kelly's suggestion, Freed asked Fred Astaire to come out of retirement and take over, which sparked the second and in many ways the more interesting second phase of Astaire's long career in the movies. After his ankle healed, Gene played D'Artagnan in M-G-M's *The Three Musketeers* (1948), and was in his element. He had loved watching Douglas Fairbanks in silent swashbuckler movies and longed to indulge in a melodramatic, action-packed project. One can say he overindulged, for this long movie perhaps has too much overacting from Kelly. Although it has no dances per se, Kelly visualized his acting in *The Three Musketeers* within the context of dancing. He noted the similarity between fencing and dancing, and later commented that all the action scenes in the movie were "extensions of dancing." *The Three Musketeers* is worth seeing for that alone, and scenes from it would later be clipped into *Singin' in the Rain* as well.[22]

Kelly provided audiences with an impressive demonstration of modern dance in *Words and Music* (1948), where he and Vera-Ellen performed a section titled "Slaughter on Tenth Avenue." It was an adaptation of a comic dance with black undertones from the Rodgers and Hart Broadway musical *On Your Toes* (1936), performed on stage by Ray Bolger. Kelly decided to delete the comic nature of the dance and turn it into a mean street melodrama in which the protagonist and his girl are gunned down in a bar. Audiences and critics alike were impressed with the virile choreography and the emotionally expressive dancing. Moreover, the entire routine was like a ballet interlude in the larger movie, allowing Kelly further opportunity to work with that concept. This routine also represented a huge turning point in Vera-Ellen's career. She had performed tricky, athletic routines in her previous films, but Kelly taught her to invest her dancing with emotion that was suited to the character she portrayed. It led to an M-G-M contract for her.[23]

Soon after, Gene Kelly came up with an idea of his own for a dance movie, simply to avoid being drafted for a Joe Pasternak project that he hated. *Take Me Out to the Ball Game* emerged from an idea he developed with assistance from Donen, and then sold to Arthur Freed. It was inspired by the story of Al Schacht, a former major league player, who later entertained baseball fans with a comic act at game time. Frank Sinatra agreed to dance again with Gene, and Jules Munshin supported both of them, making an effective trio. *Take Me Out to the Ball Game* garnered a great deal of money for M-G-M, but modern commentators tend to undervalue its dancing and its infectious spirit. The movie witnessed the culmination of many Gene Kelly traits—his fascination with his Irish heritage, his deep interest in sports, and his faith in the marriage of athletics, entertainment, and dancing. It was the last major film musical in which he played an aggressively brash character who eventually becomes domesticated. Comden and Green wrote some of the songs for this movie, and Donen again helped Gene in filming the dance numbers—director Busby Berkeley barely could handle the rest of the film. In fact, Kelly experienced a certain amount of frustration with Berkeley, whose concept of direction seemed stuck in the 1930s.[24]

Both Kelly and Donen wanted to strike out on their own in terms of taking more complete control over their projects, and Freed gave them the chance to do so in *On the Town*. It was the first time Kelly and Donen received full directorial credit, the first time Comden and Green worked closely with them, and the first of three movies that sealed Kelly's imposing stature in the rarefied world of the film musical. Typically termed "the most innovative musical of the decade," *On the Town* was based on the Comden-Green Broadway stage musical, but with significant alterations. As noted in the previous chapter, the focus shifted from Ozzy and Claire to Gabey and Ivy to accommodate Kelly and Vera-Ellen. Sinatra and Munshin rejoined Kelly in *On the Town*. Most of Leonard Bernstein's music was dropped as too serious or "highbrow" for a typical movie audience, and the storyline was made a bit more sentimental, sweet, and naïve. The most striking aspect of *On the Town* was the opening sequence, filmed on the streets of New York City within a tight shooting schedule. Kelly and Donen had to argue strenuously with M-G-M to shoot on location, and their point was worthwhile. In this sequence, edited with sharp cuts to enhance the sensation of excitement in setting the stage for the three sailors' twenty-four-hour leave in New York, *On the Town* represented the apotheosis of the sailor image in Hollywood films. It was a pivotal movie in Kelly's career, and remained his favorite work because of the impact of that "on location" opening sequence. The movie also contains "A Day in New York," the most effective ballet sequence in any Gene Kelly movie.[25] An energetic and vibrant dance, filmed on a bare stage so as to emphasize the dreamlike nature of most movie ballets, it zeroes in on the pure emotion of the storyline and never ceases to tear at the heartstrings without becoming maudlin or sentimental.

Critics recognized a new force in Hollywood with the release of *On the Town*. Morgan Hudgins wrote that Kelly, already a "triple threat man," had "gone beyond the triple-threat class." Hudgins notes that most commentators had already seen Gene as "the most versatile man on the Hollywood scene," and toted up the precise categories—writer, director, actor, dancer, choreographer, and singer.[26]

Wedged in among his three biggest musicals, Kelly took the time to co-star with Judy Garland for their last pairing together, *Summer Stock* (1950), a Joe Pasternak project about a struggling stage company trying to rehearse their big show in a barn. Garland's personal problems caused enormous delays on the set, but Kelly, ever faithful to a friend, took the time from his busy schedule to nurse the project along with the help of Phil Silvers. "I'll do anything for this girl," he told Pasternak. "If I have to come here and sit and wait for a year, I'd do it for her." In the process, he developed one of the more distinctive dance routines of his career, using a squeaky board and a newspaper as props. It became his favorite dance number because of the intricacy of developing and working out the details of this complex routine.[27]

Kelly always had a strong work ethic, but he now threw himself even more enthusiastically into his hours at the studio. *An American in Paris,* the second in the trilogy that supported the peak of his overall career, came fairly soon after *On the Town.* Developed from Arthur Freed's desire to create a film from the corpus of George and Ira Gershwin's songs, it was in some ways a direct precursor to *Singin' in the Rain.* Director Minnelli and leading man–choreographer Kelly produced a classic, based on a comparatively thin story about an American painter living in Paris and falling in love with a young French woman. Kelly chose and trained the unknown Leslie Caron, a classical ballet dancer from France, as his co-star. Barely nineteen years old and with no prior awareness of moviemaking, Caron's long career in Hollywood began with *An American in Paris* under Kelly's careful tutelage. The ballet that represented the climax of this film turned into an extravagant paean of praise to the aesthetics of French painting and to the comparatively naïve American reverence for the culture of old Europe.[28]

Brash and colorful to an extreme, the ballet is the thing that most fans of *An American in Paris* want to discuss, although it is so involved with the context of the French painters and their work that it tends to lose its focus on the storyline and the emotions of Jerry Mulligan and Lise, the star-crossed lovers of the movie. There is a lot to criticize about *An American in Paris*—the obvious twenty-year age difference between

Kelly and Caron, Caron's lack of acting ability and facial expression, the often drab contributions of co-star Oscar Levant, and the overblown nature of much of the acting. In many ways, it is the only Gene Kelly dance movie that is overrated. But audiences loved it anyway. Gene Kelly was among the few stars who could get away with excess.

Rehearsals for *An American in Paris* began June 5, 1950, a week before Comden and Green began to seriously write the initial screenplay for *Singin' in the Rain*. The filming of *An American in Paris* began August 1 and everything except the ballet was in the can by November 1, 1950. By then, Comden and Green had already finished the first draft for *Singin' in the Rain* as well as a few revisions, and returned to New York City. The expensive ballet sequence for *An American in Paris* took six weeks, with filming ending on January 8, 1951.[29] Soon after, Kelly signed on to star in and co-direct *Singin' in the Rain*.

STANLEY DONEN

Gene Kelly relied heavily on Stanley Donen to be his third eye behind the camera. The exact nature of their collaboration has never been pinpointed by scholars because the two never really explained how they worked together. Kelly referred to Donen as "an assistant, an aide, a colleague," and he admitted that it was very difficult to star in and direct a musical: "You need somebody that you can trust and that can help you." Donen's contribution lay not in choreography but in knowing how to maneuver the camera to capture dance on film in an effective way. "He alone knew what I was after in those opening scenes of *On the Town*, and what I wanted to achieve in the picture as a whole." There was tension, at least under the surface. As Kelly's most recent biographer has put it, Donen's "placid exterior hid a fragile sensitivity," and he sometimes chafed as the unknown assistant to the star. Donen's great contribution to the success of Kelly's movies lay in his technical expertise and in understanding how to film dance.[30]

Donen, like Freed, was born into the small Jewish population of South Carolina, on April 13, 1924. An awkward youth whose great obsession lay in what he saw in local movie theaters in Columbia, the state's capital, Donen eventually made his way to New York at age sixteen, only a year after Kelly opened his Broadway career. The two met when Donen joined the chorus of *Pal Joey*. Donen admitted he was then a *"shlepper. . . . A real zero,"* but he was immensely impressed by Kelly's self-confidence, athleticism, and dynamic stage presence. Hirschhorn concurs with Donen's opinion of himself, saying he "had no particular identity or evident talent . . . and was just a kid from the South who wanted to make it in show business." Kelly took a liking to him, however, and helped him into other Broadway shows, such as *Best Foot Forward* (1941), finally encouraging him to move to Hollywood where he persuaded Charles Walters, the dance director of the film version of *Best Foot Forward* (1943), to find a part for Stanley. After this movie, Donen bummed about between several studios, choreographing minor dances in forgettable movies. Kelly's need of his technical skills saved Donen's career. He took Donen as his assistant when he went to Columbia to make *Cover Girl*. Kelly groomed the young man from South Carolina in stages, and convinced the bosses at M-G-M to give him chances.[31]

Kelly was motivated as much by promoting his own career as by his innate desire to foster young talent, but there came a time when he had to let Donen take wing on his own. He persuaded M-G-M to let Stanley direct his first dance in *Take Me Out to the Ball Game* for Frank Sinatra and Betty Garrett. According to Kelly, the studio now began to look upon Donen as "more than just an assistant, . . . but as a fellow who had some very good taste and some esthetic drive of his own." Kelly felt that, "protégé of mine or not, . . . he had to strike out on his own *someday*. He wasn't going to always live in my shadow, and that was a good thing to come out of that picture." Kelly realized their relationship had reached a new level; "we weren't boss-and-assistant any more but co-creators."[32] Donen was sole director for the first time on *Royal Wedding* (1950), working with his boyhood idol Fred Astaire in one of M-G-M's best musicals.

Donen was divorced from his first wife, Nancy Hayward, for some time before he married one of Gene Kelly's assistants. Jeanne Coyne initially met Kelly as a seven-year-old student in his Pittsburgh dance studio. Eleven years younger than her charismatic instructor, she developed a schoolgirl crush that matured into a lifelong love. For decades, Coyne had to keep her affections secret from Gene, but she displayed enough talent to draw Kelly's professional attention. He helped convince her to move to New York in 1939, a year after his arrival, where she worked with choreographers Robert Alton and Jack Cole. Coyne became part of the Kelly team when she moved to Hollywood in 1942.

She also worked with other M-G-M stars, such as Judy Garland and Leslie Caron, assisting them in rehearsal and costume fitting. Donen and Coyne married on April 14, 1948, during the late preproduction phase of *Take Me Out to the Ball Game,* but the marriage did not work. They separated April 12, 1950, before Comden and Green came out to California for their new assignment from Freed. Their divorce was granted on May 17, 1951, during the preproduction planning for *Singin' in the Rain.*[33]

Donen and Coyne apparently could not make their marriage work, in part, because both loved other people. Coyne could not find a legitimate outlet for her affection for Kelly, and Donen apparently loved Kelly's wife, Betsy Blair. Kelly would not come to know all this until some ten years later, after his divorce from Betsy and his marriage to Jeanne. Blair was unaware of Donen's affection at that time. She recalled him as "a very attractive figure, eager to learn, ambitious and funny. And he had become our close and dear friend, an intimate in our household. Although he had an apartment of his own, he practically lived with us." After his separation from Coyne, Donen had a relationship with Elizabeth Taylor from about the latter part of 1950 to the latter part of 1951, during most of the planning and filming of *Singin' in the Rain*. It began when he directed her in *Love Is Better Than Ever* (1952). Betsy, Donen, and Jeanne were all of the same generation, about a dozen or so years younger than Gene. They all admired, loved, and respected him as a mentor and father-figure in a bizarre mix of feeling that was strong and mutually beneficial to each of the four in varied ways.[34]

Carol Haney was another important member of the Kelly team. Born Carolyn Haney in New Bedford, Massachusetts on Christmas Eve in 1924, she began to dance at age five and opened Miss Haney's School of the Dance at age fifteen. She went to California in 1940 and waited on tables to make a living until securing her first Hollywood job, but fell and injured her knee in rehearsal. Haney went to Broadway with Jack Cole's dance troupe and performed in several stage musicals. Kelly saw her and hired her as his assistant in 1949. Her first significant screen dance was in the ballet of *On the Town,* and M-G-M offered her a seven-year contract in 1950. Kelly used several other dance assistants over the years, but Coyne and Haney were the most important to his work. To one observer, they had "a telepathic-seeming knowledge of what Kelly wants."[35]

By early 1951, when Kelly and Donen prepared for their second film as co-directors, there was still no doubt that Kelly was the more visible and influential partner. Despite the success of *Royal Wedding* and his other directorial efforts, Donen was the junior partner in this collaboration. Art director Randall Duell, who also worked on *Singin' in the Rain*, put it bluntly twenty years later when he said, "Gene ran the show. Stan had some good ideas and worked with Gene, but he was still the 'office boy' to Gene, in a sense, although Gene had great respect for him. But they made a good team, because they were very compatible."[36]

COLLABORATION

The Kelly-Donen partnership accomplished more than the production of popular film musicals. Casey Charness believes it brought the art of film dancing to the fulfillment of an idea, that of the "cine-dance," a melding of the distinctive strengths of dancing and filmmaking that had never been done before. As Charness puts it, "The two men seem to have elevated Hollywood dance from simplistic display of either dancing or photographic ability into a perception that incorporates both what the dancer can do and what the camera can see." Charness believes Kelly and Donen "developed a balance between camera and dancer that ... encouraged both photographer and choreographer to contribute significantly to the creation and final effectiveness of a dance." This was possible because of the personal relationship between the two, which Gene Kelly often characterized as that akin to a father and son, as well as to the particular strengths and interests of Donen behind the camera and Kelly in front of it.[37]

Despite the strenuous efforts of many film scholars to detect the overriding personal influence of a single creator in various movies, the musical, in particular, tends to be immune to the "auteur" theory. It is the most complex kind of film, from the standpoint of creative input by a variety of people, so that nearly every film musical is a collaborative effort. Gene Kelly's success was due in part to the personal team he created within the Freed Unit. His main collaborator was Donen, who handled technical issues and oversaw the filming of the dances, while Jeanne Coyne and Carol Haney helped work out the details of dance routines for which Kelly developed the choreography. This devoted team helped Kelly achieve the high level of quality as well as the rapid production of one classic dance film after another. Kelly was the star and received the lion's share of recognition, but "what finally appeared on the screen was very much a team effort."[38]

Part of the Kelly team, at least temporarily, were writers Comden and Green. "Gene was one of our oldest friends from New York," they later wrote. Kelly had performed at the Westport Country Playhouse in the summer of 1939 where the Revuers also appeared. Green remembered Kelly as an "energetic young man who looked much younger than his twenty-seven years. . . . He had this terrific outgoing quality combined with a street-boy earthiness which was extremely appealing." Displaying "charm and . . . clean-cut good looks," Kelly's effect on a theater audience was immediate and compelling. "They just loved him," Green recalled. "He could do no wrong. There was this magic—this 'star quality' he exuded. His dancing was very athletic and he had the wonderful ability to make the most complicated things look ridiculously simple."[39]

Kelly became the leader in every group he entered, and eager associates sought him out. But "the guys around us were the reason we had such good musicals," Kelly later remembered. "We had real collaboration. . . . That's how it was with everyone. It was fun. We didn't think it was work."[40]

DONALD O'CONNOR

One of the first things Kelly dealt with after signing on with the new movie project was to find someone to replace Oscar Levant as Cosmo. Kelly had just finished working with Levant on *An American in Paris,* and the two were not close friends. More importantly, the sardonic quality of Comden and Green's screenplay would not have been served well by Levant's heavy-handed, morose brand of humor.

Levant recalled that he and Kelly had engaged in a heated argument during rehearsals over exactly how Gershwin's "By Strauss" should be played. Levant wanted to play it in the traditional Viennese way, which Kelly thought was not suited for dancing in the kind of movie he was making. "We had quite a fight," as Levant remembered, "but our differences were resolved and we finally achieved an agreeable relationship."[41]

Levant was born in Kelly's hometown, Pittsburgh, in 1906, six years before Kelly. The two never met, however, while growing up. Levant's father, a Russian Jew, ran a jewelry store in the city. Oscar displayed an amazing ability to play the piano, which led him to New York City for lessons. In the early 1930s, he worked at M-G-M as a songwriter and was exempted from the draft in World War II because of severe psychological problems that accompanied him throughout his lifetime. Levant was a case study of varied phobias, obsessive-compulsive behaviors, and antisocial tendencies, mixed with undeniable musical talent and a cutting wit that impressed many. The talent and the wit led to performances on radio and in minor movies by the 1940s, although what he did could hardly be called acting. Levant was only good at being Levant. His first M-G-M movie, *The Barkleys of Broadway* (1949), offered him the opportunity to perform two classical piano pieces as well as play the droll friend of Fred Astaire and Ginger Rogers. The role of Adam Cook in *An American in Paris* was essentially the same character, but as a struggling music student in Paris with no money and a more sour, downbeat view of life.[42]

Apparently Freed, who was the only person in the world wanting Levant to play Cosmo Cosgrove, foresaw a continuation of this trend in Levant's screen career in *Singin' in the Rain*. The best take on this point is that Freed saw *Singin'* as primarily a singing movie, although one has to admit that the Freed-Brown songs and the scenario of the project do not seem to fit Levant's one-dimensional screen persona at all. In contrast, Kelly wanted to make *Singin'* a dancing movie, and there was no room for Levant in the new conception.[43]

Stanley Donen later put it more bluntly. "Betty, Adolph, Gene and myself were just frantic. We wanted a dancer for the part." At least Kelly and Donen believed "the picture would be destroyed if we used Oscar." Lela Simone, a German-born pianist who came to the United States and eventually worked for Freed in a variety of technical and administrative roles, thought Freed wanted Levant for the Cosmo role, "because for seven years he paid his living." Levant was not careful with his income or in managing his career, and Freed, according to Simone, helped him out all he could. When asked why, Simone could only respond, "I don't know. He adored Oscar and maybe because Oscar was a friend of Gershwin's or . . . I don't know. . . . He absolutely worshipped Levant. And vastly exaggerated his talent."[44]

Donen later claimed that he told Freed the team wanted to replace Levant, but Freed hesitated. The impasse broke when Adolph Green impulsively told Levant he had been kicked out of the project, assuming the replacement had been approved. Instead of approaching Freed to confirm the news, Levant became very angry and walked out of the picture on his own. Freed was forced to accede to the team's desire.[45]

The role was given "on Kelly's insistence" to Donald O'Connor.[46] Born around August 28, 1925, Donald's parents later could not recall exactly where or when the birth took place: "We just know it happened somewhere around Chicago, in a small town. But we can't remember the place or the date." This resulted not from parental neglect, for the O'Connor family was knit closely by affection and business, but because the family was a vaudeville team that traveled extensively. O'Connor was literally born on the road, if not in a trunk, and had lived his entire life in the entertainment field. His father, John O'Connor, had been an acrobat for Ringling Brothers before becoming a dancer and comedian in vaudeville. His mother, Effie, was twelve years old when she married John. She had her first child a year later, and six more in later years; Donald was the youngest. "They all went in the act," O'Connor later recalled, "and the more kids you had the more money they paid you." Between having children, O'Connor's mother was a tightrope walker and bareback rider in the circus, and played accompaniment for the family group in vaudeville. Donald first appeared on stage with the group when he was three days old. His mother placed him on the piano bench while she played because there was no one available to take care of him.[47]

Donald began to perform at the age of thirteen months. "I couldn't actually dance," he admitted later, "but they held me up by the back of my skirt, and I moved my feet like crazy!" When he was only ten months old, O'Connor's six-year-old sister Arlene was killed when a car hit her as she was chasing a ball behind the theater where the family performed in Hartford, Connecticut. Thirteen weeks later John O'Connor collapsed from a heart attack on stage during a performance and passed away at age forty-seven. Donald grew up without a father and always felt bad about it. Effie continued the family act as the only way she knew how to raise money, courageously reorganizing the group and trouping on. But the double tragedy haunted her so much that she became overly protective of her youngest child, refusing to let him learn the more dangerous dance routines and monitoring his every move off stage.[48]

Vaudeville was O'Connor's world as he grew up. The family mixed a wide variety of acrobatic stunts, singing, and dancing into their act, with Donald's specialty a rousing tap dance. The vaudeville circuits had already seen their heyday; after starting in the early 1880s, this peculiar brand of lowbrow entertainment had reached its peak in the decade before O'Connor's birth. Now it was on the wane, but the family made a living at it nevertheless.[49]

"I don't remember who taught me my first routines," O'Connor later admitted. "I was just too young; I never paid any attention, I guess. Because it was second nature for me to pick up something and do the act." O'Connor recalled, however, meeting other vaudevillians at drugstores and trading new dance steps. There was little need for more education than this, for vaudeville performers depended on a formulaic approach to their craft. Teams developed something that worked and stuck with it. "I learned just two or three dance routines, and I never learned anything else," O'Connor said. Time step, buck and wing, Maxi Ford, and little else, over and over in house after house for years on end, this was the vaudeville education of Donald O'Connor. He became a good "hoofer," a term denoting someone who danced from the waist down, placing all their movement on their legs and feet instead of using their entire body.[50]

More importantly, O'Connor learned how to connect quickly and intimately with an audience. "I loved those years on the road," he remembered in 1988. "I loved fooling around in front of the audience. . . . I knew that the harder I worked, the more laughs and more applause I got. No one had to teach me *that*. I could hear it. And that was my thing. That's what I was there for. And I really *lived*, to do just that." O'Connor's energy and technique were sharpened to a fine point by this immediate contact with the audience. "It was so ingrained, being in front of an audience, that if something was inherently funny in a movie scene, I'd automatically wait for a laugh." When asked by interviewer Mindy Aloff what made dancing funny, O'Connor quickly answered, "Legomania, the way a person moves his legs like a chicken to music. Pratfalls are always funny. A performer has to answer to himself. If you think something's funny, you've got to go out there and try."[51]

O'Connor's first, uncredited movie appearance was in *It Can't Last Forever* in 1937 as a child dancer. Similar short appearances came in eleven other films for Paramount, until he returned to the family act in 1939 after his brother Billy died of scarlet fever. In 1942, Donald was lured back to Hollywood for Universal's *What's Cookin'?*, in which he created a niche for himself as a teenage heartthrob opposite Peggy Ryan, leading to contracts for both. It was a tough adjustment; O'Connor was amazed at how quickly young movie dancers picked up different routines. He could not do this because his long years in vaudeville had gotten him into a choreographic rut. The dance instructor that Universal Studios hired for him could do nothing to correct this, but producers insisted he continue in a series of spinoff movies because his charisma brought in the box-office receipts. Through hard work, O'Connor expanded his choreographic range and jelled with Ryan and the Jivin' Jacks and Jills, with whom he made fourteen movies during the 1940s. He was drafted at age eighteen in August 1943, but before he left for the war, O'Connor filmed three movies simultaneously and married Gwen Carter, whom he had dated for two years. The two performed for servicemen before he left, and O'Connor's role in the army was also to entertain troops. On his return to civilian life, his daughter Donna was born in 1946. Resuming his dance career in forgettable movies, O'Connor found success in comedic acting roles in a series of pictures with a mule. He played Peter Stirling in *Francis* in 1950, followed by *Francis Goes to the Races* in 1951. Audiences loved the corny premise of a talking mule, and O'Connor was stuck in a moneymaking series that brought little professional fulfillment.[52]

Yet O'Connor's dancing talent was obvious on the big screen. He had what was needed to graduate from the second-rank movies that had been the mainstay of his career to the type of musicals M-G-M was capable of making. Kelly and Donen both were keen on hiring him, but it was not a simple matter. Universal was willing to loan O'Connor for $50,000, but O'Connor hesitated because he knew that under the terms of his contract, he would not see a cent of that sum. He was performing at the Palladium in London when the news arrived. "I got the call as I was lying in bed writing a short story. And although I was flattered, I said no." M-G-M wanted him badly enough, and Universal was happy to accommodate, so an arrangement was made to allow O'Connor to receive the money directly. Actually, O'Connor received much more than the initial amount. Promised $5,000 per week for ten weeks, he willingly worked overtime to ensure the success of *Singin' in the Rain*, racking up 108 days on the job and receiving bonuses that amounted to an additional $40,000. This was quite a sum compared to the $25 a week that he remembered as his initial salary as a vaudeville performer.[53]

Soon after returning to the United States, O'Connor visited the Culver City studio and met Gene Kelly for the first time. He immediately became excited by the project. "And as I was driving home, I thought, 'Oh my God, which way does he turn?' I only turned to the left." This had caused problems between O'Connor and choreographers he had previously worked for, and now he was worried. The next day he met Gene and, "I was just about to ask him which way he turned, and he asked me. He said, 'Which way do *you* turn?' I said, 'To the left.' And he said, '*Thank* God. So do I!'"[54]

DEBBIE REYNOLDS

Ironically, not only O'Connor but the other actors slated to play major characters in *Singin' in the Rain* were not members of the Freed Unit. Freed often recruited promising players from other units, from other studios, or from Broadway, and not all of them became permanent members of his repertory company. For that matter, Donen sometimes directed movies for other producers and Kelly acted in movies produced by other units as well.

Yet, no one could have guessed that Debbie Reynolds would be anyone's choice for the leading lady in *Singin' in the Rain*. She was not a dancer, not quite nineteen when she was cast, and had little movie experience. After the success of the film, nearly everyone tried to take credit for choosing her, but it is likely that Louis B. Mayer was the moving force behind pushing her into Freed's new project, as a way to develop what he thought was a promising talent.

Debbie was born Mary Frances Reynolds on April Fool's Day in 1932, in El Paso, Texas. Her family moved to Burbank, California, when she was a few months old. Her father, a mechanic who ran a gas station, purchased a lot and built his own house. Reynolds remembered that her family was poorer than most in her area. Small in stature, cute, and a natural clown, Reynolds won a beauty contest in Burbank in 1948 because she joked candidly with the audience to hide the fact that she had no particular talent to entertain them, and no strong desire to win the contest. She claimed she had entered merely to obtain the prizes that went with registration. The audience loved her frankness and she was crowned Miss Burbank. Talent scouts in the audience offered her a contract with Warner Brothers for $65 a week and she accepted. It was during her short time at that studio that she allowed her name to be changed to Debbie.[55]

Warner Brothers put her in two movies, *June Bride* (1948) and *The Daughter of Rosie O'Grady* (1950), but failed to capitalize on what Reynolds had to offer film audiences. "About all I could do in the way of talent was to be exuberant," Reynolds later joked about her famous beauty contest escapade, but the same could apply to her early movie roles. Warner Brothers decided to drop her and helped Reynolds get a job at M-G-M for $300 a week. The studio insisted she continue taking classes to finish her high school education, as had Warner Brothers, and she became a classmate of Elizabeth Taylor and one other starlet in the little schoolroom on the Culver City lot. Reynolds later confessed that she did not take seriously the dancing or drama lessons that M-G-M forced her to take, even though the studio hired some of the best teachers to conduct these classes. She was part of a group of entertainers that played for soldiers in California and Korea soon after the war broke out in June 1950.[56]

Debbie's first significant role was a small but visible one in *Three Little Words* (1950), the biographical musical about Bert Kalmar and Harry Ruby. Produced by Jack Cummings and starring Fred Astaire, Vera-Ellen, and Red Skelton, it remains one of the better M-G-M musicals in terms of story, acting, and dances, although it is underappreciated by film scholars. Reynolds portrayed the singer Helen Kane, who became famous in 1928 for singing the Kalmar-Ruby tune "I Wanna Be Loved by You." Helen disliked the song initially and adlibbed a line, which so took audiences that it became her signature. All Reynolds had to do in the movie was look cute as she mouthed the line "Boop-boop-ee-doo" when Kalmar and Ruby discover her. Then she did a rendition of "I Wanna Be Loved by You" with Carleton Carpenter. Ironically—considering the plot of *Singin' in the Rain*—the real Helen Kane dubbed Reynolds in both segments of *Three Little Words*. So, in her first significant exposure on the screen, Reynolds neither spoke nor sang for herself. The role nevertheless garnered for Reynolds a multiyear contract with the studio.[57]

M-G-M allowed Reynolds to sing for herself in her next film, *Two Weeks with Love* (1950), where she and Carpenter performed a rousing rendition of "Aba Daba Honeymoon," a modernized version of a song that was popular in 1914. It was the kind of song that Reynolds could put over very effectively with her untrained voice. Simple and silly, the performance was carried by her energy and fresh, young look. Although untrained as a dancer, M-G-M devised some simple movements for her to add color to the number. "We swung in a tree and on a porch and did a little waltz clog, which is almost like a jitterbug," Reynolds later remembered. "It was such a simple dance that it was a breeze to do." Roger Edens put together a stage act for her and Carpenter by stringing together this and other odd songs. Early in 1951, they toured the old vaudeville circuit to promote the movie, giving five or six performances a day. Meanwhile, a recording of the song quickly sold a million copies. The public took to "Aba Daba Honeymoon" with remarkable fervor, and the enthusiastic crowds that flocked to see her stage show finally made Reynolds take entertaining seriously as a profession. "The audience really hooked me," she later confessed. "I suddenly realized that I enjoyed performing." The sight of 500 or 600 people, waiting in line to see her show, flabbergasted the teenager from Texas. "It was very surprising to see how popular I'd become."[58]

In an effort to capitalize on the Reynolds phenomenon, Mayer decided she should star opposite Gene Kelly in Freed's next picture. Hugh Fordin credits Freed with this decision and characterizes it as "a provocative piece of casting." Freed had supported the casting of Leslie Caron for *An American in Paris,* even though she had no movie experience and was completely unknown in the United States, so it is not impossible that he and Mayer were in complete agreement about giving Reynolds an opportunity to reach the next level in her career. Reynolds became the recipient of M-G-M's "policy of grooming young talent for star status," as Rudy Behlmer has put it.[59]

But Debbie Reynolds was not a dancer, nor was she an actress; her young career was carried mostly by her natural ability to make people laugh by saying off-the-wall things.[60] She could carry the right kind of tune, one that suited her voice and range, but she was unprepared to stand her ground as a major player in a big movie musical. It would only work if she received the same kind of patient coaching that Gene Kelly had given Leslie Caron.

But would Kelly be willing to do this? After all, he had chosen Caron and convinced Freed to sign her on with his endorsement of her ballet talent and her fresh, untrained approach to acting. But, according to Reynolds, she was foisted on Kelly by Mayer. She remembers that Mayer called her to his office early in the spring of 1951 and said, "Debbie, you are a very talented little girl, and I have a surprise for you today. You are going to make a picture with Gene Kelly and Donald O'Connor." When Kelly walked into the office and sat down, Mayer told him, "So here's your leading lady." Reynolds contended years later that his reply was "Whaaat?," but when Mayer insisted that he meant it, Kelly began to size her up. Reynolds admitted that she could not dance or sing. "L.B., w-w-w-what are you doing to me?" Kelly asked his boss, and was "very upset," according to Reynolds. She says he told her to stand up, and asked, "Can you do a time step?" and on seeing her do it, blurted, "That's not a time step, that's a waltz clog." He then asked her to do a Maxi Ford, and Reynolds tried to joke her way out of her deepening embarrassment by saying, "I don't know that car." "That's not a car, that's a *step!*" was Kelly's reply.[61]

According to Reynolds, Kelly was flabbergasted. He had barely heard of her and asked Mayer what she had done to justify the role. "It's not what she's done but what she's *going* to do that matters. We want to make her a star." As Reynolds later put it, Kelly, who remained "shocked, amazed, and not at all pleasantly surprised," had no choice. "Mayer's word was law, and Gene was lumbered with me." Reynolds, throughout her life, believed that she had been shoved into the hands of an unwilling co-star. Kelly was, it is true, a teacher at heart who loved to mold budding talent, but Reynolds had shown none of the promise of Caron in the area of dancing. "Mine is a reluctant talent," Reynolds candidly admitted. "I have tremendous energy, tremendous stamina, and the ability to work very, very hard; that's how I see myself."[62]

In sharp contrast to Debbie's story, Gene Kelly claimed that he had chosen Reynolds for the lead female role in the movie. "I thought she had great talent, so we discussed putting her in and then put her in," he said in 1958. In 1974, sixteen years later, Kelly said that after seeing her perform "Aba Daba Honeymoon" in *Two Weeks with Love,* he felt she was the right person for the role. "That's the girl who's so naïve and so inexperienced . . . she's perfect to play *Singin' in the Rain.*" Kelly went on to tell his biographer in the early 1970s that "no one else at the studio could have touched it. I *insisted* she be used, and *never* had *any* meeting with Mayer concerning *Singin' in the Rain.*" Stanley Donen supported

Kelly in this claim, arguing that Debbie's version of the story was "entirely wrong. We couldn't wait to get her. . . . I thought she was adorable. There was no one else any of us thought of for that part." Donen has said that after seeing "Aba Daba Honeymoon," he and Kelly wanted her for the part and Freed agreed.[63]

Reynolds seems to have no reason to fabricate a story about how she landed her part in *Singin' in the Rain*—yet, her version does not tell the whole story. Lela Simone recalled that several women were tested for the part, so it wasn't as if Mayer said Debbie gets the role and everyone had to agree. Simone remembered Reynolds as doing well in her audition even though she "was no actress, she was nothing. She was a high school girl." But the audition convinced everyone that Reynolds had the potential to make the part work.[64]

Whether or not the incident in Mayer's office took place, the fact that the studio auditioned several women for the female lead explains why Kelly and Donen remember Debbie's casting for the movie rather differently. They apparently saw her potential before filming started, possibly watched "Aba Daba Honeymoon" at the same time, and probably talked with each other about how perfect she was for the role.

Reynolds says the embarrassment she felt at her first meeting with Kelly soon gave way to excitement. Not until that evening did it dawn on her that this new role brought with it far more demands than she had ever shouldered. "It hadn't occurred to me that I had to *dance* with them and be as *good* as they were." With the blessings of hindsight, Reynolds later admitted that "I was about to start something more difficult, more exhausting, more horrendous than any experience I'd ever known in my short and very sheltered experience."[65]

JEAN HAGEN

Comden and Green had an actress in mind to play the character of Lina Lamont—an old friend and colleague, Judy Holliday. But the writers knew that her acting career had risen meteorically and she "was too big a star to be considered for the part," in the words of Jeff Kurtti. They then considered Nina Foch, who had just finished a secondary role in *An American in Paris* as the rich lady who tries to mold and smother Gene Kelly's character, Jerry Mulligan. Foch's screen test revealed that she was "unsuitable for the role."[66]

Jean Hagen, however, was available. Relatively unknown to this point, her career shadowed Holliday's in many ways. Hagen had performed in the off-Broadway version of *Born Yesterday*, the stage comedy that represented Holliday's breakthrough. Comden and Green had in fact kept the role of the street-smart but sensitive Billie Dawn in mind when they created Lina Lamont. If Holliday was not available (and Kelly in later years could not recall if she had even been asked to do the movie), then Hagen was a perfect substitute. Moreover, Hagen already was under contract at M-G-M. Mayer's second wife Lorena also advised the studio boss to use her as Lina. After testing about ten women for the role, everyone agreed that Hagen would work. Kelly later remembered that "the whole picture would have suffered" if they had not found her. "We tested her and she was just perfect," he said. "All the other girls who were pretty enough to be believed as a movie star, weren't funny enough. We were damn lucky to have Jean Hagen."[67]

Jean Shirley ver Hagen was born in Chicago in August 1923 (or 1924, 1925, or 1926, according to varied sources). Her father was a Dutch immigrant who came to the United States to study opera and stayed for good, marrying an American woman. When Jean was twelve years old, the family moved to Indiana. She attended Lake Forest College and Northwestern University, rooming with Patricia Neal and graduating with a degree in drama and music in December 1945. Like so many other hopefuls, Hagen went to New York City and worked at a variety of odd jobs to make ends meet. One day while ushering at the Booth Theater, she talked loudly and critically of the play *Swan Song*. The writers Ben Hecht and Charles MacArthur overheard this and took her comments seriously. They let her try out as a replacement for a sick cast member and gave her the part, but Hagen's debut was delayed by a sudden attack of appendicitis. Hecht and MacArthur kept the job open for her.[68]

When *Swan Song* ended in September 1946, Hagen worked with her friend Patricia Neal in *Another Part of the Forest*, and was noticed in the role of a "brazen trollop." Neal also introduced her to future actor Tom Seidel, who married Hagen in July 1947. Their first child, born in August 1950, when the initial screenplay for *Singin' in the Rain* had just been drafted, was named Patricia as a tribute to Hagen's friend.[69]

Hagen and several other stage actors, including Holliday, David Wayne, and Tom Ewell, made their film debut in *Adam's Rib* (1949), supplementing Spencer Tracy's and Katharine Hepburn's efforts as a feuding lawyer couple. Hagen again played the "slatternly 'other woman' who comes between" Holliday's and Ewell's roles as a married couple. This movie set all four Broadway actors on their separate careers in the movies. While Holliday garnered the most opportunities, Hagen often struggled as she increasingly became typecast as the problem woman, or she suffered through small parts in forgettable films. One of her best roles was as a "doomed girlfriend" in John Huston's *Asphalt Jungle* (1950). Although she acted very well, Hagen was overshadowed by Marilyn Monroe in this successful movie. Jean appeared in seven films before she was tapped to create Lina Lamont, a character not unlike her previous roles except that Lina had to be approached with more comedic elements than she had normally invested in her characters. Hagen was fully capable of that, but M-G-M had done little to develop her talent. The studio's "offhanded policy of casting her as a knowing dame or insipid best friend" had circumscribed her career. Hagen "became just a useful gap filler in MGM pictures," but *Singin' in the Rain* represented an important break in her career.[70]

The task of casting the movie's major roles was finished, and the smaller parts could easily be filled by tapping the large stable of character actors and bit players at M-G-M. Usually unsung and always underappreciated, these performers filled the screen of so many pictures that they constituted a recurring film population that spanned decades of Hollywood history. Many of them had acted in silent movies and were still going strong, eager to appear even for a few seconds in every movie they could get.

3
Out of Thin Air You Make a Moment Dance

Gene Kelly finished working on *An American in Paris* on January 8, 1951. Ten days later, the *New York Herald-Tribune* reported that he was to begin preproduction of a new M-G-M film based on Mark Twain's popular novel *Huckleberry Finn*. Kelly was to co-star with Danny Kaye and rumor had it that Mickey Rooney would play Huck, while E. Y. Harburg and Burton Lane would write the songs. Arthur Freed planned to begin work on the new movie in the summer of 1951, but Kelly, rested after his "long vacation," threw himself into the preproduction work for *Singin' in the Rain* in March, and *Huckleberry Finn* was put on hold. Freed often floated reports of movies he was planning, probably as a way to lay claim to new properties and get yet another line of publicity in the papers. The report about *Huckleberry Finn* appeared at the time that Kelly agreed to do *Singin' in the Rain* as his next project, when it may have been a bit too early to accurately reflect what the star had in mind.[1]

Kelly's driving work ethic allowed him only two months as a "long vacation." In contrast, Fred Astaire limited himself whenever possible to only one movie per year, taking several months off between projects. Astaire also had a strong work ethic, but he paced his career more carefully than did Kelly, who felt he had to take advantage of opportunities to accomplish his artistic goals while his health and vitality held out. Kelly was in superb physical shape, even though he "never consciously exercised," according to biographer Clive Hirschhorn. "I don't do any formalized setting-up exercises," Kelly told interviewer Helen Hover, "and I wouldn't know what to do with a vitamin pill. I get so much exercise dancing I don't have to touch my left toe with my right eyebrow ten times each morning to keep in condition."[2]

More importantly, Kelly had honed his artistic sense to a fine point by early 1951. Two years before, when he was thirty-seven years old, Kelly "began to develop something of an aesthetic sense," as he later claimed. "Not only did I know exactly what I was striving for in my pictures, but I felt that I now knew how to achieve it. And it was this constant sense of adventure I felt every time I embarked on something that kept me going." He was grateful that he retained the physical stamina necessary to achieve those goals, considering that most male dancers peaked physically in their late twenties. "But I was still taking leaps and bounds over tables in my forties," Kelly told Hirschhorn. "Without the mental stimulation my work gave me, I don't think this would have been possible."[3]

Kelly's greatest joy was in working out dance routines, rather than performing them in front of the camera. "There was something about achieving a perfection during rehearsals, which I found even more exciting than committing that perfection to celluloid." Later in his life, Kelly was more pointed in his comments regarding the relative merits of creating and performing dance. "The big thrill for me is *creating* something," he said. "There's great magic in that. You take an idea—a man coming down the street out of the blue, alone—and there's some music. And out of thin air you make a moment dance."[4]

For Kelly, creating dance for the film was, at the start, an intellectual exercise. He began by working out the basic steps of any given number in his head. "You start working out an idea in a chair," he commented twenty years after working on *Singin' in the Rain*. "You just don't get up and dance on the floor; your feet don't work it out; you work it out first in your head, just like the guy who writes the story." Action followed intellect. "When I get the idea blocked out, I fill it in with movement." For Kelly, the beginning and the end of a dance number came first because he knew what was needed to fill in the middle, based on those bookends. How to create the beginning and end depended a great deal on the context of the number, and therefore the script came into important relief as an aid to the choreography. Creating dance for the camera was quite different than for the stage, because it had to be conceived with the camera in mind. A number "should be composed for certain camera setups to *begin* with. The cutting [editing] of it, therefore, should be pretty much mechanical."[5]

Another factor in the creation of dances for *Singin' in the Rain* was, of course, Kelly's co-stars. Donald O'Connor was an old trouper with years of experience, an apt partner for the superstar, but O'Connor was not immediately available. He began a five-week engagement in England on March 12, with two weeks at the Palladium. During those two weeks, M-G-M worked out the deal to engage him for the picture. O'Connor's representative, Robert Webb, was willing to cancel the last week of the performer's tour through the smaller towns of England in order to get him to the Culver City studios as soon as possible. Webb reminded Freed that O'Connor was committed to doing another *Francis* movie, but the script for the third installment in that series of pictures had not been finalized as of early March. O'Connor committed himself to start work on *Singin'* by April 25, 1951, at the latest.[6]

Comden and Green returned to Los Angeles for three weeks in March to work on revisions of the screenplay. It was an intense experience, and quite a few important changes were made. Unlike the previous drafts, this third and final version of the script was a collaboration between Kelly, Donen, and the writers. Kelly knew Comden and Green and their Revuers material well. He recalled that they "used to do little bits about silent movies and early sound movies, so we expanded on that a lot" in the revision process.[7]

Kelly was taken by the basic premise of the film, and enjoyed helping to tweak the sardonic treatment of Hollywood's past. "Almost everything in this movie springs from the truth," he later claimed. "It's a conglomeration of bits of movie lore." Kelly explained that even the characters drew on real people: the director "Roscoe Dexter is a little bit like Busby Berkeley," while the producer "R. F. Simpson has a touch of Arthur Freed in him." Like Berkeley, Dexter was loud and used exaggerated gestures. As an in-joke regarding Freed, Simpson could not visualize a scene until he'd seen it on film. Moreover, Cosmo's role as a "mood-music pianist" on the sets of silent films was exactly what Freed did, in addition to songwriting, before his connection with M-G-M in 1929. The character of Dora Bailey was meant to be gossip columnist Louella Parsons. The script was "constantly referential but never reverential," in the words of Kelly biographers Sheridan Morley and Ruth Leon.[8]

SCRIPT REVISIONS

As soon as Kelly came on board, he and Donen started working closely with Comden and Green on script revisions. The writers were delighted with their collaboration and recalled that the four of them went "over the script shot by shot" to make changes and revisions. The co-directors also worked closely with each other to plan out the movie. "Let me assure you that Stanley Donen and I were in this very room that you and I are sitting in now, working out every shot of that film," Kelly told an interviewer at his home in 1988.[9]

Comden and Green worked hard for three weeks in March before returning to New York. They continued to work on the script while devoting time to their stage project, writing "a couple of added scenes" and working out an additional line or two through telephone conversations with Kelly and others in Culver City. They felt comfortable with this working relationship because they knew Gene and Stanley so well. "We were lucky to work with directors we were very comfortable with, so that once we had left we knew the script was going to be wonderfully handled." Kelly called them several times and remembered that their conversations often ran like this: "We're doing this now. What do you think of this line? Give me a new line." The writers, who were immersed in "doctoring a show in Philadelphia," often responded with, "Oh, call us back tomorrow. We're very busy now. Abe Burrows is here." Nevertheless, Kelly was pleased that Comden and Green were so familiar with the lyrics, music, and dialogue, and also, because they were his personal friends, he was willing to put up with these frustrations to keep production going.[10]

The exact contributions of these four people later became a point of some discussion among fans of *Singin' in the Rain*. Green said that Kelly and Donen influenced the structure of the movie more than the characterizations. Comden said they had little influence on specific lines of dialogue except when it was necessary to lead plausibly into a dance number: "We had to stay very close in touch on those things." Donen disputed these claims and insisted that he and Kelly made huge changes in the screenplay and that Comden and Green's published script for the movie "is taken off the screen after all our changes before and even during production . . . [it is] not the script Betty and Adolph gave us." Art director Randall Duell supported this view and stated that "an awful lot of the stuff [in the movie] Gene and Stanley cooked up. They spent night after night after a day of rehearsal. They'd meet in their dressing room and cook up all these ideas. I'd say they were almost totally responsible." Although Duell's final assessment gives

Comden and Green too little credit, a careful comparison of the writers' first two drafts shows mostly minor changes, even though Donen was consulting with them throughout. However, the third and final draft, which Comden and Green wrote after Kelly got involved, shows major changes and is closer to the final movie in important ways. So, putting it all together, it appears that Kelly's involvement sparked creativity between the co-directors and their input greatly improved the script.[11]

Gene Kelly's personal copy of the script for *Singin' in the Rain* was part of the personal papers and memorabilia he donated to Boston University in the 1960s, but he requested that the screenplay be returned to him in 1972. It was destroyed in the disastrous fire that leveled his home in Beverly Hills on Christmas Eve in 1983. The script had many handwritten notes on the margin, which would have been invaluable in assessing the exact contributions Kelly made to the final draft, and the production of *Singin'*.[12]

It is true that there are whole sections of scintillating dialogue and many funny situations, or blocks of sequences, that remain intact from the first two drafts to the third and final draft, and are retained in the movie as well. There was no need for Comden and Green to thoroughly rewrite the script for Kelly or any other player—it was essentially a good screenplay from the beginning. But the final draft has many important improvements over the first two drafts as well. In particular, some parts of the screenplay badly needed new ideas to improve the narrative flow of the movie and heighten the integration of song, dance, and story.[13]

The film presents a well-crafted narrative, with several critical turns. The initial turning point, which redirects the flow of the storyline and sharply defines where the interplay of characters and conflicts will take the viewer, is the first time that Lina Lamont speaks. Everything before that point is a smoothly flowing narrative that provides the background of the story. But from the moment Lina speaks, the viewer knows that *she* will be the problem everyone has to face in the picture. The next major turning point is the love song and dance between Don Lockwood and Kathy Selden on the empty soundstage, signifying that the love interest we all expected to develop has taken root. This love connection, and Lina's opposition to it, are the true centers of the movie's structure, with the problems associated with the transition from silent movies to sound pictures accentuating the narrative flow.

The rest of the movie's turning points occur in natural sequence: the bad preview of the studio's first attempt to make a talkie; the revelation that Don, Kathy, and Cosmo should remake *The Duelling Cavalier* as a musical; Lina's discovery of Kathy's dubbing and her clever plot to take advantage of it for her own career; and Lina's final comeuppance after the successful premiere of *The Dancing Cavalier*. The first and second versions of the screenplay essentially had this structure in place, but with many turning points that were not so well constructed or sharply defined. Among other things, this transition from a good script that needed work to a movie that almost seems perfect after more than fifty years of viewing indicates the significance of incorporating the dance numbers into the scheme. The songs and dances were not just the icing on the cake, they were part of the basic ingredients of the confection. The screenplay could not be finalized without them, and for that, the participation of Kelly—as the dancing star and the choreographer—was necessary in the preproduction phase.

Chapter 1 details the differences between Comden and Green's first draft of the screenplay as compared to what we see in the movie. All of those changes were in the final draft as well, and were the result of the collaboration between the directors and the writers.

Yet there are some highly visible differences between the final draft and what audiences would eventually see on the screen, and these improvements are due almost entirely to Kelly and Donen because the writers were only marginally involved with preproduction (via telephone) at this stage. Comden and Green's consistently had R. F. Simpson and his wife arrive in the same car with Don and Lina for the premiere of *The Royal Rascal,* unlike in the movie, where Don and Lina make a striking entrance on their own. In all the drafts, Lina did not kick Don in the pants (in Don's flashback told to the audience at the premiere); this was added later to nicely demonstrate the conflict that defined the stars' true relationship. In the jalopy ride, when Kathy calls out to the policeman, the scripts said that Don recognizes him, calls him Matt, and chats with him about his family. In the movie, the policeman recognizes the star, but the star does not know the cop personally, which is much more believable. Comden and Green had Kathy give Don a lengthy (two-page) explanation as to why he couldn't find her for three weeks—she said she was with a traveling nightclub unit, they were stranded in Iowa, and she finally came back when talkies were introduced to see if she could get a part in movies. The directors dropped this extraneous conversation to improve the narrative flow. All the scripts had Don cutting the cake with a knife right before Kathy jumps out of it at Simpson's party, and this was changed to his simply approaching and standing near the cake, which works much better. The villain in *The Duelling Cavalier* said "heh, heh, heh" to Lina's "no, no, no" in all the scripts, which was changed to "yes, yes, yes" in the movie, and works far better in the preview as well as when Kathy repeats it to Cosmo's amusement.[14]

Comden and Green had added a humorous scene in the final draft which was not retained in the movie, and it is not clear why this was dropped. A middle-aged woman, who is engrossed in watching the preview of *The Royal Rascal,* clutches her husband's arm and says passionately, "Don! Don! Oh, Don!" Her harried husband responds, "Hey, remember me? My name is Sam."[15]

Other changes though are understandable. The writers had "Charlie chooses chestnuts" in one of the diction coach's exercises, which was changed to the more alliterative "Chester chooses chestnuts." Also, *both* Cosmo and Don were to dance each time Cosmo tries to cheer up Don—first when Don cannot find Kathy and then after the dismal premiere of *The Duelling Cavalier.* In both cases, it is much more believable that only Cosmo would perform (as he does in the movie) to snap Don out of his gloom.[16]

Another note, surely developed by the puckish Green, was to weave the phrase "Are you anybody?" or its variant into the picture. In the beginning, at the premiere of *The Royal Rascal,* Cosmo was the butt of this blunt question, which so well summarizes the ballyhoo of early Hollywood. Later, Cosmo even said the line to himself in a mirror. In the end, the question was aimed at Spencer Tracy as he comes out of a limousine to attend the premiere of *The Broadway Rhythm.* Green hoped to highlight the irony of such a question with a cameo appearance by one of M-G-M's top stars.[17] But the trick, and the theme, were dropped from the final screen version for some reason. The only time the line is used is by Lina as a personal insult to Cosmo after he makes fun of her following the premiere of *The Royal Rascal.*

Comden and Green changed the ending considerably in the final draft. They introduced a more elaborate ceremony for the pulling of the rope to reveal that Kathy is dubbing Lina. In this version, Don recalls his role in *The Prince of Pirates,* and starts to act out the scene. Cosmo and Simpson get into the spirit of the act and ham up nautical themes, yelling, "One-two-hoist away!" and "To the ropes!" before the trio finally raise the curtain. Kathy is scared and confused as she is exposed to the audience, and the trio urge her to continue singing (in pantomime from the wings). In the end, Don, Kathy, and Cosmo "happily sing and dance" together on the stage to "You Are My Lucky Star" as the audience applauds.[18] Fortunately this version of the ending was not retained in the movie.

The final draft included certain new aspects that were kept, however, in the screen version. Many of these are discussed in Chapter 1 as changes from the initial draft. In addition, the team of writers, directors, and actors had worked out the details of Don and Cosmo's past in vaudeville, to a point in the final draft where it was almost exactly as viewers would see it on the screen.[19]

Ironically, as Comden, Green, Kelly, and Donen continued to work on script revisions, Freed was faced with a problem regarding the title of the movie. As early as August 1949, he had received a memo regarding the issue because someone had discovered that a "non-fictional inspirational book" entitled *Singing in the Rain* had been published about 1936. In March 1951, Loew's New York office suggested that Freed make it clear in the publicity of his new movie that the title came from his own song, not any other publication. This angle informed Freed's immediate decision to drop the final "g" in "singing" as the official spelling of his picture's title. This would emphasize the fact that the movie title came from his own songbook.[20]

Rudi Monta, an M-G-M staff member, pointed out that Kathy Summers was the name of a real actress. He suggested the character be called Kathy Burrows or Kathy Norwood. But the name was changed first to Kathy Sands, and eventually became Kathy Selden by May 23. Monta also discovered that there actually had been a studio called Imperial Pictures in 1928. He suggested the name be changed to Magno, Mammoth, Big-Art, or Climax Pictures. It eventually became Monumental Pictures. Bea Whitney, another M-G-M staff member, reported that Comden and Green referred to Warner Brothers' *The Jazz Singer* as the first full talkie, whereas *Lights of New York* (1928) actually held that distinction. "Mr. Freed & Mr. Edens said they knew this but didn't care," noted a secretary at the bottom of Whitney's memo.[21]

At the end of the movie, Lockwood and Selden kiss in front of a billboard advertising a new picture, in which the two of them are starring.

The name of the movie? *Singin' in the Rain!* Originally, it was supposed to be *Broadway Rhythm,* but Monta pointed out to Freed that this was already the name of a real film in 1944, and he suggested changing the billboard to *Broadway Frolics.* However, probably as a touch of humor, the directors used the name of the movie itself.[22]

Monta also suggested that the name of a movie star at the first premiere be changed from Gilda Mara to Olga Mara, and that her husband in the movie should have his title changed from "Marquis." No reasons were given for these proposed changes. The first was probably suggested to avoid a connection to Rita Hayworth's *Gilda* (1946). The second change was possibly to avoid confusion with the "marquee" at the premiere which is pronounced exactly the same. Both suggestions were accepted and the title was changed to "Baron."[23]

Joseph Fields, a writer with a long and successful career in movies and the stage, drafted some outlandish revisions of the final draft of the screenplay in late July and early August 1951, long after production of the movie had begun. These ideas included a drastic alteration of the climax of the movie. Fields suggested that Don pretend to accidentally raise the curtain on Kathy dubbing Lina in the theater, followed by an infuriated electrician chasing him menacingly with a wrench, inexplicably angry with the star for raising the curtain. Don would then climb a ladder and kick the wrench out of the man's hand as the audience roared with laughter and applause. Finally, Don would drop down beside Kathy on a rope as the audience went wild. Fields also suggested dropping several scenes that actually work very well in the movie. It is baffling why Fields proposed these ideas, especially so late in the schedule, but they were all ignored.[24]

In their published screenplay of *Singin' in the Rain,* Comden and Green write in a note that, "in this version, we are presenting an account of what is in the film itself." Although largely true, there are actually many differences between their published screenplay and the movie. Lines that were dropped from the screenplay, and descriptions or settings that were changed, are still kept in this published version; changes made in the lines are not always reflected; and some gestures that were dropped are still described. Don and Cosmo are said to be in ragged clothes as boys and also as grownups in the flashback, even though this is not so in the movie. Don is said to be at the piano and Cosmo is playing the fiddle, when it is the opposite in the movie, and with good reason—given Gene's connection to violin lessons and Cosmo being a mood-music piano player. Don and Lina are supposedly kissing in a castle garden in front of a hedge in *The Royal Rascal,* but they are actually inside the "castle" in the movie. The writers mention a "red" curtain at the premieres, when the curtains used in the movie are beige. Don supposedly bursts into laughter when Kathy comes out of the cake, but he does not do so in the film. They say that Don, Kathy, and Cosmo have half-empty plates in front of them (in the scene in Don's house), but in the movie, Don's sandwich is untouched and his glass of milk is full. He obviously has not eaten. In their published screenplay, Cosmo sings a few lines of "Fit as a Fiddle" and Don says "Whoopee!" In the movie, Cosmo does a few impromptu dance steps as well, and Don does not say "Whoopee!" The writers say Don is "cynically amused" when Cyd Charisse's character tosses him a coin and leaves, but he is clearly depressed in the film. Also, near the end, they say a voice rings out in the balcony, "Hey, cut the talk Lina, sing!"; but the man who says this is not in the balcony and it's not just a voice. They also have the order wrong for the denouement. They say the three men move to the ropes and stand there watching Lina, flapping their arms to imitate her, "and then start pulling on the ropes to raise the curtain." Actually, they flap their arms first, then pointedly walk to the ropes in the back and pull on them. Although this may seem like a minor difference, had they walked to the ropes first, the viewers would have guessed what the plan was; it works better when they walk over later and pull the ropes right away to reveal Kathy.[25]

Also, new lines added to the movie are not included in Comden and Green's published screenplay. For example, in the movie Don says sarcastically (in a voiceover for the flashback), "and of course all through those pictures, Lina was and is always an inspiration to me, warm and helpful, a real lady." This pretty substantial line from the movie was not in the final draft that Comden and Green submitted, and they seem to have missed it. With all of these and many such differences, the published screenplay is not a completely accurate account of what is in the film.

In their preface, Comden and Green also claim that "except for a few minor alterations, and the post facto descriptions of the musical numbers and montages created by director-choreographers Kelly and Donen, the other differences between the script of *Singin' in the Rain* and the film itself are covered in the Introduction."[26] This however is an exaggeration. In their Introduction, Comden and Green note that the only other differences between their script and the film were that "Make 'Em Laugh" replaced "The Wedding of the Painted Doll" and the medley with the touring routine for Gene and Debbie was replaced by one song on an empty sound stage. In truth, there is a long list of changes between the final script and the movie as discussed in this section, including the bizarre "Prince of Pirates" scene and having *all three players sing and dance* on stage to a "love" song, "You Are My Lucky Star," as the ending of their final submitted draft, but Comden and Green did not acknowledge any of this. Moreover, between the final draft and the making of the movie, the three main characters were improved and most of the songs were switched around (as will be seen in the following sections). Despite all this, Comden and Green give readers the erroneous impression that their final script was almost identical to the movie, discounting the substantial changes made by Kelly and Donen.

CHARACTERS

Don Lockwood had been conceived from the start as a flashy silent screen star who encounters problems in the transition to sound. Gene and everyone else agreed that John Gilbert was a salient example of that type. Born in Utah in 1899, John Cecil Pringle made his first film in 1917 and soon became "a vital heartbeat in the silent era and one of the brightest stars shining in MGM's galaxy." Gilbert starred opposite Greta Garbo in *The Flesh and the Devil* (1927), and the screen pair broke new ground in depicting sensuality on screen.[27]

Gilbert developed a passionate love for Garbo and a serious drinking problem. Moreover, he could never get along with Louis B. Mayer. In fact, the two literally had a couple of fistfights during Gilbert's stormy years with M-G-M. Gilbert's personal demons compounded his tough transition to talkies. Playing opposite Catherine Dale Owen in *His Glorious Night* (1929), Gilbert declaimed melodramatically, "Oh, beauteous maiden, my arms are waiting to enfold you. I love you, I love you, I love you." Several people giggled on the set during the filming, as well as in the movie theaters during the viewing of this classic example of ham acting. There is reason to believe that Gilbert was set up to fall. Director Lionel Barrymore hated him and allowed the actor to go overboard in developing his role in *His Glorious Night*. There also were rumors that Mayer might have technically altered the sound recording to heighten the ludicrous nature of the scene. At any rate, Gilbert's career took a nosedive and never recovered. He made more movies in the early 1930s, one opposite Garbo in *Queen Christina* (1933). Despite his continued passion for Garbo, which led to his divorce, and despite Garbo's love for him, the pair never married. Gilbert died in 1936.[28]

Given the visibility of Gilbert's overacting, it was almost inevitable that Gene Kelly agreed to duplicate it for *Singin' in the Rain*. The "I love you, I love you" line was repeated by Don in *The Duelling Cavalier* in the final version of *Singin'*, as was the audience laughter. But Don ended up a better person than Comden and Green initially created. In the second draft, the writers themselves dropped Don's insistence to Kathy, after *The Dancing Cavalier*'s success, that she continue to dub Lina, so the Lamont-Lockwood combination could go on. Later Kelly and Donen also dropped Don's lengthy gloating about himself as a star and a legend to Kathy in their jalopy ride.[29]

For the character of Kathy Selden, they needed a young, inexperienced, but promising actress with spunk. Kelly later admitted that Reynolds was perfectly qualified for the role because she already had those characteristics. "Debbie's own naivete took care of everything. She didn't know what the hell was going on half the time," he jokingly said twenty years later, "which was just the right quality we wanted, and she was marvelous. Just marvelous."[30]

As Don's character softened in rewrites and even after the final draft, Kathy became less combative as well, and both became more appealing individuals. Comden and Green had included a substantial scene in all their drafts that involved Kathy and her fellow dancers in the dressing room before performing at Simpson's post-premiere party for *The Royal Rascal*. Kathy fumes at length about the conceited character named Don Lockwood who has unsuccessfully made a pass at her. "Of all the raving eagle maniacs," Comden and Green have her say in a deliberate mispronunciation of the word. "You can imagine—well, I cut him down a peg or two." Defending her high-minded adherence to "art" even as she is getting ready to dance at a Hollywood party, Kathy righteously says, "I'm no Garbo. I'm a singer and dancer. What would they use me for in pictures?" All of this was wisely deleted.[31]

Lina Lamont also grew out of the career of a current star, Judy

Holliday, although she had never performed in an M-G-M movie. Holliday developed a character that mixed worldliness with a soft heart when she performed with Comden and Green in The Revuers. She further developed it for the stage version of Born Yesterday and the movie version filmed at Columbia. Everyone agreed that this was the right model for Lina, not in terms of the goodhearted aspect, but the external, brash demeanor and poor speaking skills. Ironically, Jean Hagen had performed that role in the off-Broadway tour of Born Yesterday, and knew it well.[32]

Judy Holliday was an enormously gifted but controversial actress. Born in Manhattan in 1922 as Judith Tuvim, her IQ test classified her at the genius level in school. A founding member of The Revuers, she went to Hollywood for a time during World War II where Twentieth Century–Fox changed her name to Holliday, which was a loose translation of the Hebrew name Tuvim. Back in New York, Holliday's big break came with Born Yesterday, replacing Jean Arthur in the role of Billie Dawn in 1946. Her Billie has been described as "a hard-boiled ex-chorus girl whose knowledge consists mainly of a few suggestive dance steps, some chirpy melodies, and a vast store of carnal knowledge." But the key to the success of the play and the movie was the transformation of Billie into a more socially aware, moral person who finally stands up to her domineering and sleazy boyfriend, Harry Brock. Without realizing he had been the model for Brock, Harry Cohn bought the rights to the play for Columbia. Before releasing his movie version of Born Yesterday, Cohn put Holliday, Jean Hagen, and two other stage actors in Adam's Rib. Holliday later won an Oscar for her Billie Dawn in Born Yesterday (1950). Even before the film was released, she was named along with 150 other entertainment industry people as having links to communist organizations. Her stardom coincided with vicious and unrelenting attacks by Red-baiters for years to come.[33]

The creation of Lina Lamont was inspired by Billie Dawn, but it was not a duplication of that character. The squeaky voice and the lack of intelligence are related to Billie as depicted early in the plot of Born Yesterday. But Lina did not include the transformation into a better person or the basic innocence and naïveté of Holliday's character. Billie Dawn was not a manipulative or ambitious person, and she became wiser as the film progressed. Lina remained the basic "bad-guy," outsmarted in her attempt to manipulate everyone for selfish aims, much in the way that Harry Brock was outsmarted by Billie at the end of Born Yesterday.

Ironically, Jean Hagen's "real voice was mellow and feminine," and the voice that sounded like fingernails trailing across a blackboard "was wholly self-created." Hagen also was a brunette, but she was screen-tested in a blond wig and Dore Schary liked it. The platinum blond hair seemed to accentuate Lina's cold, conniving nature. Given that her character was pretty cut and dried, Hagen seems to have participated far less in preproduction meetings than other cast members. She sometimes wandered onto a neighboring sound stage to watch rehearsals for Fred Astaire's next film, *The Belle of New York* (1952). One day she watched the famous dancer rehearse for his "Dancing Man" number in that movie, which Astaire performed with a little sand sprinkled on the floor.[34]

Zelda Zonk (whose last name was later changed to Zanders) was a more prominent character in the early drafts. Comden and Green had her performing a number with a chorus but then she is outshined by Kathy who follows with her own dance. Also, Zelda argues with Simpson against the idea of including Kathy as her kid sister in her new movie.[35] In the final product, Rita Moreno's opportunity to shine in this role was reduced, not unlike the way Kathy overshadowed Zelda in the latter's own movie.

Cosmo's character was rather sleazy in the early versions of the screenplay. In an early draft, a showgirl asks Cosmo if she'll get to sing in the picture, and Cosmo eyes her and says, "If you meet me after rehearsal, I'll . . . ." This scene was dropped by the writers but replaced by another sleazy scene, ending with an elaborate joke. In the first two drafts, there had been no scene at Simpson's party where Cosmo converses with an aspiring starlet. In the final draft, however, a starlet sits on his lap, curls his hair with her fingers, and asks flirtatiously, "Oh Mr. Brown . . . could you *really* get me into the movies?" Cosmo leads her on "with a little leer" until she asks what she would have to do. "Well, it's simple. Meet me Saturday afternoon in front of the Loew's Theater. I'll take you in—unless there's something playing I've seen already, in which case you're on your own." The starlet yells as she jumps off his lap, "Oh, so's your Aunt Tilly!" Kelly and Donen dropped this scene.[36]

The final draft also had several scenes that depict Cosmo as rather sophomoric and extremely annoying. He makes terrible suggestions to the director to "help" him with the story for *The Duelling Cavalier*, such as Don testing the guillotine and getting his head cut off. The director is not amused. Cosmo also insults Lina by singing, "The Old Gray Mare Ain't What She Used To Be," and says that her talking may bring back silent pictures. He sings like Al Jolson the whole time Simpson is seriously talking to the others about shutting down. The directors dropped all of these scenes, making Cosmo a much more likable character.[37]

Actors had to be selected to portray secondary characters, and at times they had to be replaced. Jerry Mohr was initially slated to play the part of the studio's publicity man, but he dropped out on a Friday. By the following Monday, Kelly had recruited his friend King Donovan to take over the role. Famed and feared Hollywood columnist Louella Parsons was "interested" in playing the part of Dora Beagle. Her agent contacted Freed to tell him, but the producer did not take her up on the offer. There certainly was a precedent for columnists to appear in movies. Hedda Hopper, a fierce rival of Parsons, had appeared in Norma Shearer's *Let Us Be Gay* (1930) and Buster Keaton's *Speak Easily* (1932). The directors made the links between secondary characters and real people stronger whenever possible. For example, R. F. Simpson's line, "I can't quite visualize it. I'll have to see it on film first" (as an affectionate tie-in to Arthur Freed) was added late in the production phase.[38]

Freed had offered a contract to Nacio Herb Brown to work on songs for his new project at a very early date, August 1, 1948. That one-year contract was renewed for another year, but not extended beyond August 1, 1950. Brown was therefore not on contract when Kelly, Donen, Comden, and Green worked out the final draft of the script in the early spring of 1951. Exactly what Brown did for Freed during those two years is unclear, other than writing the music for "Make 'Em Laugh."[39]

Everyone went through a brainstorming process in the spring of 1951 to select fourteen songs from the Freed-Brown catalog for inclusion in *Singin' in the Rain*. The tentative musical layout, dated April 4, included seventeen numbers beginning with "Fit as a Fiddle." Kathy and the girls were to sing "All I Do Is Dream of You" at Simpson's party, and Don was to reprise that song in his bedroom. The April 11 screenplay explains that Don is too late to stop Kathy from driving away after Simpson's party and begins to sing "All I Do Is Dream of You" in the driveway.

Then the sequence moves to his bedroom where, in his pajamas, he dances to the tune. Cosmo was to sing "The Wedding of the Painted Doll" to cheer up Don in the studio, and Zelda, Kathy, and another girl were to rehearse "We'll Make Hay While the Sun Shines," to prepare for Zelda's new picture. An unidentified piece was to be used during Kathy's audition, while Don was to sing "Should I?" to Kathy as part of their falling-in-love routine. This was to take place, for the first time, on an empty sound stage instead of the travelogue as a backdrop. Soon after, Kathy was to sing "You Are My Lucky Star" to Don's image on the billboard, and Don and Cosmo were then to do "Tongue Twisters" (not yet written) at the diction lesson. "Good Morning" was still slated to be sung at the Pink Fedora restaurant by Don, Cosmo, and Kathy, and Don was to do "Singin' in the Rain," but without mention of a venue. After that, Cosmo was still pencilled in to do "The Piano Playing Pioneer" (which was not yet written), and Kathy's dubbing sequence for Lina as yet had no song listed. Don's solo number, "The Broadway Melody," was next. Don was to perform this on a set for R. F. Simpson to sell the idea, with shots of cameras filming him as he dances, rather than creating the entire ballet sequence as a dream interruption of the narrative flow as in the finished film. Neither Don and Lina's "premiere number" nor Kathy's dubbing of Lina at the premiere had songs attached to them. However, Don was to end the movie by singing "You Are My Lucky Star" on stage after the premiere.[40]

The "premiere number" apparently referred to Don and Lina singing in *The Dancing Cavalier,* as an updated April 17 memo indicated that this number, as well as Kathy's dubbing number for Lina, would be "You Were Meant For Me." This was changed in late May to "Would You?" for both instances. In the April 17 memo, Zelda and the other girls were now to perform "I've Got a Feeling You're Fooling," but Zelda's number was later dropped, as was Kathy's audition number. Also in this memo, Kathy's dubbing sequence for Lina now had "Singin' in the Rain" listed, but Don was now joined by Kathy and Cosmo in singing "You Are My Lucky Star" in ending the movie, to match the April 11 screenplay. The montage incorporating "Beautiful Girl" and various (unnamed) musical clips to represent the Jazz Age talkie first appeared in the April 11 script. By the end of May, "Tongue Twisters" became "Moses Supposes," and in late June, "You Were Meant For Me" replaced "Should I?" as Don's number with Kathy.[41]

Don's performance of "The Broadway Melody" later evolved into the complex ballet, which included "Broadway Rhythm." A new song, "Make 'Em Laugh," replaced "The Wedding of the Painted Doll"; and "The Piano Playing Pioneer," which was never written, was dropped altogether. The musical montage shown before "Beautiful Girl" evolved to include several dropped Freed-Brown numbers—"Should I?," "I've Got a Feeling You're Fooling," and "The Wedding of the Painted Doll." Another Freed-Brown song, "Temptation," was added as background music for people dancing at Simpson's party.

A few other Freed-Brown songs were considered for *Singin' in the Rain* but rejected. Gene Kelly donated more than 200 song sheets to his collection at Boston University in the early 1990s, some of them with scorch marks from the 1983 fire that destroyed his home. He wrote short comments on nearly all of them, indicating that Freed's "Alone" "Almost made it into [the movie]," the song "Yours and Mine" was "Considered for 'Singin in the Rain' (No Go)," and Zelda's "We'll Make Hay While the Sun Shines" also "Didn't make it for 'Singin in the Rain.'"[42]

In the end, with the addition of two new songs, *Singin' in the Rain* contained sixteen songs, only two of them—"Would You?" and "You Are My Lucky Star"—not accompanied by dance or acrobatics. Both new songs composed specifically for the movie—"Make 'Em Laugh" and "Moses Supposes"—had to be written before starting production, and the backgrounds of both are rather unique.

After Donald O'Connor came on board to replace Oscar Levant, Comden and Green had "painfully wedged into the script" the Freed-Brown song "The Wedding of the Painted Doll." This had been one of the team's bestselling numbers, but it was a bit difficult to find a place for it in *Singin' in the Rain*. By placing it in the hands of a comic actor-dancer, and making it the centerpiece of Cosmo's efforts to cheer up Don, the writers hoped to make use of it. But Kelly and Donen did not like the number, nor could they find something better in the catalog. Donen says he (or he and Gene, depending on which Donen interview one reads) approached Freed with the request to write a new song. Kelly and Donen wanted something snappy and funny as a cheering-up song, something like "Be a Clown." Cole Porter had written this anthem to entertainment for *The Pirate* and Kelly performed it twice, initially with the Nicholas Brothers, and then at the end of the movie with Judy Garland.[43]

Freed seems to have taken the directors literally, for he consulted with Nacio Herb Brown and quickly produced "Make 'Em Laugh." The new song bore a disquieting resemblance to "Be a Clown." Donen went further than that, stating that it was "100-percent plagiarism, and partly we are to blame. None of us had the courage to say to him, 'For Christ sake, it obviously works for the number, but it's a stolen song, Arthur.'" No one wanted to embarrass Freed or risk incurring his anger, so they went along with the game. Porter himself was too much of a gentleman to ever raise the issue. Betty Comden could not understand why Freed and Brown did this, and concluded "it must have been an accident. . . . Arthur himself wrote so many wonderful songs, he must have subconsciously thought he was dipping into something he'd composed years ago." Rudy Behlmer writes, "No one has ever discovered whether this was an amazing coincidence, a private joke between songwriters, or an innocent and amusing pastiche."[44]

There was but a slight hint of plagiarism associated with the other new song written for *Singin' in the Rain*. Comden and Green wrote the lyrics for "Moses Supposes" while Roger Edens wrote the music. The number apparently had its origin in the days when George Abbott produced the stage version of *On the Town*. According to John Mariani, Abbott gave some tongue twisters to the actors, which included Comden and Green, to improve their diction. Another version of the story has it that Comden and Green overheard Abbott using that particular tongue twister with other actors.[45]

But the origin of "Moses Supposes" goes even further back than Comden and Green's own past. M-G-M staff member George G. Schneider discovered an old "college" song entitled "Old Man Moses," written by David Hume and copyrighted in 1887, that bore a very strong resemblance to the lyrics that Comden and Green had written. "This is the only college song on this subject which I have been able to locate and, to me, it is the basis of the song as written by Betty Comden and Adolph Green." The song had two choruses that resembled the interplay of rhyme and word similarities that infuse "Moses Supposes": "Old Man Moses, he sells posies, all he knows is the price of roses; Old Man Moses, he sells posies, red as a rose is, Moses' nose is." The second chorus was similar: "Old Man Moses now reposes where the roses deck his toes-es." It is quite possible that Comden and Green had no knowledge of the Hume song, having become familiar with a variant of it through the auspices of George Abbott.[46]

The company was ready to begin rehearsals on April 2, 1951, the day after Debbie Reynolds turned nineteen years old. Carol Haney and Ernest Flatt began working with her, starting at 10 in the morning and ending at 3:50 in the afternoon, with one hour off for lunch. Jeanne Coyne joined them after a few days. This was a typical workday for Reynolds for the next two months. Flatt had become a ballroom dance teacher at age twelve in Colorado, where he was born in 1918. He studied dance in Hollywood and performed in the touring company of *Oklahoma!* and was a featured dancer in *An American in Paris*. He assisted many dancers at M-G-M. Kelly relied on Flatt to demonstrate the basic steps to Reynolds, and trusted Haney and Coyne to take her further along in her dance education. He later joked that he sent Ernie Flatt to work with Reynolds mainly to keep her busy.[47]

Much of the intense rehearsal phase in the preparation for *Singin' in the Rain* focused on getting Reynolds up to speed with Kelly and O'Connor. She recalled that Carol, Ernie, and Jeanne took shifts with her. "Having been a gymnast made me strong," Reynolds remembered, "but soon I was overwhelmed and intimidated." The three planned to teach her all the steps both Kelly and O'Connor liked to do, so she could put them together in whatever combination was needed. "My teachers were all nice to me, and even fun," Reynolds remembered, but Kelly scared her. He popped in now and then to see how she was doing. "He was never satisfied. I never got a compliment. Ever." Kelly, however, mentions in an interview that he was not impressed by her prior dance experience, characterizing it at an amateurish, high-school level. He needed much more out of her and was convinced she was capable of it. His intensity and drive overawed Reynolds. "He was so strict, so unyielding, and so serious all the time. He had an enormous burden of creativity on his back. Who had time for a crying nineteen-year-old who didn't know how to sing or dance?" Reynolds began to feel as if she "was being thrown to the lions." Thirty years later, when writing her memoirs, Reynolds understood his predicament. "He was stuck with me. He knew he needed to drive me and so he did. But I didn't know the word *quit*. In my mind, I just had to do it."[48]

No one who worked with the inexperienced performer complained about the task. When asked if Reynolds was difficult, Lela Simone replied, "Well, I wouldn't say she was difficult to work with, but she was tedious to work with." This was only because Reynolds had to start from scratch. She wanted to succeed, and became irritated and frustrated with herself at times. One day Reynolds became "infuriated" because she had trouble pinning down a dance step. She exploded, "shouting and swearing," threw her dancing shoes at a mirror and shattered it. Later she felt "so ashamed of my behavior."[49]

On another frustrating day, Reynolds hid under a piano so no one would see her and began to cry. Soon she heard a voice asking, "Why are you crying?'" Without knowing who it was, Reynolds replied, "'Because I'll never learn any of it. I can't do it anymore. I feel like I'm going to die, it's so hard." The voice responded reassuringly, "No, you're not going to die. That's what it is to learn how to dance." Reynolds finally looked out and saw Fred Astaire standing there. "You come watch me. You watch how hard I work. I don't cry, but I do get frustrated and upset and I'm going to let you watch." She went with him to the next sound stage where he rehearsed for a routine in *The Belle of New York* and saw him getting frustrated but still going on. The point was well made. "His gesture was an enormous help to me," Reynolds concluded decades later. "It was another step in seeing that MGM was a university of hard work and pain and wonderful creativity."[50]

The pace of rehearsals continued through late May. Kelly began rehearsing as well by April 18, with Donald O'Connor beginning his rehearsals April 24. Barbara Lawrence also joined the crew to help out in rehearsals, but Jeanne and Carol were constants, assisting everyone everyday. There were no rehearsals at all on May 12 because Kelly was ill that day.[51]

Even before rehearsals started, the censors were hard at work assessing the script of *Singin' in the Rain*. Every movie project had to undergo the same process. Years before, the moviemakers had created a system of self-censorship to prevent an outside source from doing it for them. In response to contemplated censorship legislation in thirty-six states, the industry created the Motion Picture Producers and Distributors of America Association to handle a number of issues, including censorship. The organization had little ability to enforce standards, and the Production Code it created in 1930 had a negligible effect on the content of movies until the MPPDA revised the code and appointed Joseph I. Breen to enforce it. This action was taken in response to the creation of the League of Decency by Catholic bishops. Breen's office, officially called the Production Code Administration, could only issue recommendations, but it could also refuse to issue a Code Certificate for any film deemed unacceptable. Nearly all the studios paid attention to the Breen office, as it was informally known, if for no other reason than to enhance the marketability of their films.[52]

The second version of the script for *Singin' in the Rain* was the first to be submitted to Breen, on January 2, 1951. Breen in general had little trouble with it, reporting to Louis B. Mayer two days later that "the basic story seems to meet the requirements of the Production Code." But he listed several areas of concern for the studio to consider. "We assume that the girl in the safari outfit will be adequately clothed. . . . None of the show girls in the process of changing their clothes should be shown in their underwear. Also, their dancing costumes must be selected with great care." Lina's costumes also had to be "selected carefully," and the studio had to stage the scene "where Lina is 'wired for sound'" so as not to violate anyone's sense of morality. The male characters had to be watched as well. Breen did not like Cosmo's line, "She's the first dame who's said no since you were four." He also was disturbed by Don's line, "What are you doing later," spoken in response to Cosmo's injunction to "Watch my mouth!" It "approaches the element of sex perversion and we ask that it be eliminated," Breen advised. In general, he called Mayer's "particular attention" to the costumes of all women in the film. "The Production Code makes it mandatory that the intimate parts of the body—specifically, the breasts of women—be fully covered at all times." Breen wanted to review the "lyrics of all songs" to be used and concluded with a standard disclaimer, "You understand, of course, that our final judgment will be based upon the finished picture."[53]

The studio decided to send the third and final draft of the script of *Singin' in the Rain* to Breen as well. His office responded in late April with repeated suggestions that women's costumes be carefully considered. Also, Breen reminded M-G-M "that we cannot approve photographing women in their underwear. Please bear this in mind when Don runs through the dressing room."

Breen did not like the extended (and obviously suggestive) dialogue between Cosmo and the aspiring starlet at Simpson's party. But instead of asking that it be cut, he urged that it should be "delivered without any offensive sex suggestive flavor." The directors cut this dialogue anyway.[54]

The studio submitted the lyrics for at least three songs to be used in the picture, "You Are My Lucky Star," "Moses Supposes," and "Good Morning." Breen easily passed on all of them late in May. M-G-M worked closely with the Breen office to get passing reviews for *Singin' in the Rain*. Of course, the final, finished version of the film had to be screened and carefully analyzed before the office gave its final stamp of approval, but the review process headed off any trouble areas before production began. Walter Plunkett, the veteran costume designer at M-G-M who worked on the 1920s outfits for *Singin' in the Rain,* later recalled that it was easier to get things past the Breen office if you could make a case that it was authentic to the period portrayed in the film. "You didn't really have to be accurate. You just had to pretend to be."[55]

TECHNICAL ASPECTS

Singin' in the Rain was produced only twenty-four years after the introduction of talking pictures. It spoofed a revolutionary event that was closer in time to 1951 than the making of *Singin'* is to our own time. *The Jazz Singer* (1927) was not really the first talkie, for that famous movie employed the new technology only for a few songs and some dialogue. Moreover, the sound was played back on a disk rather than imbedded on the film itself. Some short movies employed both the sound-on-disk and sound-on-film techniques before 1927, and technical improvements enabled several pictures to use a lot of sound the next year. The number of talkies increased with each passing year so that they quickly became commonplace, and all studios used sound-on-film by 1930.[56]

As we have seen, dubbing the singing, even dubbing dialogue, became common from the start, especially for dance musicals. It was inspired mostly by technical issues. "The quality of the sound recording and the vocal performance can be controlled and assured in advance," noted Gerald Mast. "Filming on the set can then be much freer, concentrating exclusively on a visual interpretation of the number and a projection of its musical energy into visual space." It was a short step from prerecording the music for playback at filming, to using a different singer to substitute for a star whose voice was not up to the studio's standard. Dubbing, in one form or other, and for one reason or other, suffused the movie industry whenever it turned its attention to musical or dance numbers in pictures.[57]

Singin' in the Rain would be filmed in Technicolor, as were all M-G-M musicals since *Meet Me in St. Louis* (1944). While various methods of tinting or hand-painting film had been tried since the advent of movies, true color photography began with the creation of the Technicolor Corporation in 1918. Because of the expense involved, studios limited the number of films that employed the dominant two-strip method throughout the 1920s. Technicolor developed a three-strip color process by the early 1930s, adding a blue range that made the images "seem more real and true." *The Wizard of Oz* and *Gone with the Wind*, both released in 1939, were the most successful movies to use the three-strip process, and it became the norm for all studios who wanted to employ color. M-G-M used the three-strip process in 115 feature movies by about the time Freed began production on *Singin'*, and his newest project would employ that process too. Still, most movies of the 1950s were black and white. Even by the latter part of the decade, only one out of four feature films appeared in color.[58]

The production phase of *Singin' in the Rain* coincided with new technical developments in how movies could be presented on the big screen. Inspired in part by the challenge of television, the movie industry experimented with efforts to contrast the size and spectacle of their product with small-screen entertainment. Five different widescreen methods were current in the early 1950s, all of them using varied techniques to present the film in a larger format than the standard movie screen. None of these processes became popular and many of the movies employing them were also exhibited in the standard 35 mm format. Stereophonic sound, which offered four-channel sound rather than the standard one channel, was an added component to the widescreen methods. Moreover, 3-D technology reappeared with the widescreen techniques after the studios had ignored it since 1938, when M-G-M initially experimented with the technology. *Singin' in the Rain* employed none of these technical tricks—widescreen, stereophonic, or 3-D—with the studio opting for the traditional three-strip Technicolor and single-channel recording.[59]

M-G-M was uniquely situated to produce a movie like *Singin' in the Rain*. Arthur Freed had been a key player in the creation of early film musicals and he drew on some of the problems encountered in making *The Broadway Melody* when it came time to brainstorm about the details of *Singin'*. More importantly, many technicians at M-G-M had also lived through the transition to sound. They represented a rich resource of movie history readily available to the cast members. Kelly and others made the rounds at the studio, "talking to the veterans of the various departments to get their recollections. We gathered far more material than we were able to use, but what we did was based on actual happenings." They paid particular attention to the veterans who had worked on creating the system of recording sound at the studio, fascinated with the experimentation phase that involved hiding microphones at odd locations on the set. "This used to drive the actors crazy," Kelly recalled. Another story that caught their imagination grew out of a suggestion by sound experts imported from the East Coast, who suggested that metal nails holding the floorboards might interfere with recording. The studio apparently replaced them with wooden pegs. "We wanted to fit that story in," Kelly remembered, "but it was so expensive to show thousands of carpenters for just one or two shots. It wasn't worth it."[60]

One of the old veterans at the studio who drew Kelly's particular attention was Buster Keaton. A legend of the silent screen era, Keaton's tempestuous career hit rock bottom in the early sound period. Contrary to popular views, this was due to a variety of personal problems and his frustration at working within the studio system, rather than anything associated with his on-screen performances. Keaton became a contract player with M-G-M in 1928 and was still on the payroll in 1951, doing little more than helping out on movie projects inspired by elements of his past success, starring currently popular actors. Kelly recalled that Keaton "would hang around the area circumscribed by the commissary, shoeshine parlor, and barbershop. I used to see him almost every day for a chat." Keaton also played third base for M-G-M's amateur baseball team, the Wolves. Kelly thought he was "an all-round terrific player," even at fifty-five years of age. In one of his earlier M-G-M movies, Keaton had appeared as part of the ensemble performance of "Singin' in the Rain," the highlight of *The Hollywood Revue of 1929*. The two-strip

Technicolor image seems surreal today, as well as the wooden staging of the number itself. Unlike the rest, Keaton conspicuously refuses to sing or smile in this bizarre debut of the famous Freed-Brown song.[61]

Kelly liked and admired Buster Keaton. "A lot of his moves I certainly intuitively copied in doing certain numbers," he recalled in 1979. Kelly specifically referred to the squeaky board and newspaper number in *Summer Stock*. "I didn't look like him, but I often wish I did. He was a complete genius, and there was a lot of dance inherent in his movements." Kelly most admired Keaton's easy grace when doing physical comedy and wished he had the ability to carry off some of his dance routines with a similar comedic touch.[62]

Besides the personnel at M-G-M, the studio had an enormous storehouse of props dating back many years. Kelly and the other creators of *Singin' in the Rain* studied still photographs of the studio to get a feel for how it looked a quarter-century before. Art director Randall Duell and set director Jacques Mapes recreated as much of the look as possible in designing sets, which they began to build in April 1951. They had to build microphones as well as recording and dubbing equipment to accurately resemble what was used in the earlier period. They even used original set decorations from famous silent and early talkie movies on the sets for *Singin' in the Rain*. For example, Don's mansion is filled with furniture from the John Gilbert–Greta Garbo film *Flesh and the Devil*. Kathy Selden's car is the same used by Mickey Rooney in his Andy Hardy series. Don uses a portable dressing room when filming *The Duelling Cavalier* that had once been used by Norma Shearer.[63]

Duell and Mapes also found original lighting equipment in the M-G-M storehouse that had been used in the 1920s. Old Cooper-Hewitt stage lights were dusted off and made part of the set decoration for *Singin' in the Rain*. They found a glass sound stage from the era, which was being used at the time as a machine shop, and incorporated it into the set design scheme. Duell and Mapes also discovered the plans for a sound booth, a box typically four feet by five feet in dimension and walled in to prevent the motors of the cameras from being picked up by the microphones. It typically had no ventilation system and thus could be a trial for anyone forced to stay inside for even a few minutes. The reconstructed sound booth figures prominently in the sequence that depicts director Roscoe Dexter's frustrating efforts to get Lina to adjust to being recorded while she plays her role in *The Duelling Cavalier*.[64]

When asked more than twenty years later what proportion of the set material one sees in *Singin' in the Rain* was vintage equipment, Randall Duell could not say exactly. M-G-M "had at that time a fantastic backlog of what we call units, stock units." Art directors and set designers recycled them on a regular basis for all new movie productions. The difference in *Singin' in the Rain* was that Duell and Mapes recycled on a broader and deeper scale than ever before. The storyline and setting of the movie allowed them the opportunity to more fully explore the storehouse of props and gadgets than usual. It was, among other things, an economical way to make the film.[65]

Fortunately, Walter Plunkett was available to design the costumes for *Singin' in the Rain*. One of the M-G-M veterans, Plunkett had designed clothes for some of the most popular stars of the 1920s. He could recall all the problems associated with costume design and sound recording. "We had to use special fabrics for the costumes," he remembered of his work for an RKO film called *Rio Rita* in 1929, "because these mikes would pick up any sound and distort it terribly." The microphones especially distorted the noise created when taffeta was rustled. In fact, the technicians used that trick to recreate the sound of fire and earthquake. Plunkett found that it was best to sew the microphones into tight-fitting costumes to make sure they remained in one place. "It was really just like *Singin' in the Rain*," he laughed.[66]

When Plunkett began to recreate some of the wild designs he produced in the 1920s, he recalled that people connected with *Singin' in the Rain* howled with laughter and that they insisted on inserting a number that would highlight the fashion of the era they were spoofing. Out of this grew the "Beautiful Girl" number. "We tossed around different ideas, what are camp things of the period?—like pearls with tweed, and I said, 'monkey fur as trimming, for instance.'" This sequence therefore originated as a joke rather than an integral part of the storyline.[67]

Plunkett also indulged his memories when designing costumes for the Simpson premiere party early in the film. He used fifty pounds of beads and more than a thousand yards of "ostrich feather fringe." Olga Mara, who appears at the movie premiere and the party, wears a dress inspired by Plunkett's original design for Pola Negri, a Polish-born actress who "epitomized the image of the exotic, larger-than-life celebrity" of Hollywood in the 1920s. Negri's career floundered in the transition to sound because of her heavy European accent. Plunkett made one concession to the tastes of 1951 in making the skirts a bit shorter than they would have been in the 1920s. Freed protested the inaccuracy of this portrayal but Plunkett enlisted the aid of Roger Edens and prevailed.[68]

Plunkett also recalled that many of the costumes he designed for Jean Hagen were "as nearly as I can remember, duplicates of some I did in all seriousness for Lilyan Tashman. And she was the epitome of chic at that time." In addition to newly designed costumes, based on old models, Jean Hagen wore the same dress that Norma Shearer used in *Marie Antoinette* (1938) for the sequences in which she appears in *The Duelling Cavalier* and its remake, *The Dancing Cavalier*. Hagen also used Shearer's wig. Canadian-born Shearer became "the epitome of natural high breeding and the final word in feminine sophistication," due to her innate grace and careful management by M-G-M's publicity department. *Marie Antoinette* was one of three movies for which audiences crowned Shearer "first lady of the screen." Her older brother, Douglas Shearer, headed M-G-M's sound department for many years, and his name appears on the credits of *Singin' in the Rain*.[69]

Freed spared no expense in getting the wardrobe for his new film right. Plunkett and his assistants used more than 500 costumes for *Singin' in the Rain*. Their total cost amounted to $157,250.[70]

BUDGETS AND SCHEDULES

It was difficult to set realistic budgets during the course of preproduction because the more expensive elements of *Singin' in the Rain*—the dance numbers—were not yet well developed. Moreover, those numbers tended to evolve, sometimes even after the general filming of the movie began. Randall Duell put it well years later when he said *Singin' in the Rain* "grew from day to day, it was terribly difficult to put that down in dollars and say, 'We're going to spend $60,000 on this number.'"[71]

Because of the complexity of film musicals, it was difficult to set accurate schedules for rehearsing and filming. An initial schedule for Production Number 1546 anticipated five weeks for the rehearsing and building of sets for fourteen numbers, with sound recording of those songs beginning May 31. The actual filming of *Singin' in the Rain* was projected to start on June 11 with the black and white dueling sequence for *The Duelling Cavalier,* and then "Fit As a Fiddle." The number that became "Moses Supposes" was to undergo dress rehearsal and camera rehearsal by June 14, with filming during the next two days. Rehearsal for Kelly's rendition of "All I Do Is Dream of You" was to take place August 1–2, with filming on August 9–10. "Singin' in the Rain" was to undergo dress rehearsal and camera rehearsal by August 11, with filming August 13–14. The short number involving "The Broadway Melody" was to be filmed next. O'Connor's solo number was still referred to as "Piano (Playing) Pioneer" in an April 27 memo on scheduling. "Moses Supposes" continued to be referred to as "Tongue Twisters" as late as June 1, when a revised, but incomplete, schedule of rehearsals and filming was produced. However, this schedule more accurately identified June 18 as the start date for filming the movie.[72]

By the end of June, a few days after filming had indeed begun, a "Picture Estimate" for Production Number 1546 identified a total of forty-two days of production, fifty-four days of rehearsal, three days for the second camera unit to rehearse, and nine days for it to film its allotted part of the script. The cost thus far of *Singin' in the Rain* was $224,187. The estimate to complete the movie ran to $1,655,903, for a total estimated cost of $1,880,090. The "Picture Estimate" of June 30 also indicated that a total of 7,460 feet of film would be needed to shoot the "book," and an additional 3,620 feet to film the musical numbers. *Singin' in the Rain* would therefore require 11,080 feet of film.[73]

FINAL REHEARSALS

Other than Gene Kelly, whose dual role as star and co-director mandated he pay attention to costs and schedules, no one else among the cast members had time to worry about such things. Kelly, Reynolds, and O'Connor began to prerecord their songs on May 23, more than a week earlier than originally estimated. Still photographs of Kelly were taken on May 28, with hair and wardrobe tests for Reynolds three days later. All three main cast members were subject to wardrobe fitting on June 1. Kelly was busy in a budget meeting for more than two hours on June 4, followed by more wardrobe fitting. The next day, Kelly, Reynolds, and O'Connor prerecorded "Singin' in the Rain" for the introduction of the movie, but Reynolds was too ill to work June 6–7. Jean Hagen did a sound-only test scene on June 8, the same day that "Beautiful Girl" and

"Good Morning" were prerecorded. The latter song was prerecorded again, along with "You Are My Lucky Star" (including Debbie's version), "Singin' in the Rain," and "Would You?" on June 13.[74]

Kelly had to prerecord nine songs, given his starring role. Gene "is always a little worried about his . . . singing," recalled Saul Chaplin, who had worked on the music for *Cover Girl* and *An American in Paris*. "Gene has a very pleasant Irish voice; it's the most I can say for it." Kelly himself felt that the "public accepts lousy singers, you know. I'm stating it very boldly: I'm not a good singer." But Kelly gave his singing talents too little credit, for he had an engaging, simple, and sincere vocal style that audiences enjoyed. Fred Astaire also had limited singing talent which he made the most of to put songs across in a style that most viewers readily accepted. Kelly thought that singers like himself and Astaire had an advantage in that they tended to concentrate on the lyrics and the emotions of the song rather than the notes.[75]

In the meanwhile, rehearsals continued at a fast pace. What was termed a "PHOTOGRAPHIC RAIN TEST" took place on June 14 while dress rehearsals for "Moses Supposes" and "Good Morning" occurred two days later. True to the factory mentality that helped to make M-G-M so successful, the work schedule for Saturday, June 16, began at 9 a.m. and ended at 4:40 p.m., with one hour off for lunch.[76]

Debbie Reynolds felt the increased pressure as the first day of filming neared. She sometimes stayed overnight at the studio rather than driving back to her family's home in Burbank. Reynolds slept "in my little dressing room on the floor, with a guard stationed by the studio outside my door. Other nights I'd stay with Louise Horne, my teacher from Warners, who lived nearby in Westwood."[77]

Kelly drove forward with the project, determined to bring it off on schedule and at reasonable cost. According to Reynolds, he sometimes became angry at various delays. "It's a very short-lived temper," Reynolds recalled, "but when it breaks it's like a giant explosion and all hell is let loose." While the storm was never directed at Reynolds, she remembered it was aimed "at a lot of other people, mostly through frustration at himself."[78]

Reynolds remembered one example of Kelly's temper. She, Kelly, and O'Connor were practicing their routine at the bar stools for "Good Morning" when Kelly thought O'Connor was doing a step the wrong way. O'Connor knew he was doing it right and Kelly was actually missing it, but he had too much respect for Kelly to directly criticize him. Instead of complaining, O'Connor apologized. "He adored and worshipped Gene Kelly," Reynolds reported, "and wouldn't have dared answer back. Besides, Donald was younger than Gene, and being the very respectful type of person he is, he just kept quiet." The trio continued rehearsing, and Kelly continued to miss the step until he realized it was his fault. "*I'm* doing it wrong!" he shouted. "'Why the hell didn't you tell me?!' Then he was madder than ever at us for not pointing it out to him. And I said to him, 'But Gene, you can't win for losing with you.' Which made him furious."[79]

Kelly never recalled the temporary anger or frustrations of making *Singin' in the Rain*. He remembered the fun he had with O'Connor in rehearsing their numbers, and the fun he, Haney, and Coyne had in watching O'Connor try routines for "Make 'Em Laugh." Moreover, he had nothing but praise for his two co-stars. "Fortunately Debbie was as strong as an ox," he often remarked, "and unlike Leslie Caron could work for hours. Also she was a great copier, and could pick up the most complicated routines without too much difficulty."[80]

Several decades later, Reynolds came to recall the making of *Singin' in the Rain* with respect for the hard work Gene Kelly forced her to do. "Gene taught me discipline and he taught me how to slave. And today, if I don't drop dead from exhaustion after rehearsal, I feel I haven't accomplished a thing. And this I got directly from Gene. He taught me how to be a perfectionist." At the same time, she cannot remember that time as enjoyable. "Everyone else seemed to be having lots of fun but me. I had too much to learn, and in too short a period. There was just no time for fun. To be thrown into the Gene Kelly type of class was too formidable for fun."[81]

4

Their Feet Do All the Work

The production phase of *Singin' in the Rain* began with the first day of filming on June 18, 1951. Fred Astaire began filming his new movie, *The Belle of New York,* on the same day. The *Singin'* company sent "a horseshoe made of hundreds of flowers" to the *Belle* company at 9 a.m. for good luck. Publicity men snapped a photograph of Astaire, *Belle* director Charles Walters, and producer Arthur Freed posed with the horseshoe and a sign that read, "To the Belle of New York Company From The Singin' in the Rain Company. God help us Both. Love and Good Luck!"[1]

The *Singin' in the Rain* company had decided to start by filming "Moses Supposes," one of the trickiest numbers—a practice that was fairly common in Hollywood musicals. Astaire recalled that later in his career he preferred to start production of a new picture by filming four or five of the more demanding dances. "These are usually the ones we consider the most difficult. If an idea doesn't jell, so to speak, the staging of that one is postponed until the rest of the picture is completed." For Astaire, it was easier to save the "most important trick solos" for filming at the end of production, so he could have "plenty of time to concentrate."[2] Although Gene Kelly never spoke or wrote about this aspect of filming, he seems to have preferred starting with the more difficult dances and ending with the production of his film ballets.

Four days into filming, Louis B. Mayer cut his ties to M-G-M by resigning his position as its head. Mayer had been in a fierce power struggle with Nicholas Schenck for a long time. In addition, Dore Schary, whose movie projects were a source of heated arguments between himself and Mayer, often went over Mayer's head to Schenck to get his way. When Schary managed to control a larger number of M-G-M shares on option than anyone else, Mayer issued an ultimatum to Schenck, who once again sided with Schary. Mayer resigned on June 22, ending more than a quarter-century as manager of Hollywood's most prestigious producer of film musicals. Schary now was in the driver's seat, but at a time when a multitude of problems loomed on the horizon, including the threat posed by television, the growth of independent producers, rising production costs, and changes in audience tastes.[3]

"MOSES SUPPOSES"

The actors, dancers, and technical crew of *Singin' in the Rain* paid little attention to these boardroom power plays as they threw themselves into the first exciting days of production. "Moses Supposes," referred to as "Tongue Twisters" almost up to the start of production, was the first dance to be filmed. Ironically, the makers of *Singin' in the Rain*—a movie based on the Freed-Brown catalog of songs—started with a completely new song, not written by Freed and Brown.

Before dancing the "Moses Supposes" number, Kelly and O'Connor interact with a male diction coach who appears here for the only time in the movie. As they repeat the nonsensical words "Moses supposes his toe-ses are roses, / But Moses supposes erroneously" with mischief in their eyes, they set the mood for a playful romp to follow. Veteran character actor Bobby Watson played their foil very well. Born Robert Watson Knucher, he sold peanuts in a dance hall in Springfield, Illinois, at age ten before going on stage as a comic actor. Watson achieved success on the Broadway stage and went into films. He appeared in seventy-two movies before *Singin' in the Rain,* often in rather effeminate roles or, ironically, as Adolf Hitler. With the right makeup, Watson portrayed the German dictator effectively in eleven movies, often uncredited.[4]

The dancing in "Moses Supposes" is one of the most virile, difficult tap routines on film, but Kelly always felt its qualities were never fully appreciated. "Donald and I rehearsed that dance for days, but most critics dismiss it as a zany Marx Brothers romp. They remember the clowning around with the vocal coach that precedes the number, but not the dance itself."[5]

Casey Charness has broken down the number into individual shots. In the second, O'Connor "introduces the idea that there is going to be a dance by producing a skipping step backwards." The action explodes when he and Kelly jump onto a desk and perform a tap dance "using simple heel-toe brushes done quickly." It is a great segue into what Charness calls "a precision tap" routine that ranges across the open space of the floor, with Bobby Watson an amazed spectator. O'Connor recalled that Kelly observed his individual style and quickly incorporated "a lot of my personality, outside of his own" into their numbers, and "this hidden dimension . . . makes it look so good outside the tough, physical stuff" seen on the screen.[6]

The precision tap routine is the heart of "Moses Supposes," even if critics tend to focus on the clowning with the vocal coach. Along with "Singin' in the Rain" and "Good Morning," "Moses Supposes" takes its place among the elite number of film dances that are expressions of sheer mastery of craft. Both men dance as if doing hard things is supposed to be easy. They wear their talent gracefully.

Whether one or the other was a better dancer in general, and particularly in this dance, has been a matter of some discussion among commentators. "Kelly appears to be the sharper of the two," Charness concludes, because he "is more intent on striking the floor at precisely the right time." O'Connor "hits the floor with just as much accuracy, but his take-offs are not as light as Kelly's, nor is his attack as pronounced." But O'Connor puts much of his own style of dancing into the routine, even as he matches Kelly step for step. "His forte is throwing his whole body into the dance, using the askew elbow or the knee bent in almost the wrong direction to stand his ground and keep attention on his side of the screen." Charness wrote that O'Connor "approaches each dance with a comic attitude that invades his entire frame, with the result that whatever he does may not be as technically astute as Kelly's footwork, but that he seems to be having a much better time doing it."[7] Although both men are clearly enjoying themselves, O'Connor shows a trace of nervousness as he often glances at Kelly. Gene truly appears to be having a ball, grinning at O'Connor several times, seemingly to share the joy of performing this number.

Kelly biographers Sheridan Morley and Ruth Leon note that Gene only looks at O'Connor during this dance "when the choreography insists on it. He simply assumed that they would both be in the right place at the right time; if not, Stanley Donen would say so after the take." Yet, Morley and Leon draw the inscrutable conclusion that O'Connor was a better dancer because he looked at Kelly far more often than Kelly looked at him. A more logical conclusion is that Kelly looked at his partner fewer times because the two were engaged in a unison dance in which the aesthetic was served if they could maintain their unity *without* looking at each other. Moreover, O'Connor proved he could keep pace with Kelly technically, and in a bravura fashion, as he had never done before in a previous film. But he could not match Kelly's grace or command, and there was no need for him to attempt to do so. Yet, that may be the reason he often glanced at Kelly, just to be sure they were in unison. The important thing is that the two men worked on a level of equality in one area while allowing each other leeway to express themselves in other, individual ways. The strength of Kelly and the suppleness of O'Connor complemented each other very well.[8]

Donen's contribution to the success of "Moses Supposes" is obscure; naturally, the eye focuses on the two dancers and not on the camerawork. But Casey Charness detects "certain camera techniques which Donen had by now formularized." He refers to "the dolly in to medium shot to signify the ending of one shot and the beginning of another, the tracking shot to follow sideways movement which is nearly always present no matter what the generic nature of the dance, and the dolly in for the conclusion in medium shot." However, most fans of *Singin' in the Rain* would probably agree with Wendy Wasserstein that, in the "Moses Supposes" number, "There's no need for fancy camera angles or trick photography. Their feet do all the work."[9]

Kelly was right in bemoaning the fact that commentators too often noted the comic aspects of "Moses Supposes" rather than the artistry. For example, Walter Terry wrote in the *New York Herald Tribune* that Kelly and O'Connor "jump into a dance romp, a bit of rough-house perhaps it is, which is great fun." Similarly, film historians Richard Fehr and Frederick Vogel wrote that the lyrics of the song were "unequalled nonsensical pitter-patter, happily complementing the eccentric dance duet by Kelly and Donald O'Connor." Another film historian, Joseph Casper, went even farther by writing that "Don and Cosmo pummel the diction coach's pomposity, pedantry, and smugness by throwing his tongue twisters back in his face and by vigorously tapping around him while dismantling his sanctum." Lockwood and Brown certainly play the role of errant schoolboys more interested in making fun of the teacher than learning anything, but Bobby Watson does not play the role of the diction coach with smugness or pomposity. He is in fact a fascinated, if not completely comprehending observer of the dance, which is more playful than insulting.[10]

It was up to Stanley Donen to offer the correct, if slightly biased, assessment of "Moses Supposes." Speaking some forty years later, Donen told his biographer that this was "the best tap number that has ever been done in pictures. Ever." Only Fred Astaire's and Eleanor Powell's "Begin the Beguine" in *The Broadway Melody of 1940* came close to it, in his view. "But the one with Donald and Gene is better, for its sheer energy."[11]

"FIT AS A FIDDLE"

Freed wrote the lyrics for "Fit as a Fiddle" after his collaboration with Nacio Herb Brown had ended. Al Hoffman and Al Goodhart wrote the music for this song that saw its premiere in George White's stage show, *Music Hall Varieties,* in 1932. It also appeared in *Married before Breakfast* (1937). A few years before his death, Gene Kelly wrote on the song sheet of this number, "O'Connor & Kelly, A Couple of hams! Came off well." Actually, Kelly and O'Connor used only the chorus of the song, ignoring most of the lyrics which merely repeat the singer's happiness at his upcoming marriage.[12]

O'Connor remembered "Fit as a Fiddle" as "a pretty straightforward routine. Gene choreographed it and we went ahead and shot it without too much fuss or bother." In fact, the filming took only a day and a half of the production schedule. One reason the number may have been easy for Kelly to choreograph is that it seems similar to routines done by Gene and his brother Fred as boys, down to the rowdy audience booing them at the end despite their talent. Also, as Donen's biographer notes, the number is reminiscent of Kelly's rendition of "Take Me Out to the Ball Game" with Frank Sinatra, in the movie of the same name filmed three years earlier. Both routines occur early in their respective films to establish the camaraderie between the two male characters and provide a peppy opening for the array of dance numbers to come.[13]

The filming was not without incident, despite O'Connor's observation to the contrary. He either lost his bow while filming, or attempted to ad lib a movement with it that did not work (depending on which O'Connor telling of the tale one relies on). At any rate, Kelly became angry at the gaffe. He yelled at the prop man for providing bows of unequal length, threw his fiddle on the floor, and stalked away to his dressing room. O'Connor felt guilty about the incident and waited fifteen minutes until he could screw up enough courage to confront Kelly. Knocking on his dressing room door, ready to apologize, O'Connor was surprised to find the star lying on a sofa. Kelly invited Donald to make himself comfortable. "When I told him I expected him to be in a stinking rage, he laughed and said he only used the incident as an excuse to have a bit of rest as he was feeling a little tired." O'Connor admitted he was tired too, and both men had a good laugh at the incident. O'Connor later found it strange that Kelly could not simply call a break to rest, as if he had to hide his vulnerabilities behind a storm of anger, but the episode also drew the two together in a behind-the-scenes bond.[14]

"Fit as a Fiddle" witnessed a change in cameraman for the *Singin'* project. John Alton had managed the cinematography so far, but Kelly and Donen felt that "the scenes were coming out too dark," so they replaced him with Harold Rosson, who had worked on *On the Town.* Donen's camera staging involved only four positions, "all long shots, approximating a front-row perspective," according to Casey Charness. Kelly's choreography included "very fast, perfectly timed, complicated steps" similar to "precision flash tap." One of the most visually impressive steps in "Fit as a Fiddle" is the buck-and-wing, a normally routine, stationary step that Kelly turns into a traveling step. Instead of dancing in one place, the pair move, and moreover, "not even in a straight line but in a circle around a partner, making the execution triply cumbersome." Charness writes that the camera accompanies all the moves in "Fit as a Fiddle" with a graceful lack of ostentation. It "tracks sideways" most of the time and moves from a long shot to a medium shot at the end of three of the four scenes. Altogether, the camera "moves the audience perspective along with the dance."[15]

Walter Terry particularly liked "Fit as a Fiddle" when *Singin' in the Rain* was released. He called it the "most hilarious offering" performed "in the great tradition of eccentric dancing." As Kelly and O'Connor sing "Haven't a worry, haven't a care, / Feel like a feather, floating on air," they "tap, shuffle, strut, kick, clown, exude enthusiasm and play violins in a sequence certain to bring a smile to the lips of even the most determined grouch."[16]

The Freed-Brown song "Good Morning" had seen light in previous outings before *Singin' in the Rain,* but never in such a bright, memorable way. Judy Garland and Mickey Rooney sang it in *Babes in Arms* (1939), the first movie Freed produced. It also appeared in *Mr. & Mrs. North* (1942). In *Singin',* the number, performed by Gene Kelly, Donald O'Connor, and Debbie Reynolds, represents a happy celebration of the plan to make *The Duelling Cavalier* into a musical, making the lyrics, "Good mornin', good mornin'! / Sunbeams will soon smile through," an integral part of the plot. For their exuberant dance, the cast needed several rooms because the action moves from the dining room to the kitchen, where the dance begins, and then out into more rooms before ending on a couple of couches. Kelly had experimented with moving a dance routine across several contiguous spaces as early as "Make Way for Tomorrow" in *Cover Girl* (1944).[17]

Also, in both "Make Way for Tomorrow" and "Good Morning," Kelly incorporated ordinary objects found naturally in those spaces into his choreography. In the *Cover Girl* routine it was "garbage pails and their lids, lampposts, oars on a dock, a mailbox on a corner," as well as people such as "a milkman and a drunk." Gerald Mast calls this an example of "street-song *bricolage,*" the latter word denoting use of ordinary objects as props in a dance sequence. In the "Good Morning" routine, Kelly uses the assemblage of raincoats and hats on a hatrack and, most impressively, the two sofas. Beth Genné notes that the raincoats are used "as props for mock 'ethnic' dances . . . a cape for a Spanish dance, a skirt for a hula, and a flapper partner for the Charleston." "Bricolage," a French word used in several disciplines, often refers to the act of creating something by using diverse objects that happen to be in one's environment. French anthropologist Claude Lévi-Strauss applied the term to the versatility of humans in prescientific cultures as they used natural objects for their own purposes. Hollywood people more typically referred to "bricolage" as a "prop dance," and Fred Astaire not only pioneered but practiced the art more assiduously than any other movie dancer.[18]

"Good Morning" takes place in nine camera shots, with O'Connor, Reynolds, and Kelly singing in the kitchen in the first. Then the trio perform a "unison tap" with their "arms hung at sides." A tracking shot follows them out of the kitchen into the living room, moving "past the edge of a wall" to get from one room to another. Casey Charness believes the camera became "subverted to the dance in this number, and even serves to destroy cinematic illusion at one point," by reminding us that the dance routine is taking place on a set instead of inside a real house. The destruction of illusion is gentle, not explosive, and the number charms and excites mainly because of "its high standard of dance content" rather than because of camera-work. Jerome Delamater has also noted that at one other point in the number, the camera tracks right to follow the trio dancing up some stairs and then tracks left again, only to find that the coat rack has suddenly appeared at a spot where it had not been located earlier. As this was done in one take, a prop man obviously placed the rack there when the camera was off to the right. This is so subtle, however, that only after viewing the film through a movieola, a machine that allowed him to stop and go as he pleased, did Delamater notice it.[19]

The night before the cast began filming "Good Morning," O'Connor and Kelly went out for a few drinks. O'Connor had a hangover the next morning and could not dance properly. "I got to the set and tried to do a few steps, Gene shouts at me, 'Stop the clowning, will you!' Later on he apologized for chewing me out, 'Listen, Debbie hasn't been coming along as I'd hoped, but I couldn't bawl her out because I didn't want to lose her, so I took it out on you.'" O'Connor claimed that he said, "That's okay, Gene. I understand. But the next time you do it I'll kick you in the balls."[20] Even though said as a joke, O'Connor failed to realize that he was partly to blame for the incident. He also forgot that Gene had yelled at the prop man instead of him, in a similar incident while filming "Fit as a Fiddle." With the stress of acting, dancing, choreographing, and co-directing, it is perhaps understandable that Kelly needed to yell at someone at times when all was not going well. He chose the person who was most able to handle it and at least partly to blame in each case.

One of the days that involved filming "Good Morning" (June 25) serves as an example of a typical day of filming on the set of *Singin' in the Rain*. Kelly, O'Connor, and Reynolds worked from seven or eight in the morning until after 6 p.m. Jean Hagen was available until midafternoon while Millard Mitchell was on the set for a couple of hours to get oriented—his contract had only started two days before. Carol

Haney and Jeanne Coyne worked all day. Much of the time was spent on various scenes associated with the "Good Morning" number. From 8 a.m. until 9:19 a.m. everyone either set up equipment, rehearsed, or established the proper lighting. The crew shot three takes from 9:19 until 9:31 a.m., but the takes were useless because the rain that was directed to fall outside Don's house came into the interior of the set. For two minutes photographers took still shots, then the trio rehearsed for thirteen minutes and the cast and crew shot some more scenes—Don takes his uneaten sandwich and milk from the dining room into the kitchen, followed by Cosmo and Kathy—from 9:47 until 10:25 a.m. The records show more rehearsals, a couple of minutes to refresh makeup, and then the crew shot Cosmo as he "starts into reprise" of "Fit as a Fiddle" from 11:07 until 11:33 a.m. This pattern continued for the rest of the morning with spurts of rehearsal both on and off the set, re-touching makeup, and several more takes of various scenes exposed. It is noted that the lunch break took place between 1:03 and 2:03, and in mid-afternoon Kelly, Reynolds, and O'Connor rehearsed to the play-back of the music. The scene depicting them dancing from the kitchen into the dining room was filmed from 4:20 to 5:00 p.m., just before everyone quit for the day. A total of 2,900 feet of film was exposed, of which 356 feet was retained.[21]

The detailed notations in the assistant director's reports provide a glimpse into the rapid production pace for *Singin' in the Rain*. The sound stage was a beehive of activity as everyone understood that time was money when filming a musical. M-G-M was lavish with production money, but the bosses wanted every minute accounted for to make sure their resources were not wasted. By June 25, 1951, the cast and crew had filmed seventeen scenes. They had exposed 14,295 feet of film, but only 1,581 of it was good enough to be included in the movie. After six days of filming, and with nine scenes of "Good Morning" shot on June 25 alone, the assistant director estimated that *Singin'* was two and a half days ahead of schedule.[22]

The final outcome of this number is superb, with wonderful perfor-mances by all three. The only part where O'Connor seems a little stiff is when the trio does the bowling action in rapid succession. This may be due to the fact that the strenuous upper arm action was new to him. As O'Connor mentioned to an interviewer, he had only danced from the waist down before he met Kelly.[23]

Debbie Reynolds remembered "Good Morning" as one of the hardest parts of *Singin'* to film. She was not a dancer and had to work very hard to keep up with Gene and Donald. Although tough and determined, she still felt "worn out" after each practice or filming session with them. In fact, the famous ending of the number, with the trio somersaulting over one couch and breezily riding another as they tip it over, was the toughest scene in the entire movie for her. They did the scene what seemed "hundreds of times" to her, from eight in the morning until eleven at night. "Gene was shouting, 'Dance harder! More energy!'" At the end of one take Reynolds "just lay on the ground and with barely enough breath to talk, I said, 'I can't do it again.'" Donen signaled that it looked all right so Kelly called it a night. In her interviews, Reynolds claimed that she fainted when she got off the floor, and the others took her to her dressing room and called her family doctor who "looked at my feet and saw the blood vessels had burst. 'What are you doing to this girl?' he asked. And Gene said, 'We're making a movie.'" In her autobiography, however, when she relates this incident, there is no mention of her fainting, and she says her family doctor came to see her in the morning when she couldn't get out of bed. This version fits well with Kelly's comment to an interviewer that although Debbie worked very hard, the stories regarding her bleeding feet were apparently made up for dramatic effect, because he certainly did not remember this happening. In any case, as Reynolds noted, "The doctor forbade me to come to the set for at least three days, but I was back after one day in bed."[24] None of this shows on screen of course. The trio seem to be having a wonderful time, and this is probably the best dance of Debbie's entire career, in technical aspects as well as emotional appeal, and one that is loved widely by movie audiences.

"MAKE 'EM LAUGH"

The only song Freed and Brown wrote specifically for *Singin' in the Rain* had a checkered origin, given the quick way that they based it on "Be a Clown." Gerald Mast has noted that the comic idea of the song "Make 'Em Laugh" comes from "I Love a Mystery" in *Something in the Wind* (1947). It was clear to the cast and to the audience, however, as Mast puts it, that the "melody and lyrics" came from Cole Porter's song. Film historian Roy Hemming noted that *The Pirate* was not then well known among movie fans, and therefore Freed and Brown could get away with the close copy more easily.[25]

Irving Berlin immediately saw the similarity when he visited Freed's set as "Make 'em Laugh" was being filmed. When he heard the playback of the song, "Make 'em laugh, make 'em laugh! / Don't you know everyone wants to laugh?" Berlin was startled. "Why, why, why—that's 'Be a Clown,'" Donen recalls the conversation. Freed stammered, "Well, the kids and I —we all got together and—come on, Irving, that's enough now." Donen later commented that Freed "wasn't going to take the rap alone on that."[26]

The Breen office approved the lyrics for "Make 'Em Laugh" soon after filming of *Singin'* began, but Breen of course only was looking for objectionable language, not plagiarism. Freed gave M-G-M the right to use this song on June 22, 1951. Many viewers noticed the similarity between the two songs upon the movie's release. In response to numerous letters on this topic, Sidney Skolsky wrote in his Hollywood *Citizen-News* column that "Porter and Freed are very good friends and Porter does not care to make an issue of it." Joseph Casper concluded twenty years later that the similarity "mars the number's luster."[27]

Quite a bit more work was needed on "Make 'Em Laugh" than on most of the other numbers in the movie, in part because it was a fairly late addition. Moreover, it was a unique number, not really a dance per se but comic shtick mixed with acrobatics set to music, more akin to vaudeville than an M-G-M musical. Interestingly, O'Connor rerecorded part of the song at a slower speed to see if it would work better; it didn't. The original recording stayed.[28]

"Make 'Em Laugh" became one of the most famous numbers of the movie, so much so that Donald O'Connor felt a bit left out. "Through the years everyone takes credit for that number, and now I feel that I had nothing to do with it," he told an interviewer in 1979. "I don't think I even performed it." O'Connor gave credit to Carol Haney and Jeanne Coyne for helping him work out the routine: "They were great laughers, and I had the funny bone. I'd say hello in the morning and they'd break up." When Kelly mentioned that he played a large role in working out the number and had the notes to prove it, O'Connor said, "if he has notes they're Jeannie's and Carol's notes." Yet, in an earlier interview, O'Connor said, "Every time I got a new idea, or remembered something that had worked for me in the past, Gene wrote it down, and bit by bit, the entire number was constructed." Also, Kelly was referring not just to selecting the best moments from O'Connor's improvisations, but to the task of putting all the movements to beats, as if it was a dance. For example, they had to figure out on which note he would get slapped by the dummy, on which note he would fall off the couch, and so on. "To get the beats where he'd slap his head on the musical counts was most difficult," Kelly later remembered. O'Connor did acknowledge that Kelly contributed significantly to "Make 'Em Laugh." His "main contribution was his ability to see something very good and to utilize it. And his only other contribution was where I hit the wall and screw up my face. He thought that was very funny. I didn't. But he liked it and they kept it in. And it is funny on the screen." Gene had watched Donald make these face distortions and wanted to incorporate them into this number. "That was his idea entirely." This was called "gurning," which refers to a deliberately distorted facial expression. The name comes from an odd-looking fish called "gurnard." O'Connor said that Kelly also insisted on including a "close-up" sequence of his gurning.[29]

Kelly recalled that O'Connor did crazy things spontaneously whenever he saw Haney and Coyne, and they always laughed a lot at his antics. O'Connor, guided by Haney and Coyne as much as Kelly in selecting tricks for "Make 'Em Laugh," focused on whatever made them laugh the most. They strung the tricks together into what resembles a traveling number with O'Connor going from one set to another, encountering a variety of people and props. Prop men brought all the interesting objects they could find at M-G-M for O'Connor. Among the pile were many dummies, and O'Connor found one in particular that was fascinating. Phil Garris, his friend and a stand-in on the set, pointed it out to him. The dummy had no head, hands, or feet, "but it had symmetry," he remembered. O'Connor recalled an incident that occurred to him while riding a subway to Brooklyn in 1940. He was wearing dark glasses to remain anonymous, and a man "who looks like an ex-fighter sits down next to me." O'Connor tried to move away but the man followed him, and eventually put his hand on O'Connor's knee. "Then down to my crotch," O'Connor remembered. "So I did a gay voice and said, 'Listen, my boyfriend will beat the shit out of you if you go any further!'" He incorporated a part of this incident into his routine with the dummy, ending up fighting the headless torso behind a couch. Kelly recalled that O'Connor improvised for hours with the dummy, while he and others watched and laughed, and all this was eventually reduced to just a couple of minutes on the screen.[30]

Another element of this comic shtick was O'Connor running on his side in circles on the floor. It was a trick popularized by Jerry Howard, better known as Curly, of the Three Stooges. Curly had done this routine often since he began working with his brother, Moe Howard, and Larry Fine in 1933. He dropped out of the Stooges act in 1947 due to heart trouble, and was in poor health in the summer of 1951 when O'Connor paid him the honor of asking his permission to do the trick in "Make 'Em Laugh." He died a few months later on January 18, 1952. O'Connor thought it was "one of the highlights of the whole routine."[31]

"Make 'Em Laugh" was the ultimate mix of old vaudeville tricks put on film. It was such an impressive number that finding a proper ending for it became a problem. O'Connor felt it was leading "to such a crescendo that I thought I'd have to commit suicide as a finale." But the trick of running up a wall, and back-flipping from it, lent itself to a proper end. It was a tricky feat, but O'Connor's brother Jack had done it in vaudeville and had taught it to Donald, and Donald himself had performed it in two of his previous movies. In *Feudin', Fussin' and A-Fightin'* (1948) he ran up a board in a barn and back-flipped as he would do in "Make 'Em Laugh." Then in *Double Crossbones* (1951), a movie about pirates which O'Connor preferred to forget, he ran up a wall and back-flipped from it.[32]

The Nicholas Brothers (Harold and Fayard), a successful duo of black eccentric dancers, had dabbled with this trick before. Choreographer Nick Castle at Twentieth Century–Fox suggested it for both brothers. At first Harold did not believe it possible, but he worked for a week with a harness to catch him if he fell, and was able to do it. Apparently, Fayard could not master it, although the brothers' biographer (and Fayard) claim that both brothers did the back flip in *Orchestra Wives* (1942). Actually in that movie, at the end of a number called "Kalamazoo," Fayard jumps straight up and simply kicks off a square pillar, and then Harold runs up another square pillar and back-flips from it onto the floor, just as O'Connor does twice in a row in *Singin'*. Although Fayard claimed that O'Connor's performance of the stunt in "Make 'Em Laugh" was a tribute to the brothers' work, there is no indication from O'Connor's many interviews that this was so, especially as he himself had performed the trick in his earlier movies and his own brother had performed it years before in vaudeville.[33]

The stunt was difficult and dangerous. "I was up so high," O'Connor said as he recalled his first experience in the air. "It required a lot of energy. They put me in a harness, like a horse, to learn the back somersaults. It was weird up there when I put on that harness for the first time. The courage came with practice." Harold Nicholas had gone through the same thing. He failed the first two times he attempted the stunt in rehearsal, but nailed it on the third attempt. Then Nick Castle quietly told the prop men to only pretend to hold him with the harness rope to give Harold more confidence. He improved with each repetition, but when Castle told him the men were not holding him firmly he nearly fainted.[34] Like O'Connor, courage came with practice and Harold performed the trick confidently and impressively in *Orchestra Wives*.

Rehearsing and filming "Make 'Em Laugh" was the toughest routine O'Connor had ever done in the movies. "We began to rehearse the number and I'd get very tired. I was smoking four packs of cigarettes a day then and getting up those walls was murder. I'd roll around the floor and get carpet burns. They had to bank one wall so I could make it up and then through another wall. My body just had to absorb this tremendous shock."[35]

Kelly admired O'Connor's stamina. Talking to Hedda Hopper only three years later, he recalled that the younger man "did everything—climbed walls and knocked himself out. I'd say 'Can you do this,' . . . He'd say, 'Yes, I can do that.' You can't get people to do things like that except a crazy dancer. . . . I couldn't give anyone else in the business the beating I gave Donald in that picture." In the end, Kelly recalled that he had to trim twenty minutes of O'Connor's gags and tricks from the routine to fit it into the overall framework of *Singin' in the Rain*.[36]

For what Joseph Casper calls "O'Connor's brilliant but bruising ballet," the performer reportedly wore some "protective padding," but it must have been minimal. O'Connor himself recalled nothing but the bruises, the aches, and the pains in later years because he performed "Make 'Em Laugh" on a concrete floor. The assistant director's reports indicate that he rehearsed the number from 10:00 in the morning until 4:30 in the afternoon on June 29, and again most of the day on June 30. After several more days of rehearsal, O'Connor began to hurt in his "body, my knees, ankles, and toes, everything started to hurt," so he decided to film the routine in one hard day to get through it quickly. The preliminaries to the hard parts were filmed on July 14, depicting O'Connor carried across the room on a plank, dodging the sofa carried by workmen, and getting hit in the back of the head with a board (reminiscent of the Three Stooges).[37]

When the day for filming the tough parts came, O'Connor brilliantly withstood the pounding. Unlike Debbie's reaction when she couldn't get out of bed the day after filming "Good Morning," Donald never complained. He was an experienced dancer, used to grueling practices as well as aches and bruises. O'Connor just "went home and couldn't get out of bed for three days," he later recalled. When he returned to work, everyone applauded his effort. Stanley Donen told him the routine was "just great," as O'Connor remembered the conversation decades later. "'It's fantastic. Do you think you could do it again?' I said oh, sure, anytime. He said, 'Well great, you're going to do it again tomorrow.'" Unfortunately Hal Rosson or his assistant had overlooked the fact that the camera's aperture was incorrectly set. "It was open and it stuck, so that whole number was fogged out. It looked like a ghost doing his thing." O'Connor was a true vaudeville trouper; he took the bad news in stride and filmed the grueling number once more. In a way, he felt the repeat helped, "Because I knew it better and I was able to do better in the number." He had to recuperate in bed for another three days after the second filming.[38]

The end result was worth all the hard work and bruises. "Make 'Em Laugh" is both an acrobatic act and a clown act, as Peter Wollen has correctly put it, rather than a dance. It was filmed with remarkably few cuts, one of them taking place after his second run up a wall to give him more opportunity to prepare for the third attempted wall run, which turns out to be a crash through the plaster and a quick reemergence through the broken wall back into camera view, only to collapse in fake exhaustion. Comden and Green put it well years later when they wrote that the dance included "every piece of zany gymnastic clowning and surrealist vaudeville bit Donald had saved up in his body, and worked them into an insane classic unlike any other before or since." As Donen later testified, there was no trick photography involved in "Make 'Em Laugh." "That was all Donald. The only thing we did was make a cut near the end [of the interplay with the dummy], to get the dummy to move up to speed. But can you imagine Oscar Levant in the role?"[39]

The peppy song that highlights the post-premiere party at Simpson's house had been sung initially by Gene Raymond and Joan Crawford in *Sadie McKee* (1934). It was also used in *Hide-Out*, released in 1934 as well, and in *No More Ladies* and *Broadway Melody of 1936*, both released in 1935. Kelly and Donen filmed the number in seven shots and employed "the Charleston, the black bottom, and a few made-up steps" for Debbie Reynolds and the chorus as they sing "All I do, is dream of you, the whole night through. / With the dawn, I still go on, dreaming of you." Charness notes that "there are knee-crosses, which are shot from a crane in [shot] four showing all nine girls, and from eye level in shot five, which details the movement in a medium framing, allowing the audience to appreciate the quality of the detail more closely."[40]

Reynolds wrote some choice commentary on the filming of "All I Do Is Dream of You." "My brains were fried, my eyes were crossed inside, and my hand was squeezing my butt just to keep my concentration on the lip-synch, the steps, and the spacing." Reynolds could think only of "'Double tap, double tap / sliiiiide tap! Double tap, double tap / sliiiiide tap!'" Meanwhile, Kelly was on the sideline yelling through a microphone "'SMILE DAMN IT, SMILE!!'" He also cautioned Reynolds, "'DON'T LOOK SO PANICKED!'"[41]

What Reynolds did not realize at the time was that Kelly knew her expression was critical to the success of the dance. The camera-work was perfectly planned to highlight her, and to establish Kathy Selden as a sprightly presence on the screen. Also, it was the first dance in *Singin'* that Reynolds appears in (of only three dances that she performs in the movie), and, as such, it was a major factor in creating her film career. Jeanne Coyne is also in that number, to Debbie's right, and looks equally energetic and joyful, although she is not always on the screen.

The number was filmed on July 23, 24, and 25, almost a month after filming "Good Morning."[42] Yet, Reynolds seems to have struggled in this energetic number as well, mainly because dancing was so new to her.

When Reynolds looked back on her first major film role, she tended to remember the immensely hard work involved. "I felt under the gun so much of the time that I missed just about anything that didn't have to do with my performance." This greatly contributed to her tendency to remember the making of *Singin' in the Rain* with something less than pleasure.[43]

Gene Kelly also performed a dance to the music of "All I Do Is Dream of You," but it did not make it into the final version of the movie. It depicts Don Lockwood going home after Simpson's party and remembering the song and thinking of Kathy as he gets ready for bed. Sung in a slower, ballad style, Kelly dances for four minutes in his bedroom. Donen remembered that it took "several days to work" this number out, but he considered it "a very good number" and "athletic" in the Kelly style. Kelly also was very fond of it and "regarded it as one of his best." He consented to dropping it from the release print of *Singin' in the Rain* only because "it slowed down the narrative" of the movie. Unfortunately, no film of this dance is available today.[44]

THE MONTAGE AND "BEAUTIFUL GIRL"

A medley of Freed-Brown songs, "I've Got a Feeling You're Fooling," "Should I?," and "The Wedding of the Painted Doll," was put together as a montage designed to illustrate the excitement of shifting from silent to sound pictures. Freed and Brown's "Beautiful Girl" followed the montage directly and became the lead-in to a fashion show. Historians tend to discuss these two numbers as one because both spoof Busby Berkeley, and the fashion show is meant as a spoof as well. But it is worth noting that they are really two separate numbers and only "Beautiful Girl" is an integral part of the plot, for it leads to Cosmo spotting Kathy (one of the dancers in this number), and she is therefore rediscovered by Don.

"I've Got a Feeling You're Fooling" was sung by Robert Taylor in *Broadway Melody of 1936* (1935). It also was used in *Dancing Co-Ed* (1939) and in a movie called *With a Song in My Heart,* released in the same year as *Singin' in the Rain,* 1952. "Should I?" had been used in *Lord Byron of Broadway* (1929), and also in *Thousands Cheer* and *Pilot No. 5,* both released in 1943. "The Wedding of the Painted Doll" was slotted into the montage after it was dropped as Cosmo's attempt to cheer up Don on the movie set. This well-known Freed product initially appeared in *The Broadway Melody* (1929) and was repeated in *The Song Writers' Revue* (1930), where Freed himself sang it. It also appeared in *What Price Hollywood?* (1932), *Another Language* (1933), and *Son of the Gods* (1936). "Beautiful Girl" had been sung by Bing Crosby, before he became famous, during intermissions at a movie theater called the Orange Grove that Freed operated in Los Angeles during the 1920s. Crosby introduced "Beautiful Girl" to a wider audience in *Stage Mother* (1933), and the song was also used in *Going Hollywood* in the same year.[45]

Bits and pieces of the songs, "I've got a feelin' you're foolin', I've got a feelin' you're havin' fun," "Should I reveal, exactly how I feel? Should I confess, I love you?" and "It's a holiday, today's the wedding, of the painted doll," were used along with a full rendition of "Beautiful Girl" to become something more than an homage to the past. "We are doing Busby Berkeley here," Stanley Donen commented years later, "only we're making fun of him." The sequences in both numbers mimic Berkeley's famous "kaleidoscopic patterns," and the "Beautiful Girl" number includes a fashion show reminiscent of those to be seen in Fred Astaire's *Roberta* (1933) and Gene Kelly's own *Cover Girl* (1944).[46]

The idea of tacking the fashion show onto the songs originated with the delight Edens and Donen felt at the 1920s costumes Walter Plunkett produced. They worked up a spoof of silent era fashion to follow the Berkeley spoof. Plunkett was happy to oblige and Edens wrote the spoken narrative for the fashion show. Everyone "roared with laughter," in the words of Hugh Fordin, when the daily rushes were shown.[47] But the joke has lost its effect with the passage of time and the fashion show now comes across as the only unnecessary section in the entire movie.

Jimmy Thompson recited the narrative as well as sang "Beautiful Girl." Thompson had first appeared as an uncredited stock company member in Kelly's *Summer Stock* (1950), and worked as Kelly's personal assistant. An earlier script had Don and Cosmo finding Kathy on the lot, with Kelly doing the narrative and singing "Beautiful Girl" instead of Thompson. Gene even recorded these sections for a playback. But the revised plot, with Cosmo discovering Kathy at the end of the dance, worked better. Consequently, they had Thompson do the narrative and song instead.[48]

The montage takes the viewer through a whirlwind sequence of images redolent of movie lore, but one must recall that it was a time less than a quarter-century before the filming of *Singin' in the Rain*. Film historians John Russell Taylor and Arthur Jackson say that the frenetic pace of the montage suggests the Jazz Age atmosphere, while Casey Charness believes it "marks the first time the Hollywood musical had ever been reflexive, and amused at its own extravagant non-dancing inadequacy, at that." Berkeley's "overhead kaleidoscopic floral pattern is predominantly featured, as is the line of tap-dancing chorines, who are seen only from the knees down." Other images include "the dancing college sweethearts, the crooner with megaphone grafted to his mouth, [and] three singing sisters." "Beautiful Girl" and the montage are musical numbers, "yet with hardly a smidgin of dance content, which appears to be Donen and Kelly's statement, precisely."[49]

It was no easy matter to arrange all this. The musical montage was filmed on August 8, 11, and 13, and also on September 26 and 27. A typical day of filming the montage took place on August 11. Gene Kelly put in a full day of work, and O'Connor dubbed his taps that day. Carol Haney and Jeanne Coyne were on the set nearly twelve hours. Jeanne was in the dance as well, playing one of the three girls in the "Woo de woo de woo" segment. Twenty-one other dancers were available for filming the sequence, including Ernie Flatt. The technical crew began to set up equipment at 8 a.m. The dancers rehearsed to playback and three takes were shot from 9:44 to 9:52. Three more shots were exposed from 9:56 to 10:07, and then the dancers rested for ten minutes. Everyone worked at this pace all morning, shooting many takes. The technical crew experienced some difficulty with their equipment. Operators got a shock from one camera, and upon inspecting it found an electrical short that had to be repaired. They later discovered that the film had buckled inside the camera, spoiling three takes. In fact, many takes were spoiled by various causes—poor expressions by one of the dancers, and a breakdown in synchronization of the camera-work. After an hour-long lunch break, the pace continued. The crew used a ubangi, a device to place the camera as low as possible to the floor, so that with a "tipped lens" it could photograph the subjects from a low angle. Some images of the dancers with cocktail shakers were filmed in this way, and images of the chorines dancing from the knees down were filmed from a regular camera setup. Here, the dancers sat behind a black cloth and stuck their legs through slits in the cloth to achieve this effect. The first result was not good apparently, as the assistant director recorded in his report, "new instructions re-kicking—reh. with dancers." This took place from 5:29 to 5:35 p.m., and the scene was shot again. Finally, after a very full day for everyone, the company was dismissed at 6:07 p.m. [50]

"YOU WERE MEANT FOR ME"

The song selected for the pivotal number in which Don woos Kathy had seen quite a lot of exposure in previous movies. "You Were Meant for Me" debuted in *The Broadway Melody* (1929). It was also aired in two other movies released that same year, *The Hollywood Revue of 1929* and *The Show of Shows*.[51]

In *The Broadway Melody*, Charles King sings it in a sincere but heavy-handed way to Anita Page, who reacts rather negatively because King plays her sister's fiancé at that point in the movie. The song is repeated in another scene as dance music for a party. In *The Hollywood Revue of 1929*, the song is used in an intentionally comedic way. Charles King tells Conrad Nagle that he sang "You Were Meant for Me" to Anita Page once, and jokes that it was a good way to be romantic, as it saved money. Then Page walks in and Nagle sings the same song to her, she responds very positively, and they kiss. King looks shocked, shrinks to a tiny size, hops off his (now giant) chair, and stalks off in a huff.

The song appeared again in four movies released in 1930, *The Divorcee*, *The Lady of Scandal*, *The Ship from Shanghai*, and *The Dogway Melody*. Ten years later, in 1940, it was used in *Hullabaloo* and *Forty Little Mothers*. This was followed by *Penny Serenade* (1941), *Maisie Gets Her Man* (1942), and *The Mouse Comes to Dinner* (1945). Next, it became the title song of Twentieth Century–Fox's *You Were Meant for Me* (1948), which starred Jeanne Crain and Dan Dailey and included Oscar Levant and Percy Kilbride. Finally, only a year before *Singin'*, it was included in *Casanova Cat* (1951).[52]

After so many outings the song needed something new to set off its qualities, and Gene Kelly came up with an effective strategy. It would be the third time in his movie career that his character wooed the leading lady by imagining a movie setting in an otherwise spare venue. The two previous times occurred in "The Spanish Dance" in *Anchors Aweigh* (1945) with Kathryn Grayson, and in "You Wonderful You" from *Summer Stock* (1950) with Judy Garland. Initially, a medley of Freed-Brown songs, "Chant of the Jungle," "Would You?," and "Broadway Melody," were slated for this number, and it was to be a traveling routine among the various movie sets on the backlot. This was switched to a single Freed-Brown song, "Should I?," in April. By late June, Kelly and Donen decided to use "You Were Meant for Me" instead, and to find a different venue. Kelly called Comden and Green who were still in Philadelphia working on their stage show and asked them to rewrite the scene and mail it to Hollywood. The writers had to reorient their minds to the movie project for a few days in order to get the job done.[53]

Meanwhile, Kelly searched for the proper setting for the new arrangement. "We don't want a set," he told art director Randall Duell. "We don't want to build anything. We want to just pick something." Kelly and Duell explored the M-G-M studio and walked onto an empty sound stage. It was mostly dark, with only a few lights scattered around and a stepladder in the middle of the empty space. The two walked to the ladder and thought about it. "This is great," Kelly told Duell. "We'll use the ladder, and we'll bring in these lights. We'll bring them all in. This is all we want, a big empty sound stage with a few lights and a ladder." The basic elements were already there, saving the production a great deal of money and creating an unforgettable moment in *Singin' in the Rain*. "That was purely Gene's idea," Duell later admitted.[54]

As Don and Kathy walk onto the empty stage before the number, a billboard for a movie called *Chant of the Jungle* is seen behind them. The song "Chant of the Jungle" had only appeared in one movie, *Untamed* (1929).[55] Also, it was the only Freed-Brown song from the medley originally planned for this number that was not used elsewhere in the movie. The placement of the billboard seems to have been a way to include the song, at least at the visual level.

The "You Were Meant for Me" sequence is divided into twelve shots, with Kelly starting to sing the song in shot nine. Kelly's rendition of the song is natural and heartfelt, perfectly matching the lyrics, "But I'm content, the angels must have sent you, / And they meant you just for me." The pace of the song is faster than in the takes of the vocal prerecordings and works better, while the ladder is used "as a pivotal point for camera movements during the vocal." Kelly choreographed the dance movements to illustrate the tentative nature of their relationship, with Reynolds moving away from him at times, and the camera alternating medium and long shots, using a crane to enhance the interplay of movement and sentiment as expressed in both the song and the dance. Kathy becomes more comfortable with Don, and the two dance sweetly together.[56]

The overall development of the dance, with a tentative beginning followed by a comfortable pairing, is somewhat similar to Kelly's "Our Love Is Here to Stay" with Leslie Caron in *An American in Paris*. But the styles of the two dances are quite different—ballet moves with Leslie Caron, and simple tap and ballroom swirls with Debbie Reynolds. And although the bare stage setting is similar to Kelly's wooing dances in

Anchors Aweigh and *Summer Stock,* the three dances are very different. "The Spanish Dance" in *Anchors Aweigh* is a fantasy Kelly creates for the two of them, and he dances alone and acrobatically to bolero-type background music. "You Wonderful You" in *Summer Stock* has Kelly singing to Garland, but as a way to show her what the theater is about. Although both dance, the steps are limited and constrained to a small space, using only part of the theater stage.

Casey Charness believes "You Were Meant for Me" is a good example of cine-dance. The camera complements the dance movements superbly. Through a combination of long, medium, and close shots, it shows us how big the physical space of the stage is and yet frames the dancing in intimate ways when it is called for. The camera is the "recorder, definer, and enhancer of the space," and this "results in a restrained collaboration that is striking in how calmly yet firmly it asserts itself." Charness concludes that "You Were Meant for Me" "is eloquent in its definition and use of space, smart in its correlation between space and dancer, a connection which is achieved through the camera alone." Genné concurs, writing that as "they skip in an exhilarating circle around the floor . . . the camera swoops around" and at the "emotional high point . . . the moment of acceptance," the camera pulls back and up for "a visual 'high.'"[57] Ironically, the sequence exhibits its artificiality in obvious ways; Don Lockwood explains how illusions are created in Hollywood and then proceeds to create one of his own for Kathy, which reveals the real emotion he feels for her.

Debbie Reynolds recalled an incident during the filming of "You Were Meant for Me" that tends to bring the artistry down to earth. She had a habit of chewing gum while on the set and hastily put her wad of gum under a step of the ladder when called on to film a scene. Kelly "leaned romantically up against the ladder" and his head touched the fresh gum. It took out a chunk of hair when he moved away from the ladder. "Well, he let out a yell and I just turned pale. . . . that was the end of my chewing gum days. And very nearly the end of me."[58]

Gene Kelly and Debbie Reynolds chatting on the set.
Note the worn M-G-M equipment they are sitting on.
(SINGIN' IN THE RAIN © Turner Entertainment Co.
A Warner Bros. Entertainment Company. All rights reserved. Courtesy of the
Academy of Motion Picture Arts and Sciences, Margaret Herrick Library)

The Kelly team on the first day of production.
From left: Jeanne Coyne, Stanley Donen, Gene Kelly, Carol Haney, and
Donald O'Connor. The symbolic good-luck umbrella, filled with flowers and
trinkets (including fake mice), seems to interest everyone except Kelly and Coyne.

Alternate title scene without umbrellas, shot on a sound stage and
with Reynolds wearing her galoshes like a 1920s flapper.
(SINGIN' IN THE RAIN © Turner Entertainment Co.
A Warner Bros. Entertainment Company. All rights reserved. Courtesy of the
Academy of Motion Picture Arts and Sciences, Margaret Herrick Library)

"Not in front of all these people!"
From left: Donald O'Connor, Madge Blake, Gene Kelly, and Jean Hagen,
just before Don Lockwood is prevailed upon to tell his life story to the crowd
at the premiere of The Royal Rascal.

"Fit as a Fiddle," an energetic dance by Gene Kelly and Donald O'Connor,
shown as Don Lockwood relates his life story to his adoring fans.
(SINGIN' IN THE RAIN © Turner Entertainment Co.
A Warner Bros. Entertainment Company. All rights reserved. Courtesy of the
Academy of Motion Picture Arts and Sciences, Margaret Herrick Library)

Part of the jalopy ride sequence, when Matt the Cop, played by Robert Foulke,
recognizes Don Lockwood and reassures Kathy Selden that she is one lucky girl.

"You Were Meant for Me," a turning point in the film's plotline and one of Gene Kelly's most effective "falling in love" dance sequences. (*SINGIN' IN THE RAIN* © *Turner Entertainment Co.* A Warner Bros. Entertainment Company. All rights reserved. Courtesy of the Academy of Motion Picture Arts and Sciences, Margaret Herrick Library)

"Moses Supposes," a split-second image of what is unanimously acclaimed
as the best tap dance routine captured on film.

"IN the bush!" Douglas Fowley is the exasperated director trying to
deal with the technical difficulties of filming with sound. Kathleen Freeman,
the diction coach, is on the right. A worried Don Lockwood looks on while
Lina Lamont seems bored with these tiresome proceedings.

"Good Morning!" The only dance performed by the three principals as a trio.
It is a joyous celebration, a wonderful example of collaborative
effort, and the toughest dance Debbie Reynolds did in the movie.
(*SINGIN' IN THE RAIN* © *Turner Entertainment Co.*
A Warner Bros. Entertainment Company. All rights reserved. Courtesy of the
Academy of Motion Picture Arts and Sciences, Margaret Herrick Library)

"I'm laughing at clouds," Gene Kelly's most famous pose from his
best-loved dance number, "Singin' in the Rain." This scene was used as the
model for a proposed statue to the performer in Pittsburgh, his hometown.

While performing "Singin' in the Rain," Kelly smiles his way through a
dance routine made difficult by the need to perform in an artificial rain shower,
on a slick pavement, while recovering from a bout of flu and sinus infection.

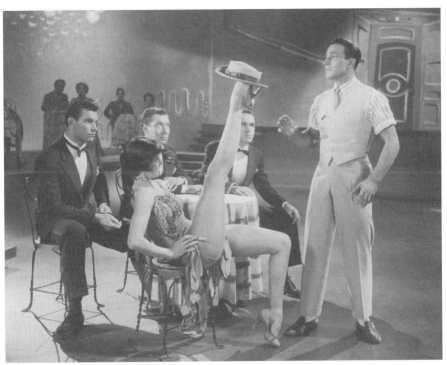

Raising the censor's eyebrow—one of the most provocative poses in a steamy sequence from "The Broadway Ballet." More than one foreign censor had trouble accepting Cyd Charisse's stunning performance when they considered allowing the movie to be shown in their countries. Carl Milletaire plays the scar-faced gangster, accompanied by two henchmen.

The fifty-foot-long "crazy veil" in Gene Kelly's fantasy dance with Cyd Charisse during "The Broadway Ballet." Charisse had to struggle against powerful fans which were used to manipulate the long silk veil.

A savings bank cashes in on publicity for the movie while celebrating
its own anniversary. M-G-M's extensive promotional plans included selling a
variety of movie posters and displays, normally to theater managers.

*Gene Kelly visiting his wax image at Movieland Wax Museum,
Buena Park, California, which opened in 1962 and closed in 2005. The set was
rigged for continuous rain accompanying a recording of "Singin' in the Rain."
Kelly's mixed feelings about the hoopla surrounding his most famous dance
number are obvious.*

5

Come On with the Rain

The title number of *Singin' in the Rain* has become the most recognizable tune in film musical history. It became a classic soon after the movie was released and has grown in stature since 1952. The conceptualization, choreographing, and filming of the number took place in the middle of production as just one of several important dances. Not until later years did the makers of *Singin' in the Rain* realize how much the number meant to viewers.

"Singin' in the Rain" was a perennial favorite among the Freed-Brown songs. It was written for a stage show called *The Hollywood Music Box Revue* in Los Angeles in 1927, but some of its lyrics were derived from an earlier song Freed had written with Abel Baer called "The Sun's in My Heart." Freed recalled how "Singin' in the Rain" came about: "I had the title for some time before writing the song," and Nacio Herb Brown "came to me one afternoon with the news that he'd just written a great tune for a coloratura soprano. He sat down and played it with all the classic trills. All I could think of was that a vamp in the bass and a few minor changes would give it the zip for some lyrics I'd written." In providing copy for the program of *Singin'*, Freed added that the lyrics "were all about a fellow in love who went around 'Singin' In The Rain.'" He later admitted that he did not spend "more than an hour and a half writing the lyrics for that song."[1]

The song's film career began with an elaborate staging in *The Hollywood Revue of 1929* where Cliff Edwards ("Ukulele Ike") sang the song while chorus girls and guys dressed in raincoats and rain hats danced behind him as "prop rain poured from overhead pipes."[2] The three Brock sisters shared one raincoat and sang the song with stiff arm movements at both ends of the trio. The entire choreography was wooden, with mechanical, synchronized moves—shrugging shoulders and waving arms. The dancers' expressions certainly did not do justice to the lyrics and even Ukulele Ike looked glum and morose as he sang about being joyful. The number was filmed in Technicolor, and in front of a big painting of Noah's Ark. A long line of M-G-M stars, also dressed in raincoats and rain hats, sang a part of the song.

Next, M-G-M used the song in five movies in 1930—*The Divorcee, The Girl Said No, The Ship from Shanghai, The Woman Racket,* and *The Dogway Melody*. It was used again in three movies in 1932—*Speak Easily, The Old Dark House,* and *Skyscraper Souls*. In *Speak Easily,* Jimmy Durante plays the tune for the director of a theatrical troupe and pretends he wrote it himself, but the director knows better. M-G-M also used the song in *Idiot's Delight* (1939), *Dulcy* (1940), *Little Nellie Kelly* (1940), and *Maisie Gets Her Man* (1942). Other studios used the song before 1952 as well. It graced RKO's *Unexpected Uncle* (1941), Paramount's *Happy Go Lucky* (1943), and Universal's *Hi Beautiful* (1944).[3]

Comden and Green had written that "Singin' in the Rain" was to be performed by Kelly, Reynolds, and O'Connor after they emerge from the Pink Fedora restaurant to celebrate their idea of making *The Duelling Cavalier* into a musical. However, Kelly wisely reoriented the original plan to make the song a major expression of love by Don for Kathy. He recognized early on that the number would work best with just him, and that it should be placed at a key moment in the story. However, he was not forthcoming when asked what exactly he intended to do with the song. Kelly later said that his idea "was so simple I shied away from explaining it to the brass at the studio in case I couldn't make it sound worth doing."[4]

Kelly recalled that Freed and Edens visited him in his office to ask what he had in mind for "Singin' in the Rain." "Well, I said rather vaguely, it's got to be raining, and I'm going to be singing. I'm going to have a glorious feeling, and I'm going to be happy again. What else?" "Well, that's logical," was the only thing Freed could say in response. Kelly tried to postpone further discussion because "they knew I hadn't come up with an idea, but I told them not to worry, that I'd think of something."[5] In a way, Kelly had given little thought to the number because its staging seemed self-evident. But a simple production of this number could sound blasé in the telling, so he did not know exactly what to tell Freed and Edens.

Just a few days after this conversation, Kelly looked at the song lyrics "to see if they suggested anything other than the obvious." At the end of the chorus he thought to add "'dancin' to the lyric—so that it now ran 'I'm singin' and *dancin'* in the rain.' Instead of just singing the number, I'd dance it as well. Suddenly the mist began to clear, because a dance tagged onto a song suggested a positive and joyous emotion." Kelly thought the best spot in the movie's narrative to place a song like this was at "my moment of greatest exhilaration," where he celebrates his love for Kathy and the joint decision to turn the failed movie into a musical. "From then on everything slotted beautifully into place."[6]

Kelly later discussed how he worked out the number. "I have to have an excuse," as he put it, "because . . . to go out and sing in the rain without looking like an idiot, one must have quite an impulse!" Kelly explained that "the easiest way—is when the number flows out of a situation." Love was among the most powerfully effective motives for anything in movie musicals, and it justified the sight of a grown man splashing in rain puddles on an empty city street. Kelly also felt that a song and dance man needed to sing his "thesis," then perform. In other words, he would begin by singing the song, and then let his feet take over. As Kelly later told interviewer Curtis Lee Hanson, "After I sing it, I dance it. At the end of the song, I state 'I'm singing and dancing in the rain.'"[7]

Kelly often commented that "a number is the same as a short story, you have a beginning, a middle and an end." For "Singin'," the ending involved an authority figure in the form of a policeman who wonders what this fellow is up to on a wet, deserted street. "And you *always* have to have some comment," Kelly told Hanson. "A fellow who is singing in the rain has to be observed if it's going to be funny. The policeman, in this case, saw it." Film scholar Peter Wollen interprets the appearance of the policeman as reminiscent of "Make Way for Tomorrow" in *Cover Girl* (1944). In that number, a policeman again provides some counterpoint to the inner joy expressed by the trio. Uncomprehending, he also stands there, slightly suspicious of what is going on. In the case of "Singin' in the Rain," however, after Don leaves the policeman, he gives his umbrella to a passing stranger as an "epilogue" to the little story just acted out.[8]

As for the choreography, Kelly's main concern was to express child-like joy. Grown-ups normally do not cavort in the rain, "they often want to, but usually they don't," Kelly remarked. "I thought of the fun children have splashing about in rain puddles and decided to become a kid again during the number." It was then easy to devise dance steps to express this emotion, especially as Kelly had two city blocks with all their accoutrements to work with in creating a classic bit of bricolage.[9]

"I think I composed the number in three days," Kelly later remembered. Edens wrote the segue notes, "Do do do, dodo dodo . . . ," the bridge that musically leads into the song itself. Kelly often commented on how important that bridge was in enabling his character to move from kissing Kathy to jumping onto the nearest lamppost, as he "always hated the Jeanette MacDonald–Nelson Eddy way of going into a song." Kelly and Edens wisely decided to use only the first verse of the song. The second verse, which Ukulele Ike included in *The Hollywood Revue of 1929*, and which Judy Garland sang at a formal dance in *Little Nellie Kelly*, was decidedly inferior in quality, for example, "Why do I get up each morning to start, / Happy and het up with joy in my heart?"[10]

CAMERA-WORK AND SET PREPARATION

Kelly thought that "Singin' in the Rain" was "not a difficult dance technically, it could be done by any dancer: it's a dance which has to be *played* more than it's danced." He and Donen planned the camera movements to keep "the dance coming into camera," that is, Kelly would always be approaching the viewer. "If I stopped, we would bring the camera up and cut and come sidewards so I would move back and forth. Always into camera. Always the forces were pushing, pushing, pushing the camera." To accomplish this they had to create a large set on which to film the number. It cost more money, but allowed the directors to "keep the dance moving down the street so that forcing the camera back all the time didn't decrease the kinesthesia, the movement in the camera." They were self-consciously creating a cine-dance, which has since been hailed as one of the better examples of collaborative effort between the choreographer and the director (in Kelly's case, he performed both roles).[11]

Film scholars agree that Kelly and Donen achieved their purpose in the camera-work for "Singin' in the Rain." Jerome Delamater writes that Kelly often took advantage of space in staging his numbers, refusing to be restricted by "an invisible proscenium arch" or constricting stage aesthetics. Within the "seemingly undefined area" in which he

danced, the camera moved in varied ways to complement his movements and "to reveal new space for the dancer; areas of off-screen space
are constantly being revealed on screen and thus become potential
dance space." As Kelly told Delamater, "What I did in 'Singin' in the
Rain' . . . was to take the whole street and keep the dance moving down
the street." Casey Charness writes that the penultimate moment of the
dance is the "fast pullback and dolly up combined with the sweeping
motion of an open umbrella twirled in space." That moment defines
the entire number and its purpose of expressing the joy of love and life.
Charness sees the movement in this number as not directly into the
camera, but more often to screen left, and thinks that this increases the
sense of movement rather than diminishes it. "Donen and Kelly contribute implied movement along with what is actually seen on screen,"
Charness writes. "It is a canny precept, and one that is integral to the
success of the dance." Given what the co-directors wanted to achieve in
this dance, Kelly needed someone with talent behind the camera, and
he gave full credit to Donen. He could not perform and direct camera
movements at the same time and considered his co-director's work as
"very important" in this number.[12]

The setting of "Singin' in the Rain" was equally important to its
camera-work. Kelly wanted to do it on an existing street in the backlot
to save money, rather than on a stage. Art director Randall Duell, Kelly,
and Jeanne Coyne explored the different streets in the backlot until
they found a suitable venue on the East Side Street in Lot 2. Then they
hauled a piano to the street and took along a tempo track to provide the
beat of the music as Kelly began to work out his steps. As he did for
"You Were Meant for Me," Kelly used whatever props were available on
the street and built them into the choreography. The classic example of
this is his jumping onto the lamppost. Another example is where Kelly
saw a wrought-iron fence nearby and did what many kids have done,
using his umbrella to make a rattling noise along it. He also added a
segment going up and down the curb. Kelly easily felt comfortable with
this setting. The musical score was fully developed to take into account
the evolving choreography, incorporating all the bricolage, especially
the umbrella.[13]

One of the factors considered in preparing the setting was the rain.
M-G-M had done other dances in the rain before—in *The Hollywood
Revue of 1929* and *Till the Clouds Roll By* (1947), both with piped-in rain

on a sound stage. The choreography and dancing in *Till the Clouds Roll By* was more sophisticated and energetic than in the earlier film.

In *The Broadway Melody of 1938*, Eleanor Powell and George Murphy danced in what appeared to be a rain-drenched outdoor setting in "Feeling Like a Million." Paramount had also featured Maurice Chevalier dancing in rain while performing "The Rhythm of the Rain" in *Folies Bergere* (1935).[14]

The technical difficulties of dancing in the rain again, with conviction, were great. Kelly needed slight puddles at key locations in order to incorporate more splashing into his routine. "We would draw a circle where that puddle was to be built," recalled Duell: "We would rearrange the architecture of the thing to accommodate the exact split second when he was there to test whatever it was. Then we would dish out the street and repave it and make all these puddles so that he hit exactly where he was going to go." Duell says the crew spent "several weeks" doing this, and he planned seven puddles. He also wanted to have at least two inches of water in the gutter pool so that Kelly could truly act like a child, joyfully splashing without worrying about making a spectacle of himself. Kelly wanted to deliberately let water from a downspout flow over himself as another touch of unrestrained joy. Duell had to cut off a nearby step to allow Kelly room to get under that downspout. Years later, Kelly enjoyed claiming that the technicians thought he "was crazy because I went to the set and had them dig holes in the ground to accumulate the rain water," but this sort of thing was not unusual while preparing numbers for filming.[15]

Although Duell planned seven puddles, it is clear from viewing the finished film that only one was cut out of the preexisting concrete of the sidewalk. It is the puddle in which Kelly taps his left foot just before jumping into the gutter pool. The hole is clearly lighter than the rest of the sidewalk, due to the excavation and the pouring of fresh cement to smooth the hollow surface. The gutter puddle, where Kelly splashes when "caught" by the policeman, is also very easy to see on film. The edges around the pool of water show where new cement meets the old concrete. Careful and minute observation of the filmed dance shows that no other puddles were cut into the sidewalk. Kelly probably suggested a plan for seven puddles before the rain pipes were set up. Once he tried the dance with water, he realized that the uneven pavement allowed him to splash very well, and with good effect, so that cutting all the other puddles was unnecessary. The one puddle allowed him to add some diversity toward the end of the dance, and the large pool in the gutter allowed him to take the number to its climax. Kelly simply talks of puddles in his interviews, without mentioning how many there were. Duell's interview took place more than twenty years after the film was made, and as he worked on numerous pictures every year, it is understandable he did not remember that they changed the proposed plan, to cut only one puddle in the pavement and the huge hole in the gutter.

BLOCKING THE SHOTS

As finally worked out, Kelly and Donen used only ten shots for the entire number, which lasts a bit less than five minutes. In shot one, Kelly kisses Reynolds goodnight, which sets the mood for the number as "the beginning of the story." He sends the car home in shot two, comes down the steps, still with a blissful smile, waves to the driver after he drives away, and also waves to a running passerby after he's gone, nicely depicting the slight absentmindedness, mixed with sweetness, of a person very much in love. He sings the "Do do do . . . " vamp, closes the umbrella, and joyously sings, "I'm singin' in the rain, just singin' in the rain, / What a glorious feelin', I'm happy again" in shot three. In the same shot, he also jumps on the famous lamppost, making it look easy in the acrobatic Kelly style. As he jumps off and sings, "The sun's in my heart and I'm ready for love," the camera zooms in for a close-up of his boyish, happy grin. In shot four, he waves to a couple who run by staring at him. As Kelly takes off his hat and sings, "Come on with the rain, I've a smile on my face," the camera cranes up above and zooms in on his smiling, upturned face. It is in shot five that Kelly starts dancing, as he sings, "Dancin' in the rain . . . " and playfully interacts with the figure of the woman on the shop window display. He uses the umbrella in different ways, including strumming it, as he sings the last line of the song, "I'm singin' and dancin' in the rain." Shot six has him now dancing without singing as he does a variety of lighthearted steps, continuing to use the umbrella as a prop or toy, and he ends the shot scraping the umbrella against the fence. The camera tracks him in shot seven as he dances along the sidewalk, twirling the now-open umbrella over his shoulder, throwing it up and catching it. Kelly approaches a gushing downspout a couple of times before going under it, first with the umbrella, then putting the umbrella down and getting thoroughly drenched.[16]

Shot eight includes the peak of the dance as Kelly runs toward and jumps off the curb with a high, acrobatic leap, and brilliantly uses the open umbrella as a prop while spinning "round and round in jubilation" across the slippery street. Film scholars have nothing but praise for this movement and the camera-work. "It is a very kinetic moment," Charness has written, "for though there is no technically accomplished dance present, the feeling of swinging around in a circle with an open umbrella is a brilliantly apt choice of movement, one that will be readily identifiable by an audience which might know nothing kinesthetically of actual dance. . . . Accompanying this movement is a breathless pullback into a high crane shot that takes place at the same time Kelly is swinging into his widest arcs with the umbrella. The effect is dizzying, perhaps the finest single example of the application of camera knowhow to a dance moment in the Donen-Kelly canon."[17]

Back on the sidewalk, Kelly performs "cross-overs at the ankle" up and down the curb in shot nine. He would do a similar step with roller skates in *It's Always Fair Weather* (1955). This is followed by a "pantomimed tight rope walk" along the edge of the curb and joyful splashing on the sidewalk in the one puddle mentioned earlier. Finally, Kelly jumps into the gutter pool and splashes around in uninhibited, childlike glee until he spots a policeman watching him, and then he gingerly steps out of the pool onto the curb. The final shot, number ten, is "an over-the-shoulder shot from the cop's point-of-view," as Kelly explains to him, "I'm dancin' and singin' in the rain." He waves to the cop somewhat nervously while leaving, generously gives his umbrella to a passing stranger, waves jauntily to the cop this time, and walks away along the sidewalk with a decidedly Chaplinesque air.[18]

FILMING THE TITLE DANCE

The filming of "Singin' in the Rain" mostly was a technical matter, as Kelly felt the dancing was comparatively simple. Since M-G-M hated to pay its employees overtime, they rigged up an elaborate covering with a black tarpaulin across the two blocks of outdoor street to create a plausible facsimile of nighttime during the day. Technicians also rigged an elaborate system of pipes, using water directly from the Culver City water system, to simulate rain for six hours each day. Technicolor filming demanded much light, and the rain could not be seen when lit in a straightforward fashion. Kelly explained that this forced Harold Rosson, the cameraman, to arrange the lighting indirectly, placing the bulbs behind the rain instead of in front of it. Rosson had to front-light Kelly and the policeman as usual. All in all, the number was very difficult for the technicians to set up, according to Kelly.[19]

Among Kelly's concerns when it came time to film was manipulating the umbrella "with the beats of the music, and not falling down in the water and breaking every bone in my body." He also developed what his wife Betsy Blair called "a frightful flu and sinus infection" several days before the scheduled filming, which made him concerned about catching pneumonia as well. Kelly's illness began on Monday, July 9, when he had an 8:45 a.m. call at the studio. He did not reach the Culver City facility until 1:40 that afternoon, and was "too ill to rehearse in rain," according to assistant director Marvin Stuart. Kelly instead "listened to playback—tried out wet sidewalk in rain and checked camera angles with Mr. Donen," and left at 5:05 p.m. Kelly was too ill to work on July 10, 11, and 12, but reported on Saturday, July 14. However, his illness reached its peak soon after, producing a 103-degree temperature. Kelly's personal physician visited his home on both Sunday and Monday morning and refused to allow him to go to work. Betsy called the studio twice to report the news, but unknown to her, M-G-M had sent its own doctor to Kelly's home on Monday to check on him. Kelly never wanted to see this doctor because he had a reputation for too freely prescribing drugs to studio stars. Betsy refused to answer the door and the doctor went away without seeing him.[20]

In fact, no one was on call Monday, July 16, one of the rare days in the production period that the *Singin' in the Rain* company did no work. Kelly was well enough to go to the studio on Tuesday, July 17, as production resumed in full force. Kelly, Reynolds, and all the bit players involved in the "Singin'" number were on call, and four scenes were shot, all of them preliminary to Kelly's dance.[21]

Kelly's dancing in "Singin' in the Rain" was filmed all day on Wednesday, July 18, and on the morning of Thursday, July 19. The first day was packed with activity as the crew set up six different camera angles. Of a total 160 scenes in the movie, forty-seven had been completed by July

18, including the day's accomplishment. The production team exposed 2,966 feet of film on July 18, but the net result was 175 feet of completed film. The total amount of footage exposed thus far in the production of *Singin'* amounted to 51,387, with only 5,095 of that listed as net. Yet, the production team was two days ahead of the filming schedule.[22]

Kelly and Donen used only two extras on July 18, Harry "Snub" Pollard, who played the older man to whom Kelly gives his umbrella at the end of the dance, and Brick Sullivan, who played the policeman. Pollard was an Australian who came to the United States in 1910 and worked first in vaudeville, then in films, usually in uncredited bit parts. Sullivan was born in South Dakota and most often played a policeman or guard in seventy-eight films from 1936 to 1951. For their work that day, Pollard was paid $15.56 and Sullivan $22.23. Carol Haney and Jeanne Coyne were on the set all day to help out, Coyne as Kelly's dance-in. One stand-in was on the set all day, another was on standby, and a third was available only for the last couple of hours of filming. Debbie Reynolds was not on call because her scenes with Kelly in this segment of *Singin' in the Rain* had been filmed the day before. Donald O'Connor was scheduled to be on the set only in the evening for some additional filming that was planned.[23]

The technical crews were in the studio by 8 a.m. on July 18 to begin setting up. The first rehearsal started at 8:06 and continued until 8:43, with Coyne dancing Kelly's part to the playback as the camera moved according to plan so every detail of what was to come could be worked out. At 9:00 a.m., Kelly limbered up for five minutes and finished his wardrobe preparation, followed by his own rehearsal to the playback for about eleven minutes. Then cameraman Rosson (guided by Donen) shot nine takes from 9:16 to 9:33, followed by more rehearsal by Kelly for about ten minutes. Kelly then spent twenty minutes practicing his dance "from drug store to music studio in rain," as the technicians rigged additional piping to extend the space to be danced in and filmed. By now it was 10:40 a.m. More rehearsal with the rain, more rehearsal to the playback, and then seven takes were shot in eleven minutes. Kelly next wanted to practice the "cascade" effect of standing under the broken downspout, and spent more than twenty minutes working out the details. Technicians then adjusted the pipes feeding water into the downspout to suit Kelly's instructions. He practiced spinning the umbrella on the sidewalk and standing once again under the spout before the company broke for lunch at 12:12 p.m.[24]

After an hour-long break, the grueling pace continued. The crew rehearsed the rain effect using stand-in Rene Barsam while they played back the music. Then Kelly rehearsed without the rain for seven minutes, and Rosson shot twelve takes in twenty minutes. It is recorded that they stopped to allow someone to "Wipe water off lens," and continued shooting several more takes. Finally, by 2:36, Kelly was ready to run through the penultimate moment of the number, noted as "dances in wide circle in street Low and to high boom shot." After trying it out, Kelly and Donen got on the boom and went up to see what it would look like as Coyne danced the part to playback, but without rain. Then Kelly continued to rehearse for a half hour as set decorators lighted and dressed thirteen second-story windows on the street, given that the high boom would bring these windows into the camera's view. Kelly and Donen probably had noticed this fact when they rode up, thus the last-minute dressing that took place. Coyne danced the part again to the playback and in the rain, then Kelly took a couple of minutes to finish his wardrobe and makeup. He rehearsed again for six minutes to the playback to get warmed up, and danced for eight takes from 4:16 to 4:29, and three more takes from 4:52 to 4:56 p.m. [25]

Everyone accomplished a great deal on July 18, but the filming was not over. Given that the "Singin'" set provided a venue for filming night scenes during the day, and the piping provided rain showers on demand, Kelly and Donen wanted to film other scenes in the movie that required either element. The crew broke up the camera setup that had been required for shooting the "Singin'" number and set up to film the scene in front of the employment office to be inserted into Don's telling of his life story, early in the picture. To do this they had to tear down part of the black tarpaulin in front of a usable building façade but retain the piping above it. Kelly changed his clothes, and O'Connor, who showed up on the set before his 5:20 p.m. call, rehearsed a bit, and then the scene was shot in two takes from 5:56 to 5:59. Kelly spent the next fifteen minutes rehearsing for the next day's shooting of "Singin'" before going home.[26]

A careful analysis of what happened on July 18, recorded in Marvin Stuart's report, reveals that the majority of activity on the set consisted of rehearsing by Kelly and Coyne, with crew setup and teardown constituting the second activity. Actual filming was comparatively short. A total of 580 minutes of activity was recorded (forty minutes more than the nine hours of time actually spent on the set because setup and teardown sometimes took place concurrently with rehearsing). Out of those 580 minutes, 380 (or 65.5 percent) were spent in rehearsing, 122 minutes (or 21 percent) were spent in setup or teardown, and only 78 minutes (or 13.4 percent) were spent in filming. So much time was spent in rehearsal on the set, despite the weeks of preparation in preproduction, because small details still had to be worked out and the directors could not know until the last minute exactly how the action would look within the context of the finished set. It is difficult to know exactly how much of what one sees in the finished product was the result of this last-minute analysis, but the assistant director's report indicates that quite a bit of it was fine-tuned at the last minute through repeated and no doubt exhausting repetitions only minutes before it was time for the cameras to roll. It is interesting that Kelly worked through these details himself, and also watched as his former Pittsburgh student, current dance assistant, and future wife Jeanne Coyne danced these famous steps in the rain in order to see how they played out from the viewer's perspective. Everything had to be worked out as closely as possible because it was expensive to roll the cameras. Forty-six takes were done on July 18 in only seventy-eight minutes.[27]

Working under the black tarpaulin on a warm summer day created problems. The set took on a hothouse atmosphere, creating the effect of a steam bath according to some who were there. Moreover, when testing out the piping system during the several days before shooting began on July 18, technicians noticed a decided drop in water pressure during the late afternoon. They checked M-G-M's water system and tanks and found no problem. Upon consulting the Culver City water authorities, they found that most residents turned on their lawn sprinklers at about 5 p.m. M-G-M was needlessly competing with hundreds of Culver City residents for water and losing the contest. Rather than endure the added expense of trying to compensate for this, the production crew decided to film only before 5 p.m., and from that point there was no problem with the "rain." The one scene in front of the employment office that was shot in the late afternoon of July 18 was not a problem either; it required only a small amount of rain on one small spot of the set, and filming lasted only three minutes.[28]

Kelly felt a bit vulnerable under these conditions, given that he had not completely recovered from his severe flu and sinus infection. Later he claimed that he still had a temperature of 103 on July 18, but that seems unlikely. His temperature had peaked over the weekend but surely had dropped some by July 18. Betsy did confirm, however, that Gene still had a fever when he performed the number. As a result, he worried about catching pneumonia and "kept rushing out into the sun to keep warm whenever I could." Donald O'Connor recalled an amusing aspect of filming "Singin' in the Rain." He arrived on the set early enough to catch a bit of the activity and found that the moisture and heat caused the tweed material in Kelly's suit to shrink. "Actually you'd be talking to him in between shots, and you'd actually see the material start to rise in his pants and his cuffs. It was really hysterical; it was funny." Kelly apparently had the same reaction. "Gene was a dignified man, and particularly in his work. When all of this started to happen beyond his control, it got to him too. He was hysterical." For his part, Kelly always downplayed the personal difficulties he encountered in filming this classic dance. "It was difficult to shoot in the water. It was a harder job for the photographer [Rosson] than it was for me. All I had to do was get wet."[29]

But the filming was not over. Everyone assembled at 7:30 on the morning of Thursday, July 19, to complete the work on the title number. Coyne danced in for Kelly for the puddle-splashing part of the number as Brick Sullivan stepped into the scene. This took place from 7:35 to 8:32 a.m. Then more rehearsal with the camera movement, the rain, and the playback took place. It is recorded that from 8:56 to 9:04, "Mr Kelly, Mr Donen in off stage discussion," followed by "Directors rehearsing boom moves with dance ins and setting new marks for camera" from 9:04 to 9:17. Then Kelly rehearsed to the playback from 9:17 to 9:25 and took two minutes to finish his wardrobe. Technicians started the rain falling at 9:27 but had to stop immediately as Kelly noticed that his pants cuffs were loose. He changed to another pair, but then the technical crew thought of putting some sawdust in the gutter puddle "for effect." One take was shot from 9:34 to 9:36, followed by the crew adding additional pipe for rain and sweeping "excess water off streets." Then eight takes were shot from 9:56 to 10:14. The crew broke up this camera setup and repositioned the equipment so as to shoot from behind the glaring cop toward Kelly from 10:15 to 10:33. While rehearsal continued, the crew laid dolly track for the boom shot that would follow Kelly as he walked jauntily down the street at the end of the number. They practiced this shot with all the actors for a bit, then Coyne rehearsed it to a playback from 11:34 to 11:50. Kelly and the other actors rehearsed it again to the playback from 11:50 to 12:01, then four takes were shot from 12:01 to 12:09, followed by several more takes from 12:11 to 12:26 before everyone broke for lunch.[30]

It took six days to rehearse "Singin' in the Rain," and after one and a half days of filming, the number had been committed to celluloid. The decision to finish it in the morning was motivated in part by the water pressure problem, but also by the fact that other scenes in the movie had to be shot on street scenes to simulate night. After lunch on July 19, the crew set up for filming the sequence during which Don and Cosmo suffer a flat tire and Don is mobbed by a crowd of adoring fans. The black tarpaulin was already in place even if the piping was not necessary.[31]

WHAT MAKES THIS NUMBER SO MEMORABLE

Stanley Donen said that everyone involved in the making of "Singin' in the Rain" considered it just another of many dances that had to be put into the can as the production schedule rolled forward. "We didn't know it was going to be such a great number. . . . We were always looking for imaginative ideas for his [Kelly's] solos, but this didn't seem to offer much." At the same time, Kelly knew instinctively that the best way for this number to work was to keep it simple and joyful. He built that premise into the choreography and it touched viewers. Very often, the most unassuming art has the longest life, and Donen came to understand this. "It works because of its utter simplicity, and there's no better idea for a movie than to dance for joy."[32]

Film scholars have universally agreed with this explanation. Joseph Casper has noted the irony in setting an ecstatic dance of joy in a rain-soaked, deserted city street, which turned "a musical cliché inside out." The environment helped Kelly to dance what Casper terms "a profound psychological portrait" by contrasting eternal joy against a dreary background. "The artless lyrics and lively melody, the ambling, jumping, and tapping and their interaction with the environment, which Kelly's rust-colored shoes never let us lose sight of, define the state of joyful childhood." Peter Wollen has noted that Kelly's early experiences in teaching children to dance, as well as his desire to incorporate children into his film dances in *Anchors Aweigh* (1945), *Living in a Big Way* (1947), and *An American in Paris* (1951), show that he "identified with children." Wollen believes this helped to prepare Kelly for dancing with childlike abandon in *Singin' in the Rain*.[33]

Moreover, Wollen concludes that the number "is an outstanding example of the use of transitions for the dramatic integration of song and dance numbers into the narrative of the film. . . . Above all, however, it is the careful articulation of music, song lyrics, gestures and pantomime, dance and tap, which ensures the success of the piece." In addition to all these aspects, a huge part of the success of this number is due to Kelly's technical prowess and charisma. Although Kelly claims that the dance was "a very easy number to do," Sheridan Morley and Ruth Leon point out that "Kelly had to hit mark after mark that he couldn't see on an underwater dance surface that was slippery and unsafe. He never missed one." Also, whereas other proficient dancers may have got the technical aspects right, Kelly had this "terrific outgoing quality . . . which was extremely appealing. There was this magic he exuded. They [audiences] just loved him." All this, together with Kelly's total immersion in acting out childlike joy and fun, make the number instantly appealing and memorable to so many.[34]

As Donen testified, however, no one thought of these things when the dance was filmed on July 18–19, 1951. They "had no idea of the impact it would have." The same could be said of the movie itself, for in many ways the dance number, "Singin' in the Rain," was emblematic of the film, a cine-dance masterpiece that germinated into a world classic.[35]

6 Everything but Dancing

In the finished film of *Singin' in the Rain,* sixty minutes consist of dance numbers or songs. The filming of the other forty-three minutes of film time proceeded in segments throughout the production period.[1] It was done efficiently, and usually with no fanfare of any kind. Often, the filming of nondancing sections of the movie took place opportunistically, fitted in to the needs of filming dance numbers.

The complex street sequence starting with Don and Cosmo's ride in Cosmo's car, his flat tire, and the "mobbing" of Don by a group of adoring young fans needed to be done in a nighttime street setting. To avoid paying overtime to a group of technicians, actors, and bit players, the production company took advantage of the black tarpaulin put up for the "Singin' in the Rain" number on the East Side Street of Lot 2. A skeleton crew had tried to film footage of Don leaping "from Cosmo's car across the top of second car to roof of street car and into Kathy's car" on the evening of July 14, before the tarpaulins went up, but the results were not satisfying.[2]

Therefore the co-directors planned to utilize the covering, right after lunchtime on July 19, after the "Singin'" number was finished. Kelly and O'Connor rehearsed the flat tire scene as Donen rode up in the camera boom to check out the shot from that angle. Next, the crew lined up all the vehicles needed for Kelly's leaping sequence and rehearsed the "street car action" from 2:45 to 3:05. Then Donen took five shots over the following twenty minutes. Kelly rehearsed with the "bit children" from 3:25 to 3:41, and the kids rehearsed by themselves for another seventeen minutes before the first take of the "mobbing" took place from 4:46 to 4:48. More rehearsal followed this unsatisfying take before a second filming took place. Now Kelly had to have his evening coat repaired because the kids had ripped it into two pieces. Donen then shot a third take from 5:04 to 5:06. The crew quickly reversed the camera setup to shoot Donald O'Connor's reaction to the mobbing scene in two takes from 5:35 to 5:38.[3]

Apparently no one was satisfied with the three takes of the mobbing scene when the daily rushes were run, for the next day, Friday, July 20, it was shot again early in the morning. The rest of the sequence was filmed that day too. Kelly did his own stunts while trying to escape his adoring fans, running between the slowly moving vehicles on the street, then climbing up to the top front of a moving streetcar and running along the top to the back. But stuntman Russ Saunders doubled for Kelly in jumping from the streetcar into the jalopy driven by a double for Debbie Reynolds. Saunders missed his first attempt, bouncing off the back seat upholstery of the open-topped jalopy onto the street behind the car. He nailed the shot on the second attempt. The car had been used as Andy Hardy's jalopy in the popular Andy Hardy series produced at M-G-M. The first of these lightweight movies, starring Mickey Rooney, came out in 1937, with thirteen more by 1946. The last, *Andy Hardy Comes Home,* appeared in 1958.[4]

Another sequence with potential difficulties was the cake-throwing scene at Simpson's premiere party. It was a big cake and Jean Hagen had no desire to go through take after take. Debbie Reynolds, who had to master the art of pie-tossing at a tender age, recalled that Hagen "was wonderful and very nice to me," quite unlike the character she had to create in Lina Lamont. But Hagen dropped the "nice guy" role long enough to warn Reynolds about getting the cake toss right on the first take. "I had an alexandrite ring I'd bought in Mexico," she recalled later, "and I told Debbie, 'Listen, get it on the first take or you'll get the cake and ring in *your* face. This is it, kid!'" Reynolds took the threat seriously. Donen later testified that the scene was filmed in one take. "If I'd flubbed it," Reynolds said, "Gene would have decked me before Jean would have." She harbored no ill feelings. The day after putting this risky scene in the can, Reynolds left a chocolate cake in Hagen's dressing room with a note that read, "Here's one you can eat with a fork."[5]

Several shots of Don and Cosmo as children were exposed on the afternoon of July 10, a day when Kelly was ill. One of the scenes involved Allen Sutherland as Don, and Dennis Ross as Cosmo, stealing fruit from a street vendor played by Angie Poulis. This scene was later dropped from the movie. Scenes depicting Don and Cosmo as boys, dancing for the players in a poolroom, were also shot late that afternoon. Young Don does a "buck and wing" and picks up coins from the floor before he is carried out of the poolroom. This may be a deliberate tie-in to what Gene's brother Fred did when they played the "cloops" as teenagers. In the scenes that follow, as Lockwood tells his life story to the audience at the premiere, a grownup Don plays the violin in a saloon while Cosmo plays the piano. This too seems to be a deliberate tie-in, as Kelly had learned how to play the violin when he was a boy.[6]

RECYCLING OLD FOOTAGE

Grauman's Chinese Theatre, which opened for business in 1927 on Hollywood Boulevard, only fifteen miles from M-G-M, was the setting of all premieres in the movie. Kelly and Donen filmed scenes that took place inside the theater on July 26–28 and July 30–31. Many of the exterior scenes at the theater, which involved quite a few extras, were filmed on August 1, 2, and 6. Kelly and Donen used footage of the exterior of Grauman's Theatre from a previous film to set the tone for the sequences that depict the premieres of both *The Royal Rascal* and *The Dancing Cavalier*. David O. Selznick's *A Star Is Born* (1937), starring Janet Gaynor and Fredric March, provided the footage. Selznick had, in turn, used Technicolor footage of the real-life premiere of his own Marlene Dietrich and Charles Boyer movie, *The Garden of Allah*, at Grauman's Theatre in 1936. Presumably, Selznick was happy to allow the use of this footage by the studio formerly headed by his father-in-law.[7] Ironically, footage of a real Hollywood event served the purposes of two movie versions of behind-the-scenes Hollywood entertainment.

In *A Star is Born*, the marquee reads "Vicky Lester," and in *Singin' in the Rain*, the same marquee reads, "Premiere Tonight—Biggest Picture of 1927—Don Lockwood—Lina Lamont in THE ROYAL RASCAL." The cars moving and stopping in front of the theater are exactly the same in both movies, but the *Singin' in the Rain* company further doctored the footage to show beams from four searchlights crisscrossing in front of the theater, which is very effective in creating the mood of a movie premiere. The searchlights were there in the original footage, as seen in *A Star Is Born*, but were not lit, and are difficult to notice unless one is looking for them.

Another movie that was mined for suitable footage to be used in

Singin' in the Rain was one of Gene Kelly's favorites, *The Three Muske-teers* (1948). As a boy, he had loved Douglas Fairbanks, Sr., and cited the silent picture *The Three Musketeers* (1921) as the most memorable film of his life. Kelly was delighted to star as D'Artagnan in the lavish M-G-M version of the Alexander Dumas story. Although not a musical, Kelly reveled in the opportunity to imitate the swashbuckling style that had so impressed him as a kid.[8]

Careful observation of both movies shows that five action-packed scenes from *The Three Musketeers,* converted to black and white, were inserted into *The Royal Rascal* sequence viewed by the premiere audi-ence in *Singin'.* Ironically, *The Three Musketeers* had been shot in Tech-nicolor, but it was necessary to show these scenes in black and white to depict a silent film. In the first scene taken from the earlier picture, a guard is rushing at Kelly, as D'Artagnan, with a huge spear poised to strike him. In the second scene, the guard lunges at Kelly who dodges him, and the weapon sticks in the door. In the third scene, Kelly throws the attacker over the staircase, just as Lana Turner in the character of Lady de Winter appears at the door. But through a quick cut, Turner is replaced by Jean Hagen, in the character of Lina Lamont playing a role in *The Royal Rascal.* Because Kelly throws the attacker at the exact moment when Turner is seen, it was apparently impossible to edit her out of the transition to avoid this split-second inconsistency. Next, a stunt double for Kelly swings over the stairs holding onto a chandelier, and lands in the foyer, kicking an opponent out of the way at the same time. Then, Kelly fences with and kills another opponent. Finally, Kelly backs out of the front door onto the landing, and throws a man rush-ing at him over the railing and into a small moat. It is interesting that these five fast-action scenes did not represent continuous footage taken from *The Three Musketeers.* Several other fight scenes with Kelly (and his double), which were interspersed with these scenes in the earlier movie, were not used.

To blend this footage for *The Royal Rascal* sequence, one scene was inserted in the middle of the footage, and several new scenes, also in black and white, where Kelly is dressed exactly as in *The Three Muske-teers,* were added at the beginning and end. Kelly kisses Hagen in the first scene, and in the second, he hears a footstep. A third new scene was inserted with the guard heading down the stairs with the spear. This may have been an outtake from *The Three Musketeers,* or perhaps the co-directors used a bit player who resembled the guard and wore the exact costume to shoot this scene. A fourth scene shows Kelly rushing out the door to confront the man. In the scene inserted in the middle, Jean Hagen replaces Turner in the doorway and reaches out to Kelly, who rushes to her side, but then turns back to face his attackers again.

At the end of the inserted footage from *The Three Musketeers,* three new black and white scenes, with Kelly in the same costume, were added to smooth out the transition to *The Royal Rascal.* In the first scene, Kelly is on the landing of the same building used in the earlier movie and jumps over the same railing, over which he had previously thrown a man into the moat. But now, instead of a moat, there's a cobbled path with a pile of dirt on it, and he lands on the dirt on his back. In the second scene, he jumps up (the dirt is now gone, as it has served its purpose in cushioning his fall), fights another man who rushes at him, and kills him with his sword. This interesting juxtaposition—moat, no moat; dirt, no dirt—is hardly noticeable unless one watches the footage carefully in repeated viewings. In the last added scene, Hagen appears on the landing, stretches out her arms to Kelly, runs down the steps, and the scene (and the movie, *The Royal Rascal*) ends as they kiss. Of the thirteen scenes in *The Royal Rascal* sequence, only five were taken from *The Three Musketeers,* but they were central to building the dramatic action.

JALOPY RIDE AND STUNTS

A close examination of the jalopy ride shows footage from five different street scenes. First, Don (played by stuntman Russ Saunders) jumps into Kathy's car on M-G-M's New York street, Lot 2, where a double for Reynolds drives the car. The street is made to look authentic as the trolley car has "Pacific Electric" displayed boldly on it and a prominent sign on a building says "Hollywood."

Next, Don and Kathy (now Kelly and Reynolds) ride in the car with the background footage of a real Beverly Hills street. On July 17, a second unit shot this footage in Beverly Hills after dark.[9] The street in the footage is South Santa Monica Boulevard; one sees real stores and the Bank of America building at the corner of North Beverly Drive and South Santa Monica Boulevard. This is the moving background for Kelly and Reynolds, who sit in the jalopy on a sound stage to film their interaction. The third street scene involves the interaction with the cop, and it is also shot on Lot 2 on the M-G-M compound. After that, Don and Kathy again are "on the move" (actually on a sound stage) with background footage shot by the camera car driving west along South Santa Monica Boulevard. This is the fourth street scene, and one can see the Bank of America building in the distance, marked by a red neon sign. The Bank of America building is still at that location today. Kathy soon appears to turn right onto North Roxbury Drive. Initially, after she "pulls" onto this street, one sees that the background shifts due to the fact that the camera car went up a slight grade, and then leveled off again. That slight grade is still there, a few feet north of the intersection of Roxbury and South Santa Monica. Vintage 1920s cars can be seen behind them, obviously included to drive behind the camera car.

Finally, when Kathy reaches Sunset and Camden, the last "street" scene depicting Don's testy farewell to Kathy was once again shot on a sound stage, but this time with a painted background that shows houses more reminiscent of a Peoria suburb than a swank part of Beverly Hills, and strikingly different from the exterior of Simpson's house (seen only a couple of scenes later), which looks like a luxurious Beverly Hills mansion.

The scenes depicting Don and Kathy interacting in her jalopy were filmed on August 4, and their stopping at the intersection of Sunset and Camden was filmed on August 6.[10] The entire jalopy ride included filming on two real California streets, a fake New York street on the Culver City lot, and a sound stage inside a building on that lot. If a viewer paid more attention to Don and Kathy, as they should, it would all seem natural.

The stunts that illustrated Don's early film career in the story of his life were filmed in early August as well. The plane crashing into a building and the shack that exploded were staged on August 9, and the motorcycle going over the cliff was filmed the next day.[11] It is ironic that real stuntmen doubled for Kelly here, even though he was supposed to portray a stuntman and he often performed his own stunts in previous films. Of course, even in *Singin' in the Rain*, Kelly performed some of his own stunts. He flipped over the bar and crashed into the stack of glasses in the flashback Don Lockwood shared with the crowd at the first premiere. In the scenes added to *The Royal Rascal*, Kelly jumped off a high railing, fell on his back, and jumped right up to confront his adversary. Finally, just before the jalopy ride, Kelly jumped onto a moving car, leaped from there to the top of the moving trolley car, and then walked back while it was still moving. But the jump into the jalopy as well as the stunts filmed on August 9 and 10 were obviously too dangerous for M-G-M to allow Kelly to attempt.

DUBBING

Sound dubbing had been a feature of filmmaking ever since the early sound era, although moviemakers were reluctant to publicize the trick. It was used if the actor couldn't sing, or if someone's singing voice wasn't right for the role. *Photoplay* magazine discussed it in July 1929, terming the process "vocal doubling," and explained the secrecy by noting that the studios "feel that it spoils the illusion, that it hurts a production's box office appeal." It seems to have reached a peak in the 1950s with stereophonic sound increasing the demand for high-quality singing. Also, the increasingly common practice of putting well-known stars with little singing experience into singing movies forced producers to increase the use of obscure performers (typically from stage or radio) who willingly submerged their own identity to make a picture work. They received no credit and no exposure for their efforts, except when their names were placed on records of hit movie songs released by M-G-M.[12]

In *Singin' in the Rain*, the production company prerecorded the songs and played them back on a disc while filming, for tape had not yet become available. Filming her first major musical, Debbie Reynolds found it particularly difficult to deal with this process. "Putting the song together with the dancing takes a very special precision," she recalled. "They had one man on the set who did nothing but watch our lips. If there was one mistake, it was 'CUT!' and we'd have to start all over again." Reynolds also had to remember where to breathe in the song in order to make it look real. "When I wasn't in front of the camera, I was off somewhere sitting listening to a record, mouthing it."[13]

If a performer dubs him- or herself, at least there is some cohesion in matching the voice with the action. But when a different person sings for a performer, the result can result in something less than perfection. Two voices seldom match precisely in their tonal quality, and often it is obvious that a particular star is not actually singing the song that appears to issue from his mouth. Also, the singer may be able to put a song across with subtle nuances that the performer cannot understand or mimic physically. As Gerald Mast has put it, the performer on screen has too often "been robbed of an expressive acting instrument" because he is not in control of the voice heard by the audience, even though singing "is the most powerful action a character can perform in a musical."[14]

Dubbing is the pivot on which the plot of *Singin' in the Rain* turns. Comden and Green have ample fun with the concept, from the scratchy, irritating voice of Lina Lamont, to Cosmo's brilliant idea to make the talkie work, to the climactic denouement wherein Lina is tricked into revealing her lack of talent before a laughing audience. Comden and Green signal what is to come with the demonstration film of talking pictures that is shown at Simpson's party. Julius Tannen portrays the inventor of a new gadget that will marry sound and image on the screen. It is the Vitaphone system, or the "sound-on-disc" technology, as opposed to the more popular and viable "sound-on-film" process. The latter "used a photo-electric cell to convert sound waves into light waves and then record them onto the edge of the film strip," according to Jeff Kurtti. This created an optical track on the film itself that could be read in the projector.[15]

But dubbing plays a deeper role in the making of *Singin' in the Rain* than to merely create laughs. Comden and Green made fun of it, to be sure, but the production company of *Singin' in the Rain* used dubbing when they felt it was necessary. Debbie Reynolds had a natural, virtually untrained singing voice that worked perfectly for simple, bouncy songs, but not so well for others. She recorded all the songs the script called for her to sing—four songs (but six versions in all)—and then the company evaluated the result. Her singing in the three peppy versions was kept—"Good Morning" and "Singin' in the Rain" (as the title number with the introductory movie credits), both of which she sang with Kelly and O'Connor, and her solo rendition of "Singin' in the Rain" for the scene at the end of the movie that reveals Lina's lack of talent. Her other three prerecordings did not work, even though one song was filmed to the playback (Kathy singing "You Are My Lucky star" to a billboard of Don Lockwood) before being dropped from the movie. The remaining two, "Would You?" and Reynolds singing "You Are My Lucky Star" as a duet with Kelly, were both dubbed by Betty Noyes.[16]

The Freed-Brown song "Would You?" had less exposure in previous movies than the other songs used in *Singin' in the Rain*. It appeared only in *San Francisco* (1936), where Jeannette MacDonald sang it to Clark Gable.[17]

Unrelated to the plot of *San Francisco*, the lyrics of the song suggest that a couple is watching a movie and describing scenes between a pair of lovers. As used in *Singin' in the Rain*, these lyrics add layers of irony because Don and Lina sing it in a movie (*The Dancing Cavalier*) within a movie (*Singin' in the Rain*), and it is a song about a couple watching movie characters and getting up their courage to imitate them.

Critical to the plot of *Singin' in the Rain*, the song became the link in a brilliant sequence that depicts Kathy's secret dubbing for Lina and Lina's painful efforts to sing for herself (using obviously older, more outdated equipment than Kathy is using) and seamlessly takes the viewer through to the finished product of *The Dancing Cavalier*. The sequence begins with Kathy, Don, and Cosmo recording "Would You?" in the studio, but Betty Noyes actually sings for (or dubs) Debbie Reynolds. We segue to Lina's attempt to record the song herself, and the vocal transition takes place in the middle of the line where Noyes sings, "But before . . ." and Jean Hagen's scratchy Lina voice takes over with, ". . . the story eeends!" Lina continues to flub the recording, forgetting the next line until the scene shifts to a depiction of the filming of *The Dancing Cavalier* as Betty Noyes once again picks up the vocal with the line, "And would you dare to say . . . ." In the fourth segment, we segue to the black and white, final version of *The Dancing Cavalier* as the preview audience will see it, where Noyes hits the high notes perfectly as she sings, "I would, would you?" and her singing works extremely well with Hagen mouthing the lyrics. The entire sequence flows seamlessly from one segment to the next.

The song is also used at the premiere of *The Dancing Cavalier*, at the end of that movie, with Kelly's and Hagen's characters singing it as a duet. Kelly sings, "I'll kiss her with a sigh, would you, would you?" and Noyes follows with, "And if the girl were I, would you, would you?" and then both sing the rest of the song together. It works very well and the audience reaction to the song and the movie is believable. The playbacks made for *Singin' in the Rain* include "Would You?" as a duet sung by Kelly and Reynolds, and Reynolds sounds terrible in this song, shrill and tinny, especially in the high notes.[18] So it is understandable why Betty Noyes was asked to dub her.

Ironically, while Noyes dubbed Debbie's singing, Jean Hagen dubbed Debbie's speaking voice in the dubbing sequence of *Singin' in the Rain*. The voice Hagen created for Lina Lamont was a fabrication of her talent. Her real voice was mellow and cultured, "quite remarkable," as Stanley Donen later put it. The few spoken words that Reynolds had to say in the dubbing sequence "was supposed to be a cultured speech," according to Donen, and Reynolds "had that terrible western noise," a byproduct of her early life in south Texas, so Hagen did the speaking part herself. Reynolds was dubbed twice in this short segment, and Hagen did double duty as dubber and dubbed. "Jean Hagen dubs Debbie Reynolds dubbing Jean Hagen!" as Ray Hagen put it in a 1968 article.[19]

It turns out to be an almost bizarre exercise. The production company of *Singin' in the Rain* focused on a deceptive, widely known "secret" in the industry while coolly practicing the deception themselves in the very sequence that makes fun of it. It adds quite another layer of irony to the lyrics, "And would you dare to say? Let's do the same as they."

"YOU ARE MY LUCKY STAR"

Freed and Brown had already squeezed a great deal of mileage out of "You Are My Lucky Star." They wrote the song in 1935 and Eleanor Powell sang it with Roger Edens in *The Broadway Melody of 1936* (1935). After that it was used in *Riffraff* (1936), *Let's Dance* (1936), *The Broadway Melody of 1938* (1937), *Lucky Night* (1939), *Fast and Furious* (1939), *Babes in Arms* (1939), *Hollywood: Style Center of the World* (1940), *Born to Sing* (1942), *The Youngest Profession* (1943), and *Three Little Words* (1950). Like several other songs included in *Singin' in the Rain*, "You Are My Lucky Star" seemed to be a favorite of audiences and producers alike.[20]

The original plan of the movie called for Debbie Reynolds to sing a full version of the song to Don Lockwood's image on a billboard, after the love dance between Kathy and Don on the studio sound stage. It was to symbolize her own falling in love with the silent film star, serving as a counterpoint to Gene Kelly's ballad version of "All I Do Is Dream of

You" after the Simpson party. Roger Edens arranged the song for Reynolds much as he arranged "You Made Me Love You" for Judy Garland in *The Broadway Melody of 1938* (1937). This had been Judy's breakthrough number, in part because Edens arranged it as a love song to Clark Gable by the juvenile Garland. Popularly known as "Dear Mr. Gable," the song prepared the way for Judy's banner year in film with *Babes in Arms* and *The Wizard of Oz*, both of which were released in 1939. It is possible that Edens and Freed consciously framed the billboard number to be Debbie's breakthrough as well, as Rudy Behlmer implies. Edens "wrote a special introduction and a recitation section between choruses" of the song, just as he had done for Garland's number.[21]

Donen filmed the billboard number on July 11, in the sunny exterior of Lot 2. Reynolds rehearsed to the playback in the morning and continued to do so after lunch. The crew shot four takes before repositioning the setup to bring a tree into view. Reynolds rehearsed moving to and leaning on the tree, and then four takes of the scene were shot. The crew then set up the camera to catch Reynolds in a medium close-up as she sat on the tree. Before shooting seven takes of this scene, the crew had to "hose down background," presumably to add luster to the vegetation. After rehearsing the pan shot which took Reynolds from the tree back to the billboard, Donen shot two takes and exposed nine additional takes of the song's ending back at the billboard.[22]

The sequence was edited and finished but at the last minute dropped from the release of *Singin' in the Rain*. It was more than four minutes long and came into a crowded section of the movie, after "You Were Meant for Me" and before "Moses Supposes." In fact, there was no need for Kathy to sing to Don's billboard because she had already admitted to being his fan before "You Were Meant for Me." Not only was Debbie's version of "You Are My Lucky Star" redundant, but her singing performance left much to be desired, as the surviving footage clearly proves. Reynolds called it "a very rangy song," and she could not do it justice.[23]

In addition, it was a poorly conceived number. The silly dialogue weakened her character and was contradictory to the plot line. She tells the billboard that she stood outside the Brown Derby for two hours to get a close look at Don, and that she's the president of the Don Lockwood fan club, yet she didn't recognize him when he jumped into her jalopy. Also, while the soppy style may have worked for Judy as a real person at a private party, particularly in her early teens, it would not have worked for a grown woman's role in a movie, especially given Kathy's strong personality.

A shortened version of "You Are My Lucky Star" remained to finish the movie. Comden and Green had planned for Don, Kathy, and Cosmo to sing and dance to this number on stage as the audience applauds, and this was unchanged right up to the final version of their script. There is even a note in April 1951 from Donen that this number would be performed by Kelly, Reynolds, and O'Connor and would last two minutes. Fortunately, this was changed, as it makes little sense for the three to dance together at such an emotional climax for the two lovers, moreover to the lyrics of "You Are My Lucky Star."[24]

So the number was sung only by Don and Kathy, ending the movie on a high emotional note as Kelly sings "You've opened heaven's portal, / Here on earth, for this poor mortal," and the scene switches to the couple locked in an embrace at a future moment in time. But Betty Noyes dubbed Reynolds in this number as she did for "Would You?" The playbacks for "You Are My Lucky Star" provide evidence that even singing along with Kelly, who sang the song very well, Reynolds could not handle it and actually got worse with progressive takes. Debbie also told John Mariani that her acting left something to be desired while filming the short duet with Gene. She was supposed to have tears in her eyes when Kelly began to sing the song to reassure her of his love. "I couldn't cry," Reynolds admitted. "Nothing sad had ever happened to me. My dog hadn't even died. So they had to put onions on my cheeks to make tears come out."[25]

OTHER MUSICAL NUMBERS WITHOUT DANCES

The "Singin'" number was reprised twice: once as the title number over the film credits and a second time at the end of the movie when Lina is exposed. An unused playback of the title number is a perkier, more lilting version in terms of the tempo of the music than the one actually used. Unfortunately, Debbie's voice is too loud and one cannot hear Gene and Donald well. There is also an unused filmed shot of the title song that looks the same as the one in the movie except that the three players do not have umbrellas. The footage selected for the release print depicts Kelly, Reynolds, and O'Connor walking stridently through an artificial rain on a sound stage, complete with umbrellas and raincoats. The voices of all three are matched well, in volume and pitch, in this version.[26] They put galoshes on Debbie's feet and kept the flaps untied so they would bounce about when she walked. This was the little-known origin of the term "flappers" in the early 1920s.

At the end of the movie, Reynolds sings "Singin'" from behind a curtain while Hagen mouths the number on stage. Reynolds does very well here. It is a version suited to her abilities—peppy and straightforward—and places no great demand on her limited vocal range. The same was true of her singing of "Good Morning." The song works very well for her voice and is appealing, but she probably could not sing "Singin'" emotionally and expressively as Kelly sings it.

Finally, "Temptation," another Freed-Brown number, is played as background music (with no words) for the tango at Simpson's party. It is a classic torch song, popularized by Bing Crosby in *Going Hollywood* (1933). The song appeared in another movie that same year, *The Barbarian*, and in two more movies in 1934, *Sadie McKee* and *Forsaking All Others*.[27]

POSTPRODUCTION WORK

Kelly's version of "All I Do Is Dream of You" was filmed last, after the ballet, and took two days to shoot. As mentioned in Chapter 4, it was cut from the movie to speed up the narrative. Unfortunately, no film of this number remains, although some stills have survived. As mentioned earlier in this chapter, Debbie's solo of "You Are My Lucky Star" was cut for a variety of reasons. Another scene that Reynolds filmed, her dialogue with fellow dancers in the dressing room before performing at Simpson's party, was cut. It is possible this was done both to tighten up the narrative flow of the movie and to soften Kathy's character, as the dialogue contained several angry outbursts.[28]

The production phase of *Singin'* reached a plateau by August 18, 1951, when most of the movie was in the can. It had taken fifty-two days of hard work to reach this point, and the production crew had adhered to the projected filming schedule precisely. But production was far from over. Given the precedent of inserting "dream ballets" into several previous Gene Kelly movies, most spectacularly in *An American in Paris*, it was almost inevitable that *Singin' in the Rain* would contain a ballet as well. Typical of previous efforts, this type of number needed an extended period of time to develop and film, so it was saved for last.[29]

While some people began to work on the ballet, others began post-production on what had already been filmed. One of the earliest and most important of postproduction tasks involved dubbing the taps for the dances. They had been filmed without sound at all, with the performers dancing to a playback of the music. Any sounds associated with the action, such as taps, had to be done later. While it sometimes happened in Hollywood that taps were prerecorded before the actual filming, it seems to have been quite uncommon, given that a smaller action would therefore guide a larger one. Also, Kelly explained that "if you pre-dub and then you get an inspiration on set, you're stuck." In short, it was much easier, although that is a relative term only, to postsynchronize the taps to the recorded image. Every film dancer from Fred Astaire to the most obscure hoofer hated this chore. "It's the most difficult thing in pictures and it galls all of us," Gene Kelly later remembered, "because you have to watch yourself do this and that, and then copy yourself."[30]

Despite rumors that someone else dubbed Kelly's taps in *Singin' in the Rain,* authors Peter Hay and Rudy Behlmer, and Lela Simone who worked on the postproduction of the movie, all report that Kelly did it himself. Carol Haney simply helped him find the right shoes for the job. Kelly also confirms this. "We tried different shoes, soft shoes, ballet slippers, you name it. But in the end I did it myself with metal taps." Music mixer William Saracino recorded the tapping as Kelly listened to the playback and watched himself on the screen. Donald O'Connor typically dubbed his own taps unless his schedule did not allow it. In that case, choreographer, tap dancer, and character actor Louis Da Pron, who usually worked for Universal, did it for him. But O'Connor could tell the difference when he watched the finished product because Da Pron was "a heavier dancer. Everyone has his own distinctive sound." For *Singin' in the Rain,* however, O'Connor was able to dub his own taps. Gene also dubbed Debbie's taps for the "Good Morning" number, and did it so well that it is impossible to know this by watching and listening to the finished film.[31]

The editorial team finished their first cutting by September 6, paving the way for the music and sound people to begin work. Initially they wanted to use Peter Tchaikovsky's *Romeo and Juliet Overture* as background music for the silent picture sequences, but after a few days they dropped that idea due to the difficulty of getting a copyright clearance.[32]

Lela Simone, an assistant to Arthur Freed who mostly worked with the more minor musical and sound chores of the Freed pictures, remembered the difficulties inherent in working on the title number of *Singin' in the Rain*. She had to consider, "Where does the rain come from? How much noise is it to make? What is the noise going to sound like once it is recorded? How are his footsteps going to sound within the rain?" In some parts of the number they found there was not enough sound on the film, or the sound of rain splashing overwhelmed the sound of Gene's feet. Simone had to make recommendations to fix problems like these, consult with Kelly for his approval, and then redub when necessary. Simone reported that for the "Singin'" number, Kelly had to record his taps on a wet floor, adding more headaches to an already unpleasant task.[33]

Simone carried out this tedious process for the entire movie. She thought Gene's, Debbie's, and Donald's voices were too low in the main title, where they stride confidently through the rain holding umbrellas, and this needed to be dubbed again. She wanted some of Dora Bailey's lines to be louder as she introduced the attendees at the premiere of *The Royal Rascal* and recommended more background music for the scene in the burlesque house as Don relates the story of his and Cosmo's early career. Simone also thought the kids' voices should be louder as they descend on Don Lockwood in the "mobbing" sequence and wanted Kathy's line in the jalopy, "swimming pools, wild parties," to be louder as well. She found many sections of music and dialogue to be too soft, including the group of show girls singing "All I Do Is Dream of You" and Cosmo's line, "Lina, you never looked lovelier," after Lina gets the cake in the face.[34]

For "Make 'Em Laugh," Simone judged that there was too much piano noise and that the dialogue was too soft as Cosmo walked across the piano keyboard. She wanted all the sound effects associated with Cosmo hitting himself on boards, walls, and the floor to be louder, and suggested that a loud smacking sound accompany him when he kisses the headless dummy. Simone calculated that Lina ought to say the line, "Of course we talk—don't ivrybody?" "a little shriller." In "You Were Meant for Me," Simone thought the taps were too loud and she wanted the sound technicians to "reverberate the Dialogue on empty stage."[35]

"Moses Supposes" fared pretty well in Simone's hands, although she wanted a louder hand-clapping noise at the start of the number and the taps to be redubbed "a little more brittle." For the finale of the movie, Simone had general recommendations. "All the Backstage scenes (in the wing) should be played—if at all possible—for more exitement. [sic] More applause, more Yelling, more 'speech—speech' etc. Over the cut to the audience during Jean Hagen's curtain speech the crowd murmur should be a little louder."[36]

Much of the fine-tuning of the finished product, which leaves such an impression on the viewer, came from Simone's suggestions in the postproduction phase. She wanted the fiddle music to be sweetened in "Fit as a Fiddle." She also wanted a bright fanfare to announce Kathy's emergence from the fake cake and asked arranger Lennie Hayton to make the steel guitar and ukulele sweeter in "Good Morning," as the trio clown around with raincoats. She recommended that a xylophone be used to make the sound of the umbrella running along the iron fence in the title number.[37]

Not all of Simone's suggestions were adopted. When Don leaves Kathy after the jalopy ride, Simone suggested, "Start music as Gene's coat rips—through dissolve to party. Continue until producer says 'Hold it.'" Simone suggested using the Freed-Brown song "Temptation" for this whole stretch, but that was not done. Instead, a musical bridge starts as Don's coat rips, and it ends almost immediately at the start of the next scene as Kathy pulls up in front of Simpson's house and converses with Simpson's houseboy. "Temptation" starts exactly with the party scene and it is much more effective this way. Also, Simone suggested that music should start just when Kathy throws the cake (which hits Lina) and continue to the end of the reel.[38] Although the music does start at that moment, it's very soft, almost inaudible, and ends almost immediately as Don enters the women's dressing room. And this sequence too is more effective as done, this time with hardly any background music.

As Simone and others worked on the music and sound through the first three weeks of October, Johnny Green, the head of the Music Department at M-G-M, geared up the famous studio orchestra for scoring the picture. Widely known for the rich sound of its orchestra, M-G-M spared little expense in the music and sound of its best productions. Scoring began October 19 and was finished in a few days.[39]

A story circulated around the studio, quite possibly manufactured by the publicity men, that the Sound Department at M-G-M thought something was wrong with *Singin' in the Rain*. They discovered that the dialogue was out of synchronization in one sequence of the picture and spent an entire weekend fixing it. When done, they were told that was the way it was supposed to be—to poke fun at the problems in the early sound movies—and the technicians had to spend another weekend putting it back together again. Whether this could be true is doubtful, but it made good copy in promotional material when the movie was released.[40]

7   *Gotta Dance!*

Every Hollywood musical had a big production number, usually located at the end of the film, to send the viewer home with a bounce. Betty Comden and Adolph Green assumed such a number was needed at the end of *Singin' in the Rain*, but they did not suggest a song from the Freed-Brown catalog in their first draft. Gene Kelly, however, did not want the big number to be at the end of this film, probably to differentiate it from *An American in Paris*. By the end of May, "Broadway Melody" was mentioned for this number, and it was no longer at the end of the movie. Moreover, there were no detailed plans or ideas about the number, which apparently was conceptualized merely as a large dance when filming began in June, but it was assumed the principal dancers would be Kelly and Donald O'Connor.[1]

Eventually, Kelly began to build the ballet around two Freed-Brown songs when he added "Broadway Rhythm" to "Broadway Melody" and extended the music for the major dance. He particularly liked "Broadway Rhythm." On the cover of his personal sheet music copy, Kelly wrote, "Loved dancing to this—," several decades after making *Singin' in the Rain*.[2]

Both songs were among the most popular in the Freed-Brown catalog. "Broadway Melody" had premiered in the groundbreaking movie of the same name in 1929, where Charles King performed it three times. The first time he sang it to an appreciative group of coworkers, the second time to his fiancée and her sister in planning for a group audition, and the third time it was filmed as a stagy performance, with a line of chubby chorus girls dancing to artless choreography. The song was parodied in *The Dogway Melody* (1930), and also appeared in *Hot Dog* (1930), *Gems of M-G-M* (1930), *The Broadway Melody of 1936* (1935), and *The Broadway Melody of 1938* (1937). The song "Broadway Melody" has been described as Nacio Herb Brown's best musical score, at least of the 1930s. "Broadway Rhythm" premiered in *The Broadway Melody of 1936*. Roger Edens arranged it as an unusually long number by repeating it five times in succession. First, Frances Langford sang it, then Buddy and Vilma Ebsen danced to it, then after two more reprises, Eleanor Powell danced to it as the finale. It then appeared in *Let's Dance* (1936), *The Broadway Melody of 1938*, *Babes in Arms* (1939), *Presenting Lily Mars* (1943), and *Casanova Cat* (1951).[3]

Plans to put together a larger than usual dance number for *Singin' in the Rain* fell apart when Donald O'Connor's prior commitments to do a television show and another *Francis* movie took precedence. The television commitment, O'Connor's first appearance as host of the *Colgate Comedy Hour*, was scheduled for October 7, 1951. It was the sixth episode of the second season, and Douglas Fowley was to appear in it as well. Work on *Francis Goes to West Point* would soon follow. Apparently the start of production for *Singin'* was delayed after O'Connor's future schedule was set, and he did not have time to hang around for the production of the big number.[4]

This forced Kelly to completely rethink the project at the last minute, while filming of the movie was in full swing. He did not want to ask Debbie Reynolds to bear the weight of a major dance number—her skills did not allow it. Moreover, Arthur Freed apparently was eager to expand the dance number into a full-blown movie ballet, following the enormous ballet that ended *An American in Paris*, which already was the talk of Hollywood even though that movie had not yet been released. In addition, both Freed and Kelly were interested in redirecting the career of dancer Cyd Charisse, who had performed in several M-G-M films since *The Ziegfeld Follies* (1946). Kelly felt she had the ability to do much more with her talent than she had so far realized. Here was an opportunity to create a showcase for her and turn the "big number" of *Singin' in the Rain* into a ballet that could rival the ballet sequence in *An American in Paris*. What to make of it was the problem. "Donald and I would have done it as a sort of a personal humorous thing," Kelly recalled in 1966. "Now we had to do it as almost a dream sequence. We had to make up something. That was tough. It was forced in, and it forced the picture." Working in a hothouse atmosphere, Kelly found that "it became like Topsy; it grew" into something much longer and far more complex than the traditional "big number" of most musical pictures.[5]

The ballet of *Singin'* naturally evolved because Kelly and the Freed Unit were experienced in creating lavish numbers that straddled the boundary between a simple dance number, which usually lasted a few minutes, and an involved dance ensemble that could take up to twenty minutes of screen time. The once sacrosanct lines between vernacular and popular dance and classical ballet began to blur in the 1930s both on stage and on film. Jazz and other popular music began to appear in modern ballet, and ballet elements of all kinds began to appear in Broadway musicals and Hollywood pictures. According to Jerome Delamater, the word "ballet" "has, in fact, become almost synonymous with any kind of dance except pure hoofing." Within the context of moviemaking, "the term *ballet* is often applied to those rather longer dance numbers—irrespective of the type of dance used in them—not usually introduced by or associated with a specific song." They often became opportunities for choreographers and directors to explore the psychological dimensions of their characters, giving rise to what often was termed a "dream ballet."[6]

The trend started on Broadway with Richard Rodgers and Lorenz Hart, whose *On Your Toes* (1936) had two ballets. George Balanchine choreographed both of them, and also worked on "Peter's Dream," a ballet in the Rodgers and Hart stage musical *Babes in Arms* (1937). Agnes de Mille's choreography for the dream segment of *Oklahoma!* (1943) "brought ballet wholesale on to the Broadway stage," in the words of film historian Peter Wollen. Half of the Broadway musicals staged in 1944 "had some kind of ballet number," and forty-six Broadway shows staged from 1945 to 1948 also had ballets, half of them dream ballets.[7]

The movie industry caught on to the trend pretty quickly. The first impressive dream ballet on screen was that in Fred Astaire's *Yolanda and the Thief* (1945). More than eight minutes long, it was in reality a nightmare ballet rather than a dream, in which Astaire's shady character dreams of being ensnared by the love offered him by the pure woman he's attempting to rob. A British production, *The Red Shoes* (1949), not only was a movie about ballet performers but had a surrealist ballet segment lasting seventeen minutes. The picture was a smashing critical and commercial success, and fueled Hollywood's interest in film ballet.

It is possible, as Wollen has suggested, that the seventeen-minute ballet in *An American in Paris* was directly inspired by *The Red Shoes*, although Gene Kelly had already choreographed a remarkable ballet in *On the Town*, which was released the same year as *The Red Shoes*.[8]

Coming so directly on the heels of *An American in Paris*, which wrapped up production only six months before Kelly had to construct the ballet for *Singin'*, it was almost inevitable that the new, expanded idea for the big number should evolve into yet another long ballet. Kelly focused on the lyrics of both songs to come up with a story line—a young hopeful "seeking fame and fortune," "show-biz," and "bright lights"—and added underworld characters and a moll to build the story. Music arranger Lennie Hayton worked on combining "Broadway Melody" and "Broadway Rhythm" into a cohesive musical score. He used a total of thirty-two bars from both songs, and rearranged the music to give Kelly four extra notes that he needed at one point.[9]

Cyd Charisse was not Gene Kelly's first choice for the ballet, however. He wanted to use his dance assistant Carol Haney in that role. She was a highly accomplished dancer who could excel in almost any category of dance. Freed, however, did not "think she photographed well," as Charisse later put it. More specifically, Freed thought that Haney's earthy, working-class persona did not fit the image of a glamorous female star that M-G-M and other studios insisted on projecting. This attitude prevented Haney from achieving the movie roles her talent warranted, but she swallowed her disappointment like a trouper. Ironically, as Kelly's dance assistant, she was given the job of prepping Charisse for the role that she lost. Charisse did not know this when she began rehearsals on September 17, but found out about it later. Haney never mentioned her lost opportunity and faithfully worked with her replacement. "She was a wonderful girl," Charisse later said. Haney's loyalty to Kelly was overpowering. "I'll always remember Carol Haney fondly for the way she helped me, when her heart must have been breaking," Charisse wrote in her memoirs.[10]

Cyd Charisse was born in Amarillo, Texas, on March 8, 1921, as Tula Ellice Finklea. Of French Huguenot heritage, her father Ernest owned and operated a jewelry store. Cyd's brother had difficulty pronouncing the word "sister" and the family adopted his version of "sis" as her nickname, "Sid." As a teenager, "Dancing was my whole life," Charisse later put it. Her family took her to Los Angeles for lessons with French-born Nico Charisse. The Ballet Russe offered her a position when she was fourteen years old, and gave her at least two different Russian names, a common practice for all their dancers. Even though Nico Charisse was sixteen years older than Cyd, the two married in 1939 and settled in Los Angeles where her first son was born three years later. Movie roles began with a dancing part in *Something to Shout About* (1943), where Charisse was billed as Lily Norwood (named after her grandmother Lily and her mother's maiden name, Norwood). Her career advanced when Freed offered her an M-G-M contract, changing the spelling of her nickname to "Cyd." Her first role was as a featured dancer in a segment of the gaudy *Ziegfeld Follies* (1946). Her most substantial role was as a self-absorbed ballet dancer in *The Unfinished Dance* (1947), where her ballet talents were showcased in a worthy but little-noticed film. Her marriage to Charisse broke up and Cyd dated a number of men before marrying singer-actor Tony Martin in 1948.[11]

Charisse nearly had her big break when she was scheduled to star opposite Kelly in *An American in Paris,* but pregnancy prevented her from fulfilling that commitment. After her second son, Tony Martin Jr., was born August 28, 1950, Charisse did some small, nondancing roles in obscure movies. About a year later, while walking into a rehearsal hall, Freed passed her and nonchalantly asked, "Cyd, how would you like to dance in the big finale with Gene Kelly?" Charisse remembered her reaction decades later. "Of course, I just had to stop breathing, because everyone was saying on the whole lot what a great picture 'Singin' in the Rain' was." Freed's off-handed way of announcing his decision covered the fact that Charisse was Kelly's second choice, and that Freed had deftly shifted the golden opportunity to someone he wanted to promote for stardom. "Arthur Freed had signed me under contract," Charisse later recalled, "and he was my mentor. He was always looking out for me." Kelly was quite happy, for he fully realized Charisse's potential and looked forward to developing it.[12]

When Haney began working with Charisse, the choreography for her role had already been "blocked out." Jeanne Coyne also helped Haney in prepping Charisse, and she and Cyd became good friends. Charisse needed all the help she could get, for this was the biggest role so far in her career and she was asked to dance in a seductive yet cold way quite unlike anything she had done before. Kelly had a precise style in mind and recalled that Charisse had some initial difficulty in adapting to it. Also, she was a bit taller than Kelly, which always caused problems in Hollywood, whether one was making a musical or a drama. Kelly cleverly disguised this by having both of them bend and twist when they danced closely together. Kelly's vigorous dance style took its toll on Charisse's body when they rehearsed together. "When he lifts you, he lifts you," Cyd recalled. "When Gene threw you on the floor, you were on the floor. I don't think Tony ever understood why I was so black and blue from simply doing a dance number."[13]

Charisse needed the right hair and costumes to complement the vamp image that Kelly wanted to create. Her hair already was very black but the styling needed to be just right. Sydney Guillaroff, famed M-G-M hairstylist, provided three different wigs for Kelly and Donen to choose from. They opted for a wig similar to one that Guillaroff had styled for the silent screen star Pola Negri. The directors also wanted Charisse to style her movements and facial expressions after one of the sexiest women in the silent movies, Louise Brooks. Born in Kansas in 1906, Brooks had danced on Broadway before going to Hollywood. Dark-haired, intelligent, and beautiful, she was considered the prototype of the onscreen flapper. Brooks had an independent streak that did not mesh well with corporate Hollywood. She starred in films in Germany before retiring from the movie business in 1938.[14]

REHEARSALS

The company used two of M-G-M's biggest sound stages to rehearse and film "The Broadway Ballet." Rehearsals began August 20 and continued through early September. It was recorded that Kelly spent August 25 "working at home," but the rest of the time he was at the studio. On September 11, he rehearsed with the treadmill that was to be used early in the ballet, to carry the stream of people one might see on the streets of New York as the hoofer makes his rounds of talent agents.[15]

Also on September 11, Kelly began to split his time between the *Singin'* production and a new movie that Freed wanted him to do, a musical version of Mark Twain's novel *Huckleberry Finn*. Freed had released news of the new project to the press as early as the previous January, and had announced that Kelly would co-star with Danny Kaye. All the principal actors, including Dean Stockwell as Huck, William Warfield as Jim, and Margaret O'Brien as part of the Grangerford family, were lined up. Director Vincente Minnelli began rehearsals on August 28, working without Kelly for two weeks until the star could find time for the new project. Kelly worked with Minnelli from 10 a.m. till noon for four days, September 11–14, and spent the afternoons working on "The Broadway Ballet." By then, Kelly had soured on the new picture. The primary reason was his desire to take advantage of a new tax law that allowed American citizens to work overseas for up to eighteen months and not have to pay U.S. income tax on their earnings. Kelly always had a love for Europe, and wanted to move there temporarily, making movies, and this seemed like a good opportunity to put that desire into effect. Freed was remarkably understanding. He decided to shelve *Huckleberry Finn* indefinitely on September 21. As Hugh Fordin has put it, this move "seems to indicate Freed's irrevocable loyalty to a man of Kelly's talent, who, for many years, had done brilliant work under his banner."[16]

Rehearsals for "The Broadway Ballet" continued after Kelly returned his full attention to the project. The crew shot tests of the set and wardrobe on October 10–11, and the songs were prerecorded October 12–13. Kelly recorded several takes of "The Broadway Melody," which begins the ballet. In the very first take, his voice seems not up to the song, but his second take was very good; he sounded exactly as in the final version. But the orchestral accompaniment was a bit different than in the release print, indicating that some musical polishing took place between the recording of the playback and the recording of the final version.[17]

FILMING

The nearly thirteen-minute ballet was filmed in fifty-six camera set-ups. It begins with Don Lockwood explaining to R. F. Simpson the only sequence yet to be filmed for *The Dancing Cavalier,* then moves to a shot of Kelly in a tuxedo (uncommon costuming for him) as he sings "The Broadway Melody" in a Times Square setting. The camera then cranes up to reveal a great deal of darkened space around Kelly. When the lights come on, some seventy extras come running toward him as "the camera dollies in and cranes back down with their movement."[18]

Making this happen visually was no easy task. Randall Duell remembered that "one of the toughest problems we had was the Times Square episode," for it took up two sound stages and demanded a lot of lights. Given that the crane shot the directors had planned for the introduction of the extras was to be taken from 180 feet up in the air, Duell noted that he had to spend an entire day riding the boom to see how to organize the lights and electric signs on the set. He used more than fifty comparatively small signs with large bulbs and had to make sure they showed up to best effect from every position the crane shot would find. Moreover, the signs had to be lighted at the precise moment to coordinate with the beats of the music as well as with the movement of the craned camera. Duell and his crew had to run through the motions many times over several days: "It would take two or three hours to move one sign. Then you had to go back and ride the crane again. Technically, it was very satisfying to finally see it completed." The program for *Singin' in the Rain* claimed that enough electricity was used in making this sequence to "light a small city for two weeks." It took three days to film the two Times Square segments, at the beginning and at the end of the ballet.[19]

The narrative begins as Kelly, dressed gaudily as a hoofer new to the big city, passes through a representation of New York street life with a treadmill carrying a wide variety of people past him. The hopeful hoofer tries his "Gotta Dance!" routine with two talent agents to no avail; the third one takes an interest and leads him to a speakeasy where excited extras dressed in colorful costumes encourage him to dance his heart out.

The speakeasy scenes, including interactions between the hoofer and the extras as well as the "vamp" dance, were rehearsed some more on October 15, with staged dress rehearsals on October 16–18, and were filmed on October 20 and 22–23. Charisse always recalled the vamp dance as one of the hardest things she had ever done in pictures, "because of all the nuances. It was really like a mini-drama within a number." She did the job extremely well. "We needed someone who could stop a man by just sticking up her leg," Stanley Donen later commented. "Cyd was stunning."[20]

But Donen felt she needed some extra coaching beyond her remarkable dancing talent. Charisse had never smoked before, but Donen insisted she do so for this sequence. In fact, Charisse recalls that he held up production a while in order to teach her. Charisse had difficulty handling the smoke; she coughed and felt sick to her stomach. Donen taught her how to blow the smoke exactly right to achieve the effect he desired, and finally she managed the task.[21]

The moment that the hoofer collides with Charisse's prominent leg is one of the most memorable in movie history. Kelly had often performed knee slides in previous films, having the crew wax the floors to make it easier for him to time the slide precisely. Charisse performs a dance of enticement to lure the innocent's heart, and he tries to ignore her, but cannot in the end. However, when she breathes smoke into his face, he throws away her cigarette and "asserts himself firmly by pulling her to him and arching her up into a lift." They look knowingly at each other, an expression of triumph but no love on her face, and then the pair perform an erotic dance. When the hoofer "lowers her to the floor," the camera achieves a "slightly overhead" view, and Charisse's "length is made more interesting as she lies on the floor by shooting her from above. She seems more his equal and less the formidable female. The high-angle shot from the crane humanizes her. But he is still a post around which she serpentines." Any idea that this is a traditional love duet is shattered when the vamp's mobster boyfriend casually lures her away from the hoofer with an expensive diamond bracelet. Kelly's character is stunned and confused, but his agent quickly leads him away to begin his career, which is neatly summarized by Kelly dancing to the same tune with the vocals "When I hear that happy beat, feel like dancing down the street" in three different, socially ascending venues—the Columbia Burlesque, Palace Vaudeville, and Ziegfeld Follies. The Burlesque and Ziegfeld sequences were shot on October 24.[22]

The scenes involved in the transition to the speakeasy sequence were filmed out of order—*after* the vamp dance. The company rehearsed the treadmill scenes on October 25 and filmed them the next day. They shot the hoofer's three auditions on October 27 and 29, and filmed his entrance into the speakeasy on October 30. Moreover, Kelly worked out his solo dance to "Broadway rhythm, it's got me, everybody dance!" inside the speakeasy on November 8–10 and 12–16. The sets for the treadmill sequence, Gene's solo in the speakeasy, and his first dance with Charisse (the vamp dance) were all designed with economy in mind. Randall Duell remembered that it was "mostly just scenic painting, exaggerated, and, obviously, it was what it was." He meant that it was not the best décor, for there were very few props, but it worked well for these sequences and numbers, and it was cheap.[23]

What Kelly termed the "Crazy Veil Dance" proved to be the most technically difficult part of "The Broadway Ballet" to film. It was, as Casey Charness writes, "a fantasy-within-the fantasy, for the ballet is still being told to the studio head as an intended project." It represents the hoofer's continued obsession with the vamp, a dream sequence within the ballet in which he fantasizes about the passion he feels after seeing her at a casino. Kelly initially thought of it "as a sort of scarf dance," but changed the scarf to a long piece of light material when he realized "there was nothing especially new" about a duet in which the lovers are connected with a scarf. For much of the dance, the piece of white China silk voile seems to be twenty-five feet in length, and some sources cite that figure. At the end of the dance, however, it clearly seems to be fifty feet long, the length Kelly, Charisse, and others have mentioned. It is likely that two different veils were used to create the different effects Kelly envisioned, and this fits with Charisse's reference to the difficulty of working with "those veils."[24]

A piece of material that long, whether twenty-five feet or fifty feet, was not easy to manage. Kelly wanted it to become the major visual element of the dance and that meant using fans to move it about. But ordinary wind machines were not powerful enough, so the company obtained three airplane motors. Strong technicians had to manhandle the motors to the instructions of Haney and Coyne. Along with Kelly, they first experimented with various ways of moving the voile to the beats of the music, "not just haphazardly" and "without blowing Cyd clean off the set," as Kelly later put it. After several days of aiming the stream of wind at the floor just in front of Charisse, or directly at her but at reduced speed, or switching one fan off in order to suddenly change the direction of the streaming material, they finally set the routine. Kelly remembered that it was "about as complicated as anything I've ever done—including the 'alter ego' and the squeaky board numbers."[25]

Charisse, who was on the receiving end of this volume of forced air, had to strain every muscle to hold her own. "I could hardly keep on my feet when the fans were turned way up and the enormous scarves tugged at me. I'd get home at night, with my shoulders sore and aching from the pressure of the wind." Charisse also had to dance into the force of the fans at times, even though she found it "difficult even to walk against them, much less perform a ballet." Kelly felt the pressure as well. Although athletically built, with very strong muscles, he had difficulty lifting Charisse within the air stream produced by the machines. "It took all my strength to do it because the force from those motors was tremendous. My stomach muscles were tightening, my arms were like steel bands, it was like lifting this room. Of course you can't let that be seen on screen."[26]

The rehearsals of the casino scenes took place on October 31 and November 1, and they were filmed on November 2. Apparently, it was not quite right, as more rehearsals of these scenes were done on November 3 and 5.[27]

By November 5, the company was filming on no less than six sets in one day in an effort to get all the shooting done. Several takes of the Palace Vaudeville sequence were shot that morning, delayed somewhat by a mix-up in the exact distance from the camera to Kelly and from Kelly to the row of chorus girls behind him, necessitating remeasuring and alterations in the setup. After a few minutes break for wardrobe change, Kelly filmed some scenes at the roulette table in the casino set and his reaction when he sees the vamp appear once again. Then he had to change clothes again, as the company set up on the exterior of the Chinese Theater set, with black tarpaulins to create the illusion of a night scene, to reshoot a few scenes of Don at the premiere of *The Royal Rascal*. After lunch, Kelly had to change wardrobe once more, and the crew filmed him in the projection room, explaining the last number of *The Dancing Cavalier* to be filmed and preparing for the dissolve into "The Broadway Ballet." Then Kelly had to change his clothes yet again, followed by "rehearsal" and more "takes" of some speakeasy scenes. While the crew set up the wall and the door to the speakeasy, and an artist continued to paint the interior décor of the speakeasy, the assistant director reported, "Mr. Kelly checking moviola for match," after which more speakeasy scenes were shot. This hectic day ended with filming the sea of hands as seventy extras added their stylized enthusiasm to the "Broadway Rhythm" dance that Kelly performed. The assistant director reports, "Directors discussing setup to get best effect of many pairs of hands clapping," but presumably he meant "waving," as that is what the extras do in the movie. This discussion was followed by several takes, trying out different versions for the sea of hands, while special effects man Irvin G. Reis worked with "black backing" and "black flooring" to try for the best effect.[28]

The crew assembled on November 6 to film the difficult "Crazy Veil Dance." They spent the time from 8 to nearly 11 a.m. setting up and rehearsing the moves with dance-ins, making sure the movements of the three airplane motors were correct. They shot three takes and then took time to repair the veil, which had ripped during the last take. After two more takes, technicians touched up the paint on the steps of the set with spray guns. After shooting take six, the crew took a fifteen-minute break so Walter Plunkett could deal with a developing problem associated with Cyd Charisse's costume. It was a bit short to begin with, and the wind pressure on the veil tended to shorten it even more. As a result, it exposed some of her pubic hair, which became easily visible when her thigh was in the camera's view. This problem was not a surprise to the crew; it had become apparent during rehearsals and Plunkett had tried to fix it several times, often commenting, according to Donen, "We've got Cyd Charisse's crotch licked." Cyd also tried shaving, but on November 6, it became obvious that the problem was not solved. Marvin Stuart, assistant director, demurely remarked in his daily report that the crew spent the time from 11:35 to 11:50 waiting, while "Fix dress to avoid showing too much thigh." Then they shot thirteen takes from 11:50 to 12:30.[29]

After lunch, the crew rehearsed with the motors and the dance-ins before Kelly and Charisse rehearsed. After shooting only one take, another eight minutes were spent to "Fix dress so that thighs are not too exposed." Several more takes were then shot, a couple of minutes taken for the still photographer to shoot some exposures as well, and a new camera angle was set up. Kelly and Charisse rehearsed the next scene, touched up their makeup as the crew cleaned the floor, and then filmed four takes, followed by additional rehearsal. The veil needed to be trimmed before six more takes were exposed. Then Kelly and Charisse rested "after strenuous dancing" from 5:53 to 5:58 p.m. They filmed several more takes before the company dismissed for the day at 6:06 p.m.[30]

When the "Crazy Veil Dance" was finished, everyone agreed that the problem of Cyd's thigh had not been solved. It was still possible to see a slight area of pubic hair just outside the border of her costume. Donen received instructions to deal with this problem in the lab. He supervised the application of white paint to cover the hairs on the print, and the paint is visible even today. In fact, Donen thought it became more prominent as time passed because the Technicolor application that created the rich color of the movie tended to fade with time, but this paint did not. As a result, Donen recalled, "Cyd's crotch started to light up like neon."[31] Actually, it is prominent only if one is looking for it; otherwise, the effect is easily missed because the viewer naturally focuses on the dancing pair instead of Charisse's thigh.

In fact, the "Crazy Veil Dance" is a surrealist experience that tends to draw everyone's attention away from earthly issues. Assistant director Marvin Stuart called it the "Infinity Set," very spare and deliberately inspired by the paintings of Salvador Dali. The most famous of the surrealist artists, whose career reached its peak in the 1930s, Dali developed what art historians call the paranoiac-critical method and linked it to surrealism. It produces an eerie feeling well suited to the dreamscape atmosphere Kelly wanted to create in the "Crazy Veil Dance." Gerald Mast has called the setting "a placeless void of pure emotion," and has noted that what appears to be a duet actually is a trio, "for two human dancers and a fluttering white scarf, . . . soaring above them, trailing behind, wrapped around, a physical extension of their emotion." Casey Charness has also noted how the scarf's movements "illustrate the depth of the set, . . . a case of a prop used to define the dance space."[32]

The end of "The Broadway Ballet" brings Kelly back to reality after the "Crazy Veil Dance," for the vamp coldly tosses him a coin and walks away with her mobster boyfriend. The hoofer leaves the casino, still dressed in his tuxedo, as the "camera cranes down and dollies in all the way, the full depth of the set to medium shot." As he stands alone, depressed, another young hoofer shows up. He's obviously fresh in town, dressed similarly to Kelly's own costume earlier in the ballet, and sings "Gotta Dance!" Instantly, the despondent hoofer is reminded of his own passion. In one of the more inspiring moments of *Singin' in the Rain*, Kelly sings "Gotta Dance!" with heartfelt and renewed passion, emblematic not only of his character but of his own personal life and career as well. The seventy extras reappear as Kelly dances enthusiastically to bring the ballet to its triumphant close.[33]

The ballet ends with an interesting technical achievement, consisting of "two pieces of film." One is "an optical matte from medium to close-up of Kelly's face," and the other is "a long to extreme long of the crowd via a crane up." As Charness has noted, this means "there are two movements within one shot: a dolly in on his face and a crane up from the crowd, accomplished by laboratory superimposition." It separates Kelly from the giddy gaggle of extras and isolates his character as a singular star, by this late time in the ballet. It is an interesting visual experience as well.[34]

In the very last shot, we dissolve back to Don Lockwood in the projection room, having finished his rendering of the final number yet to be filmed for *The Dancing Cavalier*. Playing an inside joke on producer Arthur Freed, R. F. Simpson tells Don that it sounds okay, but he would have to see it on the screen. Everyone agreed that this was one of Freed's favorite comments when presented with an oral description of a proposed film dance.[35]

COST AND EFFECT

At twelve minutes, fifty-seven seconds long, "The Broadway Ballet" cost $605,960. In contrast, the seventeen-minute ballet in *An American in Paris* cost $542,000. The big number originally conceived for *Singin' in the Rain* was estimated to cost only $85,000. Producing a movie ballet was a hefty investment of money and time. The total cost of *Singin' in the Rain* amounted to $2,540,800; nearly a quarter of that cost (23.8 percent) went into the ballet. In fact, the film came in $620,996 over budget, which was very close to the amount of money spent on the ballet.[36]

Such an expenditure of time and money on just one extended dance was justified only if the effect supported the movie and audiences were interested. All commentators agree that the ballet works within the context of *Singin' in the Rain*. Rudy Behlmer has noted that it is "a purposely designed kaleidoscope of show-business clichés, particularly those relating to early sound pictures." Charisse looks like "a combination of silent screen star Pola Negri and vintage flapper Louise Brooks." The mobster is reminiscent of "a George Raft gangster type who continually flipped a coin," and "Kelly's hoofer, with tuxedo, straw hat, and cane, suggests Broadway musical star Harry Richman." Behlmer has also noted that the crowd of extras waving their arms "was a throwback to King Vidor's *Hallelujah* (1929)." Gerald Mast has also noted that the ballet is reminiscent of the entire string of *Broadway Melody* movies M-G-M produced. Other commentators have noted that the duet with Kelly and Charisse alone was worth the effort of producing the ballet. Even if "The Broadway Ballet" is "a self-contained entity, complete with its own story and characters," as Charness has put it, and has only marginal relevance to the plot of *Singin' in the Rain,* it is a well-crafted filmic story that retains enough connection to the larger movie so that viewers are able to retain their sense of cohesion.[37]

Was the ballet really necessary for the success of the larger movie? Probably not. In contrast to the ballet in *On the Town,* it does not encapsulate the emotions or the characterizations of the larger plot in *Singin' in the Rain.* In contrast to the ballet in *An American in Paris,* it does not dazzle the eye at every scene with its colorful brilliance, which is what most viewers liked about it rather than its connections to the emotions of the characters in that movie.

Ironically, both directors thought "The Broadway Ballet" was too long. Moreover, Donen felt it "was an interruption to the main thrust" of the picture, but he also said the vamp dance was one of his favorite parts in that movie. Kelly also thought that "The Broadway Ballet" was too long, and recalled that it kept growing much more than he had originally planned. He explained that this was because he introduced a new, significant character in the form of Cyd Charisse's vamp, and needed time to develop that role on screen. "I'd have liked to trim three minutes out of it," he admitted, "but I just didn't know where."[38]

In the end, "The Broadway Ballet" received overwhelming positive responses from critics and viewers. As Kelly realized, people greatly enjoyed it despite the concern the directors felt about its length.[39]

In fact, "The Broadway Ballet" is the most balanced of the movie ballets that Gene Kelly made; it is well-crafted, well-danced, and effectively photographed, from every perspective. For this alone it is worth watching, rather than to gain added emotional connection with the characters of *Singin' in the Rain.* Moreover, the two dances that Kelly and Charisse perform together are truly memorable by any standard of judgment. Finally, Gene's own passion to dance is so well reflected in the hoofer he portrays, that it makes the backstory of the ballet very appealing to audiences.

8

Best
Musical Comedy
I've Seen

It was a tradition for movie companies to celebrate the end of production, and art director Randall Duell wanted to make the postproduction party for *Singin' in the Rain* a special event. Gene Kelly suggested holding it at one of the movie's sets on Stage 28, and Duell rearranged the walls to create a single entrance. He then piped in rain around the set and stationed prop boys to give umbrellas to everyone who arrived. The party on November 21 was a huge success, in part because of Duell's novel idea, although Donald O'Connor could not attend due to his busy schedule.[1]

Ironically, the postproduction party did not mark the end of filming. Most of the crew and cast finished their work by November 21, but there was quite a bit to be done before production ended on *Singin' in the Rain*. A second unit crew had tried to film the exterior of a private house at the corner of Sunset and Sepulveda two days before, intending to use it as footage of Don's house, but rain prevented them from doing so. Filming of the exterior and interior of Don's bedroom took place on a set at Culver City on November 20 and 21, and scenes of the exterior of Simpson's house were also filmed on the latter day. The second unit crew finally got their shots of the exterior of Don's house at Sunset and Sepulveda on November 23 and 30. All of the shots relating to Don's house and bedroom were for Kelly's solo version of "All I Do Is Dream of You."[2]

Editing began on the rest of the movie even as the ballet was being filmed. Stanley Donen reports that they were very economical when shooting so as to waste as little film as possible, but editor Adrienne Fazan had enough takes of each scene to allow her to do her job effectually. The first cut of the movie, ballet included, was finished by

December 3 and amounted to 10,745 feet of film, 335 feet shorter than the original estimate. The scriptwriters were among the first to see the finished product. "The first time Betty and Adolph saw the picture," recalled Donen, "it was fresh out of the lab and still in black and white. They loved it. That's when we knew we had pulled it off."[3]

In preparing the credits for the release print, the company adhered to a protocol already worked out a few months before. "Contractual Obligations" dictated exactly how each principal actor's name appeared on the screen. Kelly understandably received top billing, but O'Connor's agent insisted that his name be "displayed in at least SECOND OR THIRD POSITION . . . and in the same SIZE TYPE AND THE SAME STYLE TYPE as that used to display the name of Gene Kelly." Reynolds was to receive third billing. Ralph Wheelwright, the M-G-M executive in charge of advertising, explained that Gene Kelly's name would appear first in the title credit number. It would "fade out before the name of Donald O'Connor appears," O'Connor's name would fade out before Debbie Reynolds's name, and "at no time will all three names appear together on the screen."[4]

Millard Mitchell's agent jockeyed to position his client's name in the credits. If Reynolds was called a featured player, then Mitchell's name would follow hers but precede Jean Hagen's. But if Reynolds was a costar, then Hagen could be listed as the first featured player, which is how it turned out. The contract also stipulated the size and position of Mitchell's name compared to Hagen's, depending on the size of the newspaper or magazine ad.[5] The actual film credits list Hagen and Mitchell side by side and in large font, with Cyd Charisse noted in medium-sized font below, followed by Douglas Fowley's and Rita Moreno's names in the smallest font.

Arthur Freed insisted on due credit as a songwriter. When he received the information on "advertising billing" from Wheelwright, Freed complained with gentle humor, "I notice that you omitted the most important credit of the last ten years in not giving credit to those famous writers and composers of screen musicals, Nacio Herb Brown and Arthur Freed." He offered to have his credit as producer reduced in order to make room for his credit as a lyricist. "I know you will plead you have been so tied-up with 'Quo Vadis' and learning how to spell Mervyn LeRoy, and your new duties on the Executive Board of this great studio have made you a little ruthless in giving anybody else credit." In the end, Freed and Brown were fully credited as writer and composer of the songs in *Singin' in the Rain*.[6]

PREVIEWS AND RELEASE PRINT

During the late 1920s and early 1930s, Irving Thalberg pioneered M-G-M's process of previewing movies and altering their content based on viewer response. Other studios soon followed suit. *Singin' in the Rain* was no exception to this practice. The first preview took place at the De Anza Theater in Riverside, California, on December 21, 1951. A total of 193 viewers filled out comment cards, but only 184 rated the movie. Ninety of them (49 percent) rated the picture as outstanding, 57 (31 percent) considered it excellent, and 34 (18 percent) thought it very good. Only two people rated the movie as good and one as fair, and no one considered it poor. The actors were rated on a different scale, using only four assessments—excellent, good, fair, and poor. The principal actors received very high marks. Kelly rated 161 (85 percent) excellent votes, 26 good, and 3 fair. The viewers rated O'Connor slightly higher, with 168 votes (89 percent) in the excellent category, 18 good, and 2 fair. Reynolds fared less well than her two co-stars, with 146 votes for excellent (77 percent), 35 for good, and 7 for fair. Also, Reynolds was the only actor (of the five rated) who received a poor vote. Hagen and Mitchell were rated much lower than the principal actors. Hagen played a funny yet unredeemed, negative character, perhaps accounting for her rating of 114 (61 percent) excellent votes, 59 good, and 13 fair. Mitchell's role was restricted to playing an often befuddled character torn between making money and doing the right thing. He received 105 (57 percent) votes for excellent, 69 for good, and 10 for fair. Overall, 169 viewers said they would recommend the movie, and only three said they would not.[7]

When asked to name their favorite sequence, thirteen viewers identified "Make 'Em Laugh," seven chose Kelly's "Singin' in the Rain," nine said "All dancing," and five mentioned Kelly's bedroom version of "All I Do Is Dream of You." Reynolds impressed viewers as wholesome and fresh, but some thought her ability to carry the role was limited. One viewer wrote, "Donald O'Connor and Gene Kelly are a terrific team," while another gushed, "This is one of Gene Kelly's finest and greatest pictures." When asked what they didn't like, several mentioned

"Debbie's singing to the billboard," and one person wrote, "Get a feminine lead with a nice voice, please!!" If this was a reference to Hagen, this viewer missed the point of the movie! Most viewers were quick to term the entire picture "excellent," "outstanding," and "Better than 'An American in Paris.'" One viewer summed up the feelings of many to come by remarking, "Best musical comedy I've seen."[8]

Freed wanted another preview and it took place at the Bay Theatre in Pacific Palisades on December 27, 1951. Out of 250 comment cards, 108 (43 percent) rated the movie as outstanding, 92 (37 percent) as excellent, and 34 (14 percent) as very good. Eleven rated it as good, 4 as fair, and 1 as poor. The ratings seemed slightly lower compared to the first preview, but once again 80 percent marked it in the top two categories—outstanding or excellent. Not all the viewers rated the actors—236 rated Kelly and O'Connor, 230 rated Reynolds, 227 rated Hagen, and 215 rated Mitchell. However, the reactions to the actors were better compared to the first preview. Kelly's performance was rated as excellent by 205 people (87 percent), good by 26, and fair by 5. O'Connor's performance appeared excellent to 223 people (94 percent), good to 11, and fair to 1. Ironically, this time O'Connor was the only actor with one "poor" vote. Reynolds was the only actor to receive a lower rating in the second preview, with 168 excellent votes (73 percent), 48 good, and 14 fair. Hagen did very well this time, and even surpassed Reynolds, garnering 185 excellent votes (81 percent), 36 good, and 6 fair, while Mitchell received 126 excellent ratings (59 percent), 80 good, and 9 fair. In the final analysis, 207 viewers said they would recommend *Singin' in the Rain* and 8 said they would not.[9]

The two previews had an impact on the release print of the movie. Based on audience reaction, Freed dropped Debbie's version of "You Are My Lucky Star," sung to the picture of Don Lockwood on the billboard. Despite the fact that some viewers liked Gene's version of "All I Do Is Dream of You," Freed decided to drop it from the final version of the picture as well. He also cut two minutes from the "Beautiful Girl" number, and, according to Rudy Behlmer, "other bits and pieces totaling eighteen minutes." An example of scenes cut by Freed is that of a messenger handing a note to Don Lockwood's character in *The Duelling Cavalier*, right before the out-of-sync sequence at its premiere. Another example is that of Don and Cosmo as boys interacting with a fruit vendor.[10]

Cutting the small parts and the bit from "Beautiful Girl" is fully understandable. Debbie's number was poorly conceived and executed, and therefore needed to be deleted. It duplicated themes already expressed in better form by other numbers and dialogue, and Reynolds simply could not handle the song well with her limited vocal talents. But Gene's song and dance apparently was well crafted and executed, one of his best, according to Kelly. It also was, at least to a degree, repetitive, but the viewer now has no opportunity to see it because the negative and all prints were later destroyed. Only one or two stills remain as well as the playback recording of the song. Kelly later bemoaned the fact that one or two of his numbers, usually ballads sung in slow fashion, were cut from each of his movies.[11]

Kelly's rendition of "All I Do Is Dream of You" was included in a ten-inch record of the *Singin'* soundtrack issued by M-G-M. The studio actually used the soundtrack rather than re-recording the songs and music. Because the ten-inch format allowed for only fifteen minutes of play on each side, the entire "Broadway Ballet" had to be cut from the lineup. M-G-M had started marketing this recording format with *Till the Clouds Roll By* in 1946, but switched to twelve-inch disks right after *Singin'* was released.[12]

The film underwent its Technicolor application in December (before the previews) and January (before the final release) as executives planned to have release prints ready for shipment to theaters by early February 1952. They hoped to have all release prints at their destinations by March 3. The last filming actually took place on December 26, even as previews were being held. Kelly, O'Connor, and Mitchell assembled on the set of the interior of the projection room to film the scenes of Don explaining the ballet to Simpson. It is likely that the directors thought of adding their affectionate in-joke regarding Freed not being able to visualize a scene until he saw it on film, and so they added this line for Simpson at this very late filming date. O'Connor arrived at 5:40 p.m. after working for the day on *Francis Goes to West Point* at Universal. The crew shot five takes from 8:32 to 8:54 p.m., finally wrapping up the filming of *Singin' in the Rain*. But there were a few audio chores to do before production truly ended. Kelly re-recorded some songs on December 11 in time for the previews. Douglas Fowley re-recorded some of his dialogue on January 2, and Jimmy Thompson did his music loops and Jean Hagen her dialogue loops on January 10.[13]

The final version of *Singin' in the Rain,* at 103 minutes in length, was shown at a private screening at M-G-M on March 7, 1952. Invited guests included director George Cukor; actors Humphrey Bogart, Groucho Marx, and Farley Granger; screenwriter Ben Hecht; songwriter Frank Loesser; and musical director Alfred Newman. Another private screening took place in New York on March 15. Nicholas Schenck, head of Loew's Incorporated, the parent company of M-G-M, was pleased with the movie: "Everyone loved it. I was delighted with every scene and it will bring a pleasant glow to everyone who sees it." In addition, Schenck demonstrated a true sense of what made a movie good when he noted that "Kelly's singing in the rain number should become a musical classic."[14]

PROMOTION

Promotion was a key to any movie's success, and the theatrical trailer was meant to create an air of anticipation among prospective viewers. The trailer for *Singin' in the Rain* attempted to link this latest Gene Kelly film with his most recent one. "In the Spirit and Fun of 'An American in Paris,'" flashes over the main title of *Singin' in the Rain* at the start of the four-minute-long trailer. The three main characters' names were shown twice. Editors chose scenes to illustrate the various themes of the movie—the change from silent to sound pictures and the flapper culture of the 1920s. They showed excerpts from all major songs and dances, including "Singin' in the Rain," and referred to "The Unbelievable, The Sensational, Broadway Ballet" as "the most thrilling dance number ever staged." Typically hyped phrases were used, such as "The Songs you Like! The Excitement you Expect!" and the trailer ended with the prediction, "The Show you will Never Forget!"[15]

M-G-M issued an *Exhibitor's Campaign Book* for the theater owners who featured *Singin' in the Rain.* It was a large book, twelve inches by eighteen inches in dimension, with twenty-four pages packed with ideas for promoting the movie as well as interesting stories and facts concerning the picture. The book contained many illustrations of posters, lobby cards, and stills from the production, as well as specially drawn illustrations. Most of these items could be obtained for a price to adorn the theater lobby.[16]

Studio staff compiled a booklet of "12 Ideas—To Simplify Your

Promotion," which included giving free tickets to anyone who sent in the longest list of song titles that dealt with weather or who entered the theater singing if it happened to be raining, or prizes to anyone who could name previous movies that featured songs used in *Singin' in the Rain*. Other ideas included sending girls (either usherettes or models) to walk on the streets wearing raingear and signs advertising the picture, or placing a young man with an umbrella to help guests enter the theater. They also suggested that theater owners pipe in water so it would fall on cutouts of Kelly, O'Connor, and Reynolds or on theater employees dressed in raingear. Still other suggestions included inviting anyone named Kelly, O'Connor, or Reynolds to register for prizes, and holding a Charleston contest. The booklet also encouraged people to complete jingles relating to the movie (for example, "Sweet Debbie at last met her swain . . . While strollin' and 'Singin' in the Rain' . . . Said she to her Gene . . . Though the weather was mean . . .").[17]

For any theater owner not impressed by the list of twelve ideas, the M-G-M staff provided a flurry of other suggestions for promoting *Singin' in the Rain*. They emphasized the 1920s costumes that Walter Plunkett had designed for the picture, calling them "by modern standards, . . . outlandish, freakish and shapeless." Or, the theater owners could host a flapper party and award prizes for the most humorous costumes. Jean Hagen's squeaky voice could be exploited with a contest to encourage viewers to record their own "Hollywood" voice at stores that offered customers the opportunity to make a short record. These could be submitted for the voice contest.[18]

The *Exhibitor's Campaign Book* offered dozens of accessories that could be hung or set up outside the theater or inside the lobby—full-size cutouts of the principal actors, bumper stickers, fluorescent banners to be attached to umbrellas, cutouts of parasols attached to a string, and plastic stick-on posters to be rubbed onto windows without glue or tape. Cartoons of the vamp dance with Kelly and Charisse and of Kelly and O'Connor in "Fit as a Fiddle," four inches by five inches in dimension, were also available for coloring by kids. A four-foot by seven-foot "standee," or cutout, featuring Kelly and Reynolds with a changeable weather forecast and either a painted or real umbrella cost $25. The campaign book also offered four stills that theater owners could tie in with local retailers. One was of Kelly and Reynolds doing the Charleston, for a tie-in with a local dance studio. Another was of Reynolds popping out of the cake, with a tie-in to a local bakery. A third showed Kelly and Reynolds kissing at the end of the movie, and associated Kelly's sweater with a local clothing store. A fourth showed Kelly's coat tearing as he gets out of Reynolds's car for a tie-in with a local car dealer.[19]

The campaign book urged theater owners to buy radio time immediately following weather reports and suggested six different announcements. For example, "But rain or shine, everybody's going to see 'Singin' in the Rain.'" It also urged the exhibitors to exploit the popularity of the Freed-Brown songs by playing them in the lobby or even sending an employee onto the streets with a portable record player. A "rainy day outfit (slicker, galoshes, umbrella) will add a provocative touch, if weather is bad." The Robbins Music Corporation of New York planned to reissue sheet music editions of seven songs used in *Singin' in the Rain* as a tie-in to the movie. M-G-M suggested that theater owners could play these in the lobby.[20]

How seriously exhibitors took the many suggestions contained in the *Exhibitor's Campaign Book* is difficult to determine. A few theaters did buy the accessories and display them in their lobbies. At least one, the Loew's Midland Theatre in Kansas City, Missouri, went further. The owner sent models around the city with placards on their backs advertising the picture, wearing see-through raingear so the placards could easily be read by passersby.[21]

Businesses other than theater owners also tried to cash in on the anticipated windfall produced by the movie. Reynolds modeled a Rain Shedder, made of rayon and designed to repel water. The coat included a cap and sold for less than $23. Deering Milliken, the company that developed Dacron, "a new and revolutionary fabric in men's clothing" that reportedly "sheds water and holds creases!," planned full-page ads in *Look, Collier's,* and *Time* magazines featuring Kelly's soon-to-become famous pose on the lamppost in "Singin' in the Rain." The ad was careful not to state that Kelly wore the material, but it claimed that 5,000 men had worn suits made of 45 percent wool and 55 percent Dacron and liked them. Deering Milliken also planned full-page newspaper ads in sixteen cities and 5,000 brochures to be mailed directly to stores. Moreover, company attempts to market products as a tie-in to *Singin' in the Rain* continued even after the movie's release. Rain Bonnet of Los Angeles wanted to push a hat "made of waterproof Vinylite plastic" that could be inflated into an umbrella.[22]

While Kelly never participated directly in promoting products linked to *Singin' in the Rain*, Reynolds, Hagen, and Charisse modeled several products that were marketed as tie-ins to the picture. Reynolds modeled for Max Factor's full-page ads in *Life* and *Look* with the message, "Exciting, New, Easy Way for you to have that Fresh, Young *Natural* Look." Hagen joined Reynolds in modeling a variety of jewelry, clothing, and scarves that had tie-ins to the Easter trade as well, since M-G-M planned to time the release of *Singin' in the Rain* to coincide with the Easter holiday. Charisse modeled a line of "Easter-Spring Hats" but appeared awkward and uncomfortable in these photographs, unlike her usual M-G-M publicity photographs. Reynolds, however, was natural as a model, smiling broadly and seeming ideal for this type of work.[23]

EARLY REVIEWS AND PREMIERES

Newspaper reaction to the early showings of *Singin' in the Rain* were overwhelmingly positive. *Variety* noted that it had "a lot more humor than in the usual musical." Kelly received very strong endorsements, including "plays the romantic lead with style," "handles his comic parts with skill," and "his dancing is standout." O'Connor impressed the weekly *Variety* critic so much "as almost to steal the show from Kelly." Reynolds was called "a pretty, pert minx, with a nice singing voice and fine dancing ability to add to her figure and looks." The reviewer for the weekly edition of *Variety* thought the ballet "pleasing, varied, and not overlong," but the reviewer for the daily edition thought it too long and wished "the ballet bit in it" (probably referring to the "Crazy Veil Dance") had been cut. "Singin' in the Rain," however, was called a "wow sequence." The *Hollywood Reporter* called this number "a show-stopper" and said Kelly's dancing in the entire movie ranged "from the graceful to the spectacular." The reviewer in the *Reporter* could not get enough of O'Connor too, and found Reynolds pleasant enough while complimenting Fowley for his ability to portray the frustrated director. Sherwin Kane of the *Motion Picture Daily* noted the "zestful cast, rollicking tunes and solid platinum production investments" of the film, recognized Lina's voice as a duplicate of Judy Holliday's Billie Dawn, and concluded that *Singin' in the Rain* was "top-notch" entertainment. Walter J. F. Higgins, writing in *The Independent Film Journal*, called it "my idea of a perfect picture. There isn't a flaw in it."[24]

Freed received rave reviews from private citizens too. Sidney Phillips wrote to tell him it was "one of the finest musicals I've ever seen." He thought "the cast was ideally chosen and directed" and called the title number "one of the finest dances anyone has ever done." Phillips noted the artistic origins of the set upon which the "Crazy Veil Dance" was performed, believing it to be a combination of Dali and Giorgio de Chirico, the latter an Italian-Greek artist who worked in many different styles and whose paintings "are characterized by a visionary, poetic use of imagery, in which themes such as nostalgia, enigma and myth are explored." Phillips was not certain how the company "achieved such an amazing atmospheric effect" but he thought "it certainly was effective." Two college students named Jim Kason and Dick Fuselier of San Francisco wrote to movie critic Hortense Morton to praise *Singin' in the Rain* and assured her it was at least as good, if not better than, *An American in Paris*. Morton sent their letter to Freed, replete with Kason and Fuselier's hand-drawn images from both movies.[25]

Following this warm early reception, *Singin' in the Rain* received two special premieres on opposite sides of the continent before its general release across the United States in spring 1952. First, the movie premiered at the Radio City Music Hall in New York on March 27 and then at the Hollywood Egyptian Theater in Los Angeles on April 9. Kelly was in Europe at the time and could not attend either premiere. Betty Comden, Stanley Donen, Roger Edens, Nacio Herb Brown, and Alan Jay Lerner attended the Hollywood Egyptian showing. The general release occurred two days later, on April 11. Reynolds remembered attending a showing of the movie at the Pantages Theater in Hollywood, with the young Robert Wagner as her date.[26]

The New York premiere was timed to coincide with a stage show celebrating the Easter season. M-G-M commissioned another viewer poll from Film Research Surveys. The company sent researchers to talk with viewers in the lobby of Loew's 72nd Street Theater. Of the 338 viewers polled, 45 percent rated *Singin' in the Rain* as excellent, 42 percent thought it was very good, and 10 percent considered it good. When asked to rank the most enjoyable performers in the movie, 76 percent identified O'Connor and 71 percent marked Kelly as their favorite. The percentages added together exceed 100, because viewers typically mentioned more than one performer. Reynolds rated a distant 52 percent, with Hagen and Charisse at only 37 percent and 32 percent, respectively, and Mitchell at less than 12 percent. Most of the positive comments were related to O'Connor and Kelly. The comments regarding Kelly showed that viewers had enjoyed his performances many times before as well. The comments about O'Connor indicated that viewers had never seen him before, or had never seen him perform in such a way, and would like him to continue this type of high-level entertainment.[27]

Film Research Surveys worked up a "deficiency quotient" to measure what it termed "destructive publicity," meaning the flow of negative comments circulating from the preview audience. *Singin' in the Rain* got such good audience response that it marked a new low in "destructive publicity." For example, while 11.8 percent of the preview audience refused to recommend *The Pirate*, 7.3 percent had the same feeling toward *On the Town*, and 2.8 percent for *An American in Paris*, only 1.8 percent refused to recommend *Singin' in the Rain*. Film Research Surveys concluded with pride: "THIS IS THE HIGHEST RATING ATTAINED FOR ANY PICTURE THAT THIS ORGANIZATION HAS PREVIEWED."[28]

Two nights before the general release of *Singin' in the Rain*, Samuel Goldwyn held a private screening of the movie at his home. Charlie Chaplin was among the invited guests and loved the picture. He met Comden and Green the next night at a party and asked them if they had heard of the movie. "We wrote it!" they happily informed him.[29]

CENSORSHIP AT HOME AND ABROAD

M-G-M had cooperated with Joseph Breen's office early in the creation of *Singin' in the Rain* in order to head off potential censorship problems, forwarding the script for Breen's review on two occasions before production began. Still, the office had to review the entire, finished film before passing full judgment on it. The Breen office had a standardized form that its employees used to evaluate each movie. It was divided into several categories, such as how the film portrayed the professions, different races, ethnic groups, and foreign nationals. The consumption of alcohol was featured in no fewer than sixteen subcategories concerning who, how, and in what context characters drank. Crime, violence, marriage, adultery, illicit sex, and character motivation rounded out the seven-part survey. The Breen office had little difficulty passing *Singin' in the Rain* on January 3, 1952, noting only two things. One was that the gambling casino of "The Broadway Ballet" seemed a slightly shady setting for the consumption of alcohol. With regard to the vamp dance, a note from Breen mentioned an "understanding" that the dance "will be shortened on the basis of the elimination discussed."[30] Although there is no record of how and where it was shortened, careful observation of the vamp dance shows an abrupt cut when Charisse is wrapped around Kelly, indicating that a particular pose or sequence that the Breen office found objectionable might have been cut at this point.

Other censorship organizations took an even firmer stand on Charisse's steamy vamp dance. The Catholic Church's Legion of Decency reviewed *Singin' in the Rain* on March 5 and warned M-G-M that it would put the film in their Class "B" but they were willing to wait a few days to give M-G-M an opportunity to alter the vamp dance sequence. Robert Vogel, who was in charge of censorship issues at the studio, supported his New York colleague Bill Kelly (no relation to Gene) in arguing that "this number is tremendous box office and shouldn't be tampered with." Moreover, neither Bill Kelly nor Vogel thought that a B rating from the Legion of Decency would affect people's perception of the film in an appreciable way. "A top-grade picture isn't hurt by this listing (Example—*Gone with the Wind*)." Besides, as Vogel put it, "With a man named Kelly getting top billing, they are all going to see that Irishman in spite of the classification."[31]

Dore Schary completely agreed with Vogel and refused to alter the dance beyond what had already been done to satisfy the Breen office. The Legion of Decency gave *Singin' in the Rain* its B rating, due to the "Suggestive dance," on March 27. In stark contrast, Harrison's Reports rated the film "Excellent for the family" on March 22, and the Film Estimate Board of National Organizations classed it as a "Family" film on April 15.[32]

A few states maintained their own movie-rating systems and Vogel had to be somewhat concerned about their decisions. He informed Freed and Schary on March 31 that some of them "have been acting a little skittish about the Charisse-Kelly dance, but so far we have gotten away without cuts in the important states of New York, Maryland, Ohio, Pennsylvania, and Virginia." In addition, the movie was passed without any cuts by Massachusetts on March 21 and by Kansas on June 30.[33]

Vogel, who handled foreign distribution for M-G-M, knew that

Gene Kelly's films always sold well overseas. They were "Very, very big, yes. Again, you see, his language is universal." More than that, Vogel thought any American musical tended to sell well in foreign countries. But that did not mean that M-G-M got a free ride everywhere. The authorities in some nations tended to be leery of the sensual elements in many American musicals, giving M-G-M more trouble over that issue than, ironically, the Breen office. One of Vogel's jobs was to oversee the studio's response to the reports of censor boards in foreign countries. The censors advised M-G-M of their concerns and sent the release print back to Culver City. The studio's representatives in those nations did not have the capability to edit film, so the studio had to redo the print according to the request contained in the censor report. Vogel indicated that M-G-M usually caved in willingly to every detail in those reports in order to ensure overseas receipts.[34]

Islamic and Catholic countries tended to give M-G-M more concern than any others. Authorities in Pakistan reported on April 15, 1953, that the vamp dance was troubling. They asked the studio to "Delete shots of Cyd Charisse with Gene Kelly's hat hanging on her foot and her raising her foot higher." They also wanted the shots of Kelly picking Charisse up and slowly turning her around to be cut. Indonesian authorities presented Vogel with a longer list of requests in August 1953. They wanted the lyrics of "All I Do Is Dream of You" to be changed to "O, now now," and they also wanted to cut the scene of "three girls dancing in short petticoats," a reference to Jeanne Coyne and two other dancers in the montage. Indonesian authorities also wanted the entire vamp dance and veil dance to be cut from "The Broadway Ballet," effectively taking Cyd Charisse out of *Singin' in the Rain* altogether. The studio undoubtedly cut all the requested parts but obviously did not change any lyrics. It is not clear if they had to drop "All I Do Is Dream of You" as well.[35]

Gene Kelly later recalled that authorities in Spain "excised the part where I kissed her in the white thing—which we thought was very lovely and charming." It seemed to this conservative, Catholic nation too "symbolic of love-making." Kelly wrote a letter protesting the decision, "saying, 'I'm a Catholic; I don't understand your attitude.' But it didn't do any good."[36] Given the steamy nature of both of Charisse's dances with Kelly, it is surprising that *Singin' in the Rain* passed fairly smoothly through the censorship filters of the United States and raised conservative eyebrows only in three nations.

The newspaper notices and personal reactions to the premieres in March and April built up public interest in *Singin' in the Rain,* giving the movie one of the best promotions accorded an M-G-M musical. Prominent reviewers weighed in during late March and early April with their opinions, and they were overwhelmingly positive. Bosley Crowther of the *New York Times,* perhaps the most prominent film reviewer in the country, called the movie "fresh and cheerful" and "guaranteed to lift the dolors of winter and put you in a buttercup mood." But Crowther mixed his review with minor criticisms. He argued shortsightedly that the picture's title had nothing to do with the plot, but then showed through his plot summary that he did not seem to understand much of the story or its underlying motivation. Crowther admired the courage of the moviemakers to lampoon Louella Parsons, in the form of Dora Bailey, and he enjoyed the humorous take on how the actors and crew were frustrated while dealing with the new sound technology. The writing did not impress him, except that he grudgingly called it "first-class satiric burlesque." Crowther liked Kelly's dancing and singing, however, and said, "His most captivating number is done to the title song—a beautifully soggy tap dance performed in the splashing rain." He also liked "The Broadway Ballet" and called the veil number "a lovely dream dance."[37]

Regarding "lampooning" Louella Parsons, Kelly said, "I personally was never bothered by Hedda or Louella. But . . . we knew in *Singin' in the Rain* that we were all taking a chance. Fortunately, Louella adored it, and only said flattering things about us."[38]

Irene Thirer of the *New York Post* thought older viewers would appreciate *Singin' in the Rain* even more than the younger generation because of the emphasis on the late 1920s. She loved the movie's treatment of this time period and was a fervent fan of Gene Kelly, believing that each movie he made "reveals the man's genius." She also noted that Lina was modeled after Judy Holliday's Billie Dawn. *Singin' in the Rain* was, in Thirer's view, a "rowdy, gaudy, tinselly terpsichorean tussle if ever there was one." Wanda Hale, writing in the *Los Angeles Daily News,* thought the picture was too long and needed tighter editing. But she praised Freed for giving viewers "something to look at, a lot to laugh at and good music to listen to."[39]

Another consistent supporter of Kelly among the reviewers, Walter Terry of the *New York Herald Tribune,* went further than most when he called the dances in *Singin' in the Rain* "superb," incorporating "the most appealing choreography to come from Mr. Kelly. Although they are richly inventive with respect to steps, body actions, rhythmic variations and space-effects, much of their charm derives from their impulsiveness. They grow easily and naturally out of scenes and incidents." Terry found the theme of "The Broadway Rhythm" to be the driving force of all the dancing in *Singin'.* "Gotta dance" seemed to be the spirit of the movie, "communicated with gusto and imagination and fine craftsmanship." Terry's favorite dances included the one with the "incredibly long white scarf." He was greatly impressed by the choreography, which included inventive actions by the scarf designed to enhance the sense of ill-fated longing that permeates the number. "The effect is not only visually beautiful but utterly sensual, quite as sensual as those fleeting moments when the pair actually achieves physical proximity." Terry also recognized that Kelly had achieved a remarkable cine-dance in this number, exploiting "that element of space which the camera can explore so excitingly but which it does not always do when dealing with dance." The set, and more importantly, the choreography of the scarf, were the key to this. "Here is camera dance, not flat in design but rather with patterns which plunge deep into space," Terry concluded. He also liked the title number very much and praised Kelly's depiction of a man "oblivious of the elements" who "dances and splashes his joyous way along a rainy street . . . mere rain cannot dampen the spirits of one who has 'gotta dance' his happiness."[40]

Most reviewers pinpointed "Singin' in the Rain" as the most remarkable dance sequence in the picture. Harrison Carroll called it "a miracle of grace and agility . . . in the middle of a downpour." An unidentified reviewer in the *New Statesman and Nation* reportedly continued to hum the tune a week after viewing the movie. Kelly's dance "revives all one's romantic enthusiasm," for it had "a rapture, an expressiveness" unlike any other. It was more effective than any ballet sequence in sweeping "together the relevant feelings and actions" of Kelly's character. While some reviewers noted that "The Broadway Ballet" contained "some first-rate ballet," others thought it too long or stagy, making "up in size what it lacks in sparkle."[41]

Many reviewers were taken by Donald O'Connor's performance,

for they saw him shine as he had never done in previous movies. Otis Guernsey had often been irritated by O'Connor's "furious comedy style," but not in *Singin' in the Rain*. "He plays on a reasonable level of wise-cracking flippancy," he wrote. Carroll noted that O'Connor "with a real opportunity, at last shines brilliantly both as a dancer and as a comedian." Dick Williams concurred that *Singin'* "marks the emergence of Donald O'Connor as a major Hollywood star." But Williams went further and relayed rumors that some of O'Connor's best numbers were deleted from the release print of the movie, which was not true. He concluded that what was left allowed O'Connor "to steal the picture from its nominal star, Gene Kelly, who is in fine form." O'Connor was not pleased when he read the Williams article. He called Arthur P. Jacobs, who ran a public relations firm in Hollywood, and explained that he had never said anything that could be construed into the rumors that Williams relayed. "O'Connor was so upset," Jacobs wrote to Kelly, "I promised to let you know immediately—cause he has only the very highest regard and appreciation for you."[42]

Debbie Reynolds consistently received mildly good notices, often described as "sweet-faced" and able to at least keep up with Kelly and O'Connor in the dance numbers. Cyd Charisse brought "some real dancing excitement to the film," according to *Time* magazine, while Jean Hagen impressed many reviewers with her comic talent. In the end, despite the impression that O'Connor made, most reviewers recognized the film was primarily Kelly's. The *New Statesman and Nation* called him "a persuasive figure; he dances brilliantly" and "when he dances he controls not only his own movements but the movements of the camera. . . . His films dance, and in his hand ballet becomes something more than ballet screened—a dance brilliantly designed for the camera."[43]

Arthur Knight called *Singin' in the Rain* "a big, bouncy, Technicolored show that has just about everything you could ask of a musical," and most reviewers endorsed it as an entertaining way to celebrate Easter. Virginia Graham noted that it offered "a refreshing change from the normal run of musicals, carrying in its coloured bosom not one seed of sentimentality." Guernsey thought it broke the formula for film musicals with its "near-perfect synchronization of verbal gags and sight gags strung together with the production numbers in a bounteous entertainment." *Singin' in the Rain* "wins [the audience] subtly with its smooth style and witty point of view, and it glides along in a kind of effortless levitation of spirits." Kelly and Donen's direction left "no trace of strain, mugging, short-cuts . . . or other evidences of trying to sell tarnished goods by sheer force of delivery. . . . The manner of this show is easy and confident." *Seventeen* magazine called *Singin' in the Rain* the "Musical of the Year" as well as "the best musical in years" a month after its general release, and many reviewers predicted it would be a box-office behemoth.[44]

Freed continued to receive letters from people who saw and loved the movie. Barbara Derix of DeKalb, Illinois, told him that she "was so overjoyed at what I saw last night that I wanted to shout it to the world." She thought Kelly was "simply great" but was very taken by Debbie Reynolds, "a little bundle of charms" who seemed to Derix "the most refreshing, sparkling and appealing personality on the screen today." Doyle L. McCuller of Houston liked *Singin' in the Rain* but confessed to Freed that "the only reason I went was to see Cyd Charisse dance." He had seen her performance in *Fiesta* (1947) and became an instant fan. "I've gotten to think of her as an Ava Gardner who dances." Other correspondents also liked Reynolds, especially in combination with Kelly and O'Connor, and many thought *Singin' in the Rain* was better than *An American in Paris*. Michael Keller of Jackson, Michigan, wrote a letter to "Gene, Don, Debbie, and the other one with the squeaky voice," explaining how much he loved the movie.[45]

AWARDS, FOREIGN RELEASE, AND BOX OFFICE

Despite the glowing response, *Singin' in the Rain* was destined to be overshadowed by Gene Kelly's previous film for some time to come. Freed released *An American in Paris* on November 9, 1951, when Kelly was deeply involved in creating "The Broadway Ballet." It took off like a rocket, garnering unusually good reviews and eventually taking in more than $8 million during its initial release period. The presentation of annual awards by the Academy of Motion Picture Arts and Sciences in March 1952 became a showcase for *An American in Paris*. The movie won the Oscar for Best Picture of 1951, becoming only the third musical to achieve that honor, following *The Broadway Melody* (1929) and *The Great Ziegfeld* (1936). *An American in Paris* also won Oscars for Best Cinematography, Best Screenplay, Best Art Direction, Best Musical

Direction, and Best Costumes. Kelly won a special Oscar for his "extreme versatility as an actor, singer, director, and dancer, but specifically for his brilliant achievement in the art of choreography on film." As biographer Hirschhorn put it, "for Gene, *An American in Paris* was an unqualified triumph."[46]

But that triumph had a negative impact on *Singin' in the Rain*. Dore Schary had expected his big historical epic *Quo Vadis* to win several of the eight Oscars for which it received nominations, but it failed in every case. *An American in Paris* was the surprise Oscar magnet that year. Schary quickly decided to cash in on the latter film's success by rereleasing it in late March and cutting promotional efforts for *Singin' in the Rain*.[47]

Hope for *Singin'* in the next round of Oscar awards in the spring of 1953 also fell short. The picture was nominated twice; Jean Hagen was up for Best Actress in a Supporting Role and Lennie Hayton for Best Music, Scoring of a Musical Picture. Both lost. Gloria Grahame won the best supporting actress award for her performance in *The Bad and the Beautiful* (1952), and Alfred Newman won the best music and scoring award for his work in *With a Song in My Heart* (1952). Many people, including Debbie Reynolds, thought Hagen deserved the Oscar. Comden and Green later commented that "we felt comparatively ignored" by the industry, and Stanley Donen was frustrated that *The Greatest Show on Earth* (1952), which he thought "one of the worst movies ever made," won the Oscar for Best Picture of the year. It is quite possible that the industry did not consider *Singin' in the Rain* to be more than "a good, solid studio product," according to film historian Jeff Kurtti, or that it "didn't seem significant because people were laughing and doing odd things" in the movie, as Adolph Green put it.[48]

Several other organizations, besides the Academy, paid more attention to *Singin' in the Rain* in 1953. The Directors Guild of America nominated Kelly and Donen for their award for Outstanding Directorial Achievement in Motion Pictures, and the British Academy of Film and Television Arts nominated *Singin'* as the Best Film From Any Source. The movie won neither award, but Donald O'Connor won a Golden Globe as Best Motion Picture Actor in a Musical or Comedy, and the Writers Guild of America gave Comden and Green its award for Best Written American Musical.[49]

M-G-M released *Singin' in the Rain* in England in mid-April 1952, coinciding with its U.S. release. The next international release was in the summer of 1952, premiering in Brazil on June 30. The film had its Swedish premiere on September 29, and other international releases followed: Denmark (October 20), France (November 21), the Philippines (November 27), Finland (November 28), Portugal (December 18), and Australia (December 25). The distribution of the picture continued across the world in 1953 with release dates in Italy (January 7), Hong Kong (February 12), West Germany (March 30), Japan (April 15), and Austria (July 3). International notices were positive. *The Times* of London noted O'Connor in addition to singing Kelly's praises. Max van Wesel, Hollywood correspondent for a film newspaper sold in France, Holland, and Belgium, endorsed *Singin' in the Rain* and informed Freed that his readers "in general have already anough [*sic*] trouble of their one [*sic*] in Europe and they want escapist entertainment." Wesel especially liked Jean Hagen, "a girl of Dutch descent and so to speak a landman of mine." The Dutch correspondent thought Hagen "continually steals te [*sic*] whole show I never thought she had it in her."[50]

Despite the fact that it was released in the wake of *An American in Paris, Singin'* plowed ahead to garner a rich lode of income for M-G-M. It cost $2,540,800 to make, and grossed $95,000 on the first day of its official release. *Singin' in the Rain* went on to bring in $7,665,000 during the entire run of its initial release.[51]

You Dance Love, and You Dance Joy, and You Dance Dreams

9

The making of *Singin' in the Rain* represented the high point in the career of many people involved in the movie. For some, no matter how many films they subsequently worked on, *Singin'* became the one their fans most talked about, the one most often seen time after time, and the one that kept their legacy alive. While a few of the many people involved in *Singin'* went on to do movies that were well known, none were considered better or more lasting in the hearts of viewers.

FREED AND BROWN

Arthur Freed, the producer and lyricist of *Singin' in the Rain*, never made another catalog movie. He continued to produce successful films even though the threat of television, financial difficulties, and the dismantling of the studio system forced M-G-M to slash costs beginning in 1953. The Freed Unit laid off technicians and switched from Technicolor to Eastmancolor to save money. Dore Schary was forced to deal with significant downsizing within a changing climate that affected all the studios in Hollywood. The Freed Unit, however, continued to provide continuity in quality and commercial success for several years, with a total of seven films coming from the unit from 1953 to 1958, when Freed made his last musical, *Gigi*. It turned out to be the biggest-grossing film of Freed's career, although it had hardly any dancing in it, and it won ten Oscars. The man who was immortalized in *Singin'* as R. F. Simpson became the producer "who orchestrated MGM's musical golden age, virtually defining its trajectory," in the words of film historian Thomas Schatz. He fostered the directorial careers of Gene Kelly, Stanley Donen, Robert Alton, and Charles Walters, to name four dancers or choreographers who initially came to the Freed Unit to do something other than direct.[1] Freed also carefully nurtured the dancing and acting careers of many others, including Cyd Charisse and Debbie Reynolds, and played a huge role in their lives.

Freed's days as a major producer ended by the late 1950s. He continued to work for M-G-M even in its waning days, retiring in December 1970. Less than two and a half years later, on April 12, 1973, Freed died suddenly of a heart attack, and M-G-M stopped making movies altogether six months later. His erstwhile partner, Nacio Herb Brown, had died several years earlier on September 28, 1964, in San Francisco, after having lived obscurely since his marginal involvement in the making of *Singin' in the Rain*. His songs, most of which were written with Freed, appeared in at least eighty films from *The Broadway Melody* in 1929 to *Hollywood Ending* in 2002.[2]

COMDEN AND GREEN

Betty Comden and Adolph Green seemed to realize they had written the screenplay for a classic film musical when moviemakers they admired began to compliment their work. In the late 1960s, after *Singin' in the Rain* had a few years to make the rounds through Europe, the screenwriters were visiting Paris when Francois Truffaut, a famous French director, waxed eloquent in his praise for the movie after meeting the pair at a party. As Comden and Green proudly put it, Truffaut "had seen the film many many times, knew every frame of it, felt it was a classic." It had played in some theaters of Paris for several months at a time.[3]

Of course, Comden and Green had plenty of evidence from appreciative American audiences that their work had not "been in vain for nothing," as they had Lina express it at the premiere of *The Dancing Cavalier*. But to receive reinforcement of the point from respected European directors cinched it for them. *Singin' in the Rain* was by no means the last film to come from the prolific pens of the team. It was soon followed by another near classic of the genre, *The Band Wagon* (1953), with Fred Astaire and Cyd Charisse, and *It's Always Fair Weather* (1955) with Gene Kelly and Charisse. The pair also continued to write successful Broadway shows, including *Wonderful Town* (1953) and *Bells Are Ringing* (1956), and they wrote the lyrics for a couple of songs in the Jerome Robbins staging of *Peter Pan* in 1954. These shows were followed by the movies *Auntie Mame* (1958), *Bells Are Ringing* (1960), and *What a Way to Go!* (1964) to continue the Comden and Green resume at Hollywood.[4]

The writers never lost their desire to appear on stage or on the screen, and indulged themselves in a few choice supporting roles. Betty Comden appeared on the television sitcom *Frasier* and in the movie *Garbo Talks* (1984). Adolph Green appeared on several television series as well as movies such as *Simon* (1980) and *My Favorite Year* (1982), and joined Comden for *Garbo Talks*. But the pair made their mark as writers rather than actors. They won a total of six Tony Awards and received the Kennedy Center Honors in 1991.[5]

Singin' in the Rain was "a thing we were very proud of, a picture we loved," Green once told an interviewer. He coupled it with *The Band Wagon* and called both movies "very special." Including *It's Always Fair Weather*, the writers said that these three satires are "filled with invention on everybody's part. They have what no other musicals are ever allowed to have—individuality and eccentricity." Comden and Green referred to *Singin'* as an "exuberant, joyous expression of love of life" in their introduction to the published screenplay of the movie. They also revealed that they received only a salary for writing the film; contrary to many viewers' assumption, the screenwriters did not "get a penny out of" the release of the movie. Comden recalled in her memoirs that after her husband passed away in 1979, she accepted "free first-class passage" on the *Queen Elizabeth II* in exchange for "doing my *Singin' in the Rain* comments."[6]

Betty Comden and Adolph Green were able to attend the fiftieth anniversary release of *Singin'* in late September 2002 at the Academy of Motion Picture Arts and Sciences theater in Beverly Hills. Both came in wheelchairs; Comden had "slipped and bruised her hip at a *Singin' in the Rain* screening at the Telluride Film Festival," and Green was suffering from a broken leg. He died a month later, leaving behind his wife of forty-two years and two children who had gone into show business. Comden survived the passing of her husband and of her son Alan, and died on November 23, 2006, leaving Susanna behind.[7]

JEAN HAGEN

Singin' in the Rain was the salient point in Jean Hagen's film career. She received more attention for her brilliant creation of Lina Lamont than for any other of her movie roles. Her second child, a son, was born August 19, 1952. While this forced her to drop out of one movie, Hagen appeared in three films released in 1953, the year after *Singin' in the Rain* premiered. But M-G-M never gave her another role like Lina, and Hagen opted for television. In September 1953, she began to play the wife of Danny Thomas on a new sitcom called *Make Room for Daddy*. It was an enormous popular success, garnering two Emmy nominations within two years. Hagen played what has been termed a "forceful, pleasantly caustic wife." She left the series, however, after the third season, having grown tired of the limitations of her character. Hagen appeared in a number of movies and many guest appearances on various television shows before retiring in 1964. She died of throat cancer on August 29, 1977.[8]

CYD CHARISSE

Singin' in the Rain was the springboard for Cyd Charisse's leap into stardom. In September 1952, after *Singin' in the Rain*'s grand premiere and just before *The Band Wagon* began filming, Arthur Freed reported in a letter to Lela Simone that Charisse and Fred Astaire were working well together in rehearsals for the movie. "I have Gene to thank for bringing Cyd to life," Freed wrote. He understood the pivotal role Kelly played in taking Charisse's dancing to a new level of sophistication and appeal. Kelly also realized it. "I sexy-ed her up in 1952's *Singin' in the Rain*," he told an interviewer in 1994, "for which she has always been grateful." The famous vamp dance, which gave Charisse her first opportunity to dance in a powerful and expressive way, turned her entire career around.[9]

In an article about "The Women in My Dancing Life," published in July 1952, Kelly praised Charisse as an ideal dancing partner. She "moves like a dream, she has a perfect figure and a beautiful face— everything a dancer could ask for." He also noted her rigorous training in classical ballet, and argued that Charisse deserved better roles than she had been offered before *Singin'*. Neither Freed nor M-G-M made that mistake again. Charisse's next movie, dancing with Astaire in *The Band Wagon,* was another huge success with critics and viewers alike. Charisse called it "a great triumph for me." She was the female star of *Brigadoon,* opposite Gene Kelly, in 1954. While that movie's many problems limited its success, Charisse perhaps had her best role as a Soviet official in *Silk Stockings,* again opposite Astaire. This movie, released in 1957, was Astaire's last musical and one of the best produced by the Freed Unit. Charisse had learned how to smoke while filming "The Broadway Ballet" in *Singin',* and she continued the habit for years to come. It apparently did not inhibit her ability to film, but she gave it up to gain more stamina when she developed a nightclub act with her husband, singer Tony Martin, years later. Charisse died of a heart attack on June 17, 2008.[10]

DEBBIE REYNOLDS

For Debbie Reynolds, *Singin' in the Rain* played an even more pivotal role in her career. She was largely unknown before 1952, with few assets as a performer and a slim track record of success. It had been a miracle that she was chosen to create the role of Kathy Selden, and an impressive accomplishment of pluck, hard work, and sheer determination that she had been able to pull it off. In an important way, the experience of being a part of *Singin'* convinced her to take her career as an entertainer seriously, to work hard at learning her craft, and to never take her opportunities for granted. It was the making of Debbie Reynolds.

But, in the immediate aftermath of her grueling ordeal on the set, Reynolds could hardly understand all this. As soon as her filming ended in November 1951, Reynolds spent a week at Lake Tahoe with a friend where she slept eighteen hours on the first day, and until noon each day thereafter. A week and a half after returning to Culver City, she began filming *Mr. Imperium* with Lana Turner and Ezio Pinza. It was a forgettable movie that failed at the box office, but soon after filming ended, M-G-M released *Singin' in the Rain.* Having barely turned twenty, she attended one of the showings with Robert Wagner, driving "an old car like the one in the movie," and was enthralled. "There she was," Reynolds wrote of herself years later, "popping out of that cake, dancing up and down those stairs, singing and smiling and holding her own with those two dancing geniuses. If there was ever a single moment when Mary Frances was transformed into Debbie, it might have been then. I thought, hey, I'm good! All that pain and the kid is good!

I was amazed." It had been the hardest acting job of her short life to date, and the results were spectacular. "I knew then and there where I belonged."[11]

The executives at M-G-M were happy too, but they also wanted Reynolds to work at improving herself. They urged her to work on lowering her voice so she didn't always sound like a high school kid. Debbie agreed, saying, "My voice could get real high and real squeaky at certain moments." She studied for hours with M-G-M's diction coach Gertrude Folger to tame her Texas accent and put her "voice in its proper channel," as she later phrased it. The studio also planned a whirlwind publicity campaign to boost her visibility in the wake of the movie's success. Debbie's face appeared on numerous magazine covers and she exhausted herself in personal appearances. M-G-M placed Reynolds in a succession of movies, most of which made money and steadily boosted her girl-next-door qualities.[12]

Very few of these films involved dancing, however. An exception to that rule was I Love Melvin, released in 1953. It gave Reynolds an opportunity to co-star again with Donald O'Connor, and it is possible that Gene Kelly might have been a part of this project if he had not gone to Europe to work on other films. I Love Melvin was not a product of the Freed Unit; George Wells produced it, Don Weis directed it, and Robert Alton handled the choreography. Almost the exact technical crew that had worked on Singin' also worked on this picture. O'Connor paid one of the earliest tributes to Kelly's "Singin' in the Rain" number by jumping onto a lamppost, designed to look like the one Kelly used, during a dance routine filmed in Central Park. Greatly overlooked today, the film has a certain amount of charm and innocent fun, and contains the second-best dancing that Reynolds did in her career, next to her performance in Singin'.[13]

Virtually all of her subsequent film roles were in nondancing, nonsinging movies. Her films ranged from Tammy and the Bachelor (1957), to How the West Was Won (1962), to Debbie's favorite, The Unsinkable Molly Brown (1964). She thought Molly Brown was her best acting job and best character, next to Kathy Selden, although she readily pointed out that creating Kathy was comparatively easy (except for the dancing), while Molly was a difficult person to create on the screen. She did some dancing in Molly Brown, but not on the same level as that of Singin' or even *I Love Melvin*. She performed in at least thirty-seven movies since *Singin'*.[14]

Debbie's personal life had its share of ups and downs. Her marriage to singer Eddie Fisher led to a messy and very public divorce after Fisher jilted her for Elizabeth Taylor. Her marriage to Harry Karl, heir to a family fortune built in the shoe business, ended with Karl wasting his and her money in a gambling addiction. Reynolds was forced, after several years of retirement, to rebuild her fortune for her own and her children's welfare by starring in *Irene* on Broadway for two years. She also had a keen sense of history and purchased a huge amount of movie memorabilia when M-G-M sold many of its assets at a public auction in 1970. Reynolds also pursued a risky venture in Las Vegas as the owner of a hotel, casino, and movie museum in 1992. Here she performed in a 500-seat theater for several years, displayed her movie artifacts, and signed photographs of Kathy Selden while telling visitors, "I don't forget my fans. Once you commit that treason, it's over." This Vegas venture also failed by 1997, but around the same time, Reynolds had a successful appearance in *Mother* (1996) with Albert Brooks. Her daughter, Carrie Fisher, also became a successful actress, most notably in the *Star Wars* film series.[15]

Throughout her long life, Reynolds always remembered that *Singin' in the Rain* was the beginning, that Gene Kelly was instrumental in creating that beginning, and that she owed him a great deal in return. "*Singin' in the Rain* and childbirth were the hardest things I ever had to do in my life," she once said. "The pain from childbirth was in the lower body but in *Singin' in the Rain* it was everywhere—especially my feet and my brain." Most of this pain stemmed from the fact that she knew so little about moviemaking and had to learn quickly and well, but part of it also stemmed from Kelly's hard, driving personality. He pushed her because he fully realized how far she needed to go and how little time there was to get there. Reynolds resented it at the time, and spoke about her feelings in guarded but clear ways for several years to come.[16]

Yet, by the time Clive Hirschhorn researched his biography of Kelly, Reynolds was able to speak appreciatively of her mentor to him. "Gene taught me discipline, and he taught me how to slave," she told Hirschhorn. Later in her career, Reynolds admitted to being a perfectionist, and that Kelly had taught her that value. She was grateful to him. "But at the time I could have done without his perfection. And his temper." Reynolds also recalled in her memoirs, published a few years later, that Donald O'Connor confided to her why Kelly had yelled at him once on the set. Gene actually was frustrated with Debbie, but knew that she might collapse if he directed his anger at her. Yelling at O'Connor, who could take it and keep going, was his way of venting steam without endangering the production.[17]

Gene took Debbie's public comments about his temper and unrelenting work schedule in stride. His only public reaction to it was to interviewer Marilyn Hunt in 1975, when he remarked that Reynolds told the story of the making of *Singin'* in entertaining ways. He laughingly noted that Debbie's versions of some stories were not accurate. Nevertheless, he characterized her as hardworking and capable, but too inexperienced at the time to understand much of what he was trying to teach her. Kelly acknowledged that she grew a great deal as an actress in succeeding years and that he felt proud of her accomplishments and her tough work ethic. Several years after Kelly's death, Reynolds told an interviewer that she still hears Gene's voice at the back of her mind, saying, "Smile, Debbie! Give it more!" and she gives it "all I have to give. He was a great teacher."[18]

Stanley Donen's biographer has expressed exasperation with the fact that Reynolds spoke more admiringly and approvingly of Kelly as she grew older, for his book criticizes Kelly at every possible opportunity in order to enhance our view of Donen's career. But it was natural and noble of Reynolds to honor Kelly as she grew to understand more fully what he was attempting to do in 1951—not only to get a movie made, but to teach a green kid something that could serve as the bedrock of a lifetime of success in a tough business. Her public comments when news of Kelly's death circulated in February 1996 bear this out. "He made me a star in 'Singin' in the Rain,' he taught me how to dance and how to work hard, to be dedicated and yet still loving as he was to his family and friends."[19]

DONALD O'CONNOR

Gene Kelly's co-star continued his frenzied work schedule immediately after finishing *Singin' in the Rain.* Donald O'Connor's *Francis*

Goes to West Point was also released in 1952, followed by *I Love Melvin, Call Me Madam, Francis Covers the Big Town,* and *Walking My Baby Back Home,* all released in 1953. O'Connor continued with *Francis Joins the WACS* and *There's No Business Like Show Business* in 1954. He also conducted the premiere of his own symphonic composition entitled *Reflections d'un Comique* with the Los Angeles Philharmonic in 1956. O'Connor's frenetic pace reached a plateau of sorts when he made *The Buster Keaton Story* (1957). The movie was a commercial and critical failure, and O'Connor redirected his career more firmly toward television.[20]

O'Connor was a happy hoofer with a phenomenal work ethic. He seemed to thrive on nonstop appearances on the screen, on the stage, and on television. Looking back at his career, he was "most pleased" with the dances in *Call Me Madam,* partnering Vera-Ellen, but his favorite movie was *There's No Business Like Show Business.* O'Connor had a love-hate relationship with the most successful movie series he ever made, playing opposite a talking mule. "When you've made six pictures and the mule still gets more fan mail than you do, you start wondering," he confessed to an interviewer in 1980. "I thought it was ruining my career. But I was wrong. The Francis movies made more money than any of my other pictures."[21]

Ironically, O'Connor never cited *Singin' in the Rain* as his favorite film, nor the dances in it as his favorite numbers. He recognized the unique opportunity it gave him to work with Gene Kelly and learn from his experience, but O'Connor's career was on a divergent path from Kelly's. The question of why O'Connor never made another film with the superstar has often circulated among movie buffs. Freed thought of O'Connor as Kelly's dancing partner in *Brigadoon,* but O'Connor's M-G-M contract expired before the movie could be made and O'Connor was off to another project without looking back. Van Johnson, with less dancing talent than O'Connor, was brought in as his substitute.[22]

O'Connor also regretted that he did not have the opportunity to work again with Kelly. His contract with M-G-M did lead to one other movie besides *Singin',* which was *I Love Melvin,* made with Reynolds at a time when Kelly was in Europe. By the time Kelly returned, the opportunity to pair him with O'Connor had vanished. Nevertheless, "It was instant camaraderie between Gene, Debbie and me," O'Connor said when Kelly passed away in 1996. "Gene and I had a relationship like George

Burns and Jack Benny. We'd just look at each other and start to laugh." O'Connor admired Kelly enormously. "He could do anything and he was wonderful," he said of Gene in 2002, only a year before his own passing.[23]

Kelly also regretted that he did not make another movie with O'Connor. He told Hedda Hopper in 1954, "I've been trying to get a picture with Donald O'Connor ever since we worked together." Kelly commented on Donald's talent and especially his work ethic in several interviews over the years: "He never stopped working at his craft." "When I'd ask if he could do something—anything from dancing on his head to climbing walls—he'd say 'Sure.' I've seen him rehearse a step a thousand times." Kelly called O'Connor "not only a great dancer but also a great clown" and said "He was a great partner for me to work with."[24]

Some viewers continued to see evidence in *Singin' in the Rain* that O'Connor was a better dancer than Kelly, or they simply liked him better than his co-star. Mindy Aloff, a dance student, conducted a long interview with O'Connor in 1979. She admired the way he "visualized his entire dancing figure in the frame and paid attention to how his entire body would read on the screen." Aloff believed O'Connor was better than Kelly "in terms of allegre facility, offhanded elegance, or precision of stylistic detail in complex footwork." She also praised O'Connor as a dancer with "style, speed, lightness, elegance, rhythmic wit; he partnered his female co-stars with respect and charm; his line readings were understated and droll."[25]

The two men, however, never felt any sense of competition between them. O'Connor guest-starred on "The Gene Kelly Show," an episode of the *Pontiac Star Parade,* on November 21, 1959. It is easy to see the rapport they shared, even several years after the making of *Singin' in the Rain.* Both men appear to genuinely have fun working with each other, and this segment is one of the high points of both dancers' television careers.[26]

O'Connor's personal life hit trouble spots soon after he finished *Singin'.* His nine-year marriage to Gwen Carter became shaky as Gwen, frustrated that her own acting career was going nowhere, wanted a divorce. She began to date Dan Dailey, who was playing O'Connor's father in *There's No Business Like Show Business* at the time, creating a certain amount of tension on the set.

O'Connor began dating Gloria Noble, an actress at M-G-M, in 1954 and married her two years later. This marriage was for keeps, but not without its ups and downs. O'Connor's brother Jack died of a heart attack in the late 1950s, reminiscent of their father's death thirty years before. Not long after, O'Connor developed a dependence on alcohol that led to a health crisis, followed by a heart attack a few years later. A tough man, O'Connor pulled through these crises and resumed work, appearing in dozens of television shows and movies during the 1970s through the 1990s.[27]

Debbie Reynolds remembered Donald O'Connor as a "kind" man. He was widely known for his humility and his "easy-going" manners. "I'm basiclly [sic] a hoofer," O'Connor once said of himself, "a tap dancer. I was always very good from the waist down, moving with the feet, but I never had anything as far as line is concerned" until he worked with Gene Kelly, Robert Alton, and Louis Da Pron. O'Connor said that Kelly's ballet training led him to teach O'Connor to move the top part of his body as well. "Then I became what's known as a total dancer, using the entire body in order to express what you want to express." O'Connor understood himself very well, and he was fully aware that the public tended to recall only a handful of certain points in his long, eventful career. "People remember three things about me. A scene in a low-budget musical where [Peggy] Ryan and I are groping for a cherry in a dish of vanilla ice cream, Francis the Mule, and the 'Make 'Em Laugh' routine in 'Singin' in the Rain.'"[28]

O'Connor was an admirable figure in the making of *Singin'*, and in the general tone and sincerity of his entertainment career. He was a very practical performer who enjoyed the basics of his craft but seldom aspired to reach beyond those comfortable familiarities. Kelly had to draw the astounding performances in *Singin'* out of him; O'Connor never really tried to do that himself in other movies. He did a great deal of dancing in most of his films, but it tends to have rather mundane choreography. Only in some dances contained in *I Love Melvin* and *Call Me Madam* did O'Connor come remotely into the neighborhood of stellar performances like "Moses Supposes" and "Good Morning." Mostly, he was content to do the old routines, mixing a great deal of acrobatic fun into his routines so that they often, like "Make 'Em Laugh," became comedy stunts rather than dances. He seemed content to make a great deal of money dancing his way through potboilers that did not tax his talents too deeply. This was the real reason O'Connor did not take advantage of the exposure *Singin' in the Rain* offered him—he was happy being a second-level success.

Yet, O'Connor cherished his moment of glory in the best musical ever made. "Every so often I'll get it out to watch here at home in order to refresh my memory on some of the steps," he confessed to an interviewer late in life. He did a nightclub act and often was asked by audience members to perform "Fit as a Fiddle" and "Moses Supposes." "The idea that they think I can do it! It's wonderful." When pressed to name his favorite number from *Singin'*, O'Connor chose "Moses Supposes," because it "was so well planned out." He lived long enough to see the fiftieth anniversary release of the movie in DVD and thought it was "absolutely wonderful." It seemed like reliving the premiere of the movie all over again. A year after the half-century celebration of *Singin' in the Rain* was over, O'Connor died of heart failure at his home in Calabasus, California, on September 27, 2003.[29]

STANLEY DONEN

Stanley Donen and Debbie Reynolds had a "falling out" soon after the making of *Singin' in the Rain*. While making another movie, *Give a Girl a Break,* which was released in 1953, disagreements over how to choreograph the picture arose between Gower Champion and Bob Fosse. This escalated into a feud that divided the entire cast, with Reynolds taking Champion's side and director Donen siding with Fosse. This messy episode seems to have colored Donen's view of Reynolds for the rest of his life. In 1992, although Donen still labeled Reynolds as "adorable" in *Singin'*, he now said that she was "a royal pain in the ass" to work with in that movie. "She thought she knew more than Gene and I combined—she knew everything and we knew nothing. For what reason I don't know, but she was very difficult to manage and get to do anything. Nobody else on the picture gave us problems like that. Debbie was very dogmatic, very tough, a real bulldog of a little girl. She used to love the Girl Scouts. She was the leader of her Girl Scout troop, and I guess she was used to bossing people around."[30] However, there is no evidence to support Donen's contention that Reynolds caused trouble for anyone on the set of *Singin';* exasperation, yes, due to her lack of experience, but no bossy behavior. Apparently, forty years after the fact,

Donen remembered his relationship with her on the set of *Give a Girl a Break* and transposed the bad experience onto that of the previous movie.

In contrast, Reynolds had trouble remembering very much about Donen's presence on the set of *Singin'*, but she did give him credit for working to line up "all those great shots for our huge dance numbers." She thought of him as a mere technician who ran the film equipment while Kelly bore the weight of directorial duties. "Stanley just operated the camera, because Stanley didn't dance," she told Donen's biographer. When told that Donen had started his show business career as a chorus boy in *Pal Joey*, Reynolds replied, "I wouldn't have known he was a dancer. He didn't contribute in that fashion . . . his talent was stronger in other areas . . . camera, editing." Most people would agree with this assessment of Donen. In her memoirs, Reynolds reinforced this view by noting that Donen "handled the technical end, working with Gene in setting up the shots. Gene directed all the actors." At the same time, she noted that Kelly and Donen "worked very well together."[31]

Indeed, Donen's relationship with Kelly began very well and was particularly smooth in the making of *Singin' in the Rain*. As Joseph Casper has noted, their collaboration was not unlike that of Don and Cosmo, a close personal relationship as well as a professional collaboration. The two also appeared in a cameo in the picture *Love Is Better Than Ever*, which Donen directed just before *Singin'* began production. The movie was not released until February 1952 because of controversy over the politics of its star, Larry Parks. More evidence of their close working and personal relationship at the time is seen from the fact that Donen accepted Kelly's special Oscar award on his behalf in March 1952, because the star was in Europe at the time. "Kelly is the most stimulating person to work with I have ever known," Donen wrote in a short magazine article, published about the time of Kelly's Oscar award, and added, "He is constantly striving for new heights. He loves to work— and people love to work for him."[32]

This wonderful collaboration began to go sour with the making of another Comden-Green musical, *It's Always Fair Weather*, released in 1955. Comden and Green wanted to satirize television (much as they had satirized Hollywood), as well as to recreate the magic of *On the Town* by portraying the three sailors ten years later in their respective lives. Kelly and Donen were slated to co-direct, as they had done so effectively with *On the Town* and *Singin' in the Rain*. Frank Sinatra and Jules Munshin were not available to recreate their roles, however, and Kelly co-starred with veteran hoofer Dan Dailey and choreographer Michael Kidd, who was making his screen debut. The three sailors became three army buddies. *It's Always Fair Weather* remained a musical, but unlike *On The Town* there was little chemistry among the three stars and the story line about how their characters' lives descended into banality and wrecked dreams represented a dark departure from the norm in movie musicals. *It's Always Fair Weather* wound up being a good movie, in the end, with several spectacular dances, but making it was no easy matter for anyone involved.[33]

Similar to what happened on the set of *Give a Girl a Break,* the company of *It's Always Fair Weather* was rife with dissension. Donen and Kidd argued with Kelly on many matters related to the making of the picture, and Donen's biographer unwittingly provides information about their repeated sophomoric reactions to Kelly's attempts to direct the movie in serious and thoughtful ways.

Dailey remained aloof from it all, and Freed was preoccupied with his own affairs at this time, so Kelly had to deal with the antagonistic duo by himself, and to his credit, he insisted on doing the right thing no matter how unpleasant his colleagues made it for him. Ironically, Donen consistently told interviewers for decades to come, "I didn't really want to co-direct another picture with Kelly at that point. We didn't get on very well and, for that matter, Gene didn't get on well with anybody. It was the only picture during which the atmosphere was really horrendous." Donen seemed to have conveniently forgotten the bitter feud he was involved in on the set of *Give a Girl a Break* only two years before. He did say he liked many aspects of the finished product, most importantly Kelly's famous roller-skating dance entitled "I Like Myself." But Donen also said, "We had to struggle from beginning to end. I can only say it was an absolute one hundred per cent nightmare." He told interviewers he could not understand why the making of the movie was such a trauma or why people could not get along with each other. Yet, Donen's biographer mentioned that Donen "didn't believe in the project 100%" and was "aching to do his own thing."[34] Also, Donen was the only person involved in two feuds that were strikingly similar. And the irony is, that in this case at least, he was the one who could have very easily prevented any ill feelings.

Much of the animosity seems to have stemmed from the issue of whether a solo for Michael Kidd was good enough to remain in the film. Kidd was a gifted choreographer fresh from successes with *The Band Wagon* (1953) and one of the most impressive dances ever filmed, the barn-raising sequence of *Seven Brides for Seven Brothers* (1954), a movie that Donen directed. In fact, the two became close in working on that movie, and Donen "was eager to have" Kidd perform this role. But Kidd had never acted before and his screen presence left a lot to be desired. "Jack and the Space Giants," a ten-minute routine with three children in a kitchen, was at issue. In this number, Kidd told a story melding elements of Jack and the Beanstalk with modern space exploration, and demonstrated how he escaped being eaten by the giants by cooking a meal for them. After it was filmed, Kelly wanted to drop it. He explained that it had been planned as a professional courtesy for Kidd, because audiences did not know who he was, but the end result did not "come across—it didn't work out." Donen thought it was good enough to keep, although years later the best he could say of the sequence, "It wasn't terrible. It could have stayed in," amounted to no recommendation at all. Kelly eventually won this argument, and Kidd took it as a personal insult, vehemently criticizing Kelly as a dancer, actor, and person. Andre Previn, who wrote the ten-minute score for this number, was apparently disappointed that his effort had been in vain, and thoughtlessly attributed the cutting of the number to jealousy. Donen went much further and broke off his collaboration and friendship with Kelly for the rest of their lives.[35]

Ironically, the DVD release of *It's Always Fair Weather* includes the footage of "Jack and the Space Giants," and it is clear to even a casual viewer that Kelly was right, and in fact was very kind not to say all he could have to justify dropping it. The number is less of a dance and more of a comic shtick, with none of the comic genius of O'Connor, and a complete lack of chemistry between Kidd and the three children, who look as if they are being forced to stand around and watch Kidd make graceless and jerky movements from one steaming pot to another. No one, least of all Kelly, could be jealous of such a performance. Moreover, it was completely extraneous to the story line. Keeping it would not have helped the movie, and might even have hurt Kidd. An unbiased director ought to have seen that. In addition, Kelly had no trouble with the fact that the only duet involving himself and Cyd Charisse was dropped on the cutting-room floor as being unnecessary for the movie. Despite good dancing, it did not advance the plot. There was no rancor in Kelly's heart about either number; he wanted whatever was good for the picture.[36]

Kelly could not understand, or at least refused to express his views on, the rift between himself and Donen. While admitting "we didn't have a lot of fun" while making *It's Always Fair Weather*, Kelly nevertheless recalled that he and Donen worked very well with each other on the set.[37] For the rest of his long life, Kelly never said a cross or critical word about his former partner, in contrast to the virulent criticism heaped on him by both Donen and Kidd.

Donen went on to develop a long, full career as a director in his own right after *It's Always Fair Weather*. He married Marian Marshall in 1952, the year that *Singin' in the Rain* was released, and eventually married a total of five times, the last one ending in 1994. He was involved in at least forty-four movies, including his work as director, choreographer, and producer.[38]

So why did Donen continue his lifelong feud with Kelly? Although Kelly was a take-charge person, who had strong opinions and usually got his way, this does not seem to have hampered his interactions with Donen. On matters of direction and camera-work, they seemed to be exactly on the same page prior to *It's Always Fair Weather*. It is much more likely that Donen's fragile ego played a role, and some of Kelly's comments over the years may have fueled the rift. Donen became riled whenever Kelly referred to him in interviews as his former assistant, or took credit for helping to get Donen's directorial career started. Kelly once stated that "I was captain. I was the senior," when asked who was the dominant partner in the Kelly-Donen collaboration, and this blunt statement must have hurt the younger man's ego. In fact, Donen nurtured a deep resentment about his legacy the older he became, jealous of any publicized or spoken insinuation of Kelly's directorial work that involved a film he also worked on. Now and then, Donen was able to say nice things about his mentor, especially in terms of his extraordinary dancing performance, but he maintained that whatever he owed Kelly for his help in getting his own career started had been paid back, "ten times over. And he got his money's worth out of me."[39]

Kelly always acknowledged that he and Donen made a good team and that it had been advantageous for both of them. He offered a balanced assessment of Donen, and always showed his unwavering affection for his onetime protégé. He mentioned Donen's limitations ("Stanley was never a choreographer in the inventive sense"), but he also praised Donen's "critical faculty" and "great understanding of mood." Kelly admired Donen's ability to know "when a dance was right" for the camera's eye, and always referred to him as "a dear friend and trusted colleague." As late as 1988, he said that Donen "turned out to be one of the best things that happened to me professionally." And two years before his passing, Kelly even said of Donen, "He was like a son to me."[40]

Donen's views on Kelly and on *Singin' in the Rain* seemed to change with the tide. After his initial excitement in working with Gene, Comden, and Green, during the making of this movie, Donen seemed to develop reservations about the film that came to garner more attention than any of the pictures he directed alone. On viewing it again in 1968, he found it "creaky," and thought there were only four good things in the movie, namely, "Fit as a Fiddle," "Make 'Em Laugh," "Singin' in the Rain," and the sequence depicting the problems of early sound recording. He specifically referred to "Fit as a Fiddle" as O'Connor's number, revealing his continuing resentment against Kelly and his attempt to belittle Kelly's work. In 1983, he seemed to have regained a soft spot in his heart for the film, calling it "great fun, with an ingenuous script and some of the most wonderful performances in a musical." He also mentioned that one of the highlights for him was Charisse's vamp dance. Then, in 1992, Donen questioned the title of the movie, arguing shortsightedly that it had nothing to do with the weather but everything to do with moviemaking. "The title should have been *Hollywood*," he thought. He seemed to have forgotten that the title *Singin' in the Rain* vividly evokes the exuberance and joy of being in love.[41]

Moreover, Donen was uninterested in recreating the effective working relationship with Kelly that contributed to the success of *Singin' in the Rain*, but which foundered on the shoals of the ironically titled *It's Always Fair Weather*. His public comments on the man, who was in essence a father figure to him, continued to waver. In thanking six men for helping his career, when presented with an honorary doctorate from the University of South Carolina in his home state in 1989, Donen carefully avoided mention of Kelly. He gave credit to Roger Edens for fostering his directorial career at M-G-M rather than to Kelly. And yet, after his early mentor passed away in 1996, Donen wistfully said, "We have the films, but we've lost him. And we've lost the ability to thank him for giving us that. And that's our loss, that he's no longer here to be loved and appreciated." If this had been his final view of Gene, it would have put an end to the years of needless resentment and ingratitude. But Donen was very guarded in talking about Kelly when everyone else involved was effusive at the fiftieth anniversary celebration of *Singin' in the Rain*. And in a televised interview in 2006, he continued to ignore or downplay Kelly's achievements and his personal help to himself, said co-directing with Kelly was very difficult, and inflated the accounts of his own contributions in all their joint endeavors.[42]

A perpetual argument exists among students of the film musical as to the exact division of Kelly's and Donen's contributions to their collaborative efforts. It is on one level an academic discussion, for it is not easy to tease out contributions from a close collaboration; nor is it necessary to do so. Betty Garrett, who saw them work together on two pictures, *Take Me Out to the Ball Game* and *On the Town,* still could not answer that question "because they worked so closely together, and they seemed to think in the same direction." Jerome Delamater writes that "as Donen did little choreography on his own, one can hardly determine the nature of his input." But Delamater wisely notes that it is "probably unnecessary to discern or to determine who contributed what" in that collaboration. Contemporaries had an opinion on the issue, nevertheless. Musician Saul Chaplin called Kelly "the prime mover," and Donen "the eager and talented pupil," and said, "Stanley Donen, who had been a chorus boy in New York, owes his entire career as director to Gene." Kelly's ex-wife Betsy Blair wrote that Gene was "the central creative force in their initial collaboration," and that the two were "really good collaborators" on their films. She also noted that Gene "was always generous about Stanley's contribution." She was "surprised and bemused," and mystified as well, by Donen's being "less than gracious" about Gene's contributions and help. In contrast, some film historians assign far more credit to Donen for his contributions to the Kelly-Donen movies than contemporaries of the era in which they were made. For example, Donen's biographer writes as if *Singin' in the Rain* (as well as *On The Town* and *It's Always Fair Weather*) were solely the result of Donen's genius—as if Kelly did not direct these movies at all.[43]

There is no question that Kelly co-directed all three movies, and that he shouldered this burden in addition to his considerable acting and dancing responsibilities. To claim otherwise is not only untrue but poor scholarship. Moreover, as far as *Singin' in the Rain* is concerned, Debbie Reynolds has consistently related that Kelly directed the actors, and that she did not remember interacting with Donen at all. Donald O'Connor also recalled that Donen was "behind the scenes, he was never in front in any way." Kathleen Freeman, who played the diction coach Phoebe Dinsmore in the movie, recalled that people from all over M-G-M came to the set frequently and asked Gene if they could speak to him for a minute to share a personal story about the transition to sound, suggesting that most M-G-M employees viewed Kelly as the principal director.[44]

But it was even more complex than that. The camera-work for all the dances (which accounted for more than 60 percent of the movie) was worked out between both directors prior to filming. Moreover, evidence from the assistant director's reports for *Singin' in the Rain* indicate that in filming the dances, Kelly often stepped out of his starring role and took breaks to consult with his partner, and then the camera setup was adjusted to better film a particular shot. The reports also show that Kelly rode the camera boom to check out the planned camera angles for the dances. This high level of contribution was typical of Gene. For example, Leslie Caron talks of his extreme technical alertness and total involvement in camera movement for the musical numbers in *An American in Paris*. Finally, it is worth listening to what the co-directors had to say about this issue. Donen told interviewer Stephen Harvey in 1972 that he and Kelly "really worked as a team," that their partnership "was a collaboration. There was no question about it." Kelly too always acknowledged that he and Donen "were a good team. I thought we complemented each other very well." In view of the wide and varied evidence, it is clear that both Kelly and Donen deserve substantial credit for directing this masterpiece.[45]

GENE KELLY

Gene Kelly entered a pivotal era in his personal life and career right after finishing work on *Singin' in the Rain*. Without realizing it yet, he reached the pinnacle of his popularity. The critical and commercial success of *An American in Paris* and *Singin' in the Rain,* coming as they did back to back, gave him unprecedented clout with the executives at M-G-M and set up a host of possibilities and new directions in his career.

The superstar decided to leave the United States and work in Europe on a risky film that he had dreamed about for eleven years. His idea was to feature the work of dancers from different countries, performing in a variety of dance styles. He wanted it to be entirely a dance film, with no dialogue. The financial opportunity to produce the movie in Europe came about because the U.S. Congress had recently passed a law allowing an American citizen to work for up to eighteen months outside the country without paying income tax to Washington. M-G-M supported Kelly's plan but he had to agree to star in two M-G-M films to be made in Europe before he began to work on *Invitation to the Dance*. The setup was that Kelly would develop the scenarios for each part of *Invitation*, as well as choreograph and direct them. He would co-produce the picture with Arthur Freed through long-distance phone calls, telegrams, and letters. The M-G-M studio at Borehamwood, just north of London, would furnish the facilities.[46]

Kelly traveled to Europe in late February 1952, but events soon took a turn for the worse. He had straight acting roles in the two movies he starred in, and his performances were good. But both dramas, *The Devil Makes Three* (1952) and *The Crest of the Wave* (1954), were box-office disappointments. When *An American in Paris* swept the Oscars and the Academy gave Kelly a special Oscar for his multitalented contributions to movies (kind of an early "Lifetime Achievement" award), he was unable to be present in California to receive it or to rejoice with his collaborators on *An American in Paris*.[47]

Finally able to begin work on *Invitation* by August, Kelly encountered one problem after another as he tried to realize his dream. The studio facilities at Borehamwood were inadequate and the technical crew inexperienced at making dance films. He had almost no staff to help him handle the many logistical and planning difficulties involved in making such a film, and many of his dancers had never stepped in front of a camera before. Moreover, the executives at M-G-M, nervous at this risky and expensive venture, insisted that Kelly also star in each episode, burdening him with yet another role to play in a movie that became the closest example of an auteur film to be found in the musical genre. Even when Freed dispatched Lela Simone to help Kelly, the going was very rough. In the end, Kelly finished two episodes of the film before his time was out, forcing him to do the third, mostly animated, episode at the Culver City studio in 1953.[48]

Kelly's *Invitation to the Dance* presented a problem to the marketing department at M-G-M, for it did not know how to position an art film for general consumption. Kelly also became frustrated that the studio trimmed the picture and delayed releasing it. When finally made public in 1956, a full two years after the heavy animation work was finished, the film received mixed reviews from the critics. M-G-M slashed its promotional support, and the movie flopped at the box office.[49]

This film, which Kelly called "an homage to the dancers of the world," had taken him from the United States at a time when he could have enjoyed the fruits of his hard work in Hollywood. Its "failure" probably broke his heart, according to Betsy Blair. Ironically, even though Kelly was not yet aware of it, Betsy began to have affairs in Paris while he was making the movie in England. Twelve years younger than Kelly, and married to him when she was only seventeen, Blair felt she needed to grow and experience the world on her own but could not bring herself to confront her husband with this problem until 1956.[50]

Moreover, Kelly had to deal with some degree of discomfort regarding his previous and highly visible support for leftist causes that had identified him as a target of communist hunters in Hollywood. In fact, some writers have argued that a secondary reason for his decision to leave the United States in 1952 had been to avoid a second wave of persecution that seemed to be brewing by late 1951, when *Singin'* was being filmed. The first wave had culminated in the infamous Hollywood Ten hearings before the U.S. Congress in 1947, and Kelly had joined several organizations which sought to support the writers and producers who were targeted. Kelly was never a communist or socialist himself; he always identified his beliefs as landing solidly in the liberal Democratic mold. Like most other Hollywood figures who were criticized for their support of the Ten, he fought merely to protect freedom of thought and speech. The Ten mostly stood their ground before Congress, but all the major studios applied pressure on their stars, including Kelly, to stop their public support or lose their jobs. He also was a prime target of the Fact-Finding Committee on Un-American Activities of the California State Assembly headed by Jack B. Tenney. Kelly summed up his reaction to all this by writing, "It's a good old American custom to stand up and *disagree* with anyone we please."[51]

Commie-hunting in Hollywood took a hiatus until March 1951, a month before rehearsal for *Singin'* began, when the House Committee on Un-American Activities began its second round of investigations of Hollywood figures. The atmosphere of tension and fear was greatly intensified in December 1951, when J. B. Matthews published a controversial article in the *American Legion Magazine*. Matthews, a former socialist who had become a virulent anti-communist, asked the rhetorical question, "Did the Movies Really Clean House?" He listed everyone who had been suspected of working for left-wing causes in the first wave of investigation and pointed out that most of them were still active in the movie industry. Gene Kelly was prominent among them, and Matthews mentioned that his current project was *Singin' in the Rain*. He also mentioned *An American in Paris* and *Huck Finn*. The movie industry quickly caved in as nearly three dozen ex-communists named some 300 friends and acquaintances to satisfy investigators.[52]

By March 1952, just before *Singin'* was released and just after Kelly had gone to Europe, efforts began to "rehabilitate" those people who had "confessed" their sins and wished to work again in Hollywood. Roy Brewer, head of an important labor union for electricians in the movie industry, served as the most effective mediator in this process. Kelly seems to have consulted with him and offered public praise for the "anti-Commie position of the American labor movement" in a speech before the Film Council of the American Federation of Labor, soon after his return from England. This was taken as a sign that he had been rehabilitated and was no longer tainted with left-wing convictions.[53]

Kelly's political tribulations never hurt his popularity with movie audiences, but they troubled his sense of justice. He disliked being used by communists who participated in organizations he was a visible part of, without telling him of their true convictions, but argued that there was no real harm done by any of the card-carrying communists in Hollywood. He stoutly maintained that his working trip to Europe in 1952 was motivated solely by the tax law, not by a desire to avoid further exposure to a conservative political litmus test.[54]

Kelly's personal life reached a crisis in the years following the release of *Singin'*. Betsy continued to have affairs and although Kelly suspected she was being unfaithful, he decided to be patient and wait for her. When offered a plum role in *Marty* (1955), Blair was told she would have to write a letter to the American Legion explaining and apologizing for her left-wing political views. Kelly went to bat for her, demanding that Dore Schary intervene so she could avoid the humiliation of writing such a letter, and Schary did as Kelly asked. However, the marriage did not last. Blair admitted her affairs to Kelly in the summer of 1956. They separated and then were divorced the next year. Jeanne Coyne, who was a close family friend, soon moved into quarters at the Kelly home to help take care of Kerry, now a young teenager who adored her. Kelly married Jeanne in 1960, and they had two children, Tim and Bridget.[55]

Ironically, *Singin' in the Rain* became a milestone in Kelly's career in the minds of nearly every author who has written of his life, because they view it as the peak that presaged the fall. From the first biographer to the last, everyone sees Kelly's career as sliding into near oblivion after 1952. This is entirely unfair, for the superstar had an enormous reservoir of energy, talent, and creativity within him that he used on numerous other movie projects and a number of television performances for more than thirty years to come. Given that *Singin'* became recognized as the best movie musical ever made, by definition anything that followed it in Kelly's career would be something less; but that does not mean he stopped making meaningful contributions. After *Singin' in the Rain,* Kelly performed in seventeen more movies. He also starred in a television series, *Going My Way* (1962–1963), and performed in seventy-one television shows, all after *Singin' in the Rain.* As his dancing decreased, Kelly's other talents came to the forefront. He directed thirteen movies and produced seven others.[56]

"When I look at myself on the screen," Kelly once told an interviewer, "I'm never satisfied." The perfectionist in Gene relentlessly placed more demands on himself than on his partners or colleagues. As he grew older, Kelly often remarked that choreography was his "first love," and that he was "a teacher at heart." He continued to pursue his many dreams for the rest of his life. On television, as part of the Omnibus series, *Dancing: A Man's Game* (1958) offered him an opportunity to teach millions of viewers that dancing was not for sissies. "Many men make the mistake of confusing beauty of movement with effeminacy of movement," he explained, "and that's nonsense. . . . Every motion a good athlete makes is as beautiful as any a dancer makes." *Jack and the Beanstalk* (1967), a delightful television special with a great deal of animation, allowed Kelly to continue his interest in creating cinedances and won an Emmy. When Jeanne died in 1973, Kelly brought up his children alone and emerged in the following years as a sort of ambassador of dance culture in America. In his approaching older age, Kelly met and eventually married a producer of documentaries, Patricia Ward, who was more than forty years his junior. It was a controversial third marriage for Kelly, and it alienated him from many friends and family members. Suffering a series of strokes beginning in early 1995, Kelly passed away on February 2, 1996, at age eighty-three.[57]

GENE KELLY AND *Singin' in the Rain*

All writers have agreed that *Singin' in the Rain* represents the greatest artistic and commercial triumph of Kelly's long career. Clive Hirschhorn has argued that it set him up "as Hollywood's greatest one-man band . . . a quintuple threat as choreographer, director, dancer, actor and singer." For the rest of his life, Kelly's fans would focus on *Singin'* more than on any of his other numerous film and television projects. In fact, the heavy attention paid to what Kelly once referred to as "that old thing" began to wear a bit on his patience. It was not his favorite movie—that place belonged to *On the Town*—and he did not think he necessarily did his best dancing in *Singin'* either. It began to irk him that fans seemed at times to forget he had ever appeared in any other picture.[58]

The title number in *Singin'* became the most talked-of dance in Kelly's career. As Clive Barnes put it after his death, it was a "miraculously deft and daft" number that was "calculated to the degree of resembling an off-the-cuff improvisation of genius. That was the Kelly the camera will always remember and freeze in history."[59]

Of course, Kelly always maintained his patience when asked once again by fans or interviewers the inevitable questions about their most favorite movie. He developed an appreciation for its phenomenal success and never regretted the hard work he invested in the film. He could be droll about it at times, referring to "the crazy kind of foolery" to be seen in some of its numbers. "*Singin' in the Rain* was a picture that I liked doing very much," he commented in 1958, a sentiment he repeated several times in later years as well. He recognized that the title number was a good example of cine-dance, and felt proud of all his dancing in the film. Kelly recognized that this movie would last longer in public view than anything else he had ever done. He also took pride in helping Debbie Reynolds to start her career in entertainment, much as he had done for Leslie Caron in *An American in Paris,* and bristled at any suggestion that Reynolds had been forced on him by Louis B. Mayer. "That is patently untrue," Kelly once stated.[60]

Kelly was surprised whenever critics or film analysts read too much into his dances, especially "Singin' in the Rain." Recalling a conversation with a critic who had devised a number of complex interpretations as to why Don Lockwood was dancing in the rain, Kelly told him that it was far less complicated than that. He had always interpreted the number as very directly expressing the giddy emotions of a man who has just fallen in love. "I wanted to bring audiences back to their childhoods, when they would cavort in the rain even though their mothers would give them hell. . . . A fellow in love does silly things." For Kelly, the number was literally nothing more complex than a simple, genuine emotion expressed in five minutes of heartfelt dancing. He downplayed the artistry of this most memorable number of his career, and joked that only an old song-and-dance man could handle an umbrella so that it became an effective prop in a dance routine. *Singin' in the Rain* "was done with joy, and it brings joy," Kelly once told an interviewer, "That's what I always tried to do." Over the years, he consistently believed that "the purpose of a musical is to make people happy."[61]

Kelly found out fairly early how people all over the world felt about him and *Singin' in the Rain.* In June 1953, he and his family were invited to witness the procession leading to the coronation of Elizabeth II in London. The street was crowded and it began to rain as the Kellys made their way to the office of Jules Stein of the talent agency MCA. Suddenly, a man with a loudspeaker announced, "Now ladies and gentlemen, I'd like you all to join Gene Kelly in 'Singin' in the Rain.'" Someone connected a recording of the song to the loudspeaker, filling the street with its music. "A few seconds later," Kelly recalled after twenty years, "thousands of lovely, cold, wet, shivering Englishmen and women started to sing. It was the biggest thrill of my life. It beat anything I'd ever known. . . . and I felt if I never achieved another thing . . . I'd have justified my existence."[62]

This was the beginning, hardly more than a year after its release, of the movie's impact on Gene Kelly's life. He naturally incorporated many numbers from the film in his television shows throughout the 1950s and 1960s. In *Dancing: A Man's Game* (1958), Kelly did a vigorous tap dance routine to "The Broadway Melody" with boxer Sugar

Ray Robinson. In his first *Pontiac Star Parade* program, aired on CBS on April 24, 1959, Kelly was singing "You Wonderful You" when prop men off-camera threw a hat and umbrella his way and rain began to sprinkle on the sound stage. The audience began to applaud as Kelly grinned and started to do the number with gusto. He became thoroughly soaked as he went through a shortened version of the song and a toned-down dance accompaniment. In his second special for the *Pontiac Star Parade,* aired on NBC on November 21, 1959, "Singin' in the Rain" cropped up more than once. Donald O'Connor's entrance started with a reference to the tune as he joked that he was still drying out since the last time the pair worked together. He pretended to squeeze his lapel, accompanied by sound effects of water, and the two grinned at each other. Later in the hour-long program, Kelly and O'Connor sat down and tapped out a medley of the tunes widely associated with each man's dancing. Suddenly, O'Connor asked for a glass of water, ostensibly to quench his thirst, but he sprinkled it in Kelly's direction. Kelly said, "Not again," and O'Connor insisted and hummed the vamp that Roger Edens wrote for the song, "Do do do . . . ." Kelly began to tap quietly at first, but then finished the number vigorously, and with a smile, as the audience roared with applause.[63]

Kelly could not escape the famous number, and, despite his periodic frustration, reprised it repeatedly for years to come. When guest starring on *The Julie Andrews Show,* broadcast on November 28, 1965, he and Andrews began the program with a medley of "Singin' in the Rain" and "The Rain in Spain." The rain was really a curtain that sparkled and both performers carried umbrellas. Kelly was a guest on Johnny Carson's *The Tonight Show* at least three times, in 1975, 1976, and 1985, and every time the band played "Singin' in the Rain" as he walked on stage. At the end of his television special, *Gene Kelly: An American in Pasadena,* broadcast on CBS on March 13, 1978, Kelly's thirteen-year-old daughter Bridget handed him an umbrella before he performed a brief version of the song and ended the show with "You Are My Lucky Star." Kelly's reluctance to reprise "Singin'" yet another time was well known in Hollywood. When he guest-starred on *The Muppet Show* in 1980, the writers worked this reluctance into the show. By the end of that episode, however, Kelly, at age sixty-eight, was "persuaded" by his cloth-bound and insistent co-stars to reprise a few lines of "Singin'" and walk with an umbrella across a wet stage that recreated the "Singin'" set.[64]

In England, Kelly's fame remained as strong as in the United States since his sojourn at Borehamwood to make *Invitation to the Dance*. In the early 1970s, The Roundhouse at Chalk Farm held a festival of his musicals one Saturday, ending late in the evening with *Singin' in the Rain*. Kelly made an unannounced appearance right after the movie ended, doing a time step to "rapturous applause." In some ways, Kelly seemed to feel more open before an English audience. On May 27, 1980, Variety Club Tent 36 hosted a luncheon in London for Kelly to raise money for charity. He was escorted in "by an umbrella honor guard," and watched clips from his films. Kelly reportedly said that he "had to sit through so many reruns of 'that number' ['Singin' in the Rain'] that 'I can't enjoy it anymore—but I enjoyed it today.'" He never spoke so pointedly on this issue before a public gathering in the United States.[65]

While Kelly felt some exasperation about the public's obsession with "Singin' in the Rain," he never let it override his sense of gratitude that he had the opportunity to touch so many people's lives with such a simple dance number. The American Film Institute honored Kelly with its Thirteenth Annual Life Achievement Award in 1985. Donald O'Connor, Debbie Reynolds, Cyd Charisse, Betty Comden, and Adolph Green performed "You Are My Lucky Star" as an homage to Kelly. Comedian Steve Martin brought the house down with an unexpected joke about the making of Kelly's most famous number. He claimed to know Kelly better than anyone in the audience (which included nearly all surviving members of Kelly's family and Fred Astaire), and then proceeded to tell a story about how he had offered advice to Kelly and Donen when they were frustrated by continual rain showers that were holding up the filming of one of their co-directed pictures. He told them to go ahead and film the number anyway. When Kelly asked him what to do about the lamppost that was in the way, Martin told him to jump on it. Keeping the audience glued to every word, Martin ended his joke by announcing that the number was filmed for *On the Town* and was later cut from the release print, and neither director ever spoke to him again.[66]

But the AFI salute ended with the most poignant statement Kelly ever made about *Singin' in the Rain* and its title number. When George Stevens Jr. presented the award to Kelly, the band played "Singin'" as his signature tune. Kelly graciously accepted the award with a modest story about how his only ambition as a youngster had been to play shortstop for the Pittsburgh Pirates. But his life had taken him in a different direction entirely. Referring to the many clips that had been shown during the ceremony, he ended by saying, "And you know, that's what you do up there, you dance love, and you dance joy, and you dance dreams, and I know if I can make you smile by jumping over a couple of couches, or running through a rainstorm, then I'll be very *glad* to be a song and dance man."[67]

Kelly's public appearances dwindled after the AFI salute, but his mind remained active. Before sending a shipment of more than 200 song sheets to his personal papers in Boston, he wrote cryptic messages on many of them. One of the song sheets was entitled, "Gene Kelly— Favorite Film Hits" and included almost all the songs from *Singin' in the Rain*. It was saved from the fire that destroyed his house at Christmastime in 1983 and has singe marks. "Saved from the Fire!" he wrote on the cover, and "Can't find this anymore—." On the cover of the song sheet for "Singin' in the Rain," Kelly wrote, "What can I say?—GK." Kelly's last public appearance was at Dodger Stadium on July 16, 1994, to attend a Three Tenors concert. Placido Domingo, Jose Carreras, and Luciano Pavarotti sang "Singin'" "with much goodwill but surprisingly little understanding," according to English biographers Morley and Leon. Yet Kelly stood and waved his appreciation at the audience before going home.[68]

After Kelly's death, local efforts to honor one of Pittsburgh's most famous sons began. A committee of twenty people chose local sculptor Susan Wagner to create a bronze statue of Kelly swinging from the lamppost in the "Singin'" number, surely one of the most famous images of the dancer and of any movie musical. It was to be fourteen feet tall and would cost half a million dollars. After some controversy, the chosen location was the end of the broad median on Liberty Avenue, a downtown street close to the waterfront. Controversy also developed over the rendering as Wagner's past work was somewhat limited in scope and not universally liked. The latest word is that efforts to realize the dream to honor Pittsburgh's famous son continue behind the scenes.[69]

The fiftieth anniversary of *Singin' in the Rain* brought the surviving cast members and crew together in spirit, and their commentary was suffused with memories of Gene Kelly and heartfelt tributes to him. Debbie Reynolds, now seventy years old, could admit that she knew very little about dancing or moviemaking half a century before and had felt "very insecure and frightened that I wouldn't be able to keep up" with her two co-stars. Reynolds praised Kelly as "the mastermind of the picture" upon whose shoulders rested the film's success or failure. Admitting that Kelly was "exacting, highly disciplined, and demanding," Reynolds accepted that this "was his way, which, well why not, he was only the greatest, so it should be his way." Reynolds had by now passed through her resentment at Kelly's demands on her limited talent at the time, as well as the fact that he had never praised her efforts in rehearsal. "He would come in," Reynolds said in 2002, "watch my rehearsals, and say 'work harder.' And I wanted so much to prove to him that I could pull this off. So, I worked harder." She was grateful for the chance to work on *Singin'* and for the opportunity "to work under the tutelage of Gene Kelly," to "learn from such a determined, powerful, and gifted man. He taught me an incredible work ethic. And after all these years it lives on. So thank you, Gene."[70]

Cyd Charisse called Kelly "absolutely brilliant" and "terribly talented," a perfectionist who "knew just what he wanted. He didn't want to hear no, he always said that's the way it's going to be and that's the way it is. And he was right." Donald O'Connor praised Kelly as a "great director," and talked about how he accommodated everyone's style in dancing or acting. O'Connor "gurned" one last time on screen, saying, "Here you are, Gene!" Stanley Donen managed to curb his resentment long enough to say that the tensions he and Kelly experienced probably resulted in better movies, but he did not specifically indicate that any tensions had surfaced during the filming of *Singin'*. He did not claim for himself, nor did he allow Kelly to be accorded, "full credit" for their collaborative directorial efforts.[71]

But perhaps the most poignant statement made by anyone among the gathered alumni of *Singin' in the Rain* in 2002 was uttered by Kathleen Freeman, who played the diction coach Phoebe Dinsmore in the picture. Speaking of the title number, which she watched being filmed, Freeman called it "brilliant stuff," and enthused, "you can still see that thing after all these years and get the same elation, the same excitement. And we've got it—for however long this stuff holds out. How grand, how wonderful." And finally, "The dance that he does is not even about dance, it's about love. And he was *magical!*"[72]

10 Legacy

The impact of *Singin' in the Rain* on American popular culture grew over the course of half a century following its initial release in 1952. Its exposure and fame grew steadily until the movie began to be cited as among the best, and then finally the best, of Hollywood's musical films.

Six years after the initial release, M-G-M rereleased *Singin'* with other musicals as a "classics package" in 1958. The movie garnered more fans with the advent of each new generation, and the spread of color television sets in the mid-1960s gave average viewers an opportunity to catch a glimpse of its original glory in their own living rooms.[1]

For those who preferred to see the movie on the big screen, many theaters ran festivals of old musicals for their clientele, especially after *That's Entertainment* was released in 1974. *That's Entertainment* sought to highlight the legacy of M-G-M musicals by presenting excerpts from them in a feature-length film intended for screenings in movie-houses across the country. The picture started with four different filmed versions of the song "Singin' in the Rain," as performed by Ukulele Ike and the M-G-M dancers in *The Hollywood Revue of 1929*, Jimmy Durante in *Speak Easily*, Judy Garland in *Little Nellie Kelly*, and Gene Kelly, Donald O'Connor, and Debbie Reynolds in the title scene of *Singin' in the Rain*. Frank Sinatra hosted the first segment of *That's Entertainment*, and pronounced *Singin'* to be the best musical ever made. In addition, Kelly hosted a segment on Fred Astaire, O'Connor hosted a segment on Esther Williams, and Reynolds hosted a segment which included an excerpt from "Make 'Em Laugh." Astaire hosted the segment devoted to Kelly's work, featuring excerpts from seven numbers and ending with the entire sequence of Kelly in "Singin' in the Rain." Astaire called it "a classic routine that audiences would never forget" and identified the dance as his favorite number in the movie.[2]

Inspired by the popularity of *That's Entertainment,* the MGM Theater in Westwood hosted a series of fifty-two films in December 1974, with each movie running a full week. *Singin' in the Rain* was the second in the series. It also ran for a week at Radio City Music Hall in New York during the month of May 1975. Vincent Canby of the *New York Times* rejoiced that this "extraordinarily exuberant, always youthful, joyously indestructible musical" was once again in the theater. Canby admitted that he had seen the movie half a dozen times since it was made. "I've seen it in fancy first-run theaters, in dumpy last-run theaters, on a 16-millimeter projector in the apartment of friends, in a shoebox-shaped theater in Paris with French subtitles. Most recently I watched it as I sat hunched up and freezing in a peculiarly air-conditioned New York screening room." Calling it an "original," he argued that "enjoying 'Singin' in the Rain' has nothing to do with nostalgia or with sentimentality. It is, simply stated, a Hollywood masterpiece."[3]

The success of *That's Entertainment* led to the making of *That's Entertainment II* in 1976. Instead of a series of hosts, this second installment was hosted entirely by Astaire and Kelly, who danced together for the second and last time in their careers. The movie highlighted "Good Morning" and included excerpts of the montage in *Singin',* which were shown in black and white to illustrate the 1920s era. *That's Entertainment II* also highlighted Cyd Charisse's vamp dance with Kelly in "The Broadway Ballet."[4]

From the mid-1970s on, fans increasingly named *Singin'* their top choice among musicals. When the first VHS edition of *Singin'* was issued in 1983, Rex Reed explained this by noting that M-G-M musicals were made to entertain, not to send socially relevant messages to their audiences, and *Singin'* did this better than any others. The movie "does not insult or compromise its audience," Reed continued. It represented "real moviemaking, real talent and sophistication at work." Because it was "timeless," *Singin'* had become "a motion-picture classic."[5]

The fiftieth anniversary of the movie led to a digitally renovated version of the film being shown at the Academy of Motion Picture Arts and Sciences in Hollywood in September 2002. A reunion of the cast and crew was also held at the same time, with Debbie Reynolds, Donald

O'Connor, Cyd Charisse, and Rita Moreno in attendance. The same digitally restored version was shown at the Film Forum in New York on November 15, 2002, and at the Egyptian Theater in Hollywood in December, with Arthur Freed's daughter, Barbara Saltzman, introducing the film to the audience.[6]

The international distribution of *Singin' in the Rain* took place in stages over a long period of time. It had been released to eight countries in 1952 and five the following year. The movie was rereleased in Finland in 1964 and again in 1988. Denmark saw a rerelease in 2000, Japan in 2003, and France in 2006. The title of *Singin' in the Rain* was translated into a variety of languages as a result of its international distribution. French-speaking residents of Belgium, Canada, and France knew it as *Chansons sous la pluie,* while German-speaking audiences responded to *Du sollst mein Glucksstern sein.* In Finland, the popular movie was called *Laulavat sadepisarat;* in Portugal, it was *Serenata a Chuva;* in Spain, *Cantando bajo la lluvia;* and in Denmark it was *Syng I sol og regn.* It is difficult to know how many of these countries recorded a dialogue track in their own language, but the French-language version is not very successful. Some of the dialogue was not translated well. Moreover, the woman who dubbed Lina Lamont could not reproduce her squeaky voice and sounds almost normal, thus eliminating a major element of the premise as well as the enjoyment of the movie.[7]

The most unusual international distribution of *Singin' in the Rain* involved cold war politics. The U.S. International Communication Agency selected ten American films for viewing in China as part of the implementation of the U.S.-Chinese Cultural Agreement signed in 1979. The agency wanted to offer movies representing different genres that were popular in the United States and linked to "the span of time during which the Chinese didn't see American films." The Chinese government, however, retained the right to choose from among the ten films. It viewed prints of them and passed on such pictures as *To Kill a Mockingbird* (1962), *On the Waterfront* (1954), and *Patton* (1970), but chose *Singin', The Black Stallion* (1979), *Shane* (1953), *Snow White and the Seven Dwarfs* (1937), and *Guess Who's Coming to Dinner* (1967).[8]

The five films were shown in festivals in Beijing and four other cities from May 6 to July 14, 1981. The president of the Academy of Motion Picture Arts and Sciences led an American delegation, which included Cyd Charisse, to open the first festival. In exchange, a slate of Chinese films was scheduled to tour American cities in the fall of that year. Critics pointed out that the Chinese wanted to avoid movies that contained sex and violence, and that most of the five films were quite old already by 1981. They also noted that "pirated prints of American musicals such as 'Singin' in the Rain' have reportedly been circulating in China for years." Given the subordination of art to political purposes under Mao's regime, *Singin'* was probably puzzling yet also a breath of fresh air for Chinese viewers. As one Chinese official told a comrade, "That was made just for fun," after the pair finished seeing *Singin' in the Rain* with Chinese subtitles.[9]

The picture also rose steadily in international rankings as the decades rolled by. Only one critic listed *Singin' in the Rain* for inclusion in *Sight and Sound* magazine's Top Ten movies list in 1962. Ten years later, five critics listed it. After the pivotal exposure accorded the film in *That's Entertainment,* seventeen critics promoted *Singin'* for the Top Ten list in 1982, and the movie was ranked number four on that list beginning that year. It was superseded by *Citizen Kane* (1941), *La Regle du jeu* (1939), and *The Seven Samurai* (1954), suggesting how difficult it was for a musical to make headway among the weighty fare normally filling such lists. By 1998, the American Film Institute ranked *Singin'* the number one film musical of all time, and the tenth best movie of any genre ever made. The institute also ranked the title song as the third best song in movie history, behind "Somewhere Over the Rainbow" from *The Wizard of Oz* (1939) and "As Time Goes By" from *Casablanca* (1942). By 2000, the institute ranked *Singin' in the Rain* as the sixteenth funniest movie of all time, and two years later as the sixteenth most passionate movie as well. It rated *Singin'* the fifth best movie of all time in 2007.[10]

An online rating system available on the Internet Movie Database led 32,161 fans to record their evaluation of *Singin'.* Almost 40 percent of them rated it ten out of a possible ten points. Altogether, more than three-fourths of those voting ranked the movie as an eight or above. Positive voting was consistent across all categories of age and gender. The continuing international appeal of *Singin'* is also apparent. As recently as 2007, when the monsoon rains hit west central India, *The Times of India* listed "Singin' in the Rain" as number one among its choice of five best "rain songs."[11]

The surviving cast members came to be almost baffled by the

incredible popularity of their movie as the twenty-first century arrived. Donald O'Connor remarked, "It's incredible that it's become like a cult movie." Betty Comden expressed some surprise "with the enormity of its fame and the acclaim that its [sic] gotten in all kinds of circles." Kathleen Freeman recalled that everyone considered it a special project because of all the talent assembled to make it. But, "I don't think there was anybody in it who considered it the greatest American musical ever made. They were doing that kind of work called, 'this is a joyful piece, let's do it.'"[12]

FILM SCHOLARS

Given its quality and highly visible place in public view, film scholars from about the 1970s began to pay attention to *Singin' in the Rain*. Rick Altman has divided the musical film into three subgenres. The Show Musical "involves the spectator in the creation of a work of art," while the Fairy-Tale Musical "creates a utopian world like that of the spectator's dream." Finally, the Folk Musical "projects the spectator into a mythicized version of the cultural past." Peter Wollen believes that *Singin' in the Rain* contained important elements of all three categories.[13]

Other film students have pointed out the fundamental importance of song and dance to the success of any musical, and those songs and dances need to be varied so as to express strength, love, and ensemble performances in different numbers. As Timothy Scheurer has put it, film musicals need "a balanced yet varied score." *Singin' in the Rain* has all these varied moods expressed in its diverse numbers. Of course, variety tends to negate unity of story and plot, and there is always a tension in musical films between storytelling and vigorous entertainment on the dance floor. Gene Kelly wanted both in order to create a vibrant string of varied dances and to tell a coherent story as well, and achieved that purpose probably better in *Singin'* than in his other pictures. Even so, as Peter Wollen has put it, "his films were about dance, not about drama."[14]

In attempting to analyze the popularity of *Singin'*, Jeanine Basinger has noted "its genuinely funny and undated comedy plot," the "richly varied musical numbers," and its "satiric core, a hilarious (although loving) spoof of the transition-to-sound period in Hollywood." Most film critics agree wholeheartedly with these points. Of all the elements, perhaps the most unique feature of *Singin'* is the self-reflexive nature of the plot line. Judy Gerstel has called it "presciently postmodern" because of its "slyly subversive and deliciously entertaining" deconstruction of the process of filmmaking. *Singin'* explored "the medium's preposterous artifice" in a way that failed to destroy the viewer's faith in that artifice, a remarkable achievement by any standard of measurement. And the reason is not difficult to see; it lies in the movie's obvious love for its subject, its tongue-in-cheek quality of not taking itself or Hollywood too seriously. A reviewer in *The Times* of London, no less, compared "the self-conscious attempt at art" found in *An American in Paris* with *Singin' in the Rain*'s light style. The latter film was done "with affection not affectation." It "never forgets that it's about snappy entertainment—its [*sic*] serious about being funny." For this, and other reasons, *Singin' in the Rain* "actually improves with age," as Rudy Behlmer has put it.[15]

Sometimes ignoring their own point about the success of *Singin'* being largely dependent on its lightheartedness, many film scholars have probed relentlessly to interpret every nuance of its writing and filming. Some have noted similarities between it and the story of Hans Christian Andersen's *The Little Mermaid,* wherein the heroine's voice is stolen by a witch, thus preventing her from marrying her prince until a solution to the dilemma is found. In this scenario, Lina Lamont is the witch who appropriates Kathy Selden's voice until upstaged by Kathy's Prince Charming.[16]

Other scholars have made much of the use of color in *Singin' in the Rain*. Judy Gerstel has noted that white symbolizes "dissembling and falseness," from Lina's bleached blond hair to flashy white costumes worn by her and Don at the premiere of *The Royal Rascal,* to the "extravagant white costumes" worn in the period silent movies themselves. This "chilly, vapid whiteness is a stark contrast to the vivid blue and golden yellow of the opening credits, the colors that throughout the movie connote high spirits, imagination, and sincerity triumphing over fakery, cunning, and gloom." Joseph Casper believes that the colors in all the major dance numbers contribute to this scheme. The "colors move, along with the action, camera, and cutting, to the music's beat."[17]

Christopher Ames has dwelled on the ironies inherent in the dubbing theme of *Singin' in the Rain,* noting this was probably the first indepth exploration of the topic in any movie plot. Ames writes that the viewer is given a foreshadowing of this important element when a guest at Simpson's premiere party assumes someone is standing behind the movie screen, talking, as the sound picture demonstration proceeds, and the movie ends with Kathy singing behind the curtain for Lina. It is true that the film has a "slippery attitude toward the falseness of dubbing." The plot sends up Lina Lamont as a bad guy for indulging in it to fool her fans, while Cosmo, Don, and Kathy are heroes for using it to save the team of Lockwood and Lamont. Ames has also pointed out that Lina's desire to use Kathy for her own needs was more consistent with reality in Hollywood, where dubbing was an accepted fact of life for many decades, than was Simpson's initially high-minded refusal to go along with such a scheme.[18]

Ames misses an important point, however, when he argues that the slippery attitude toward dubbing in the movie is never resolved.[19] The point was that Don, who initially was like Lina, improved as a character as he fell in love with Kathy. In fact, he did not want her to do any dubbing at all, for fear she would lose her own chance at a career in the movies, and had to be talked into it. Near the end of the movie, Don refused to go along with Lina's selfish desire to keep Kathy as a sort of dubbing slave, and that is the reason Lina was exposed and run out of town in ridicule. Dubbing itself was not the issue, but treating people in a moral way. (Whether that was true of the real Hollywood is another issue.)

Dubbing is at the heart of the postmodernist interpretation of *Singin' in the Rain*. Based on an idea that words and truth are relevant, not only to each individual but to any given point in time, postmodernism makes of the world a scattering of temporary and loosely related personal experiences. "Dubbing, here, represents the cinematic form of writing," Peter Wollen asserts, "through which sound is separated from its origin and becomes a potentially free-floating, and thus radically unreliable, semantic element."[20]

Wollen has also tried to interpret *Singin' in the Rain* within the context of the second wave of the Red Scare in Hollywood, convinced as many British writers are that Gene Kelly fled the United States to escape political persecution immediately after making the movie. He notes that "the story hinges on the thwarting of a plot to blacklist Kathy Selden, launched by an informer and enforced by using the media to pressure a weak-willing studio, which ultimately puts profit before principle."

Wollen even sees the potential for political interpretation of the title number, suggesting it "represents Kelly's determination to be optimistic in a miserable political climate, insisting that he may have behaved in an unorthodox, uninhibited way, but that basically he is joyous and generous and American whatever the law may think as it holds him in its disapproving gaze."[21]

SONGS AND DANCES

The songs and dances that grace *Singin' in the Rain* are a major attraction of the picture. "This happy movie floats on music from beginning to end," wrote Tony Thomas of *Singin'*. Many of the dances which that music accompanies are "of such breathtaking complexity that dancers the world over" have studied them ever since. The quality of each dance number, carefully crafted as "emotional exclamations and flourishes evolving naturally from exuberance, tenderness, desire, and sheer joie de vivre," mark *Singin' in the Rain* as an unusually successful marriage of dance, song, music, and plot. As John Mariani put it, "only a very few musicals are as well integrated as *Singin' in the Rain*—and none is funnier or more literate." Casey Charness believes that the exceptional quality of the dance routines help to make *Singin'* "a thoroughly American picture."[22] That is, the movie uses cinematic dancing to create and increase international awareness of an exuberant American spirit in American-made movies in the early years of the cold war.

Given the widespread view that the dance routines in *Singin'* are of exceptional quality, commentators have often focused their attention on them during the past half century. "Make 'Em Laugh" stands out as the exemplar of comedy married, however furtively, to dance. It "remains the most hilarious routine ever recorded on film," according to Rusty E. Frank. Some film students have recognized that the apparent plagiarism of this song by Freed and Brown tainted its luster, or that it played an "inglorious finale" to "Brown's impressive career as a pioneer songwriter for movie musicals." But most writers have ignored this issue much in the same way that Cole Porter ignored it, and continued to cite "Make 'Em Laugh" as "a brilliant and frantic piece of comic dancing" that represents a "dance *tour de force*" of film history. It marked O'Connor as a major talent in screen dancing in the eyes of most commentators.[23]

The big, impressive ballet in *Singin' in the Rain* garnered a lot of attention as well. The number did not come away unscathed. Some commentators have argued, along with Kelly and Donen, that it is too long. Others believe it is a bit too much, in every way, for the average viewer to take, but most writers have praised the ballet. Basinger calls it a "slightly more coherent and accessible" dance routine than the ballet in *An American in Paris*.[24]

The ballet is so complex that elements of it can easily be singled out for exceptional quality, or criticism. The "Crazy Veil Dance," for example, has been cited by Basinger as "a lyrical and moving passage, beautifully danced and delicately designed." Walter Terry was also very much moved by this sensual number and its cine-dance qualities, as discussed in Chapter 8. In contrast, John Russell Taylor and Arthur Jackson have criticized Kelly's "attempts" at "the proper soulful expression for 'serious dance,'" and Charness has called it "the only sour note in the ballet."[25] Divergent judgments such as these for the same dance number are inevitable when choreographers and dancers attempt to push the envelope of popular dance toward deeper expression.

Overall, however, nearly everyone agrees that "The Broadway Ballet" works as a whole. Even Charness thought the ballet "perhaps best exemplifies the principles of cine-dance" among the movies co-directed by Kelly and Donen, because it was "conceived entirely by, for, and with camera." The execution of that conception succeeded admirably. "Both dance and film are balanced, and each technique is pushed to the extreme of excellence."[26]

Among the many fine dances in *Singin' in the Rain*, the title number rightfully garnered more attention from film critics, students, and fans alike. Nearly all of them agree that it is Kelly's ultimate film dance. As John Cutts has written, it's "a minor classic of its kind. A thing of beauty, lyric grace, joyous communication and overwhelming appeal." Clive Hirschhorn, Kelly's first biographer, has termed the number "the apotheosis of his art and the climax of an adventurous career," while composer Leonard Bernstein has called it "a reaffirmation of life."[27]

Freed's lyrics and Brown's music add immeasurably to Kelly's triumph in this number. The song asserted "the power of one's outlook to overcome external obstacles," which Ames believes has been "a significant theme in American popular culture." Kelly provided the right physical expression of that optimism in his choreography. Basinger has pointed out that nearly everyone imagines doing what Kelly did, cavorting unconcernedly in a downpour. "The sight of a happy man skipping on the sidewalk, climbing a lamppost, letting a drainpipe of rainwater cascade on his face and jump around in puddles is a sight marvelous to behold," writes Tony Thomas.[28]

The release of the *Singin' in the Rain* DVD package in 2002 enables us to hear the playback Gene Kelly prerecorded for the number. In listening to it with nothing but an orchestral accompaniment, no sound effects and no visuals, one realizes it still is a great performance. Although he often denigrated his own singing talent, Kelly sings this song with so much genuine joy in his heart that it is a true expression of happiness and love even without the dance.[29]

Many commentators have argued that "Singin' in the Rain" is "the most famous solo dance number ever put on film." They praised the fluid choreography, the seamless camera-work, and the simple but highly effective set design. It may well have presented "the optimism and innocence of postwar America," but even by the turn of the twenty-first century, reviewers called it "sublime cinema," demonstrating how timeless is the number's appeal.[30]

The Freed-Brown songs included in *Singin' in the Rain* continued to have exposure in future movies after 1952. "Temptation" appeared in five movies, as well as in the first episode of *The Muppet Show* in 1976. "All I Do Is Dream of You" was used in *The Affairs of Dobie Gillis* (1953) and in *The Boy Friend* (1971). "Make 'Em Laugh" appeared in a Spanish movie titled *Boca a boca* (*Mouth to Mouth*) in 1995. "I've Got a Feeling You're Fooling" was used in *Blue Cat Blues* in 1956, and "Should I?" found its way into *The Subterraneans* in 1960. "You Were Meant for Me" appeared in five movies from 1953 to 1999, but "Good Morning" appeared in only one film, *Wonder Boys,* in 2000. "Singin' in the Rain" was used in no fewer than eleven movies after 1952, and at least one television episode (*Fame,* in 1983). In contrast, "The Broadway Melody" appeared in only one more movie, in 1992, and "Broadway Rhythm" was used in two films released in 1953 and 1954. "You Are My Lucky Star" was used in *The Boy Friend* (1971), *New York, New York* (1977), and *Somebody, or The Rise and Fall of Philosophy* (1989).[31]

While all of these moviemakers utilized the Freed-Brown songs in innocuous or respectful ways (and probably had the idea to do so only because they became famous in *Singin' in the Rain*), Stanley Kubrick used

"Singin' in the Rain" as the background music of a horrible sequence in *A Clockwork Orange* (1971) that depicted violent rape and mutilation. Why and how M-G-M or Freed allowed this to happen is unclear, but Kubrick invited Stanley Donen (with whom he had formed a friendship in Europe) to view the sequence before the movie's release and asked if it offended him. Apparently, Donen was nonplussed by the gratuitous violence, saying it "didn't affect the movie *Singin' in the Rain*," and therefore he did not care how the song was used. Kubrick told Donen that he had filmed the sequence without the music, but added it later to show that the main character "was very happy," in Donen's words, while he committed this horrible crime. The incident indicates that both Kubrick and Donen failed to respect what made the "Singin' in the Rain" song and dance by Kelly so magically appealing to people—touching as it did a common chord of love and uplifting joy. Everyone who has expressed an opinion on Kubrick's use of the song has done so with a tone of outrage or befuddlement. For instance, Comden and Green bemoaned that this joyous, life-affirming song was "devastatingly and chillingly used" to depict "mindless violence," while Peter Hay called its use in Kubrick's film "bizarre" and "an aberration."[32]

CHARACTERS

Commentary on the characters in *Singin' in the Rain* has naturally focused on two salient roles. Don Lockwood appears to some writers as somewhat like the character Serafin that Gene Kelly created in *The Pirate*. Joseph Casper has noted that both roles incorporate the typical actor's narcissism and insecurity with "the prankishness at the heart of every man." Casper also believes Kelly drew on and "spoofs his own personality" in creating both characters. Lina Lamont also drew commentary from various writers over the years. Tony Thomas referred to her as the "horrible-voiced" villain, while Judy Gerstel thought "Jean Hagen plays Lamont as Judy Holliday with PMS."[33]

GOOFS AND GAFFES

Initially, no one paid attention to the fact that, although a masterpiece of its kind, *Singin' in the Rain* contains a number of technical errors. As the picture became famous and more people saw it repeatedly, they began to notice little mistakes that only endeared the movie to them rather than detracted from their enjoyment of it. In fact, there is a cottage industry in tabulating these interesting mistakes, which range from lapses in continuity and editing problems to illogical scenes and "deliberate" goofs. Some errors overlap several categories.

Among the lapses of continuity that have been noted by film buffs is the fact that the string on Cosmo's violin bow breaks in "Fit as a Fiddle," and it is easy to see it flapping as he moves. Yet in the next scene, it is magically fixed. Another example is that in the jalopy ride, Kathy shouts "Officer!" and reaches with her right arm toward the policeman, but in the next scene she is reaching toward him with her left arm. Also, in "Make 'Em Laugh," the couch is exactly in front of the painted hallway backdrop at first, but then moves to the right at the end of the routine.[34]

How can such lapses in continuity be explained? The co-directors probably decided to use the take with the broken violin string, because other than that the dance segment was perfect, and viewers were unlikely to notice the gaffe during one viewing in a theater. Debbie's scenes switching arms were shot on different days, and as explained in Chapter 6, both were different scenes, one filmed on a sound stage and the other on a lot. She and everyone else forgot the need for continuity here. Finally, the reason the couch is exactly in front of the hallway at first is that it makes an interesting backdrop for O'Connor's antics with the dummy. But at the end he needs room to run up the backdrop and back-flip from it, so stagehands moved it out of the way. In both scenes, the couch is in its most appropriate place, and that was more important than continuity as defined today.

Among the editing problems is the scene in *The Royal Rascal* where Lana Turner appears for a second before being replaced by Jean Hagen. But perhaps the most obvious editing gaffe is an amusing double-take in "Moses Supposes." At the end of the diction coach's rendition of that tongue twister, he sees for the first time that Cosmo is "gurning" behind his back. Two different shots of that moment, one at close-up and another at medium shot, are included.[35]

The likely reason for the first editing gaffe was discussed in Chapter 4. It was impossible to edit Lana Turner out from the scene taken from *The Three Musketeers* and still retain Kelly's complete and dramatic action sequence. In the case of the double-take at Cosmo's gurning, whether this was really a mistake, a deliberate duplication for comic effect, or the only way the editor could think of to make the sequence flow smoothly is unknown, but it works very well even though it bluntly reminds the viewer that one is watching a movie.

Some examples of gaffes that have been reported on the Internet are not gaffes after all.[36] For example, the fact that Don was holding the umbrella with two hands when the cop appeared but in the next scene he holds it with only one hand is not a gaffe. People can and do change hand positions that way. Also, Cosmo's mention of *Variety* is not an anachronism as claimed. The first issue of *Variety* appeared in 1905. A third example lies in Lina's claim to sing in "A Flat" before Kathy belts out "Singin'" for her behind the curtain. The song is actually played in "E," but we can easily forgive the discrepancy because Lina says "A Flat" much funnier than she could say "E." Finally, in the vamp dance, Charisse's body position changes abruptly when she is wrapped around Kelly. This has been cited as an editing problem, but the likely cause of this was a cut made to remove a "suggestive" pose, based on the memo from Breen's censorship office as discussed in Chapter 8.

Then there are a number of other goofs that the authors of this book have noticed, which no one has yet documented. Don Lockwood's profile painted on the billboard for the supposed upcoming movie *Singin' in the Rain* (starring Lockwood and Selden) looks nothing like Gene Kelly, and it is anything but a smooth transition when Kelly's real profile singing "You Are My Lucky Star" switches to the billboard profile. The artist created a good likeness of Reynolds on the same billboard, so why such a poor job was done for Kelly's profile is unclear. One possibility is that it was painted from a low angle because viewing a snapshot of the billboard horizontally makes the face look a little more like Kelly. This would also explain why no one caught the discrepancy in time because they all were looking at the billboard from a low angle as well.

For a brief moment in "Fit as a Fiddle," O'Connor is holding his violin incorrectly, but he quickly realizes and corrects the position. As with the broken violin string, the directors may have thought it unnecessary to re-do this segment. In the segment where "Beautiful Girl" is being filmed, Cosmo, R. F. Simpson, and Sid are all talking loudly while standing close to the camera. As Cosmo had not yet "invented" dubbing, presumably they were audio recording at the same time as filming and everyone was expected to be quiet. It is possible no one realized this discrepancy. Near the end of "The Broadway Ballet," lighted letters appear on the floor among the dancers in one scene, although they were not in that spot before or after that scene. It is not clear why this was done.

Other previously undocumented gaffes may be deliberate, however. Many details associated with the premiere of *The Duelling Cavalier* are illogical. It is difficult to believe that even a studio operated by R. F. Simpson would not have checked the audio on their first talking picture, and noticed the elevated sounds of Lina's pearls clicking, the soft and loud effect as she turned her head away from and toward the microphone, and the exaggerated noise created when she tapped Don on the shoulder with her folded fan and when Don's staff hit the ground. The probable reason these were built in (despite being difficult to believe) is that they made the sequence funnier. Of course, the sound suddenly jumping out of synchronization during the preview is something that could have happened in reality.

It is also noteworthy that *The Dancing Cavalier* ends with Don and Lina singing "Would You?" in period costume. This period segment of the film was supposed to be the hoofer's hallucination after he is hit by a sandbag—did the main character not recover consciousness and return to the modern world? Again, logic seems to have been abandoned for a more interesting and appealing ending that the audience at the premiere could react to.

Finally, there are other mistakes that people have noted, but the authors believe the filmmakers knowingly put these in for a variety of reasons. There is an interesting breakdown in discontinuity, if one can be allowed to put it that way—the same extras are used for the audience at the premiere of both *The Royal Rascal* and *The Dancing Cavalier;* they are even sitting in exactly the same chairs. In filming *The Duelling Cavalier,* when the sound technician in the booth says to Dexter about Lina, "She's got to talk into the mike," his lips don't move. Another such example is at the end of *The Royal Rascal* segment where Gene Kelly throws a man off the balcony into a moat, but then jumps off and lands in a pile of dirt, which disappears in the next scene.[37]

Using the same audience for both premieres was obviously a cost-cutting, time-saving plan, and either it did not occur to the filmmakers that anyone would notice or they decided not to worry about it. In the second case, the original plan was obviously to have the sound technician simply shrug and shake his head and that clearly indicates (at least to modern audiences) that he cannot pick up the sound. But the film editors seem to have thought that movie audiences of the time might not understand these gestures, and so they dubbed the line over the scene. Lastly, as explained in Chapter 4, the scene that shows Kelly throwing a man into the moat is taken from *The Three Musketeers,* and to segue into *The Royal Rascal,* the filmmakers used new scenes that focused on the continuity of dramatic action (which works extremely well), and sacrificed the continuity of the background.

Singin' in the Rain is not the only M-G-M musical with technical errors in it. During the finale of *Take Me Out to the Ball Game* (1949), a reprise of "Strictly U.S.A.," Frank Sinatra completely forgot a step while dancing with Gene Kelly, Esther Williams, and Betty Garrett. He moved his right shoulder back as if about to step back, stopped dancing altogether, and looked right and left at his partners until he realized what had happened. Then Sinatra quickly rejoined the group's rhythm. All of this took but a couple of seconds to transpire, and the viewer easily misses it unless they look at Sinatra instead of the other three dancers. And yet, M-G-M kept this take in the release print of the movie, which was a strong financial success for the studio.

M-G-M was a movie factory. The studio produced a major picture every week for years running. Its crew of technicians worked on several of them every year, going from one project to the next as fast as they could do so. With demanding schedules to meet, no time to leisurely think about what they were doing, and little opportunity to fix mistakes, these classic films dazzled audiences of the day and subsequent years despite the little flaws that can be seen only when one has the opportunity to view them over and over again on videotape or DVD.

CONNECTIONS

Singin' in the Rain influenced moviemakers as well as television show producers as it gained widespread popularity. French director Francois Truffaut loved it and allowed the movie to influence his own work, especially in *Le Nuit Americaine* (1973). Peter Bogdanovich allowed it to influence some of his work in *Nickelodeon* (1976). The makers of *Next Stop, Greenwich Village* (1975) and *Madame Rosa* (1977) also felt the influence of *Singin'.* When Dick Van Dyke recreated Kelly's dance in "Singin' in the Rain" for an episode of *The Carol Burnett Show*, it appeared to at least one viewer as a tribute that evolved into a parody "due to Van Dyke's comic persona and the relative budgets of the two productions." Observers have compiled lists of movie connections, linking *Singin' in the Rain* to more than a hundred films or video/DVD productions, and more than forty television shows, from 1952 until today. These connections include references to the title of the movie in dialogue or as a background poster, as well as attempts to duplicate or mimic the well-known dance numbers of *Singin'*.[38]

Connections of a different sort occurred when companies tried to link the public admiration for *Singin' in the Rain* with one of their products. Volkswagen wanted to incorporate the title number into an ad to sell its GTI Golf car, but ran into difficulties. While the ad agency acquired permission from Turner Movies, EMI, and Warner Brothers, Kelly's widow, Pat Ward Kelly, refused to go along with the plan. She denied permission to broadcast the ad in the United States, although allowing it to be shown on television in Great Britain and on the Web in both Britain and the United States. The ad was filmed on a set in England, duplicating somewhat the set of "Singin'," except that the VW car is prominently parked on the street. Three breakdancers performed for the camera, with either Kelly's face or that of the policeman superimposed on theirs. Rumor had it that Betsy Blair, Kelly's first wife, saw the ad and liked it when it ran in England in March 2005. The VW ad was part of a trend in which agencies used screen legends, including Fred Astaire, Lucille Ball, Humphrey Bogart, James Cagney, Steve McQueen, and John Wayne, to sell products long after they had passed away. One reporter found a student at the University of California, Berkeley, who liked the Kelly VW ad but had never heard of Kelly or of *Singin' in the Rain*.[39]

Singin' is also connected to the stage as a result of a recent trend to recycle old movies as stage shows. The first time this happened with *Singin'* was in 1983, when Tommy Steele (as Don Lockwood), Roy Castle (as Cosmo Brown), and Danielle Carson (as Kathy Selden) appeared on the stage of the London Palladium. Described as "a riot of misdirected energy," the show nevertheless had a Broadway premiere in New York on July 2, 1985, with Don Correia as Don, Mary D'Arcy as Kathy, and Faye Grant as Lina. The opening of the stage version was delayed several days due to problems inherent in working out the details. Jerome

Robbins and Mike Nichols were called in to help choreographer Twyla Tharp, who directed the show. Fifty gallons of water were rigged to fall on Correia during the title number, recycled so as to be reused for successive performances. The total cost of the stage production amounted to $5 million, double the cost of the original movie thirty-three years before, and the tickets sold for $45 each. It was "a radical reworking of the London show," but closed in May 1986.[40]

The show did not strike anyone as a success. One reviewer thought it offered "no new values whatsoever" to the movie, "but merely apes and re-creates [the original]—word for word, song for song." The touring version of the show pleased critics even less. Starring Donn Simione as Don and Cynthia Ferrer as Kathy, it was termed a "crude" attempt to capitalize on popular taste for the Kelly original, a show that made "the stage look like the most old-fashioned way in the world to tell a story." Audiences in Los Angeles applauded with "a dutiful quality" to be polite. "Each gag is underlined," complained critic Dan Sullivan, "each character played like a stereotype, so the folks in the balcony will get the idea. A deft movie becomes a rube show." Only during some of the choral numbers and when Don and Kathy "reconcile at Grauman's Chinese," did the show appeal.[41]

As if putting *Singin' in the Rain* on the stage had not been tried enough, the show opened again at the West Yorkshire Playhouse in England in 1999. This second English edition of the stage version of *Singin'* received the Outstanding Musical Production Award for the 2000 season. The reworked choreography received critical praise, and the show moved to Sadler's Wells in London by 2004, where classical ballet dancer Adam Cooper played Don Lockwood. But the theater production of this classic film musical never caught on in America. As Gerald Mast wrote, it was simply not "interesting as a stage musical." Another major reason theater performances of *Singin'* did not strike a chord with audiences is the stars people love and associate with the movie. Even if they had good stage actors, these people were not Gene Kelly, Jean Hagen, Donald O'Connor, or Debbie Reynolds, and so it simply did not work. Some movies were successfully converted into stage shows, as exemplified by *The Wizard of Oz*, which became *The Wiz* in 1978. But many movies such as *Meet Me in St. Louis*, *Singin' in the Rain*, *Seven Brides for Seven Brothers*, and *Gigi* failed to make the transition.[42]

Many people have been touched by the grace, charm, humor, and exuberance of *Singin' in the Rain*—people in the public eye and especially the private sphere. The picture has been a presence in their lives that was significant and meaningful, and many have written publicly of how they felt about the film.

Frank Sinatra wrote the foreword for Clive Hirschhorn's biography of Kelly, initially published in 1974. "To me, all film musicals before and since look a bit Neanderthal by comparison. Whenever I project my precious print of *Singin' in the Rain,* I still ooh and ahh at his intensity of effort, and the emotional pictures he could paint with his dancing."[43]

Born in New Zealand in 1939, Murray Ball became a cartoonist with a wacky sense of humor. In a book entitled *Tarzan, Gene Kelly and Me,* Ball related that his identification with Kelly began with *The Three Musketeers,* for the sight of this man "leaping about on rooftops, turning somersaults and sword fighting" amazed him. "Then I saw him dance in *Singin' in the Rain.* I was stunned. . . . He was quite obviously the best dancer in the world." Ball tried to imitate him but failed. "The thing Gene Kelly and I had in common was dancing—he could, I couldn't. The closest I ever got to moving to music was watching him. For me he was dance. He absorbed music like a lightning conductor absorbs lightning. He seemed to pull the music out of the air, pass it through his body and release it through his feet." Ball concluded that, despite his own futile attempts to dance, "deep down inside me there is still a Gene Kelly fighting to get out. And for that I thank him. I believe it is the better part of my nature."[44]

David Fantle and Tom Johnson "discovered" M-G-M musicals when they were in college in Minnesota during the 1970s. As a result, they rearranged their lives and started a company to show prints of these movies at retirement homes for a small fee, mostly so they could have an opportunity to see them as well. This was in the days before video recorders and a multitude of dedicated movie channels on television. Fantle and Johnson were especially taken with *Singin':* "when Charisse sinuously wrapped her legs around Gene Kelly's torso and then rubbed his steamed-up eyeglasses on her inner thigh, enough heat was generated to melt stone."[45]

Bryan Goetzinger was a worker at the old M-G-M studios in Culver City when Lorimar Telepictures took over the facility in 1986. Orders were issued to clean out the props and papers that had accumulated over the decades. For several weeks the collective history of M-G-M was cruelly trashed, never to be recovered. Some of the workers felt there was something tragic in all this. When Goetzinger came across twenty lampposts used in the "Singin'" number, he dug up the blueprint that listed where each one was located on the set, based on their identification numbers. In this way, he found the exact post Gene Kelly had jumped onto before beginning his dance routine. It was ten feet tall, made of fiberglass, and painted green. Goetzinger obtained permission to take it home as a souvenir and set it up in his front yard. Four years later, someone stole it. Goetzinger was convinced the thief had no idea of its sentimental value, and pleaded through the newspaper for its return, but apparently it was never brought back.[46]

English film critic Philip French remembered *Singin' in the Rain* as the movie that "Changed My Life," as he put it in a newspaper article in 2000. He had initially seen the picture on its English release in 1952, on the last day of his first six weeks of basic training in the British army. French hated army life and was depressed when he walked into the theater, expecting little from the film which some English critics had already compared unfavorably with *On the Town*. Although the movie had already started (French walked in when the "Beautiful Girl" number was on), he immediately became enchanted with it when "You Were Meant for Me" appeared. "This was pure cinema," French recalled nearly fifty years later, "the most romantic thing I had ever seen. I was raised from the spiritual lower depths, my heavy army boots exchanged for ballet shoes as I imagined I was Kelly dancing with Reynolds." He watched the rest of the film and then waited to see it in full twice before returning to his army barracks.[47]

Although he did not like "The Broadway Ballet" too well, French was elated by *Singin'*. It made him want to go to America and become an American citizen (an ambition he later dropped) and to become a newspaper film critic (which he eventually managed). Viewing the picture "every couple of years over the next two decades," French's admiration for it deepened. When it was shown on television, his family "taped the sound track, and we'd listen to the playback, recreating the images in our minds." Its issue on videotape allowed French to see it more often, and he began to play games with the film, such as trying to remember the names of the shops along the soaked street where Kelly danced his joy in the title number.[48]

"It is, to me," French concluded, "a perfect cocktail of wit, elegance, ebullience and grace, intoxication without a hangover, an innocent Eden to be visited by those well acquainted with good and evil." French thought it ought to be preserved for posterity and even prescribed as therapy for those who are depressed. "Does any work of art have a more agreeably therapeutic title?" he asked.[49]

Wendy Wasserstein would agree with French. She consumed a helping of the "movie's positive energy whenever I became melancholy." Wasserstein was convinced that the "giddy, infectious immediacy" of *Singin'* could "transform even the most dyspeptic cynic," and do so "without being cloying or campy or annoyingly wholesome. Somehow the movie remains sophisticated and wry while being good-hearted." Her three-year-old daughter insisted on twirling her umbrella when it rained on the way to school one day, and burst into the song that many people think of when the raindrops fall and they feel happy.[50]

Indeed, ordinary people, critics, and entertainment professionals in the United States and abroad share French's enthusiastic approval of the movie and echo Pauline Kael's assertion that *Singin' in the Rain* is "probably the most enjoyable of all American movie musicals." This unique masterpiece has played a living role in American culture with each new generation for more than half a century already. And as long as an American screen culture lives on, so will the beauty, charm, and magic of *Singin' in the Rain*.[51]

CAST AND CREW LIST AND MINI-BIOGRAPHIES

It took the combined efforts of 237 people to make *Singin' in the Rain*. The following list of cast and crew members who contributed to the project comes from several sources, including the Internet Movie Database (IMDB), the "Call Bureau Cast Service" list dated November 9, 1951, and M-G-M Wardrobe Department records. The combined information from these three sources constitute as complete a list of everyone who worked on *Singin'* as one could hope to find.[1]

Six of the 237 people were principal actors (Gene Kelly, Donald O'Connor, Debbie Reynolds, Jean Hagen, Millard Mitchell, and Cyd Charisse). Another six of the total were supporting actors (Douglas Fowley, Kathleen Freeman, Rita Moreno, Bobby Watson, Madge Blake, and King Donovan). Forty bit players spoke lines, and another ninety-six bit players had no lines at all. Eighty-nine crew members worked off screen to create this classic musical.

To put it in a different perspective, the largest category of people who worked on *Singin'* were the bit players who spoke no lines; they constituted 40.5 percent of the 237 people on the cast and crew list. The second biggest category contained the crew members, accounting for 37.6 percent. The third largest group consisted of bit players with lines, representing 16.8 percent of the whole group. In contrast, the principal and supporting actors together represented only 5 percent.

The amount of information available on the cast and crew, other than the principals, is uneven. For some of the more active character players, bit players, and crew members, there is quite a lot of material. For many others, no biographical information is available, only a list of films that they appeared in or worked on. For five women identified as "fashion show girls," no information of any kind is to be found. For five bit players, some biographical information is available, but their roles in the movie cannot be identified. Moreover, the sources consulted to compile this list usually do not provide enough information to confidently identify exactly what roles many of the character or bit players performed in the movie. This is unfortunate but perhaps fitting, for Hollywood's golden era ran on a mobile population of obscure players whose desire to appear on screen was so great that they put up with obscurity, uncertain paychecks, and all too brief moments in the sun, just to be a tiny part of the magic.

Some of these players were not obscure. Bess Flowers, nicknamed "Queen of the Hollywood Extras," appeared in 727 movies and television shows from the silent era to the mid-1960s. Her face was seen in five Oscar-winning films, reportedly more than any other actor. Dawn Addams, an English-born newcomer to Hollywood, appeared as a lady-in-waiting in *The Duelling Cavalier* (a movie portrayed within *Singin'*) and shortly afterward married a European prince. Mike Lally appeared in 293 films and television shows from the start of the sound era to the mid-1980s, and performed stunts in some of them. The godson of New York governor Alfred E. Smith, Lally helped Ronald Reagan and Douglas Fairbanks Jr. to organize the Actors' Guild in Hollywood. Bill Ryan, manager of the Freed Unit production schedule, was the brother-in-law of soon to be vice-president Richard Nixon.

Many character actors in *Singin'* performed roles they had created many times in other movies. Leon Lontoc was typecast as a Chinese or Filipino character, Jac George was typecast as an orchestra leader, and Brick Sullivan was typecast as a policeman. Bobby Watson fortunately did not have to recreate his stereotypical role for *Singin'*; Watson's bread and butter during the years of World War II was to play Adolf Hitler in war movies.

This comprehensive cast and crew list is an attempt to give credit to the hundreds of obscure people who rarely saw their names on the screen, but whose enthusiasm and love for the industry contributed greatly to the steady stream of pictures, clunkers and classics alike, that their work made possible.

THE CAST AND CREW OF *Singin' in the Rain*

Dorothy Abbott (fashion show girl): Born December 16, 1920, in Kansas City, Missouri, and died December 15, 1968, in Los Angeles. Abbott was a Las Vegas showgirl, model, and real estate agent. She appeared in several musicals, including *Annie Get Your Gun* in 1950 and *Jailhouse Rock* in 1957.

Martha Acker (hairstylist): Worked in makeup on her first film in 1935. *Singin'* was her last movie.

Dawn Addams (Teresa, lady-in-waiting): Born September 21, 1930, in Suffolk, England, and died May 7, 1985, in London. Married to Don Vittorio Emanuele Massimo, Prince of Roccasecca, 1954–1971. Addams appeared in her first film in 1951, and performed in two other pictures besides *Singin'* in 1952. She became very active on television in the United States and in European films after her marriage to the prince.

John Albright (ad libber): Born April 4, 1913, and died October 24, 2001. Albright appeared as a bit player in twenty-seven movies and television shows 1936–1963.

Dorothy Aldrin (script supervisor): Worked as a script supervisor on twelve projects in film and television up to 1978. *Singin'* was her first project.

Jack Aldworth (script supervisor): Worked as script supervisor on eleven projects 1948–1952, of which *Singin'* was his last. He also worked as second unit or assistant director on eighteen projects 1955–1980, as television producer on five projects 1956–1962, and as production manager on three projects 1955–1977.

Jeff Alexander (music arranger, vocal arrangements): Born Myer Goodhue Alexander on July 2, 1910, in Seattle and died there on December 23, 1989. Alexander studied at the Becker Conservatory and wrote popular songs as well as pieces for symphonic orchestras. He worked as composer on fifty-six film and television projects 1952–1980.

Shirley Allard (fashion show girl): Also known as Shirlee Allard, she appeared in four movies 1951–1954, including *Phffft* (1954).

Betty Allen (girlfriend in "Beautiful Girl"): Appeared in seven films and television shows 1935–1956.

Sue Allen (girlfriend in "Beautiful Girl"): Also known as Susy Allen. *Singin'* was her first movie. Allen appeared in a handful of later films and television shows as late as 1980.

John Alton (additional photographer): Born Johann Altmann October 5, 1901, in Sopron, Austria-Hungary, and died June 2, 1996. Alton began as a lab technician at M-G-M when the studio was formed in 1924, and began to work as a cinematographer three years later. He worked in Argentina in the early 1930s, training cinematographers, and shooting and directing films. Alton won an Oscar for Best Cinematography for his first color film, *An American in Paris*. He was widely quoted for saying, "It's not what you light—it's what you DON'T light." He is credited as cinematographer on 101 projects 1933–1966, the last of which was the pilot for the television series *Mission Impossible*. Alton also wrote a book, *Painting with Light*, which was published in 1945.

Marie Ardell (dancer, "Beautiful Girl"): Four appearances in films, 1950–1956, the last of which was in *Around the World in Eighty Days* (1956).

Bette Arlen (ad libber): Also known as Betty Arlen, born November 9, 1904, in Providence, Kentucky, and died August 4, 1966, in Farmington, New Mexico. Her first film was *Neptune's Daughter* (1949), and her tenth and last film was released in 1956.

Helen Auer (secretary to Arthur Freed): Credited, as Freed's secretary, for one other film besides *Singin'*, *Ziegfeld Follies* in 1946.

Peter Ballbusch (montage technician): Born 1902 in Switzerland, and died September 1966 of an accidental fall in a park in Utah. He is credited as a member of the editorial team on sixty-five movies, 1937–1954 (eleven in 1952 alone), including *Gone with the Wind*, for his work on montages. He also was credited on three projects for special effects work. Ballbusch wrote two movies, acted in one, and served as second unit director for *Gone with the Wind*.

Rene Barsam (stand-in): Her only movie project was in *Singin'*.

Mary Bashe (body makeup artist): Her only movie work was in *Singin'*.

Jane Bateman (fashion show girl): No information available.

Jimmie (or Jimmy) Bates (bit boy): Played a four-year-old boy in *The Merry Monahans* (1944), and the boy in Fred Astaire's number "Drum Crazy" in *Easter Parade* (1948). In *Singin'*, he was one of the kids who mob Don Lockwood when he and Cosmo get a flat tire.

Marcella Becker (dancer, "Beautiful Girl"): Her only appearance was in *Singin'*.

Lee Bergquist (fashion show girl): No information available.

Margaret Bert (played wardrobe woman): Born Margaret Birtwistle on June 4, 1896, in Blackburn, Lancashire, England, and died May 1, 1971, in Sacramento, California. Bert played bit parts in 118 movies and television shows 1933–1964, appearing in most of the great musicals M-G-M produced.

David Blair (bit boy): Appeared in *The Three Musketeers* (1948) as Gene Kelly's little brother. After *Singin'*, Blair appeared in only two other movies in 1953 and 1956.

Madge Blake (played gossip columnist Dora Bailey): Born May 31, 1899, in Kinsley, Kansas, and died February 19, 1969, in Pasadena, California. Blake started her career at age forty with a bit role in *Adam's Rib* (1949) and became a regular, racking up a total of thirty-eight films by 1966. They included bit parts in *An American in Paris* (1951), *Brigadoon* (1954), *The Long, Long Trailer* (1954), and *It's Always Fair Weather* (1955). Blake is credited with thirty-one appearances on television, and was a regular on *Leave It to Beaver* (as Larry Mondelo's mother) and *Batman* (as Aunt Harriet).

Gail Bonney (first woman): Born December 15, 1901, in Columbus, Ohio, and died December 7, 1984, in Los Angeles. From 1948 to 1978, Bonney appeared 121 times on television (mostly) and in movies.

Richard Borland (rigging grip): Worked as a grip in rigging, camera, and electrical work on fifteen films and television shows 1948–1978. His first work was on *The Pirate* (1948).

Carol Brewster (fashion show girl): Born Miriam Elizabeth Hechler on February 25, 1927, in Los Angeles. Performed as part of a specialty act called the

Brewster Twins in *Little Miss Broadway* in 1938, and did bit parts in many films up to 1970.

Nacio Herb Brown (music): Arthur Freed's songwriting partner. *Singin' in the Rain* is based on the Freed-Brown catalog of songs. See biographical information in Chapters 1 and 9.

Eric Carpenter (still photographer): Born in 1909 and died on June 16, 1976. Carpenter worked as a still photographer on five movies, from *The Wizard of Oz* (1939) to *Ben-Hur* (1956). His work involved taking still photographs of movie productions for publicity.

Gwen Carter (bit girl at party): Wife of Donald O'Connor. Her only film appearance was in *Singin'*, as the girl who asks Cosmo how she can break into the movies. Carter appeared on several episodes of *The Colgate Comedy Hour* hosted by O'Connor, and at least one of them also saw the appearance of their daughter Donna.

Cyd Charisse (vamp in "The Broadway Ballet"): *Singin' in the Rain* was pivotal in Charisse's career as she had only danced in a traditional ballet style earlier. See biographical information in Chapters 7 and 9.

Bill Chatham (dancing and singing quartette): Appeared in only three movies, including *Singin'*, where he was part of the montage number.

Lyle Clark (ad libber): Appeared in twelve movies, including *The Clock* (1945). *Singin'* was his last appearance.

Mae Clarke (played hairdresser): Born Violet Mary Klotz on August 16, 1910, in Philadelphia and died April 29, 1992, in Woodland Hills, California. A show business veteran, she appeared in 106 movies 1929–1970. Her first husband was Lew Brice, the brother of Fanny Brice. Clarke was the model for Lorelei Lee in *Gentlemen Prefer Blondes* (1953), and she was the wife of Frankenstein in *Frankenstein* (1931). Clarke's most famous role was as the uncredited Kitty in *The Public Enemy* (1931), where James Cagney hit her in the face across the breakfast table with a grapefruit. She has one line in *Singin'*, telling Lina Lamont that her French wig looks great.

Dorinda Clifton (fashion show girl): Appeared in seven films 1945–1953, including *Annie Get Your Gun* (1950) and *The Belle of New York* (1952).

M. D. Cline (gaffer): Worked on two films, *Singin'* and *Annie Get Your Gun*. (A gaffer is an electrician or lighting technician.)

Harry Cody (bit man): Born Van Doak Covington on May 10, 1896, in Tennessee and died October 22, 1956, in Hollywood. He appeared in twenty-three film and television projects 1935–1957, including *Adam's Rib* (1949) and *Three Little Words* (1950), but mostly in television 1954–1957.

Chick Collins (fencer, stunts): Died November 25, 1981. Did bit parts in twenty-eight movies 1932–1952, including *Singin'*, which was his last film.

Betty Condon (script writer): Collaborated with Adolph Green on the script. See biographical information in Chapters 1 and 9.

Pat Conway (plays a projectionist and ad libber): Born Patrick Douglas Conway on January 9, 1931, in Los Angeles, and died April 24, 1981, in Santa Barbara County, California. He was the grandson of Francis X. Bushman, a silent screen star. Conway began his career on television in 1951 and appeared in thirty-eight other roles on the big screen and small until 1975.

Alexander Courage (orchestrator): Born December 10, 1919, in Philadelphia and nicknamed Sandy Courage, he is credited as the composer on thirty projects 1950–1993 and as orchestrator for eighty-eight other projects during the same time period. Many of the best M-G-M musicals benefited from his talent. Courage also wrote music for many *Star Trek* movies and for television episodes of *Star Trek: The Next Generation.*

Jeanne Coyne (dancer, montage and "All I Do Is Dream of You," dance-in for "Singin' in the Rain," second assistant dance director): Born February 28, 1923, in Pennsylvania and died May 10, 1973, in Los Angeles. Nicknamed Jeannie as a child, Coyne was one of Gene Kelly's many dance students in Pittsburgh. She later became one of his dance assistants, was married briefly to Stanley Donen, and later became Kelly's second wife. Coyne appeared in the chorus of *Summer Stock* (1950) and was a featured dancer in *Kiss Me Kate* (1953). Coyne was the dance-in for Kelly in the title number of *Singin' in the Rain* (see Chapter 5 for more details). She also danced on screen in the chorus of "All I Do Is Dream of You" and in the "Woo de woo de woo" segment of the montage.

Tommy Crawford (props): His only project was *Singin'.*

Fred Datig Jr. (played movie usher): Born September 9, 1925, in Hollywood. Datig, who also was known as Fred A. Datig, won many international military decorations for service as an infantry scout in the European theater of World War II. After the conflict, he wrote technical studies of various guns that were published as books, and appeared in fifteen films 1946–1952.

Bert Davidson (bit part as sound engineer): Appeared in thirty-three films 1946–1954.

Mark Davis (cinematographer, matte painting): Worked at matte painting, special effects, and visual effects on six movie projects 1943–1946, before *Singin'.*

Robert Dayo (part of dancing and singing quartette): Appeared in only two movies, *Singin'* and *Around the World in Eighty Days* (1956).

Peter P. Decek (music mixer): Worked in the sound department on three movies, all classics. The other two were *The Wizard of Oz* (1939) and *The Cockeyed Miracle* (1946).

Patricia Denise (dancer, "Beautiful Girl" and "All I Do Is Dream of You"): Appeared in five movies 1946–1958.

Kay Deslys (ad libber): Born September 28, 1899, as Kathleen M. Herbert in London and died August 15, 1974, in West Covina, California. Also known as Kay de Lys, she began her career working as a comedian with Hal Roach in 1923. Deslys later played Mrs. Hardy in two Laurel and Hardy films in 1928 and 1929. She appeared in a total of sixty-six movies 1924–1952. *Singin'* was her second-last film.

Gloria DeWerd (dancer, "Beautiful Girl"): *Singin'* was her first movie, and she went on to perform in only two others.

John Dodsworth (Baron de la Ma de la Toulon): Born John Cecil Dodsworth on September 17, 1910, in London, and died September 11, 1964, in Los Angeles. He appeared in thirty projects, from 1945 to 1958, many of them television episodes.

Stanley Donen (co-director): *Singin' in the Rain* was the second in the trio of Kelly-Donen directorial triumphs. See biographical information in Chapters 2 and 9.

King Donovan (played publicity man Rod): Born on January 25, 1918, in New York and died on June 30, 1987, in Hartford, Connecticut. Donovan performed in sixty-three films 1941–1984. He appeared in fourteen films in 1951, five in 1952, and twelve in 1953. His best-known roles were in science fiction films such as *The Beast from 20,000 Fathoms* (1953), *The Magnetic Monster* (1953), and *The Invasion of the Body Snatchers* (1956). Married to Imogene Coca, Donovan often co-starred with his wife on stage, and guest-starred in forty-four television shows from 1954 to 1970.

Randall Duell (art director): Born July 14, 1903, in Russell County, Kansas, and died November 28, 1992 in Los Angeles. Worked as assistant art director on twenty-two movies 1937–1946, and as art director on thirty-eight more from 1942 to 1959. Duell also formed a successful company that designed many theme parks since the early 1960s, including the Six Flags series of parks, King's Island, King's Dominion, and Astroworld.

Michael Dugan (ad libber): Appeared in forty-one movies 1948–1967 and a number of television shows. Dugan also did stunts on eight movie projects up to 1970.

Phil Dunham (ad libber): Born Philip Gray Dunham on April 23, 1885, in London and died September 5, 1962, in Los Angeles. He sometimes spelled his first name as Phillip, and appeared in 212 projects 1913–1952. *Singin'* was his second-last movie appearance. Dunham is also credited as a writer on forty-one movie projects, 1926–1940, but most of them were silent films for which he wrote the scenarios. He directed four silent movies in 1917.

Helen Eby-Rock (bit woman): Born July 18, 1896, in Pennsylvania, and died July 20, 1979, in Woodland Hills, California. She sometimes spelled her first name as Helyn, and appeared in forty-two projects from 1929 to 1968.

Roger Edens (music coordinator): Born November 9, 1905, in Hillsboro, Texas, and died July 13, 1970, in Los Angeles. He had thirty-eight credits as songwriter 1947–1957; thirty-seven credits as musical adaptor or arranger 1934–1960; twenty-two as producer 1944–1969; eight as composer 1933–1950; and one as second unit director (for "Old Man River" in *Show Boat,* 1951). Edens also made three cameo appearances in *Broadway Melody of 1936* (1935), *The Clock* (1945), and *Funny Face* (1957). Edens helped to groom the teenaged Judy Garland for stardom, and became "the only man who ever came close to qualifying as a second father" to Garland, according to her daughter Lorna Luft. Edens lived a "discreet gay life."[2]

William Edmondson (sound mixer): Born William Robert Edmondson on July 4, 1906, and died April 18, 1998, in Portland, Oregon. He went by many aliases, including Bill or William E. Edmondson, W. Edmondson, William R. Edmondson, and Bill Edmonson. He appeared in thirty-one projects 1931–1977, many of them television episodes.

Marietta Elliott (ad libber): Appeared in six movies, several of them top-notch M-G-M musicals, 1950–1952.

Richard Emory (played Phil, cowboy hero in barroom brawl): Born Emory Johnson Jr. on January 27, 1919, in Santa Barbara, California, and died February 15, 1994, in Moab, Utah. The son of silent screen actress Ella Hall, Emory appeared in forty-seven projects 1949–1963, many of them western movies and television episodes.

Betty Erbes (dancer, "Beautiful Girl"): Appeared in only two movies, including *Singin'*.

Charles Evans (irritated audience member): Also known as Charlie Evans, appeared in 121 projects 1944–1966, many of them television episodes.

Tommy Farrell (played assistant director Sid Phillips): Born Thomas Farrell Richards, son of actress Glenda Farrell, on October 7, 1921, in Hollywood and died May 9, 2004, in Woodland Hills, California. Also credited as

Tom Farrell, he appeared in thirty-seven films 1944–1967 and in forty-one television projects 1954–1978.

Adrienne Fazan (film editor): Born May 9, 1906, and died August 23, 1986, in Los Angeles. Nominated for an Oscar for *An American in Paris* (1951), she won an Oscar for editing *Gigi* (1958). Fazan edited sixty-nine films from 1933 to 1970, including many Gene Kelly musicals.

Norwood A. Fenton (sound): Also known as A. Norwood Fenton and Norwood Fenton, worked on the sound of thirteen movies and television shows from 1943 until the last, an episode of *The Munsters* entitled "Dance With Me Herman" (1965), in which Gene Kelly's name is mentioned.

Don Fields (ad libber): Appeared in only two projects, *Singin'* and on television in 1968.

Joseph Fields (writer): Born Joseph Albert Fields on February 21, 1895, in New York, and died March 3, 1966, in Beverly Hills. He wrote a new ending and other changes for *Singin'* that were not used. The son of vaudeville and movie performer Lew Fields and brother of writers Herbert Fields and Dorothy Fields, Joseph wrote fifty scripts for movies and television 1931–1964. He also wrote many stage works, won two Tony Awards for *Wonderful Town* in 1953, and was nominated for a Tony Award for *Flower Drum Song* in 1959.

Ernest Flatt (part of dancing and singing quartette): Born Ernest O. Flatt on October 30, 1918, in Denver, Colorado, and died June 10, 1995, in Taos, New Mexico. He was a dancing assistant and specialty dancer in some movies, and prolific choreographer on television during the 1950s and 1960s, especially on *The Carol Burnett Show*. He won two Tony Awards for *Sugar Babies* in 1980.

Bess Flowers (bit part): Born November 23, 1898, in Sherman, Texas, and died July 28, 1984, in Woodland Hills, California. Nicknamed "Queen of the Hollywood Extras," Flowers appeared in 727 movies and television shows from *Hollywood* (1923) to an episode of *Perry Mason* in 1965. She appeared in twenty-four other movies, besides *Singin'*, in 1952 alone. Flowers appeared in more Oscar-winning films (five in number) than any other actor.

Hank Forester (grip): Worked as a grip on four movie and television projects.

Robert Fortier (gangster extra in ballet): Born November 5, 1926, in West Hollywood and died January 1, 2005, in Orange, California. Also known as Bob Fortier, he appeared in thirty-eight projects, including a specialty dance he performed in *Texas Carnival* (1951), but mostly on television.

Dan Foster (played an assistant director): Born Dante J. Ferrante on April 13, 1920, in New York, and died January 2, 2002, in Apple Valley, California.

Foster appeared in twenty-one projects from 1948 to a television appearance in 1953. After that, he opened a store called Dan Foster's Hobby Junction.

Robert Foulke (Matt the cop in jalopy ride sequence): Born May 5, 1908, in Philadelphia, and died February 25, 1989, in Los Angeles. Also called Robert Faulk, Bob Foulk, and Robert C. Foulk, he appeared in 202 projects 1948–1977 and in sixteen other films besides *Singin'* in 1952 alone. Foulke also worked as dialogue director on eleven movies 1940–1947.

Douglas Fowley (played director Roscoe Dexter): Born Daniel Vincent Fowley on May 30, 1911, in the Bronx, and died May 21, 1998, in Woodland Hills, California. Fowley moved to California, attended Los Angeles City College, and served in the Navy during World War II. He appeared in his first movie, *The Mad Game,* in 1933 and his last film was released in 1979. Married at least five times, he appeared in 246 films and television episodes, 190 of them before *Singin'* and fifty-six of them television appearances. Fowley worked in another classic musical, *The Band Wagon* (1953), and also played Doc Holliday on television's *The Life and Legend of Wyatt Earp* (1955–1961).

Robert Franklyn (orchestrator): Born Robert Alan Franklyn on April 30, 1918, and died November 5, 1980, in Ventura County, California. Worked as orchestrator on twenty-six films 1940–1964, and on six as composer 1946–1949.

Arthur Freed (producer and lyricist): Freed's lyrics, set to music by Nacio Herb Brown, appeared in at least 144 movies from 1929 to 2005. He was co-producer or producer of fifty-one movies 1939–1962, and hosted five Annual Academy Awards television shows. Freed dubbed the singing for Leon Ames in *Meet Me in St. Louis* (1944), and did two cameo roles, as a bystander in the rehearsal room in *The Broadway Melody* (1929) and as the man who offers a match in Grand Central Station in *The Clock* (1945). He was a writer for two movies, but his writing for *The Wizard of Oz* (1939) was uncredited, as was his role of co-producer for that movie. See biographical information in Chapters 1 and 9.

Kathleen Freeman (played diction coach Phoebe Dinsmore): Born on February 17, 1919, in Chicago, and died August 23, 2001, in New York. As a music student at the University of California, Los Angeles, Freeman caught the acting bug and became one of the most respected character actors in the business. She appeared in 123 films from 1948 to 2001, eight other movies besides *Singin'* in 1952 alone. Her movie roles included Sister Mary Stigmata (alias The Penguin) in *The Blues Brothers* (1980), and she appeared in ten movies with Jerry Lewis. She also appeared in 133 television episodes from

1951 to 1999, including *The Dick Van Dyke Show, The Lucy Show,* and *The Golden Girls.* Freeman performed on Broadway in *The Full Monty* until five days before her death. She was nominated for a Tony Award for that performance.

Lance Fuller (unidentified bit role): Born December 6, 1928, in Somerset, Kentucky, and died December 22, 2001, in Los Angeles. Married to another bit player in *Singin'*, Joi Lansing, 1951–1953, Fuller appeared in forty-nine movies and television episodes 1943–1975. Part English, French, and Cherokee, Fuller almost starred in *The Yearling* (1946) but grew out of the role due to delays in production.

Jeanne Gail (ad libber): Appeared in seven movies and television episodes.

James F. Gaither Jr. (sound recording): Born December 2, 1903, and died on June 1, 1994, in Los Angeles. Also known as James Gaither, he was sound mixer or recorder on three other movies besides *Singin'*, including *The Wizard of Oz* (1939).

Glen Gallagher (ad libber): Appeared in *Adam's Rib* (1949) in addition to *Singin'*.

Jon Gardner (bit kid): Appeared in nine movies from *Singin'*, his first, to *Ma and Pa Kettle at Waikiki* (1955).

Diane Garrett (usherette): Married to dancer Bobby Van 1952–1962, she appeared in six movies, four of them in 1952 alone. Her bit part in *Singin'* was apparently dropped.

Phil Garris (stand-in): Appeared in seventeen projects as a bit player, many of them featuring his friend Donald O'Connor, including two of the *Francis* movies. Garris also appeared as himself in an episode of *The Donald O'Connor Show.*

Jack George (played orchestra leader): Also known as Jac George, he appeared in ninety-five projects, many of them on television. George was typecast as an orchestra leader, playing that role twenty times. He played a musician in fourteen other projects, and a bandleader in two others.

Cedric Gibbons (art director): Born Austin Cedric Gibbons on March 23, 1893, in Dublin, Ireland, and died July 26, 1960, in Hollywood. His architect father moved the family to the United States where Cedric graduated from art school. He began working in the movies in 1915 and became art director at M-G-M when the studio was created in 1924. During his thirty-two-year tenure at M-G-M, his name was put on every movie the studio produced. Gibbons supervised the art direction for 1,050 films during his career, worked on set design for seventy-two films, and as production designer for five movies. He directed one film, *Tarzan and His Mate,* in 1934, and appeared as himself in two pictures. Gibbons, a founding member of the Academy of Motion Picture Arts and Sciences, designed the Oscar statuette and was nominated for and won more Academy Awards than any other art director.

Shirley Glickman (dancer, "Beautiful Girl"): Appeared in only two movies, *Royal Wedding* (1951) and *Singin'*.

James Gooch (color consultant, Technicolor): Worked on forty-five films 1948–1956, including the best M-G-M musicals made during those years.

Al Goodhart (music for "Fit as a Fiddle"): Born on January 26, 1905, in New York and died November 30, 1955, in the same city. Goodhart was a composer, pianist, agent, and radio announcer, and collaborated with Al Hoffman on many songs. He is credited as a composer for four movies 1930–1936, and for contributing to the soundtrack on ten other movies.

Inez Gorman (Mrs. R. F. Simpson): Born October 31, 1912, in Massachusetts, and died December 6, 1986, in Glendale, California. Appeared in four movies 1951–1953. Her small role in *Singin'* was dropped.

A. Cameron Grant (second man): Born Alexander Cameron Grant on August 27, 1901, in Canada and died January 18, 1972, in Los Angeles County. Appeared in forty-two projects from 1950 to 1959, including several episodes of *I Love Lucy*.

Beatrice Gray (ad libber): Born March 3, 1911, in Hollywood. Appeared in thirty projects 1943–1996.

Marion Gray (second woman): Appeared in fifteen projects 1944–1957.

Adolph Green (script writer): Collaborated with Betty Condon on the script. See biographical information in Chapters 1 and 9.

Johnny Green (musical director): Born John Waldo Green on October 10, 1908, in New York and died May 15, 1989, in Beverly Hills. Attended Harvard University and ran the Harvard Gold Coast Orchestra between semesters. Green completed his Master of Arts in English literature, then worked six months as a stockbroker at the insistence of his father before making music his career. He wrote many hit songs and went to Hollywood where he and Conrad Salinger improved the sound of the M-G-M orchestra. His songs appeared in fifty-three films from 1930 to 2004, and he conducted or arranged music for sixty-two movies from 1930 to 1969. He is also credited as composer for thirty-two movies, as producer for five, and as actor for one movie and a television show.

John Greenwald (second assistant director): Also known as Johnny Greenwald, was second unit or assistant director on three projects. On *Singin'*, which was his first project, he worked with assistant director Marvin Stuart.

Sydney Guilaroff (hairstylist): Born on November 2, 1907, in London and died May 28, 1997, in Beverly Hills. Also known as Sidney Guilaroff and Sidney Guilleroff, he was the chief hairstylist for M-G-M from 1934 till nearly the 1980s. Guilaroff was responsible for the hairstyles of most of the studio's successful actresses, and was credited as hairstylist for 390 projects starting with films in 1938 to television shows in 1989. In addition, he acted in three projects and selected costumes for one. He worked on twenty-seven other movies besides *Singin'* in 1952 alone. Guilaroff also became the first bachelor in America to legally adopt a child.

Jean Hagen (Lina Lamont): *Singin' in the Rain* offered Hagen her best-known role, as M-G-M tended to underutilize her talents before and after this movie. See biographical information in Chapters 2 and 9.

William R. Hamel (bit man): Born on March 14, 1906, in Pennsylvania and died March 8, 1958, in Los Angeles County. Also known as Bill Hamel, he appeared in fifteen projects from 1948 to 1958.

Carol Haney (first assistant dance director): Born Carolyn Haney on December 24, 1924, at New Bedford, Massachusetts, and died May 10, 1964, in Saddle Back, New Jersey. Gene Kelly's longtime dance assistant, Haney was an uncredited chorus dancer in *Wonder Man* (1945) and featured dancer in *On the Town* (1949), *Kiss Me Kate* (1953), and *Invitation to the Dance* (1956). She won a Tony Award for *The Pajama Game* on Broadway (1955), and performed the same role on film in 1957. Haney did the musical staging for several Broadway shows and appeared on many television shows as well. Her career was cut short by pneumonia, complicated by diabetes.

Betty Hannon (dancer, "All I Do Is Dream of You"): Appeared in eight projects 1945–1952, including several musicals. *Singin'* was her last appearance.

Ed Hartzke (assistant editor): *Singin'* was his only project.

Timmy Hawkins (bit boy): Appeared in twenty-four projects 1944–1955. *Singin'* was his second-last film.

Lennie Hayton (musical director): Born Leonard George Hayton on February 13, 1908, in New York and died April 24, 1971, in Palm Springs, California. He is credited as composer on forty-two projects 1941–1968, and as conductor for thirty-two other movies 1933–1968. His second wife, Lena Horne, was a regular singer in many M-G-M movies.

Wally Heglin (orchestration): Born September 20, 1904, in South Dakota and died November 3, 1972, in Los Angeles County. Heglin was music arranger on thirty movies 1939–1952. *Singin'* was his last project.

Dean Henson (unidentified bit role): Appeared in three movie and television projects, of which *Singin'* was the last.

Jean Heremans (fencer, stunts): Born January 13, 1914, in Belgium and died August 2, 1970, in Los Angeles County. Heremans performed as a stuntman on nine films 1939–1954, as an actor in five projects from 1948 to a television show in 1959, and as fencing consultant or fencing choreographer for two other movies. His most prominent work was as stuntman, actor, and fencing consultant on Gene Kelly's *The Three Musketeers* (1948).

Al Hoffman (music for "Fit as a Fiddle"): Born September 25, 1902, in Minsk, Russia, and died July 21, 1960, in New York. Hoffman came to America in 1908, graduated from high school in Seattle, and became a bandleader in that city until he moved to New York in 1928 as a drummer. He collaborated with Al Goodhart in producing many successful songs. Hoffman's songs appeared in thirty-six movies from 1933 to 2006, and he is credited as composer on six other films and as part of the miscellaneous crew on five more.

Stuart Holmes (J. Cumberland Spendrill III): Born Joseph Liebchen on March 10, 1884, in Chicago and died December 29, 1971, in Hollywood. Appeared in 460 projects from *The Way of the Cross* in 1909 to *Seven Days in May* in 1964. At least 150 of his movie appearances were in silent films. Holmes appeared in thirty-two pictures in 1939 alone. In addition to many forgettable movies, Holmes also played bit parts in many classic films.

Joyce Horne (dancer, "Beautiful Girl" and "All I Do Is Dream of You"): Appeared in six projects 1942–1952.

Ed Hubbell (still photographer): Was the still photographer on the set of ten movies 1948–1952. *Singin'* was the last movie on which he worked.

Don Hulbert (part of dancing and singing quartette): Appeared in five projects, most of them in the 1930s. *Singin'* was his last appearance.

Charles J. Hunt (production manager): Born April 8, 1881, in Fort Lee, New Jersey, and died February 3, 1976, in Los Angeles. Also known as Charles J. Hundt, Charles Hunt, and Charley Hunt, he was editor of twenty-nine movies 1921–1940 and production manager for eighteen films 1923–1952, of which *Singin'* was his last. Hunt also directed sixteen movies, mostly silents in the 1920s, worked as second unit director (eight films), producer (seven movies), writer (two films, one of them a silent movie for which he wrote title cards), sound editor (one picture), and actor (he played a chauffeur in a 1912 film).

Frank Hyers (ad libber): Appeared in fifteen projects 1947–1953. His last film was *I Love Melvin*.

Pat Jackson (dancer, "Beautiful Girl" and "All I Do Is Dream of You"): Appeared in two projects, the last of which was *Singin'*.

Henri Jaffa (color consultant, Technicolor): Born Henry C. Jaffa on April 13, 1905, in California, and died August 14, 1988, in Los Angeles. Also known as Henry C. Jaffa and Henry Jaffa, he worked as color consultant on 139 movies from 1937 to 1976. He also served as associate color director (nine movies) and associate art director (four films).

Ivor James (ad libber): Appeared in four projects from 1950 to 1952. *Singin'* was his last film.

J. James (assistant to chief lighting technician): Also known as Jimmie James, he worked as electrician, gaffer, or lighting technician on three movies, the last of which was *Singin'*.

Van Allen James (sound editor): Born June 23, 1904, in Oakland, California, and died February 27, 1985, in Los Angeles. James worked as sound editor on sixty-one projects, beginning with *The Wizard of Oz* (1939) and including many M-G-M musicals. In addition to a lot of television work, his last movie project was *That's Entertainment* (1974). He also was a bit player in one movie.

Morgan Jones (ad libber): Appeared in eighty-three projects, of which *Singin'* was his first. Most of his work was on a wide variety of television series.

David Kasday (bit kid): Appeared in seventeen projects, of which *Singin'* was his second. Kasday appears in the second scene in the movie, where he is sitting in a tree watching the celebrities arrive for the premiere of *The Royal Rascal*. His first movie appearance was as one of the kids surrounding Kelly in "I Got Rhythm" in *An American in Paris* (1951). He also appeared briefly in a group of children watching a puppet show in the ballet of that film. In addition to doing many television appearances, Kasday co-starred with Gene Kelly as the dancing genie in the "Sinbad the Sailor" segment of *Invitation to the Dance* (1956), the same year that marked his last appearance on television.

Jan Kayne (second usherette): Appeared in nine projects 1949–1952. Her bit part in *Singin'* was apparently dropped.

Gene Kelly (Don Lockwood, co-director, and choreographer): *Singin' in the Rain*, and especially the title number, became Kelly's trademark as audiences everywhere associated him closely with it. See biographical information in Chapters 2 and 9.

Jimmy Kelly (bit man): Also known as Jimmie Kelly, or as "Tiny" Jim Kelly. Unrelated to Gene Kelly, he appeared in eighteen projects 1941–1978.

Kenner G. Kemp (police escort at premiere): Born Kenner G. Kempe on January 3, 1908, in Arizona, and died May 13, 1985, in Los Angeles. A stand-in for Walter Pidgeon in two movies, Kemp appeared in 202 projects from 1933 to 1972, including some television roles.

Mike Lally (man in audience at *The Dancing Cavalier* premiere): Born June 1, 1900, in Manhattan, and died February 15, 1985, in Woodland Hills, California. Also known as Mike Lally Sr., Michael Edward Lally, Michael Lalley, Mike Edward Lally, and S. Mike Lally, he appeared in 293 projects 1930–1986. Twenty of those appearances took place in 1952 alone. His last was an appearance in *The A-Team* on television. Lally also did stunts in six films from 1936 to 1947. His godfather was Alfred E. Smith, governor of New York. Lally helped Ronald Reagan and Douglas Fairbanks Jr. form the Actors' Guild in Hollywood.

Judy Landon (Olga Mara): Appeared in a dozen projects from *Annie Get Your Gun* (1950) to an episode of *The Brady Bunch* on television in 1973.

Ben Lane (makeup artist): Did makeup work on 125 projects from 1950 to 1982, mostly on television.

Belva Lannan (secretary to Roger Edens): Involved with two movies, *Singin'* and *Ziegfeld Follies* (1946).

Joi Lansing (ad libber, audience member, or beautiful blonde): Born Joyce Wassmansdorff on April 6, 1929, in Salt Lake City, Utah, and died August 7, 1972, in Santa Monica, California. Also known as Joyce Lansing, Joy Lansing, and Joy Loveland, she appeared in seventy-nine projects from 1937 to 1970. Lansing worked as a model in the 1940s, and did a lot of television work in the 1950s and 1960s, most notably as the wife of Lester Flatt in *The Beverly Hillbillies*, 1965–1968.

Janet Lavis (dancer, "Beautiful Girl" and "All I Do Is Dream of You"): Appeared in five projects from 1940 to 1952, including *Wonder Man* (1945) and *Royal Wedding* (1951). *Singin'* was her last project.

Virginia Lee (unidentified bit role): Also known as Virginia Lindley, appeared in eleven movies and television projects from 1946 to 1958. *Singin'* was her last film.

William F. Leicester (man in black/audience member): Born August 25, 1915, in Illinois and died January 9, 1969, in Van Nuys, California. Also known as Bill Leicester, William Leicester, William Lester, or Bill Lester, he appeared in twenty-one projects as actor from 1947 to 1960, many of them on television. He is credited as a writer for ten television episodes and executive story consultant for the television series *The High Chaparral*, 1968–1969.

Peggy Leon (bit woman): Also known as Peggie Leon, she died in 1968. Leon appeared in forty projects from 1934 to an episode of *Ben Casey* on television in 1962.

Diki Lerner (male tango dancer): Also known as Dikki Lerner. He appeared in eighteen projects, the first of which was *Singin'*, and the last was in 1992.

William LeVanway (supervising editor): Born as William N. LeVanway on September 7, 1896, in Oregon, and died November 1, 1957, in Hollywood. He was credited as editor on thirty-six projects, including *Bright Lights* in 1925 and *His Glorious Night* four years later. His only credit as supervising editor is for *Singin'*.

Bill Lewin (played Bert, cowboy villain knocked out in barroom brawl): Appeared in eight projects as a bit actor 1946–1953, and in one as a stuntman in 1951.

Sylvia Lewis (female tango dancer): Born in York, Pennsylvania, was a child actor in vaudeville, and studied at the Peabody Conservatory of Music. Lewis moved to California at age twelve, and is credited as dancer, actress, and choreographer. She appeared in thirty-five projects from 1952 to 1969, many of them on television, choreographed thirteen TV shows, and played Flossie in an episode of *The Andy Griffith Show*.

John Logan (ad libber): Born February 7, 1924, in California, and died December 7, 1972, in San Pedro, California. Also known as John W. Logan, he appeared in thirteen projects, the first of which was *Singin'*. Logan also played the mechanic in *The Long, Long Trailer* (1954).

Tom Long (grip): Worked as a grip on five projects, the last of which was *Singin'*.

Leon Lontoc (Filipino butler): Born February 20, 1908, in Manila, Philippines and died January 22, 1974, in Los Angeles. Also known as Leon M. Lontoc or Leon Lontok, he appeared in fifty-one projects from 1943 to his last, an episode of *Mission Impossible* in 1973. He often played Chinese or Filipino characters.

Shirley Lopez (dancer, "Beautiful Girl"): Appeared in two classic musicals, *Singin'* and *The Band Wagon* (1953).

Alma Maison (stand-in): Her first movie was *Singin'*. She later appeared in bit parts in three movies, 1952–1953, including *I Love Melvin* (1953).

Joan Maloney (unidentified bit role): Born January 16, 1935, in Illinois and died October 28, 1992, in Tarzana, California. She appeared in four movies, of which *Singin'* was her first, and her last was *Silk Stockings* (1957).

Jacque Mapes (set decoration, set director): Born June 4, 1913, and died May 4, 2002, in Beverly Hills. Mapes grew up in the Los Angeles region, served in the Navy during World War II, and was the life partner of Ross Hunter for more than forty years. He worked on a project as set dresser in 1945, as set director on twenty-six movies 1945–1961, and as producer on eight projects 1967–1979.

Skip Martin (orchestration): Born May 14, 1916, in Robinson, Illinois, and died in February 1976 in Hollywood. Also known as Kip Martin, he worked as orchestrator on twenty movies 1950–1957, among them the best musicals M-G-M produced. Martin orchestrated the "Moses Supposes" number in *Singin'*. He is also credited as composer for an episode of the television series *Stagecoach West* in 1960.

Paul Maxey (skeptical party guest, or dancing fat man at party): Born March 15, 1907, in Wheaton, Illinois, and died June 3, 1963, in Pasadena, California. Also known as Paul R. Maxey, he appeared in 124 projects 1937–1963, a great many of them television shows. Maxey appeared in thirteen projects in addition to *Singin'* in 1952, almost all of them feature films.

Harry McAfee (set decoration): McAfee was associate art director on thirty-four projects 1934–1944 and art director on twenty-four 1933–1950. *Singin'* was his last project.

Dorothy McCarty (girlfriend in "Beautiful Girl"): Appeared in three movies 1937–1954.

Ann McCrea (second girl, or girl at party): Born on February 25, 1931, in Dubois, Pennsylvania. Appeared in forty projects, mostly on television, from 1952 to her last, an episode of *My Three Sons* in 1970.

Johnny McGovern (bit boy): Appeared in nine movie and television projects 1946–1956.

M. J. McLaughlin (music mixer): Also known as Michael J. McLaughlin. He worked as sound recordist, music mixer, or music recordist on twenty-one projects from 1934 until his last, which was *Singin'*.

Joseph Mell (played a projectionist): Born June 23, 1915, in Chicago and died August 31, 1977, in Los Angeles. Also known as Joe Mell, he was a bit actor in 136 projects 1951–1977, many of them on television.

Sheila Meyers (dancer, "Beautiful Girl" and "All I Do Is Dream of You"): Appeared in two movies and is credited as choreographer in one other.

Carl Milletaire (villain): Born June 21, 1912, and died May 4, 1994, in New York. Appeared in thirty-four films 1947–1962, and in twenty-five television shows 1950–1970. Appeared as the villain in *The Duelling Cavalier* and as the coin-tossing mobster in "The Broadway Ballet" of *Singin'*.

Millard Mitchell (R. F. Simpson): Born August 14, 1903, in Havana, Cuba, and died October 13, 1953, in Santa Monica. He performed in radio and stage shows during the 1930s and appeared in thirty-four projects 1931–1953.

Singin' was his third-last film. In another movie in 1952, *My Six Convicts,*
Mitchell had top billing.

Leo Monlon (key grip): Worked as a grip in five projects from 1948 to his last,
Singin'.

Gloria Moore (ad libber): Appeared in seven movie and television projects
1947–1956.

Marylyn Moore (usherette): Was only associated with one movie, *Singin',* but
apparently her bit part was dropped.

Rita Moreno (Zelda Zanders): Born Rosita Delores Alverio on December 11, 1931,
in Humacao, Puerto Rico. Her role was progressively shortened until Zelda
appears in only four scenes, and speaks only two lines, "What did I tell you,
Lina?" and "Oh, any time Don," both in her last scene. Moreno went on to
become the first person to win an Oscar, a Tony, an Emmy, and a Grammy.
She appeared in forty-seven films 1950–2005 (*Singin'* was her fourth movie)
and made fifty-eight guest appearances in television shows. Probably her
greatest triumph was the role of Anita in *West Side Story* (1961), for which she
won an Oscar for best supporting actress. Moreno also had a recurring role
on the television series *The Rockford Files,* for which she won an Emmy.

Forbes Murray (first man): Born Murray Forbes Barnard on November 4, 1884,
in Hamilton, Ontario, and died November 18, 1982, in Oregon. He played bit
parts in 257 movies 1936–1967, many of them M-G-M musicals.

Peggy Murray (dancer, "Beautiful Girl"; fainting girl): Born January 12, 1907,
and died July 2, 1976. Murray played the girl who faints at the sight of
Don Lockwood blowing a kiss at the premiere of *The Royal Rascal.* She also
appeared in *The Band Wagon* (1953) and her last appearance was in a picture
released in 1967.

Sally Musie (fashion show girl): No information available.

Warren Newcomb (special effects): Born April 28, 1894, and died in August
1960. Also known as Warren E. Newcombe, he is credited for special effects
on 204 movies 1932–1957, twenty-three of them in 1952 alone. Newcomb
worked on an impressive string of classic movie musicals. He also is credited
as a matte painter on six films, including *The Wizard of Oz* (1939), as
producer and director for two silent films, and for art effects on one movie.
Newcomb won two Oscars for special effects, in 1945 and 1948.

Anne Neyland (dancer, "Beautiful Girl"): Appeared in fourteen projects from
Singin', her first, to 1957, many of them on television.

Vicki Nichols (wardrobe): Credited for wardrobe work on two movies, the first in
1939, and the second, *Singin'.*

John M. Nikolaus Jr. (camera operator): Born May 18, 1913, and died February 10, 1985, in Malibu, California. Also known as John Nicholaus, John Matthew Nicholaus Jr., John Nickolaus Jr., Jack Nicholaus, John M. Nicholaus, and John Nicholaus, he is credited for work as camera operator on eleven movie projects from 1944 to his last, *Singin'*, and as cinematographer on forty-seven movies and television shows from 1956 to 1983.

Betty Noyes (singing dubber, "Would You" and "You Are My Lucky Star"): Born as Elizabeth Noyes on October 11, 1912, in Oklahoma, and died December 24, 1987, in Los Angeles. Normally uncredited because of the industry's attempt to keep dubbing a trade secret, nevertheless Noyes was credited for her work on the soundtrack of two movies, *Singin'* and *Seven Brides for Seven Brothers* (1954). She acted in two movies as well as in a television episode of *I Love Lucy* (1956).

Donald O'Connor (Cosmo Brown): *Singin' in the Rain* gave O'Connor an opportunity to dance brilliantly and in ways he never did before or since. See biographical information in Chapters 2 and 9.

Tom Ordoqui (props): Worked with props on three movies, the last of which was *Singin'*.

Betty Orge (fashion show girl): No information available.

Ruth Packard (ad libber): Died May 19, 1978, at Jamestown, New York. She appeared in eight movie and television projects 1951–1966.

Maurice de Packh (orchestrator): Born November 21, 1896, in New York and died May 24, 1960, in Beverly Hills. After studying music, he led the DePackh Ensemble 1928–1931, arranged music for Broadway shows, and went to Hollywood in 1933, where he wrote popular songs while orchestrating movie music. He is credited for 136 projects 1933–1959, as music arranger, orchestrator, or composer.

Helene Parsons (hairstylist): Worked as hairstylist on only one movie, *Singin'*.

Dorothy Patrick (second usherette, audience member): Born June 3, 1921, in St. Boniface, Manitoba, and died May 31, 1987, in Los Angeles. Also known as Dorothy Patrick David and Dorothy Patric, she appeared in fifty-two projects from 1939 to 1956. Her part as second usherette was dropped from the movie.

Ralph A. Pender (re-recording and effects mixer): Born August 31, 1901, in Maine and died June 15, 1961, in Los Angeles. Pender worked as sound re-recording mixer, dialogue editor, and effects mixer on ten projects from 1936 to his last, *Singin'*.

Betty Jane Pettit (fashion show girl): Appeared in only one other movie, *Champagne Music* (1946).

Frank V. Phillips (camera operator): Born April 7, 1912, in Illinois and died April 29, 1994, in Los Angeles. Phillips is credited as assistant camera operator on two projects, as camera operator for *Singin'*, and as director of photography on fifty-two projects 1955–1982.

Betty Jane Pike (fashion show girl): No information available.

Allen Pinson (fencer, stunts): Born 1916 and died January 22, 2006. Also known as Alan Pinson, he appeared in fifty-three movie and television projects from 1944 to 1974. Thirty of those credits are as stuntman but one is as associate producer.

Walter Plunkett (costume designer): Born June 5, 1902, in Oakland, California, and died March 8, 1982, in Santa Monica. Nicknamed Plunky, he studied at the University of California and went to New York in 1923, where he acted and designed sets and costumes for the stage. Back to California as an extra in the movies, Plunkett eventually found his niche designing costumes for M-G-M. He worked on 157 projects 1927–1966, and lived for many years with his gay partner Lee.

Harry "Snub" Pollard (old man in "Rain" number): Born Harry Fraser on November 9, 1889, in Melbourne, Australia, and died January 19, 1962, in Burbank, California. Fraser came to the United States as part of a vaudeville troupe in 1910, stayed when the troupe dissolved, and changed his name to Pollard. He worked in films from 1911, appeared in the *Lonesome Luke* series, and supported Laurel and Hardy in their movies. Pollard created his own film production company, twice, but failed to make a go of it either time. Among his greatest successes was his role as Pee Wee, the comic sidekick of Tex Ritter. He appeared in 301 projects 1911–1961 and played bit parts such as "Man at Dance" (*Loaded Pistols*, 1948), "Sailor With Baby" (*Stand By for Action*, 1942), and "Soup customer" (*'Neath Brooklyn Bridge*, 1942). In addition to playing the role of the old man to whom Kelly gives his umbrella after his dance in the title number of *Singin'*, Pollard appears to be the old man who stops in the rain in front of the theater at the preview of *The Duelling Cavalier* and asks the ticket taker, Fred Datig Jr., if a comedy is playing.

Dorothy Ponedel (key makeup artist): Died in 1981. After growing up in Chicago, Ponedel moved to Los Angeles in 1920, and acted as an extra in three silent films before working in makeup from 1930. She worked with Judy Garland and became her friend, and is credited with eleven projects as key makeup artist from 1935 to her last, *Singin'*. Ponedel retired after contracting multiple sclerosis in 1951.

Angie O. Poulis (fruit peddler): Worked on six projects from 1943 to 1952. Her scene as a fruit peddler with Don and Cosmo as boys was filmed but cut from the final release print of *Singin'*. This would have been her last movie appearance.

Charles Regan (saloon keeper): Died December 26, 1978, in Santa Monica. Also known as Charlie Regan, appeared in forty-nine projects from 1935 to 1955, often as a heavy.

Irving G. Reis (special effects): Born May 7, 1906, in New York, and died July 3, 1953, in Woodland Hills, California. Reis attended Columbia University before moving to California to work as director of twenty-one movies 1925–1952, as writer on five movies in the late 1930s and early 1940s, as cinematographer on four projects 1922–1929, and as sound director on one film. The Assistant Director's Reports as well as the screen credits for the movie acknowledge Reis for special effects in the making of *Singin'*.

Debbie Reynolds (Kathy Selden): *Singin' in the Rain* gave Reynolds her first major movie role and jump-started her film career. See biographical information in Chapters 2 and 9.

Shirley Jean Rickert (dancer): Born March 25, 1926, in Seattle, Washington. She is also known as Gilda, Shirley Jean, Shirley Jean Measures, Shirley Jane Rickert, Shirley Jean Ricketts, and Shirley Ricketts. Rickert won a baby contest at age one and a half, moved to Hollywood with her mother as a young girl, and played Shirley in the *Our Gang* movies. She appeared in thirty films from 1927 to her last, *Singin'*. She then performed in burlesque shows as a stripper and retired in Buffalo, New York.

Joanne Rio (dancer, "Beautiful Girl"): Born as Joanne Gloria Rotunno on December 15, 1931, in Illinois, and died November 29, 1984, in Los Angeles. Often a stand-in for Elizabeth Taylor, she appeared in three movie projects. *Singin'* was her first project, and the last was in 1955.

Joette Robinson (dancer, "Beautiful Girl" and "All I Do Is Dream of You"): Appeared as a dancer in three movies from 1943 to her last, *Singin'*.

Joey Robinson (dancer): Miss Robinson appeared in only one movie, *Singin'*, as a dancer.

Anthony Rocke (man in forecourt): Appeared in only one movie, *Singin'*.

Dennis Ross (Cosmo as a boy): Appeared in six movies and two episodes of *The Lone Ranger* on television, 1951–1954. His last role was in *The Long, Long Trailer* (1954).

Harold Rosson (director of photography): Born on August 24, 1895, in Genaseo, New York, and died September 6, 1988, in Palm Beach, Florida. Rosson began his movie career in 1908 as an actor for Vitagraph Studios in Brooklyn. Then he went on to do almost every job imaginable in the industry—as a handyman, selling tickets, and assisting directors. Rosson worked as a cinematographer for many film companies in New York and Hollywood, served in World War I, and worked for Metro before it merged to become M-G-M. Rosson's work for M-G-M from 1924 until his semiretirement in 1958 allowed him to collaborate with the studio's best directors. He developed effective ways to light and shoot in Technicolor, and was nominated for five Academy Awards, the first of which was for *The Wizard of Oz* (1939). He also shot the sequence that depicted the burning of Atlanta in *Gone with the Wind* (1939). Rosson is credited as cinematographer on 147 movies 1915–1966, about three per year. He is also responsible for the difficult backlighting of the rain in the "Singin'" number.

Bill Ryan (assistant to Arthur Freed): Worked as unit manager for the Freed Unit for many years, and as assistant to Freed on several movies. As unit manager, Ryan was responsible for plotting out the logistics and timetables for all movies produced by the Freed Unit. He also was assistant director for six movies, including Gene Kelly's first film, *For Me and My Gal* (1942). Ryan was the brother of Pat Nixon, Richard Nixon's wife. Nixon was a member of Congress, and accepted the Republican nomination for vice president a few months after the release of *Singin' in the Rain*.

Paul Salata (ad libber): Also known as Paul T. Salata, appeared in thirteen projects 1951–1960.

Conrad Salinger (orchestration): Born on August 30, 1901, in Massachusetts and died July 6, 1961, in Pacific Palisades, California. Worked on eighty-one movies 1931–1962, many of them classic M-G-M musicals, including *The Pirate* (1948) and *On the Town* (1949).

Dave Saltuper (wardrobe): Worked on only one movie, *Singin'*.

William Saracino (music mixer): Born October 22, 1912, and died July 18, 2002, in Santa Clarita, California. Also known as Bill Saracino, he worked as music editor or music mixer on forty-eight projects from 1939 to 1987.

Audrey Saunders (dancer, "Beautiful Girl"): Appeared in five projects as acrobat, dancer, or nun, and in four as stuntwoman, all 1948–1975.

Russell Saunders (fencer and stunt double for Gene Kelly): Born Russell Maurice Saunders on May 21, 1919, in Winnipeg, Manitoba, and died May 29, 2001, in West Los Angeles. A winner of the Canadian National Championship in gymnastics and diving, Saunders had a long career as a stuntman in Hollywood, and doubled for many actors. He appeared in thirty-five films as a stuntman, from the first, *King Kong* (1933), to the last, *Mississippi Burning* (1988), and including disaster movies such as *The Towering Inferno* (1970) and *The Poseidon Adventure* (1972). Saunders also played bit parts in twenty-five movies and television shows 1940–1981. His work included classics such as *The Three Musketeers* (1948) and *An American in Paris* (1951), where he doubled for Gene Kelly. In the latter film, there were no stunts, but Kelly and Nina Foch were doubled in a long shot, showing the couple in a car in Paris. Saunders also served as the model for a Salvador Dali painting, *The Christ of St. John of the Cross,* completed in 1951.

William Schallert (messenger): Born July 6, 1922, in Los Angeles. Also known as Bill Schallert, he was the son of drama editor Edwin Schallert of the *Los Angeles Times.* Bill graduated from the University of California at Los Angeles and has had an astonishingly long history of movie and television work, appearing in 310 projects from 1947 to today, most of them on television. Schallert appeared in fourteen films in 1952 alone. His one scene in the script of *Singin',* as a messenger who brings Don a message in *The Duelling Cavalier,* and his only line, "A message, Pierre!," was cut from the release print of the movie to save running time.

Betty Scott (dancer, "Beautiful Girl" and "All I Do Is Dream of You"): Her first project was *Singin'.* Her only other appearance was in a 1956 television episode of *I Love Lucy.*

Wes Shanks (gaffer): Worked as a set lighting foreman on one film in 1935, and as gaffer, or lighting technician, on five others from 1939 to *Singin',* which was his last.

David Sharpe (fencer and stunt double for Gene Kelly): Born David Hardin Sharpe on February 2, 1910, in St. Louis and died March 30, 1980, in Altadena, California. Nicknamed the "Crown Prince of Stuntmen," Sharpe's first appearance in the movies was at age twelve with Douglas Fairbanks in *Robin Hood* (1922). After winning the United States National Tumbling Championship for two years in a row, Sharpe returned to the movies in supporting roles, mostly in comedies, until he began to do stunt work in westerns and war pictures in the early 1940s. He appeared as a stunt double in 199 movies 1922–1978, including classics such as *The Three Musketeers* (1948), and as an actor in 154 projects 1923–1974. Sharpe also is credited as writer of three movies in 1935.

Douglas Shearer (recording supervisor): Born November 17, 1899, in Westmount, Quebec, and died January 5, 1971, in Culver City, California. Shearer began to work for M-G-M before the advent of sound pictures, and headed the newly created sound department by 1928. Credited with developing the idea for the playback method of filming musical numbers, Shearer's name is on 910 projects as sound recorder from 1928 to 1955, and one as a director, in 1940. He was director of technical research at M-G-M from 1955 to 1968. Shearer won twelve Oscars for Best Sound Recording, and was the brother of the famous actress Norma Shearer.

Robert Shirley (re-recording and effects mixer): Worked as sound re-recording and effects mixer on twenty-seven projects 1930–1956, including *The Wizard of Oz* (1939). *Singin'* was his second-last project.

Cliff Shirpser (assistant camera, Technicolor): Born August 3, 1906, in California and died December 18, 1977, in Los Angeles. Also known as Cliff Schertzer, Clifford G. Shirpser, and Clifford M. Shirpser, he worked as assistant cameraman, or as Technicolor assistant, on 110 projects 1921–1982, among them some of the classic silent and sound films of Hollywood. Shirpser also worked on special effects for eleven projects, as cinematographer for six (mostly television shows), and on visual effects for four projects.

Lela Simone (music coordinator and assistant to Arthur Freed): Born Magdaline Lela Saenger on August 26, 1907, in Berlin, Germany, and died January 23, 1991, in San Diego. A concert pianist, she fled Nazi Germany in 1933 and worked as piano soloist for the M-G-M orchestra by the latter part of that decade. She subsequently did many things at the studio, including vocal coaching, teaching piano, and editing music until she resigned in 1958. She is credited with only four projects as musician, or music coordinator, however, including *Singin'*.

William Steinkamp (sound mixer): Worked as sound mixer, effects mixer, and in re-recording on twenty-eight projects from *Bombshell* in 1933 to *Doctor Zhivago* in 1965.

Michael Steinore (re-recording and effects mixer): Born 1901. He won an Oscar and was nominated for three others for his work in Best Effects or Special Effects. Steinore is credited for sound effects, re-recording, and effects mixing on twenty-one projects from 1934 to his last, which was *Singin'*.

Elaine Stewart (lady-in-waiting): Born Elsy Steinberg on May 31, 1929, in Montclair, New Jersey. Stewart appeared in twenty-eight projects from 1952 (*Singin'* was her third movie that year) to 1964. She played Gene Kelly's fiancée, whom he ditches for the character played by Cyd Charisse, in *Brigadoon* (1954).

Ben Strobach (unidentified bit role): Appeared in one other movie besides *Singin'*. Although IMDB lists Strobach as "leading man," he was not the leading man in the barroom fight scene, and it is not clear what role he played in *Singin'*.

William C. Strohm (production manager): Worked on only one movie, *Singin'*.

Marvin Stuart (assistant director): Born May 6, 1901, and died June 22, 1968. Stuart worked as assistant director on fifty projects including many musicals from 1937 to 1960, and on four as production manager from 1962 to 1967. He was responsible for writing the Assistant Director's Reports that have been extremely useful in detailing the filming of *Singin'* throughout this book.

Brick Sullivan (cop in "Rain" number): Born July 28, 1899, in South Dakota and died September 4, 1959, in Los Angeles. Also known as James Brick Sullivan, he appeared in 105 movies 1936–1959, and in half a dozen television shows 1953–1955. Sullivan appeared in seven films released in 1952, and played a policeman or guard in four of them.

Allen Sutherland (Don as a boy): Appeared in only one film, *Singin'*. He danced very well, for such a young boy, in the poolroom scene.

Julius Tannen (man in talking pictures demonstration): Born March 16, 1880, in New York and died January 3, 1965, in Woodland Hills, California. Tannen appeared in fifty films 1934–1959, forty-three of them before *Singin'*.

Ray Teal (studio worker): Born January 12, 1902, in Grand Rapids, Michigan, and died April 2, 1976, in Santa Monica, California. Teal played the saxophone while a student at the University of California at Los Angeles and formed a band in the 1920s and early 1930s. He appeared in 313 projects 1937–1974, many of them on television. Teal had a small but prominent role in *The Best Years of Our Lives* (1946) and as a judge in *Judgment at Nuremberg* (1961). His most famous role, however, was as Sheriff Roy Coffee on *Bonanza;* he appeared in ninety-five episodes of that long-running television western.

Harry Tenbrook (workman): Born Henry Olaf Hansen on October 9, 1887, in Oslo, Norway, and died September 14, 1960, in Woodland Hills, California. Tenbrook appeared in 326 projects 1911–1960, his last role as a courtroom extra in *Inherit the Wind,* which co-starred Gene Kelly. He appeared in more than forty silent films and worked on eight movie projects in 1952 alone.

Beverly Thompson (fashion show girl): Born June 2, 1925, in Hampton, Iowa, and died on June 4, 1992. She appeared in thirty movie and television projects 1945–1988.

Jimmy Thompson (male lead in "Beautiful Girl"): Appeared in nine projects 1950–1973. Thompson was a member of the stock company in *Summer*

Stock (1950), his first movie, and was Gene Kelly's dance assistant on two
film projects. His most visible roles were as Charlie Chisholm Dalrymple
in *Brigadoon* (1954), starring Gene Kelly, and as Youngerford in the science
fiction classic *Forbidden Planet* (1956). Thompson had a fine voice and sang
"Beautiful Girl" for himself in *Singin'*. (Ironically, he was dubbed in *Brigadoon*
because Michael Maule, who was supposed to play the role of Dalrymple, had
to leave at the last minute after John Gustafson had recorded the song, and
the studio did not want to waste that dubbing playback.[3])

John True (makeup): Worked on only one movie, *Singin'*.

Dee Turnell (ad libber): Born November 27, 1925. She appeared, often as a dancer,
in sixteen projects from 1947 to 1955, many of them classic M-G-M musicals.

William Tuttle (makeup): Born April 13, 1912, in Jacksonville, Florida. Also
known as Bill, Bob, or William J. Tuttle, he left school at age fifteen and
worked in burlesque as a comedian until forming his own band. Moving to
Hollywood at age eighteen, Tuttle entered the movie industry as a makeup
artist, worked for thirty-five years with M-G-M, and was married to Donna
Reed. Tuttle also taught classes at the University of Southern California film
school, and later created his own line of cosmetics. His brother Thomas also
was a makeup artist. Tuttle worked on 341 projects 1935–1981.

Gwen Verdon (sound effects in "Rain" number): Born Gwenyth Verdon on
January 13, 1925, in Culver City and died October 18, 2000, in Woodstock,
Vermont. The daughter of English immigrants to the United States (her
mother worked in vaudeville and her father as an electrician at M-G-M),
Verdon began dancing lessons at age three to counteract the effect of rickets.
She worked with choreographer Jack Cole and taught dance lessons in
Hollywood. Although listed on IMDB as assistant choreographer, her only
involvement in *Singin'* was to help dub some of the sloshing sound effects
of Gene Kelly's splashing in the large water puddle of the title number. Her
big break came the year after *Singin'* was released when she got a role in Cole
Porter's stage show *Can Can*, and received the first of four Tony Awards for
her performance. Verdon appeared in forty-six projects 1943–2000.

Tommy Walker (ad libber): Also known as Tom Walker, he appeared in seventeen
projects 1941–1974.

Audrey Washburn (ad libber): Appeared in only one movie, *Singin'*.

Bobby Watson (diction coach): Born Robert Watson Knucher. At age ten, he
sold peanuts at the Olympic Theatre in Springfield, Illinois, and began to do
comic routines after watching the shows there over the next three years. He
performed on the road with the Kickapoo Remedies Show. By 1918, Watson

was in New York doing comedy roles on stage, often in female roles or as an effeminate male. He gained popularity as a male dressmaker in *Irene* in 1919. Watson appeared in eighty-two projects from 1925 to 1962, eleven of them as Adolf Hitler because he bore a viable resemblance to the German dictator. In fact, his role just before *Singin'* was as Hitler in *The Whip Hand*, but his scenes were deleted when that picture was released in 1951.

Lynn Wilder (fashion show girl): Born Mary Lyn Wilde on October 10, 1922, in East St. Louis, Illinois. Also known as Lou Lee, Lyn, and a member of The Wilde Twins, Wilder appeared in fifteen projects 1941–1953, including several M-G-M musicals.

Robert B. Williams (policeman): Born September 23, 1904, in Illinois and died June 17, 1978, in Orange County, California. Williams appeared in 169 movies 1936–1968, and ninety television shows 1949–1969. He most often appeared in pictures as a cop, and in *Singin'*, he played one of the policemen at the premiere of *The Royal Rascal*.

Edwin B. Willis (set decoration): Born January 28, 1893, in Decatur, Illinois, and died November 26, 1963, in Hollywood. Also known as Edwin Booth Willis, he worked as set decorator on 602 projects from *Ben-Hur: A Tale of the Christ* (1925) to *Don't Go Near the Water* (1957). Many of his films were classic M-G-M musicals, and Willis worked on thirty-four pictures in 1952 alone. He also worked in the art department on 192 movies 1933–1955, and as art director on eighteen movies 1925–1938. Nominated thirty-two times, Willis won eight Oscars.

Wilson Wood (Rudy Vallee impersonator with megaphone): Appeared in eighty-nine projects 1946–1963, including many M-G-M musicals. Wood not only performed as the Rudy Vallee impersonator, but his voice was used in the brief rendition of "Should I?" as part of the montage number in *Singin'*.

Adam York (publicity man): Appeared in only one other movie besides *Singin'*.

Norma Zimmer (dancer in "Beautiful Girl"): Born Norma Beatrice Larsen on July 13, 1923, in Larsen, Idaho. She sang background vocals for Frank Sinatra, Judy Garland, and other singers under the names Norma Larson, Norma Larsen, and Norma Zimmer. She appeared in only three films, but on many television shows, including *I Love Lucy* and *The Lawrence Welk Show* (the latter 1960–1982). Zimmer continued to perform with the Lawrence Welk Orchestra at Lawrence Welk Champagne Theater in Branson, Missouri, and hosted some Welk show reruns on PBS.

\\\\\ *Notes*

ABBREVIATIONS

AMPAS

Academy of Motion Picture Arts and Sciences, Margaret Herrick Library, Beverly Hills, California

BU

Boston University, Howard Gottlieb Archival Research Center, Boston, Massachusetts

CU

Columbia University Libraries, Oral History Research Office, Popular Arts Project, New York, New York

DD-NYPL

New York Public Library, Library for the Performing Arts, New York, New York

UAL

University of Arizona Libraries, Tucson, Arizona

UI

University of Iowa Libraries, Special Collections Department, Iowa City, Iowa

USC

University of Southern California, Archives of Performing Arts and Warner Bros. Archives, Los Angeles, California

PREFACE

1. Thomas, *Films of Gene Kelly*, 139; Mariani, "Come On with the Rain," 7; Mast, *Can't Help Singin'*, 266; Kael, *5001 Nights*, 535; Gerstel, "Singin' in the Rain (1952)," 264; F. X. Feeney review in *LA Weekly*, September 5, 1997, *Singin' in the Rain* Clippings, Core Collection, Herrick Library, AMPAS.

2. Jack Martin Smith interview with Jerome Delamater, November 19, 1973, in Delamater, *Dance in the Hollywood Musical*, 255.

CHAPTER I. ALL WE WERE TOLD WAS TO WRITE A MOVIE

1. Comden and Green, *Singin' in the Rain*, 1.

2. Ibid.; Fordin, *M-G-M's Greatest Musicals*, 351.

3. Comden and Green, *Singin' in the Rain*, 3.

4. Arthur Freed biography and filmography, imbd.com.

5. Comden and Green, *Singin' in the Rain*, 3.

6. Ibid.

7. Fordin, *M-G-M's Greatest Musicals*, ix–x; Arthur Freed biography, imbd .com.

8. Hemming, *Melody Lingers On*, 324; Fordin, *M-G-M's Greatest Musicals*, 347; Thomas, *Films of Gene Kelly*, 133, 135; Nacio Herb Brown biography, imdb.com.

9. Thomas, *Films of Gene Kelly*, 135; Nacio Herb Brown biography, imdb.com; Hemming, *Melody Lingers On*, 324.

10. Thomas, *Films of Gene Kelly*, 135; Fordin, *M-G-M's Greatest Musicals*, 7; "An Oral History with Robert M. W. Vogel," by Barbara Hall, 1990, 270, Oral History Program, Herrick Library, AMPAS.

11. Higham, *Merchant of Dreams*, 65–70; Parish and Bowers, *MGM Stock Company*, 791.

12. Higham, *Merchant of Dreams*, 5–6, 11–12; Parish and Bowers, *MGM Stock Company*, 791, 796.

13. Parish and Bowers, *MGM Stock Company*, 792, 797.

14. Crafton, *The Talkies*, 294; Kreuger, "Birth of the American Film Musical," 45; Hay, *MGM*, 63; Silverman, *Dancing on the Ceiling*, 143–145.

15. Kreuger, "Birth of the American Film Musical," 45; Delamater, *Dance in the Hollywood Musical*, 24; Mast, *Can't Help Singin'*, 92–93.

16. Fordin, *M-G-M's Greatest Musicals*, 350; Crafton, *The Talkies*, 295; Kreuger, "Birth of the American Film Musical," 45; Hemming, *Melody Lingers On*, 324; Hay, *MGM*, 63.

17. Harry Beaumont quoted in Crafton, *The Talkies*, 294.

18. Fordin, *M-G-M's Greatest Musicals*, 351; Kreuger, "Birth of the American Film Musical," 46; Hemming, *Melody Lingers On*, 324; Kobal, *Gotta Sing, Gotta Dance*, 29; Hay, *MGM*, 61, 70. See excerpts of the "Singin' in the Rain" number from *The Hollywood Revue of 1929* in *That's Entertainment III*, 1994.

19. Delamater, *Dance in the Hollywood Musical*, 17; Kreuger, "Birth of the American Film Musical," 48.

20. Kreuger, "Birth of the American Film Musical," 48; Astaire, *Steps in Time*, 200.

21. Delamater, *Dance in the Hollywood Musical*, 23; Silverman, *Dancing on the Ceiling*, 145n; Fordin, *M-G-M's Greatest Musicals*, 81n.

22. Parish and Bowers, *MGM Stock Company*, 792–793; Kobal, *Gotta Sing, Gotta Dance*, 201.

23. Delamater, *Dance in the Hollywood Musical*, 67–68, 100.

24. Hemming, *Melody Lingers On*, 326.

25. Arthur Freed quoted in Kobal, *Gotta Sing, Gotta Dance*, 201.

26. Comden and Green, *Singin' in the Rain*, 2; Roger Edens biography, imdb .com; Fordin, *M-G-M's Greatest Musicals*, 1, 3.

27. Basinger, *American Cinema*, 185; Hirschhorn, *Gene Kelly*, 159; Minnelli, *I Remember It Well*, 125.

28. Mast, *Can't Help Singin'*, 267.

29. Gene Kelly interview by Graham Fuller, 1994, in Boorman et al., eds., *Projections 4*, 281.

30. Fordin, *M-G-M's Greatest Musicals*, 253–254; Hay, *MGM*, 218–219.

31. Mast, *Can't Help Singin'*, 267.

32. Fordin, *M-G-M's Greatest Musicals*, 252–253; Parish and Bowers, *MGM Stock Company*, 793.

33. Parish and Bowers, *MGM Stock Company*, 794, 797.

34. Basinger, *Gene Kelly*, 90.

35. Previn, *No Minor Chords*, 61–62, 64.

36. Gene Kelly quoted in Thomas, *Films of Gene Kelly*, 140, and in Hirschhorn, *Gene Kelly*, 159–160.

37. Fordin, *M-G-M's Greatest Musicals*, 350. Silverman, *Dancing on the Ceiling*, 147, incorrectly reports that Freed sold his collection of songs to M-G-M in 1950 for $25,000. Wollen, *Singin' in the Rain*, 31, repeats this inaccuracy and also cites the year as 1949. The $25,000 was simply a fee M-G-M paid Freed to use his songs in their movies. This possibility was mentioned in Freed's original employment agreement but not acted upon by M-G-M until 1950. Memo from the Vice-President of Loew's to Freed, August 26, 1950, *Singin' in the Rain* Folder, Arthur Freed Collection, USC.

38. "'Singing in Rain' on Freed's MGM Slate," *Hollywood Reporter*, March 15, 1949, *Singin' in the Rain* Microfiche, Core Collection, Herrick Library, AMPAS; Behlmer, *America's Favorite Movies*, 254. Hirschhorn, *Gene Kelly*, 178, incorrectly reports that the project did not have a title at this point. Freed had decided on the title *Singin' in the Rain* for this project in 1949.

39. "Original Singing in the Rain-Cp rough draft of story outline from Ben Feiner, Jr.," January 28, 1949, Folder 1229, Turner/MGM Script Collection, Herrick Library, AMPAS; Behlmer, *America's Favorite Movies*, 254–256; Freed speech, undated and unpaginated, Box 21, Folder 2 of 2, Arthur Freed Collection, USC.

40. Freed speech, undated and unpaginated, Box 21, Folder 2 of 2, Arthur Freed Collection, USC.

41. Thomas, *Films of Gene Kelly*, 133.

42. Comden and Green, *Singin' in the Rain*, 1.

43. Comden, *Off Stage*, 20–22, 103, 115, 117; Betty Comden biography, imdb.com.

44. Richard Severo, "Adolph Green," imdb.com; Adolph Green biography, imdb.com.

45. Richard Severo, "Adolph Green," imdb.com; Kurtti, *Movie Musical Trivia Book*, 25–26.

46. Richard Severo, "Adolph Green," imdb.com.

47. Ibid.; Behlmer, *America's Favorite Movies*, 255; "Reminiscences of Betty Comden and Adolph Green: Oral History, 1959," 27, Popular Arts Project, Oral History Research Office, CU.

48. Comden, *Off Stage*, 68–69, 124; Richard Severo, "Adolph Green," imdb.com.

49. Previn, *No Minor Chords*, 66.

50. Richard Severo, "Adolph Green," imdb.com; Comden, *Off Stage*, 137.

51. Richard Severo, "Adolph Green," imdb.com.

52. Comden and Green interview with Tina Daniell and Pat McGilligan, McGilligan, 1989, ed., *Backstory 2*, 87; Leslie Caron in "Gene Kelly," *A & E Biography*, February 3, 1996.

53. *Singin' in the Rain* screenplay, October 14, 1950, Comden's and Green's address is written in a pencilled note on the cover, Folder 1235, Turner/MGM Script Collection, Herrick Library, AMPAS. The authors of this book have seen the house where Comden and Green wrote the script of *Singin' in the Rain*. It is on the southwest corner of the intersection of Camden and Carmelita. As of 2007, it was obviously the same house as in 1950, Spanish-style, not much renovated, and still solid.

54. Comden and Green, *Singin' in the Rain*, 7.

55. Ibid., 4; Comden and Green interview by Tina Daniell and Pat McGilligan, 1989, in McGilligan, ed., *Backstory 2*, 82.

56. Casper, *Stanley Donen*, 44; Stanley Donen quoted in Silverman, *Dancing on the Ceiling*, 149; Comden and Green interview by Tina Daniell and Pat McGilligan, 1989, in McGilligan, ed., *Backstory 2*, 82.

57. Comden and Green, *Singin' in the Rain*, 5.

58. Ibid.

59. Morley and Leon, *Gene Kelly*, 115; Gerstel, "Singin' in the Rain (1952)," 265; Kelly, "Dialogue on Film," 39; "Gene Kelly Interview," 251–252, Marilyn Hunt, 1975, Oral History Program, DD-NYPL. Casper, *Stanley Donen*, 239, mentions that *Show Girl in Hollywood* (1930) dealt with early sound film production. But there is no evidence that any of the creators of *Singin' in the Rain* had seen this film.

60. Comden and Green, *Singin' in the Rain*, 6–7.

61. Ibid., 7–8.

62. Comden, *Off Stage*, 119–121.

63. *Singin' in the Rain* screenplays, August 10, September 14, October 5, 14, 20, 1950, Folders 1230 to 1235, Turner/MGM Script Collection, Herrick Library, AMPAS; Behlmer, *America's Favorite Movies*, 257–258.

64. *Singin' in the Rain* screenplay, August 10, 1950, Folder 1230, Turner/MGM Script Collection, Herrick Library, AMPAS.

65. Ibid., 68–69; Mariani, "Come On with the Rain," 12; Behlmer, *America's Favorite Movies*, 257; Silverman, *Dancing on the Ceiling*, 150–151.

66. *Singin' in the Rain* screenplay, August 10, 1950, 69, Folder 1230, Turner/ MGM Script Collection, Herrick Library, AMPAS.

67. Ibid., 1, 7, 18.

68. Ibid., 7, 38, 64.

69. Ibid., 29, 32, 41, 47–48, 51; Behlmer, *America's Favorite Movies*, 257–258.

70. *Singin' in the Rain* screenplay, August 10, 1950, 60–61, 63–66, 70, 72, 74, Folder 1230, Turner/MGM Script Collection, Herrick Library, AMPAS.

71. Ibid., 80–81.

72. Ibid., 76, 81–88.

73. Ibid., 88.

CHAPTER 2. THE REASON WE HAD SUCH GOOD MUSICALS

1. Comden and Green, *Singin' in the Rain*, 6; Silverman, *Dancing on the Ceiling*, 149.

2. Comden and Green interview by Tina Daniell and Pat McGilligan, 1989, in McGilligan, ed., *Backstory 2*, 82. Donen insisted that he and Kelly met for weeks with Comden and Green, who then wrote the part specifically for Gene, because it was already decided he would be in it. Stanley Donen interview, 1973, in Harvey, "Stanley Donen," 5. Hirschhorn, *Gene Kelly*, 179, supported this scenario and added that when the script was given to Kelly and Donen, it was already decided that they were to co-direct it. Later in his life, at age eighty-two or so, Donen remembered the origin of the movie differently: Freed called him and Gene and said, "Let's do a movie with songs that Herb Brown and I wrote together," and he and Kelly looked at the sheet music and said, "these songs are all about when sound films came about, so the movie *has* to be about talkies, so Comden and Green were brought in," and they agreed with that idea. Stanley Donen interview with Robert Osborne, *Private Screenings*, 2006.

3. Comden and Green, *Singin' in the Rain*, 8. Hirschhorn, *Gene Kelly*, 179,

incorrectly reports that even at this stage, when the scripts were given to Kelly and Donen to read, the project did not have a title, and it was called *Singin' in the Rain* only after they began to work with Comden and Green on rewrites. Not only had Freed decided on this title in 1949, but the title also appears on each script of the movie from the earliest to the latest. "'Singing in Rain' on Freed's MGM Slate," *Hollywood Reporter*, March 15, 1949, *Singin' in the Rain* Microfiche, Core Collection, Herrick Library, AMPAS; *Singin' in the Rain* screenplays, Turner/MGM Script Collection, Herrick Library, AMPAS.

4. Hirschhorn, *Gene Kelly*, 5, 8–9, 14–15; Gene Kelly quoted in Hirschhorn, *Gene Kelly*, 14; Gene Kelly biography, imdb.com, 4. Hirschhorn incorrectly notes Gene's birth date as August 3, 1912 (instead of August 23, 1912) and says the scar is on his right cheek (although it is on his left cheek).

5. Hirschhorn, *Gene Kelly*, 10–11, 13–14, 16, 20–22; "Reminiscences of Gene Curran Kelly: Oral History, 1958," 1–2, Popular Arts Project, Oral History Research Office, CU.

6. Hirschhorn, *Gene Kelly*, 17, 21–24, 28–29.

7. "Reminiscences of Gene Curran Kelly: Oral History, 1958," 3, Popular Arts Project, Oral History Research Office, CU; Fred Kelly interview, 1989, in Frank, *Tap!*, 173–174; Hirschhorn, *Gene Kelly*, 30–31, 37–38; Yudkoff, *Gene Kelly*, 15, 19.

8. Hirschhorn, *Gene Kelly*, 25, 27–28, 33–34; Yudkoff, *Gene Kelly*, 18, 21, 25, 27, 32; "Reminiscences of Gene Curran Kelly: Oral History, 1958," 1, Popular Arts Project, Oral History Research Office, CU.

9. Hirschhorn, *Gene Kelly*, 43, 45–47; Gene Kelly interview with Ron Haver, 1984, in Haver, "Kelly," 58.

10. Gene Kelly interview with Ron Haver, 1984, in Haver, "Kelly," 58; Hirschhorn, *Gene Kelly*, 50; Yudkoff, *Gene Kelly*, 54; Gene Kelly quoted in Hirschhorn, *Gene Kelly*, 58.

11. Hirschhorn, *Gene Kelly*, 62–63, 65–67, 69, 86, 155; Yudkoff, *Gene Kelly*, 63; "Gene Kelly Interview," Marilyn Hunt, 1975, 6, Oral History Program, DD-NYPL.

12. Fordin, *M-G-M's Greatest Musicals*, 60; Gene Kelly quoted in Hirschhorn, *Gene Kelly*, 94.

13. Hirschhorn, *Gene Kelly*, 72, 76, 80; Gene Kelly interview with Ron Haver, 1984, in Haver, "Kelly," 58; Mast, *Can't Help Singin'*, 181–182.

14. Fordin, *M-G-M's Greatest Musicals*, 61; Hirschhorn, *Gene Kelly*, 101.

15. Fordin, *M-G-M's Greatest Musicals*, 63n; Hirschhorn, *Gene Kelly*, 98–100.

16. Hirschhorn, *Gene Kelly*, 83–84; Kelly, "Dialogue on Film," 41; Gene Kelly interview with Ronald L. Davis, 1974, 20, SMU/Ronald L. Davis Oral History

Collection, Herrick Library, AMPAS; Gene Kelly quoted in Thomas, *Films of Gene Kelly*, 27; Gene Kelly quoted in Flatow, "Through a Lens Brightly," 15; Kelly, "Some Notes," 49; Gene Kelly quoted in "The Rise of a New Dancing Star, *Everyday Magazine*, April 28, 1944, clipping in Box 8, Scrapbook 6, Gene Kelly Collection, BU.

17. Hirschhorn, *Gene Kelly*, 104–105, 109–112; Gene Kelly interview with Ronald L. Davis, 1974, 33, and Stanley Donen interview with Ronald L. Davis, 1983, 8–10, SMU/Ronald L. Davis Oral History Collection, Herrick Library, AMPAS; Chaplin, *Golden Age*, 59–60; Yudkoff, *Gene Kelly*, 133–134; Gene Kelly to Marc Houlihan, May 27, 1953, Box 3, Folder 13, Gene Kelly Collection, BU; Gene Kelly quoted in Flatow, "Through a Lens Brightly," 15; Kobal, *Rita Hayworth*, 154–155.

18. Hirschhorn, *Gene Kelly*, 113, 115–116; Gene Kelly interview with Jerome Delamater and Paddy Whannel, 1973, in Delamater, *Dance in the Hollywood Musical*, 208; Fordin, *M-G-M's Greatest Musicals*, 122, 128; Vincente Minnelli interview with David Fantle and Tom Johnson, 1981, in Fantle and Johnson, *Reel to Real*, 263–264; Mueller, *Astaire Dancing*, 248.

19. Hirschhorn, *Gene Kelly*, 121–123.

20. Ibid., 123, 126–128, 131.

21. Ibid., 136, 138; Siegel, "The Pirate," 22.

22. Hirschhorn, *Gene Kelly*, 132, 139–140; Gene Kelly interview with Ronald L. Davis, 1974, 52, SMU/Ronald L. Davis Oral History Collection, Herrick Library, AMPAS.

23. Hemming, *Melody Lingers On*, 233; Basinger, *Gene Kelly*, 57; Yudkoff, *Gene Kelly*, 192.

24. Hirschhorn, *Gene Kelly*, 142–143; Gene Kelly interview with Ronald L. Davis, 1974, 50–51, SMU/Ronald L. Davis Oral History Collection, Herrick Library, AMPAS; Gene Kelly and Stanley Donen, "Take Me Out to the Ball Game," September 27, 1946, Folder 5, Turner/MGM Scripts Collection, Herrick Library, AMPAS; Fehr and Vogel, *Lullabies of Hollywood*, 213.

25. Hirschhorn, *Gene Kelly*, 153–156; Flatow, "Through a Lens Brightly," 11, 14; "Reminiscences of Gene Curran Kelly: Oral History, 1958," 19, Popular Arts Project, Oral History Research Office, CU; Genné, "Freedom Incarnate," 90; Yudkoff, *Gene Kelly*, 202.

26. Morgan Hudgins, "Directed by Kelly," unidentified newspaper clipping in Box 8, Scrapbook 5, Gene Kelly Collection, BU.

27. Charles Walters interview with Ronald L. Davis, 1980, 32, SMU/Ronald L. Davis Oral History Collection, Herrick Library, AMPAS; Clarke, *Get Happy*, 262–266; Pasternak, *Easy the Hard Way*, 231–232; Gene Kelly quoted in Thomas,

Films of Gene Kelly, 116; Gene Kelly interview with John Russell Taylor, 1980, in Britton, ed., *Talking Films*, 195–196; Gene Kelly quoted in Knox, *Magic Factory*, 139; Hirschhorn, *Gene Kelly*, 165–166.

28. Fordin, *M-G-M's Greatest Musicals*, 306–307, 309, 318–319, 322–324; Hirschhorn, *Gene Kelly*, 168–174. Although it is often reported that Leslie Caron was only seventeen in *An American in Paris* (Hirschhorn, *Gene Kelly*, 169), she was nineteen (born July 1, 1931, Leslie Caron biography, imdb.com) when the production started on August 1, 1950, Fordin, *M-G-M's Greatest Musicals*, 314.

29. Yudkoff, *Gene Kelly*, 211–212.

30. Hanson, "An Interview with Gene Kelly," 24; Gene Kelly quoted in Hirschhorn, *Gene Kelly*, 156, 158; Yudkoff, *Gene Kelly*, 202.

31. Stanley Donen biography, imdb.com; Stanley Donen quoted in Hirschhorn, *Gene Kelly*, 73–74; Hirschhorn, *Gene Kelly*, 103; Fordin, *M-G-M's Greatest Musicals*, 240; Kelly, "Dialogue on Film," 37.

32. Gene Kelly interview with Ronald L. Davis, 1974, 51, SMU/Ronald L. Davis Oral History Collection, Herrick Library, AMPAS; Gene Kelly interview with Jerome Delamater and Paddy Whannel, 1973, in Delamater, *Dance in the Hollywood Musical*, 207; Gene Kelly quoted in Thomas, *Films of Gene Kelly*, 20.

33. Silverman, *Dancing on the Ceiling*, 97; Hirschhorn, *Gene Kelly*, 102; Stanley Donen biography, imdb.com; Blair, *Memory of All That*, 165–166; Billman, *Film Choreographers and Dance Directors*, 278.

34. Blair, *Memory of All That*, 114–115; Silverman, *Dancing on the Ceiling*, 138.

35. Billman, *Film Choreographers and Dance Directors*, 349; "A Tribute to Larry Blyden: Remembering Carol Haney," larryblyden.net; Carol Haney biography, imdb.com; Carol Haney biography, thefreedictionary.com; Stephen Watts, "On Arranging Terpsichore for the Camera Eye," *New York Times*, September 14, 1952.

36. Randall Duell interview with Jerome Delamater, 1973, in Delamater, *Dance in the Hollywood Musical*, 247.

37. Charness, "Hollywood Cine-Dance," 6; Gene Kelly interview with Graham Fuller, 1994, in Boorman et al., eds., *Projections 4*, 281.

38. Hirschhorn, *Gene Kelly*, 158.

39. Comden and Green, *Singin' in the Rain*, 5; Hirschhorn, *Gene Kelly*, 63–64.

40. Hanson, "An Interview with Gene Kelly," 1966, 26.

41. Levant, *Memoirs of an Amnesiac*, 200–201.

42. Ibid., 40–41, 52, 95, 111, 178, 180, 193–195.

43. Wollen, *Singin' in the Rain*, 32.

44. Stanley Donen quoted in Fordin, *M-G-M's Greatest Musicals*, 354; "An Oral

History with Lela Simone," Rudy Behlmer, 1990, 316, Oral History Program, Herrick Library, AMPAS; Silverman, *Dancing on the Ceiling*, 153.

45. Silverman, *Dancing on the Ceiling*, 154.

46. Donen's biographer claims that Donen thought of Donald O'Connor and mentioned it to Freed. Silverman, *Dancing on the Ceiling*, 154. However, Donald O'Connor's biography reports that Gene Kelly thought of and insisted on getting O'Connor for the role of Cosmo. "Donald O'Connor," *A & E Biography,* December 29, 1999. Historian Peter Wollen supports Kelly's role in obtaining O'Connor as well (Wollen, *Singin' in the Rain*, 32).

47. Donald O'Connor biography, imdb.com; Michael Blowen, "Donald O'Connor," *Boston Globe,* September 28, 2003; Donald O'Connor interview with Karen Idelson, 2002, dvdfile.com; Donald O'Connor interview, 1988, in Frank, *Tap!,* 146.

48. Donald O'Connor interview, 1988, in Frank, *Tap!,* 146–147; "Donald O'Connor," *A & E Biography,* December 29, 1999; Michael Blowen, "Donald O'Connor," *Boston Globe,* September 28, 2003; Donald O'Connor interview with Mindy Aloff, 1979, danceviewtimes.com; Donald O'Connor interview with Karen Idelson, 2002, dvdfile.com.

49. Donald O'Connor interview, 1988, in Frank, *Tap!,* 144–146.

50. Ibid., 147, 151; Donald O'Connor interview with Mindy Aloff, 1979, danceviewtimes.com.

51. Donald O'Connor interview, 1988, in Frank, *Tap!,* 152; Donald O'Connor interview with Mindy Aloff, 1979, danceviewtimes.com.

52. Donald O'Connor biography, imdb.com; "Donald O'Connor," *A & E Biography,* December 29, 1999; Michael Blowen, "Donald O'Connor," *Boston Globe,* September 28, 2003; Donald O'Connor interview, 1988, in Frank, *Tap!,* 146, 151.

53. Behlmer, *America's Favorite Movies,* 259–260; Silverman, *Dancing on the Ceiling,* 154, 155n.

54. Donald O'Connor interview, 1988, in Frank, *Tap!,* 151–152. Despite their relief at learning that they both turned to the left, Kelly and O'Connor perform a series of impressive turns to the right in the "Moses Supposes" number, underscoring the versatility of both dancers. O'Connor acknowledged that both of them could indeed turn to the right and that Kelly did it better than him, but the left side was stronger for both, and this was another reason they danced so well together. Donald O'Connor in Commentary, *Singin' in the Rain,* DVD, 2002.

55. Reynolds, *Debbie,* 12, 22–24, 38–40, 46, 51; Debbie Reynolds interview with Robert Osborne, *Private Screenings,* 2002.

56. Debbie Reynolds biography, imdb.com; Debbie Reynolds quoted in Parish and Bowers, *MGM Stock Company*, 606; Reynolds, *Debbie*, 63, 65, 73; Debbie Reynolds interview with Robert Osborne, *Private Screenings*, 2002.

57. Reynolds, *Debbie*, 61; Mueller, *Astaire Dancing*, 309.

58. Reynolds, *Debbie*, 69, 73–75; Behlmer, *America's Favorite Movies*, 260.

59. Fordin, *M-G-M's Greatest Musicals*, 354; Behlmer, *America's Favorite Movies*, 260.

60. Yudkoff, *Gene Kelly*, 217, inaccurately characterized Reynolds as a dancer when she was cast in *Singin' in the Rain*.

61. Reynolds, *Debbie*, 86–87.

62. Debbie Reynolds quoted in Hirschhorn, *Gene Kelly*, 180; Reynolds, *Debbie*, 11.

63. "Reminiscences of Gene Curran Kelly: Oral History, 1958," 17, Popular Arts Project, Oral History Research Office, CU; Gene Kelly interview with Ronald L. Davis, 1974, 28, SMU/Ronald L. Davis Oral History Collection, Herrick Library, AMPAS; Gene Kelly quoted in Hirschhorn, *Gene Kelly*, 180–181; Stanley Donen quoted in Silverman, *Dancing on the Ceiling*, 153; Stanley Donen in *What a Glorious Feeling*, DVD, 2002. The Internet Movie Database (IMDB) reports that Kelly wanted Carol Haney for the Kathy Selden role but no other source supports this claim. *Singin' in the Rain*, Trivia, imdb.com. Silverman, *Dancing on the Ceiling*, 152, "quotes" Kelly as saying "in 1991" that Mayer thrust Debbie on him, but Silverman apparently did not interview Kelly himself and he does not provide a source for this claim. The authors have examined all of Kelly's published and broadcast interviews and found nothing to substantiate Silverman's claim. Instead, Kelly and Donen consistently stated that they suggested Reynolds for the part, as cited in this note.

64. "An Oral History with Lela Simone," Rudy Behlmer, 1990, 296–297, Oral History Program, Herrick Library, AMPAS. Hirschhorn, *Gene Kelly*, 180, indicates that Freed considered Kathryn Grayson (not young enough), Pier Angeli (wrong quality), June Allyson (also not young enough), and Jane Powell (too operatic) for the part of Kathy Selden.

65. Reynolds, *Debbie*, 87.

66. Kurtti, *Movie Musical Trivia Book*, 24; Fordin, *M-G-M's Greatest Musicals*, 354.

67. Fordin, *M-G-M's Greatest Musicals*, 354; Mariani, "Come On with the Rain," 9; Wollen, *Singin' in the Rain*, 55; Kurtti, *Movie Musical Trivia Book*, 24; Silverman, *Dancing on the Ceiling*, 155; Hanson, "An Interview with Gene Kelly," 26; Gene Kelly quoted in Hirschhorn, *Gene Kelly*, 181.

68. Hagen, "Jean Hagen," 7; Parish and Bowers, *MGM Stock Company,* 309; Jean Hagen biography, imdb.com; Jean Hagen biography, msn.com.

69. Hagen, "Jean Hagen," 7–8, 10; Jean Hagen biography, imdb.com.

70. Parish and Bowers, *MGM Stock Company,* 309–310; Hagen, "Jean Hagen," 8–9; Jean Hagen biography, imdb.com; Jean Hagen biography, entertainment .msn.com.

CHAPTER 3. OUT OF THIN AIR YOU MAKE A MOMENT DANCE

1. Behlmer, *America's Favorite Movies,* 258; *New York Herald-Tribune,* January 18, 1951, clipping in Box 8, Scrapbook 6, Gene Kelly Collection, BU.

2. Astaire, *Steps in Time,* 206, 242; Hirschhorn, *Gene Kelly,* 161; Gene Kelly quoted in Hover, "Popping Questions at Gene Kelly," *Motion Picture* 68, no. 3 (October 1944): 94, Box 7, Scrapbook 2, Gene Kelly Collection, BU.

3. Gene Kelly quoted in Hirschhorn, *Gene Kelly,* 160–161.

4. Ibid., 123; Gene Kelly quoted in Flatow, "Through a Lens Brightly," 38.

5. Gene Kelly quoted in Knox, *Magic Factory,* 156, 171; Hanson, "An Interview with Gene Kelly," 24; Kelly, "Dialogue on Film," 37–38.

6. Robert Webb to Arthur Freed, March 7, 1951; F. A. Datig to C. Hunt, May 11, 1951, Box 21, Folder 1 (2 of 2), Arthur Freed Collection, USC.

7. Gene Kelly quoted in Behlmer, *America's Favorite Movies,* 258; transcript of unidentified interview with Gene Kelly, Box 56, Folder 6, Arthur Freed Collection, USC; "Gene Kelly Interview," Marilyn Hunt, 1975, 251–252, Oral History Program, DD-NYPL.

8. Gene Kelly quoted in Mariani, "Come On with the Rain," 10; Gene Kelly interview with Gavin Millar, 1974, *An Evening with Gene Kelly;* Hirschhorn, *Gene Kelly,* 182; Wollen, *Singin' in the Rain,* 34; Morley and Leon, *Gene Kelly,* 115.

9. Comden and Green, *Singin' in the Rain,* 8; Gene Kelly quoted in Singer, *A Cut Above,* 148.

10. Comden and Green, *Singin' in the Rain,* 9; Comden and Green interview with Tina Daniell and Pat McGilligan, 1989, in McGilligan, ed., *Backstory 2,* 82; Kelly, "Dialogue on Film," 38–39.

11. Comden and Green interview with Tina Daniell and Pat McGilligan, 1989, in McGilligan, ed., *Backstory 2,* 78, 81; Stanley Donen quoted in Casper, *Stanley Donen,* 44; Randall Duell interview with Jerome Delamater, 1973, in Delamater, *Dance in the Hollywood Musical,* 251; *Singin' in the Rain* screenplays, First Draft: August 10–September 14, 1950 (Folder 1230), Second Draft: October 5–20, 1950 (Folders 1231–1235), Final Draft: April 11–June 25, 1951 (Folder 1236), Turner/ MGM Script Collection, Herrick Library, AMPAS.

12. Inventory of Gene Kelly Collection, BU.

13. *Singin' in the Rain* screenplays, First Draft: August 10–September 14, 1950 (Folder 1230), Second Draft: October 5–20, 1950 (Folders 1231–1235), Final Draft: April 11–June 25, 1951 (Folder 1236), Turner/MGM Script Collection, Herrick Library, AMPAS. At least four script versions are also filed in the Arthur Freed Collection, USC.

14. *Singin' in the Rain* screenplay, April 11, 1951, 3, 12, 22, 31, 47–48, 63, 69, Folder 1236, Turner/MGM Script Collection, Herrick Library, AMPAS.

15. Ibid., 14A.

16. Ibid., 36, 53A, 67.

17. Ibid., 2, 19; *Singin' in the Rain* screenplay, October 14, 1950, 91, Folder 1234, Turner/MGM Script Collection, Herrick Library, AMPAS.

18. *Singin' in the Rain* screenplays, October 14, 1950 (88, Folder 1234), April 11, 1951 (97, Folder 1236), Turner/MGM Script Collection, Herrick Library, AMPAS.

19. *Singin' in the Rain* screenplay, April 11, 1951, 6, Folder 1236, Turner/MGM Script Collection, Herrick Library, AMPAS.

20. Ralph Wheelwright to Freed, August 10, 1949, Milton Brecher to Freed, March 7, 1951, and Freed to Brecher, March 12, 1951, Box 56, Folder 3 of 6, Arthur Freed Collection, USC.

21. *Singin' in the Rain* screenplays, October 5, 1950 (21, Folder 1231), April 11, 1951 (23, Folder 1236), Turner/MGM Script Collection, Herrick Library, AMPAS; Rudi Monta to Arthur Freed, March 16, April 20, 1951, Bea Whitney to Freed, May 2, 1951, and handwritten note by M. M., May 11, 1951, Box 56, Folder 1 of 6, Arthur Freed Collection, USC.

22. *Singin' in the Rain* screenplays, August 10, 1950 (88, Folder 1230), October 14, 1950 (91, Folder 1234), Turner/MGM Script Collection, Herrick Library, AMPAS; Rudi Monta to Arthur Freed, March 6, 1951, Box 56, Folder 1 of 6, Arthur Freed Collection, USC.

23. Ibid.

24. Joseph Fields biography, imdb.com; suggestions from Joseph Fields for revisions of *Singin' in the Rain* screenplay, July 26, 1951, 95, 97, Folder 1237, Turner/MGM Script Collection, Herrick Library, AMPAS. It is possible that Comden and Green asked Fields to work on *Singin' in the Rain* because they were too busy with *Two on the Aisle* in Philadelphia, and he decided to go far beyond what was really needed. Fields worked closely with Comden and Green immediately afterward, winning two Tony awards for the stage production of *Wonderful Town* in 1953.

25. Comden and Green, *Singin' in the Rain*, ix, 15, 17, 20, 21, 30, 58–59, 65, 73–74.

26. Comden and Green, *Singin' in the Rain*, ix.

27. Wayne, *Leading Men of MGM*, 79, 81, 83.

28. Ibid., 104–107, 110; Higham, *Merchant of Dreams*, 112, 150, 152.

29. *Singin' in the Rain* screenplays, August 10, 1950 (20, Folder 1230), October 5, 1950 (82, Folder 1231), October 14, 1950 (82, Folder 1233), April 11, 1951 (23, Folder 1236), Turner/MGM Script Collection, Herrick Library, AMPAS.

30. Gene Kelly quoted in Hirschhorn, *Gene Kelly*, 183.

31. *Singin' in the Rain* screenplays, August 10, 1950 (24–25, Folder 1230), April 11, 1951 (26–27, Folder 1236), Turner/MGM Script Collection, Herrick Library, AMPAS. The phrase "raving eagle maniacs" was intended to poke fun at the Kathy Selden character, who supposedly did not know that the correct terminology was "ego maniacs." The phrase was changed to "tinhorn sheikhs" in the April 11 draft.

32. Hanson, "Interview with Gene Kelly," 26; Hirschhorn, *Gene Kelly*, 182.

33. Holtzman, *Judy Holliday*, 28, 36, 53, 89, 93–94, 111, 117–118, 132–133, 136, 141, 145, 148.

34. Mariani, "Come On with the Rain," 9–10; Margaret to Freed, May 10, 1951, Arthur Freed Collection, USC.

35. *Singin' in the Rain* screenplays, August 10, 1950 (43, Folder 1230), October 5, 1950 (44–45, Folder 1231), Turner/MGM Script Collection, Herrick Library, AMPAS.

36. *Singin' in the Rain* screenplays, October 5, 1950 (46, Folder 1231), April 11, 1951 (27–28, Folder 1236), Turner/MGM Script Collection, Herrick Library, AMPAS.

37. *Singin' in the Rain* screenplay, April 11, 1951, 37–38, 42–44, Folder 1236, Turner/MGM Script Collection, Herrick Library, AMPAS.

38. Mariani, "Come On with the Rain," 10; Behlmer, *America's Favorite Movies*, 261; Wynn Rocamora to Freed, November 13, 1950, Box 21, Folder 1 (1 of 2), Arthur Freed Collection, USC; Parish and Bowers, *MGM Stock Company*, 643; Dialogue Cutting, March 17, 1952, Folder 1236, Turner/MGM Script Collection, Herrick Library, AMPAS.

39. Rudi Monta to Thau, Schenck, Sidney, Green, and Freed, February 22, 1950, Arthur Freed Collection, USC.

40. Tentative Musical Layout, April 4, 1951, Box 56, Folder 1 of 6, Arthur Freed Collection, USC; *Singin' in the Rain* screenplay, April 11, 1951, 33, 36, 50, 51, Folder 1236, Turner/MGM Script Collection, Herrick Library, AMPAS.

41. Musical Numbers, April 17, 1951, Box 56, Folder 1 of 6, Arthur Freed Collection, USC; *Singin' in the Rain* screenplay, April 11, 1951, 45, 97, Revisions (50A,

June 25), (53A, May 29), (73, May 23), Folder 1236, Turner/MGM Script Collection, Herrick Library, AMPAS.

42. "Alone" (song sheet #3, Folder 1), "Yours and Mine" (song sheet #216, Folder 5), "We'll Make Hay While the Sun Shines" (song sheet #183, Folder 4), Box 27, Gene Kelly Collection, BU.

43. Comden and Green, *Singin' in the Rain*, 9; Behlmer, *America's Favorite Movies*, 261–262; Fordin, *M-G-M's Greatest Musicals*, 359; Hemming, *Melody Lingers On*, 327; Silverman, *Dancing on the Ceiling*, 158.

44. Stanley Donen quoted in Fordin, *M-G-M's Greatest Musicals*, 359; Fordin, *M-G-M's Greatest Musicals*, 359; "An Oral History with Lela Simone," Rudy Behlmer, 1990, 315, Oral History Program, Herrick Library, AMPAS; Betty Comden quoted in Hirschhorn, *Gene Kelly*, 183; Behlmer, *America's Favorite Movies*, 262. Kelly later claimed that he created the title, "Make 'Em Laugh," for O'Connor's number, and Freed and Brown followed through with the song. "Gene Kelly Interview," Marilyn Hunt, 1975, 247–248, Oral History Program, DD-NYPL.

45. Comden and Green, *Singin' in the Rain*, 9; Kurtti, *Movie Musical Trivia Book*, 30; Thomas, *Films of Gene Kelly*, 136; Mariani, "Come On with the Rain," 11; Silverman, *Dancing on the Ceiling*, 146n; Fehr and Vogel, *Lullabies of Hollywood*, 229, claim incorrectly that Nacio Herb Brown wrote the music for "Moses Supposes."

46. George G. Schneider to Rudi Monta, copied to Johnny Green and Roger Edens, April 28, 1952, Arthur Freed Collection, USC; David Hume, "Old Man Moses," in Goodwin, ed., *Song Dex Treasury*, 217, in Hill Collection, UAL.

47. Assistant Director's Report, *Singin' in the Rain*, April 2–15, 1951, Box 21, Folder 2, Arthur Freed Collection, USC; "Gene Kelly Interview," Marilyn Hunt, 1975, 120–121, 124, Oral History Program, DD-NYPL; Billman, *Film Choreographers and Dance Directors*, 319. Fordin, *M-G-M's Greatest Musicals*, 357, and Yudkoff, *Gene Kelly*, 218, mistake the date for the start of rehearsals as April 12, 1951. Reynolds, *Debbie*, 87, also mistakes the start date as two weeks after her nineteenth birthday, which would make it April 15, 1951.

48. Reynolds, *Debbie*, 88; "Gene Kelly Interview," Marilyn Hunt, 1975, 249–250, Oral History Program, DD-NYPL.

49. "An Oral History with Lela Simone," Rudy Behlmer, 1990, 238, Oral History Program, Herrick Library, AMPAS; Reynolds, *Debbie*, 88.

50. Reynolds, *Debbie*, 88–89; Debbie Reynolds interview with Robert Osborne, *Private Screenings*, 2002. Likely based on Silverman's biased and unsubstantiated version of Debbie's story regarding this incident, IMDB distorts this incident by stating, "Gene Kelly insulted Debbie Reynolds for not being able to dance. Fred Astaire . . . helped her with dancing." Silverman, *Dancing on the Ceiling*, 152;

Singin' in the Rain, Trivia, imdb.com. There is no evidence that Kelly ever insulted Reynolds. He used great restraint even when frustrated with her limited dancing talent. Kelly was demanding because he had to draw out the best performance from her, but he was more demanding on himself than on others. Reynolds grew to understand what Kelly taught her and was grateful to him for developing her strong work ethic.

51. Assistant Director's Reports, *Singin' in the Rain,* April 18–May 22, 1951, Box 21, Folder 2, Arthur Freed Collection, USC.

52. Basinger, *American Cinema,* 185–186.

53. Joseph I. Breen to Louis B. Mayer, January 4, 1951, MPAA Production Code Administration Records, Herrick Library, AMPAS.

54. Breen to Mayer, April 23, 1951, MPAA Production Code Administration Records, Herrick Library, AMPAS. A copy of Breen's letter is in Box 56, Folder 3, Arthur Freed Collection, USC.

55. Breen to Mayer, May 23, 1951, MPAA Production Code Administration Records, Herrick Library, AMPAS; Walter Plunkett quoted in Mariani, "Come On with the Rain," 10.

56. Basinger, *American Cinema,* 228.

57. Mast, *Can't Help Singin',* 92.

58. Basinger, *American Cinema,* 226; Hay, *MGM,* 292; Kreuger, "Birth of the American Film Musical," 47.

59. Basinger, *American Cinema,* 230; Hay, *MGM,* 292–293.

60. Kobal, *Gotta Sing, Gotta Dance,* 31–32; Gene Kelly quoted in Mariani, "Come On with the Rain," 10; Kelly, "Dialogue on Film," 39; Gene Kelly quoted in Thomas, *Films of Gene Kelly,* 135; "Gene Kelly Interview," 253, Marilyn Hunt, 1975, Oral History Program, DD-NYPL. In contrast to Kelly's relating the extensive research they did for the movie, Donen said in 2006, "We didn't do any research for *Singin' in the Rain.* Our lives were the research." Stanley Donen interview with Robert Osborne, *Private Screenings,* 2006. Yet none of the principals had been through the transition to sound, so this was not literally true.

61. Gene Kelly quoted in Meade, *Buster Keaton,* 192, 244. The tape of Kelly's telephone interview with Meade can be found in Marion Meade/Buster Keaton Research Files, UI.

62. Kelly, "Dialogue on Film," 43.

63. *Program,* 6, *Singin' in the Rain* Microfiche, Core Collection, Herrick Library, AMPAS; Behlmer, *America's Favorite Movies,* 264; Kurtti, *Movie Musical Trivia Book,* 33, 35; Fordin, *M-G-M's Greatest Musicals,* 355.

64. *Program,* 6, *Singin' in the Rain* Microfiche, Core Collection, Herrick Library,

AMPAS; Fordin, *M-G-M's Greatest Musicals*, 355; Kobal, *Gotta Sing, Gotta Dance*, 35; Kurtti, *Movie Musical Trivia Book*, 33.

65. Randall Duell interview with Jerome Delamater, 1973, in Delamater, *Dance in the Hollywood Musical*, 250. IMDB puts an erroneous twist on this subject by reporting that "just as Gene Kelly and Stanley Donen reused a huge repertoire of popular songs from earlier musicals, the duo also looted MGM warehouses for props and vehicles." *Singin' in the Rain*, Trivia, imdb.com. It was Freed's idea to make a movie based on the Freed-Brown catalog of songs, and M-G-M employees *always* used the studio's inventory to minimize costs. Debbie Reynolds jokingly said that "Duell pilfered the MGM warehouses" in *What a Glorious Feeling*, DVD, 2002, which IMDB apparently understood as "duo" and jumped to these conclusions.

66. Walter Plunkett quoted in Kobal, *Gotta Sing, Gotta Dance*, 30.

67. Walter Plunkett quoted in Behlmer, *America's Favorite Movies*, 264.

68. *Program*, 12, *Singin' in the Rain* Microfiche, Core Collection, Herrick Library, AMPAS; Fordin, *M-G-M's Greatest Musicals*, 355; Kurtti, *Movie Musical Trivia Book*, 33; McCaffrey and Jacobs, *Guide to the Silent Years*, 205–206.

69. Walter Plunkett quoted in *Program*, 11–12, *Singin' in the Rain* Microfiche, Core Collection, Herrick Library, AMPAS; Kurtti, *Movie Musical Trivia Book*, 35; Jacobs and Braun, *Films of Norma Shearer*, 213; Parish and Bowers, *MGM Stock Company*, 640, 646.

70. Fordin, *M-G-M's Greatest Musicals*, 355.

71. Randall Duell interview with Jerome Delamater, 1973, in Delamater, *Dance in the Hollywood Musical*, 244.

72. "Days & Dates, 'Singing in the Rain'" (April 27, 1951), "Estimated Dates, 'Singing in the Rain'" (undated), and "Days and Dates, 'Singin' in the Rain'" (June 1, 1951), all in Box 21, Folder 1, Arthur Freed Collection, USC.

73. "Picture Estimate, Production No. 1546," June 30, 1951, Box 21, Folder 1, Arthur Freed Collection, USC.

74. Assistant Director's Reports, *Singin' in the Rain*, May 23–June 13, 1951, Box 21, Folder 2, Arthur Freed Collection, USC; Reynolds in *What a Glorious Feeling*, DVD, 2002.

75. Saul Chaplin and Gene Kelly quoted in Knox, *Magic Factory*, 54–55.

76. Assistant Director's Reports, *Singin' in the Rain*, June 14–16, 1951, Box 21, Folder 2, Arthur Freed Collection, USC.

77. Reynolds, *Debbie*, 89.

78. Debbie Reynolds quoted in Hirschhorn, *Gene Kelly*, 185.

79. Ibid.

80. Gene Kelly quoted in Hirschhorn, *Gene Kelly*, 185; Gene Kelly quoted in Michael Blowen, "Donald O'Connor," *Boston Globe*, September 28, 2003; Kelly, "Dialogue on Film," 43.

81. Debbie Reynolds quoted in Hirschhorn, *Gene Kelly*, 181, 185.

CHAPTER 4. THEIR FEET DO ALL THE WORK

1. Fordin, *M-G-M's Greatest Musicals*, 357, 362–363; J. J. [Cohn] to Freed, June 18, 1951, Box 21, Folder 1 (1 of 2), Arthur Freed Collection, USC. Debbie Reynolds misdated the beginning of production as June 19, 1951. Reynolds, *Debbie*, 89.

2. Astaire, *Steps in Time*, 201.

3. Higham, *Merchant of Dreams*, 406–410; Hay, *MGM*, 279, 282; Reynolds and Silverman incorrectly state the date of Mayer's resignation as June 21, 1951. Reynolds, *Debbie*, 92; Silverman, *Dancing on the Ceiling*, 155. Fordin cites the correct date but incorrectly reports it as three days after the start of filming *Singin' in the Rain*, instead of four. Fordin, *M-G-M's Greatest Musicals*, 353n.

4. Bobby Watson biography, imdb.com; all lyrics quoted are taken directly from the movie unless otherwise indicated.

5. Gene Kelly interview with David Fantle and Tom Johnson, 1978, in Fantle and Johnson, *Reel to Real*, 70.

6. Charness, "Hollywood Cine-Dance," 103; Donald O'Connor in Commentary, *Singin' in the Rain*, DVD, 2002.

7. Charness, "Hollywood Cine-Dance," 103–104.

8. Morley and Leon, *Gene Kelly*, 114–115; Delamater, *Dance in the Hollywood Musical*, 159.

9. Charness, "Hollywood Cine-Dance," 103; Wendy Wasserstein, "After 50 Years, It's Still a Glorious Feeling," *New York Times*, November 3, 2002, clipping in *Singin' in the Rain* Clippings File, Core Collection, Herrick Library, AMPAS.

10. Walter Terry, "Kelly's Exhilarating Dance Tonic for April: 'Singin' in the Rain,'" *New York Herald Tribune*, April 13, 1952, clipping in Scrapbook 8, Box 9, Gene Kelly Collection, BU; Fehr and Vogel, *Lullabies of Hollywood*, 229; Casper, *Stanley Donen*, 51.

11. Stanley Donen quoted in Silverman, *Dancing on the Ceiling*, 161.

12. Kurtti, *Movie Musical Trivia Book*, 30; Fehr and Vogel, *Lullabies of Hollywood*, 229; Fordin, *M-G-M's Greatest Musicals*, 355, 357; Silverman, *Dancing on the Ceiling*, 146n; Arthur Freed filmography, imdb.com; Gene Kelly notation on "Fit as a Fiddle" song sheet #35, Box 27, Folder 1, Gene Kelly Collection, BU.

13. Donald O'Connor quoted in Hirschhorn, *Gene Kelly*, 184; Donald O'Connor interview with Tony Bray, 2002, tv-now.com; Hirschhorn, *Gene Kelly*, 43; Silverman, *Dancing on the Ceiling*, 96.

14. Donald O'Connor quoted in Mariani, "Come On with the Rain," 11; Donald O'Connor quoted in Hirschhorn, *Gene Kelly*, 184.

15. Stanley Donen quoted in Silverman, *Dancing on the Ceiling*, 157; Fordin, *M-G-M's Greatest Musicals*, 357; Charness, "Hollywood Cine-Dance," 98–99.

16. Walter Terry, "Kelly's Exhilarating Dance Tonic for April: 'Singin' in the Rain,'" *New York Herald Tribune*, April 13, 1952, clipping in Scrapbook 8, Box 9, Gene Kelly Collection, BU.

17. Hemming, *Melody Lingers On*, 327; *Program*, 11, *Singin' in the Rain* Microfiche, Core Collection, Herrick Library, AMPAS; Nacio Herb Brown biography, imdb.com; Basinger, *Gene Kelly*, 87; Delamater, *Dance in the Hollywood Musical*, 140.

18. Mast, *Can't Help Singin'*, 248; Genné, "Film Musicals," 372; Feuer, *Hollywood Musical*, 4–5.

19. Charness, "Hollywood Cine-Dance," 104–105; Randall Duell interview with Jerome Delamater, 1973, in Delamater, *Dance in the Hollywood Musical*, 246–247.

20. Donald O'Connor quoted in Mariani, "Come On with the Rain," 11.

21. Assistant Director's Report, *Singin' in the Rain*, June 25, 1951, Box 21, Folder 2, Arthur Freed Collection, USC.

22. Ibid.

23. Donald O'Connor interview with Mindy Aloff, 1979, danceviewtimes.com.

24. Debbie Reynolds interview with Robert Osborne, *Private Screenings*, 2002; Debbie Reynolds quoted in Mariani, "Come On with the Rain," 11, and in Behlmer, *America's Favorite Movies*, 265; Reynolds in *What a Glorious Feeling*, DVD, 2002; Reynolds, *Debbie*, 90–91; "Gene Kelly Interview," Marilyn Hunt, 1975, 125, Oral History Program, DD-NYPL.

25. Thomas, *Films of Gene Kelly*, 136; Hemming, *Melody Lingers On*, 327–328, 331; Mast, *Can't Help Singin'*, 261.

26. Stanley Donen quoted in Fordin, *M-G-M's Greatest Musicals*, 359; Mariani, "Come On with the Rain," 11. Lela Simone later said that Irving Berlin also claimed some of the music used in *Singin' in the Rain* was his own, but there is no supporting evidence from other sources for this point. "An Oral History with Lela Simone," Rudy Behlmer, 1990, 315, Oral History Program, Herrick Library, AMPAS.

27. Joseph I. Breen to Dore Schary, June 29, 1951, MPAA Production Code Administration Records, Herrick Library, AMPAS; Use Agreement, June 22, 1951, Box 21, Folder 1 (1 of 2), Arthur Freed Collection, USC; Sidney Skolsky column,

Hollywood Citizen-News, May 3, 1952, clipping in *Singin' in the Rain* Microfiche, Core Collection, Herrick Library, AMPAS; Casper, *Stanley Donen*, 50.

28. Playbacks, *Singin' in the Rain*, DVD, 2002.

29. Donald O'Connor interview with Mindy Aloff, 1979, danceviewtimes .com; Donald O'Connor quoted in Hirschhorn, *Gene Kelly*, 183–184; "Gene Kelly Interview," Marilyn Hunt, 1975, 245, 247–248, Oral History Program, DD-NYPL; Wollen, *Singin' in the Rain*, 34; Gene Kelly quoted in Behlmer, *America's Favorite Movies*, 262; Kelly, "Dialogue on Film," 38. "Gurning" originated in rural England where it is still practiced in some small villages. Egremont, in Cumbria, hosts a World Gurning Championship every year. Wikipedia.org; Donald O'Connor in Commentary, *Singin' in the Rain*, DVD, 2002.

30. "Gene Kelly Interview," Marilyn Hunt, 1975, 246–247, Oral History Program, DD-NYPL; Kelly, "Dialogue on Film," 38; Donald O'Connor interview with Karen Idelson, 2002, dvdfile.com; Donald O'Connor interview with Mindy Aloff, 1979, danceviewtimes.com; Donald O'Connor quoted in Mariani, "Come On with the Rain," 11; Hirschhorn, *Gene Kelly*, 183. Ironically, O'Connor had done similar shtick and stunts before (mimicking a fight behind a sofa, legs flying up from behind the sofa, pummeling a sofa cushion and falling to the floor with it—all exactly as he does with the dummy) in the Universal film *Something in the Wind* (1947). Clips of this routine can be seen in "Donald O'Connor," *A & E Biography*, December 29, 1999.

31. Donald O'Connor quoted in Hirschhorn, *Gene Kelly*, 184; Curly Howard biography, imdb.com.

32. Donald O'Connor interview with Mindy Aloff, 1979, danceviewtimes .com; O'Connor in *What a Glorious Feeling*, DVD, 2002; Gene Kelly quoted in Hirschhorn, *Gene Kelly*, 183; Wollen, *Singin' in the Rain*, 34; Donald O'Connor quoted in "Hollywood Reunion," *LA Weekly*, September 20, 2002.

33. Along with Fayard Nicholas and Hill, Delamater incorrectly claims that both Nicholas brothers did the back-flip off the wall and that O'Connor copied them. Fayard Nicholas interview, 1998, jitterbuzz.com; Hill, *Brotherhood in Rhythm*, 177–178, 187, 192; Delamater, *Dance in the Hollywood Musical*, 82.

34. Donald O'Connor interview with Tony Bray, 2002, tv-now.com; Hill, *Brotherhood in Rhythm*, 178.

35. Donald O'Connor quoted in Mariani, "Come On with the Rain," 11; Donald O'Connor quoted in Susan King, "50 Years Later, Still Singin' Praises of a Classic," *Los Angeles Times*, September 3, 2002, in *Singin' in the Rain* Clippings File, Core Collection, Herrick Library, AMPAS; Donald O'Connor quoted in Behlmer,

America's Favorite Movies, 262. Near the end of his life O'Connor claimed that he did not smoke at the time he made *Singin' in the Rain*, but he probably did not remember such details clearly, for his earlier interviews indicate that he smoked heavily in 1951. Donald O'Connor interview with Tony Bray, 2002, tv-now.com.

36. Transcript of Hedda Hopper interview with Gene Kelly, June 3, 1954, File 1342, Hedda Hopper Collection, Special Collections, Herrick Library, AMPAS; Kelly, "Dialogue on Film," 38.

37. Casper, *Stanley Donen*, 50; Kurtti, *Movie Musical Trivia Book*, 22; Donald O'Connor interview with Karen Idelson, 2002, dvdfile.com; Assistant Director's Reports, June 29–30, July 14, 1951, *Singin' in the Rain*, Box 21, Folder 2, Arthur Freed Collection, USC.

38. Donald O'Connor interview with Karen Idelson, 2002, dvdfile.com; Donald O'Connor quoted in Mariani, "Come On with the Rain," 11; Donald O'Connor quoted in Susan King, "50 Years Later, Still Singin' Praises of a Classic," *Los Angeles Times*, September 3, 2002, *Singin' in the Rain* Clippings File, Core Collection, Herrick Library, AMPAS.

39. Wollen, *Singin' in the Rain*, 34; Comden and Green, *Singin' in the Rain*, 9; Stanley Donen quoted in Silverman, *Dancing on the Ceiling*, 160.

40. *Program, Singin' in the Rain* Microfiche, Core Collection, Herrick Library, AMPAS; Arthur Freed filmography, imdb.com; Charness, "Hollywood Cine-Dance," 99–100.

41. Reynolds, *Debbie*, 89–90.

42. Assistant Director's Reports, July 23–25, 1951, *Singin' in the Rain*, Box 21, Folder 2, Arthur Freed Collection, USC.

43. Reynolds, *Debbie*, 90–91.

44. Stanley Donen quoted in Silverman, *Dancing on the Ceiling*, 158; Behlmer, *America's Favorite Movies*, 268; Hirschhorn, *Gene Kelly*, 189.

45. Fordin, *M-G-M's Greatest Musicals*, 348n; *Program*, 11, *Singin' in the Rain* Microfiche, Core Collection, Herrick Library, AMPAS; Hemming, *Melody Lingers On*, 328–332; Arthur Freed filmography, imdb.com.

46. Stanley Donen quoted in Silverman, *Dancing on the Ceiling*, 161; Mast, *Can't Help Singin'*, 261.

47. Fordin, *M-G-M's Greatest Musicals*, 359; transcript of Hedda Hopper interview with Gene Kelly, June 3, 1954, File 1342, Hedda Hopper Collection, Special Collections, Herrick Library, AMPAS.

48. Jimmy Thompson biography, imdb.com; playbacks, *Singin' in the Rain*, DVD, 2002; *Singin' in the Rain* screenplay, August 10, 1950, 41, Folder 1230, Turner/MGM Script Collection, Herrick Library, AMPAS.

49. Taylor and Jackson, *Hollywood Musical*, 88; Charness, "Hollywood Cine-Dance," 100.

50. "Fashion Show Number," MGM Wardrobe Department Records, Folder 228, Herrick Library, AMPAS; Assistant Director's Report, August 11, 1951, Box 21, Folder 2, Arthur Freed Collection, USC. Hirschhorn credits Kelly with inventing the ubangi "in conjunction with the MGM camera department" for taking a low-angle shot in *The Pirate*, 1948. Hirschhorn, *Gene Kelly*, 138.

51. Arthur Freed filmography, imdb.com; *Program, Singin' in the Rain* Microfiche, Core Collection, Herrick Library, AMPAS; Excerpts, *The Hollywood Revue of 1929*, Film and Television Archives, UCLA.

52. Arthur Freed filmography, imdb.com; Nacio Herb Brown filmography, imdb.com; Hemming, *Melody Lingers On*, 328–332.

53. Hirschhorn, *Gene Kelly*, 190; Basinger, *Gene Kelly*, 45; Behlmer, *America's Favorite Movies*, 263; Comden and Green, *Singin' in the Rain*, 9–10; *Singin' in the Rain* screenplay, October 14, 1950, 50, Folder 1230, Turner/MGM Script Collection, Herrick Library, AMPAS; "Musical Numbers," April 17, 1951, Box 56, Folder 1 of 6, Arthur Freed Collection, USC.

54. Randall Duell interview with Jerome Delamater, 1973, in Delamater, *Dance in the Hollywood Musical*, 250.

55. Arthur Freed filmography, imdb.com.

56. Playbacks, *Singin' in the Rain*, DVD, 2002; Reynolds in *What a Glorious Feeling*, DVD, 2002; Charness, "Hollywood Cine-Dance," 101–102; Taylor and Jackson, *Hollywood Musical*, 87–88.

57. Charness, "Hollywood Cine-Dance," 101, 103, 131, 134; Genné, "Film Musicals," 367.

58. Debbie Reynolds quoted in Hirschhorn, *Gene Kelly*, 185–186.

CHAPTER 5. COME ON WITH THE RAIN

1. Behlmer, *America's Favorite Movies*, 263; Arthur Freed quoted in Fordin, *M-G-M's Greatest Musicals*, 351; Arthur Freed quoted in *Program, 7, Singin' in the Rain* Microfiche, Core Collection, Herrick Library, AMPAS; Arthur Freed quoted in Kobal, *Gotta Sing, Gotta Dance*, 201.

2. *Program, 10, Singin' in the Rain* Microfiche, Core Collection, Herrick Library, AMPAS; Hay, *MGM*, 289; Thomas, *Films of Gene Kelly*, 135; Kobal, *Gotta Sing, Gotta Dance*, 33; Morley and Leon, *Gene Kelly*, 112.

3. Hemming, *Melody Lingers On*, 328, 330–332; Arthur Freed filmography, imdb.com; Nacio Herb Brown filmography, imdb.com.

4. Gene Kelly quoted in Thomas, *Films of Gene Kelly*, 138; Gene Kelly quoted

in Mariani, "Come On with the Rain," 11. In the introduction to the published screenplay of the movie, Comden and Green wrote, "We knew from the start, there was a scene where there was rain, and the leading man was singin' in it." Comden and Green, *Singin' in the Rain*, 9. However, in all of their scripts and revisions in 1950, they consistently had the three main characters—Don, Kathy, and Cosmo—singing the song together as they emerged from the Pink Fedora restaurant. *Singin' in the Rain* screenplays, August 10–September 14, 1950 (65, Folder 1230), October 5, 1950 (66, Folder 1231), October 14–20, 1950, (67, Folder 1234), Turner/MGM Script Collection, Herrick Library, AMPAS. It was only in the final script, after Kelly's close involvement, that the song was first written in for Don Lockwood alone. *Singin' in the Rain* screenplay, April 11, 1951 (71, Folder 1236), Turner/MGM Script Collection, Herrick Library, AMPAS.

5. Gene Kelly quoted in Hirschhorn, *Gene Kelly*, 186. Many writers have noted this episode wherein Kelly admitted he had not worked out an impressive staging for "Singin' in the Rain" early on, but they often put an added spin on the basic story. One version, told by Yudkoff, *Gene Kelly*, 214, and Silverman, *Dancing on the Ceiling*, 146–147, has Kelly and Donen laughing at it as a joke and deliberately irritating Freed. Morley and Leon, *Gene Kelly*, 112, claim that Kelly did not want to do the song because it "already had at least two airings." According to them, when Freed asked about the staging of the number, Kelly "grumped" in reply, "'What can I tell you?' . . . 'It's going to be raining and I'm going to be singing.'" However, there is no support for the notion that Kelly was reluctant to do the number, or that he was deliberately irritating Freed by being vague. He simply had not decided how to work the number yet. Hirschhorn, *Gene Kelly*, 186.

6. Gene Kelly quoted in Hirschhorn, *Gene Kelly*, 186; Gene Kelly interview with Jerome Delamater and Paddy Whannel, 1973, in Delamater, *Dance in the Hollywood Musical*, 211.

7. Gene Kelly interview with John Russell Taylor, 1980, in Britton, ed., *Talking Films*, 192; Hanson, "An Interview with Gene Kelly," 24; Gene Kelly interview with Graham Fuller, 1994, in Boorman et al., eds., *Projections 4*, 284; Gene Kelly quoted in Delamater, *Dance in the Hollywood Musical*, 157.

8. Gene Kelly quoted in Thomas, *Films of Gene Kelly*, 139; Hanson, "An Interview with Gene Kelly," 24; Delamater, *Dance in the Hollywood Musical*, 157; Wollen, *Singin' in the Rain*, 12.

9. Kelly, "Dialogue on Film," 41; Gene Kelly quoted in Hirschhorn, *Gene Kelly*, 186.

10. Gene Kelly interview with John Russell Taylor, 1980, in Britton, ed., *Talking Films*, 192; Hanson, "An Interview with Gene Kelly," 24; Gene Kelly quoted in

Fordin, *M-G-M's Greatest Musicals,* 357; Gene Kelly interview with Graham Fuller, 1994, in Boorman et al., eds., *Projections 4,* 284; Kelly, "Dialogue on Film," 41; lyrics of second verse from "Singin' in the Rain" song sheet #143, Box 27, Folder 3, Gene Kelly Collection, BU.

11. Gene Kelly interview with John Russell Taylor, 1980, in Britton, ed., *Talking Films,* 192; Hanson, "An Interview with Gene Kelly," 24; Gene Kelly interview with Jerome Delamater and Paddy Whannel, 1973, in Delamater, *Dance in the Hollywood Musical,* 211. Kelly explained that early movie musicals such as *The Broadway Melody* were filmed in a stagy way that prevented any development of the cine-dance ideal. "Gene Kelly Interview," 22, Marilyn Hunt, 1975, Oral History Program, DD-NYPL.

12. Delamater, *Dance in the Hollywood Musical,* 139; Gene Kelly quoted in Delamater, *Dance in the Hollywood Musical,* 139; Charness, "Hollywood Cine-Dance," 108, 130; Casper, *Stanley Donen,* 53; Kelly, "Dialogue on Film," 40.

13. Randall Duell interview with Jerome Delamater, 1973, in Delamater, *Dance in the Hollywood Musical,* 245–246; Mariani, "Come On with the Rain," 11–12.

14. Mast, *Can't Help Singin',* 261.

15. Randall Duell interview with Jerome Delamater, 1973, in Delamater, *Dance in the Hollywood Musical,* 246; Fordin, *M-G-M's Greatest Musicals,* 356, 358; Wollen, *Singin' in the Rain,* 16. Fordin includes Duell's hand-drawn plan of the locations of the seven puddles on the sidewalk (356), with a note that it is from the Gene Kelly Collection. We looked thoroughly through all the material in the Gene Kelly Collection at Boston University, as well as in the Arthur Freed Collection at USC, but this plan was not to be found anywhere.

16. Wollen, *Singin' in the Rain,* 25–26; Charness, "Hollywood Cine-Dance," 105, 107.

17. Charness, "Hollywood Cine-Dance," 107; Wollen, *Singin' in the Rain,* 26.

18. Charness, "Hollywood Cine-Dance," 107–108; Wollen, *Singin' in the Rain,* 27.

19. Hirschhorn, *Gene Kelly,* 186–187; Gene Kelly interview with John Russell Taylor, 1980, in Britton, ed., *Talking Films,* 192; Kelly, "Dialogue on Film," 40; *Program,* 12, *Singin' in the Rain* Microfiche, Core Collection, Herrick Library, AMPAS; Gene Kelly quoted in Thomas, *Films of Gene Kelly,* 138–139; Gene Kelly quoted in Morley and Leon, *Gene Kelly,* 116. IMDB incorrectly reports that the "rain consisted of a mixture of water and milk so it would show up better on film." *Singin' in the Rain,* Trivia, imdb.com. Wikipedia repeats this myth, *Singin' in the Rain,* wikipedia.org. Wollen incorrectly reports that ink was added to the rain to make it more visible. Wollen, *Singin' in the Rain,* 16.

20. Assistant Director's Reports, July 9–12, 14, 16, 18–19, 1951, Box 21, Folder 2, Arthur Freed Collection, USC; Blair, *Memory of All That*, 164–165; Gene Kelly quoted in Hirschhorn, *Gene Kelly*, 186.

21. Assistant Director's Report, July 17, 1951, Box 21, Folder 2, Arthur Freed Collection, USC.

22. Assistant Director's Reports, July 18–19, 1951, Box 21, Folder 2, Arthur Freed Collection, USC.

23. Assistant Director's Report, July 18, 1951, Box 21, Folder 2, Arthur Freed Collection, USC; Harry "Snub" Pollard biography, imdb.com; Brick Sullivan biography, imdb.com.

24. Assistant Director's Report, July 18, 1951, Box 21, Folder 2, Arthur Freed Collection, USC.

25. Ibid.

26. Ibid.

27. Ibid.

28. Fordin, *M-G-M's Greatest Musicals*, 357; Mariani, "Come On with the Rain," 12; *Program*, 12, *Singin' in the Rain* Microfiche, Core Collection, Herrick Library, AMPAS. IMDB incorrectly notes that there was "a severe water shortage in Culver City" at the time Kelly shot this number. *Singin' in the Rain*, Trivia, imdb.com.

29. Gene Kelly quoted in Hirschhorn, *Gene Kelly*, 186; Betsy Blair in *Anatomy of a Dancer*, DVD, 2002; Donald O'Connor interview by Karen Idelson, 2002, dvdfile.com; Hanson, "An Interview with Gene Kelly," 24.

30. Assistant Director's Report, July 19, 1951, Box 21, Folder 2, Arthur Freed Collection, USC.

31. Gene Kelly interview with Gavin Millar, 1974, *An Evening with Gene Kelly;* Assistant Director's Report, July 19, 1951, Box 21, Folder 2, Arthur Freed Collection, USC.

32. Stanley Donen quoted in Mariani, "Come On with the Rain," 12.

33. Casper, *Stanley Donen*, 52–53; Wollen, *Singin' in the Rain*, 17.

34. Wollen, *Singin' in the Rain*, 28; Gene Kelly interview with Gavin Millar, 1974, *An Evening with Gene Kelly;* Morley and Leon, *Gene Kelly*, 116; Adolph Green quoted in Hirschhorn, *Gene Kelly*, 63–64.

35. Stanley Donen quoted in Mariani, "Come On with the Rain," 12.

CHAPTER 6. EVERYTHING BUT DANCING

1. *Program*, 6–7, *Singin' in the Rain* Microfiche, Core Collection, Herrick Library, AMPAS.

2. Assistant Director's Report, July 14, 1951, Box 21, Folder 2, Arthur Freed Collection, USC.

3. Assistant Director's Report, July 19, 1951, Box 21, Folder 2, Arthur Freed Collection, USC.

4. Assistant Director's Report, July 20, 1951, Box 21, Folder 2, Arthur Freed Collection, USC; Reynolds in *What a Glorious Feeling*, DVD, 2002; *Exhibitor's Campaign Book*, fifth page, for *Singin' in the Rain*, Ron Haver Papers, Special Collections, Herrick Library, AMPAS; Kurtti, *Movie Musical Trivia Book*, 35.

5. Reynolds, *Debbie*, 91; Jean Hagen and Debbie Reynolds quoted in Mariani, "Come On with the Rain," 10; Silverman, *Dancing on the Ceiling*, 158; *Exhibitor's Campaign Book*, third page, for *Singin' in the Rain*, Ron Haver Papers, Special Collections, Herrick Library, AMPAS.

6. Assistant Director's Report, July 10, 1951, Box 21, Folder 2, Arthur Freed Collection, USC; Cast List, *Singin' in the Rain*, imdb.com; Hirschhorn, *Gene Kelly*, 20–21, 29–30. Comden and Green incorrectly identify Dennis Ross as "Don as a Boy." Comden and Green, *Singin' in the Rain*, vii.

7. Assistant Director's Reports, July 26–28, 30–31, August 1–2, 6, 1951, Box 21, Folder 2, Arthur Freed Collection, USC; Kurtti, *Movie Musical Trivia Book*, 18.

8. Gene Kelly and Saul Chaplin interviews by Ron Haver, 1984, in Haver, "Pas de Deux," 23.

9. Assistant Director's Report, July 17, 1951, Box 21, Folder 2, Arthur Freed Collection, USC. The report simply mentions Roxbury Drive for the street footage at night. The authors of this book explored several streets in Beverly Hills near Roxbury Drive to discover and document the streets filmed and the route taken for the moving background of the jalopy ride.

10. Assistant Director's Reports, August 4 and 6, 1951, Box 21, Folder 2, Arthur Freed Collection, USC.

11. Assistant Director's Reports, August 9–10, 1951, Box 21, Folder 2, Arthur Freed Collection, USC.

12. Wagner, "I Dub Thee," classicimages.com; Kreuger, "Dubbers to the Stars," 49, 51–54.

13. Silverman, *Dancing on the Ceiling*, 162; Reynolds, *Debbie*, 89. Late in his life, Donald O'Connor misremembered the numbers in *Singin' in the Rain* as being recorded live on the set, instead of being prerecorded as they actually were. Donald O'Connor interview by Tony Bray, 2002, tv-now.com. Also, IMDB incorrectly reports that a microphone hidden in Debbie's blouse recorded her heartbeat during a dance number, "mirroring what happens to Lina Lamont in the movie

itself." *Singin' in the Rain,* Trivia, imdb.com. The fact is that no sound recordings were done during the filming of the dances. Instead, the dances were performed to prerecorded songs, as explained in the chapter.

14. Mast, *Can't Help Singin',* 93–94.

15. Drysdale, "Soundmatters," 67; Kurtti, *Movie Musical Trivia Book,* 21.

16. Playbacks, *Singin' in the Rain,* DVD, 2002; Behlmer, *America's Favorite Movies,* 267. Fordin, *M-G-M's Greatest Musicals,* 358, misnames the dubber as Betty Royce instead of Betty Noyes, and so does Reynolds, *Debbie,* 92.

17. Arthur Freed filmography, imdb.com; *Program,* 10–11, *Singin' in the Rain* Microfiche, Core Collection, Herrick Library, AMPAS.

18. Playbacks, *Singin' in the Rain,* DVD, 2002.

19. Stanley Donen quoted in Fordin, *M-G-M's Greatest Musicals,* 358; Hagen, "Jean Hagen," 9; Wagner, "I Dub Thee," classicimages.com; Reynolds, *Debbie,* 91.

20. Arthur Freed filmography, imdb.com; Nacio Herb Brown filmography, imdb.com; Hemming, *Melody Lingers On,* 329–331; *Program,* 10, *Singin' in the Rain* Microfiche, Core Collection, Herrick Library, AMPAS; Fordin, *M-G-M's Greatest Musicals,* 3.

21. Behlmer, *America's Favorite Movies,* 268.

22. Assistant Director's Report, July 11, 1951, Box 21, Folder 2, Arthur Freed Collection, USC.

23. Hirschhorn, *Gene Kelly,* 189; Reynolds, *Debbie,* 91–92; playbacks, *Singin' in the Rain,* DVD, 2002; *What a Glorious Feeling,* DVD, 2002.

24. *Singin' in the Rain* screenplay, April 11, 1951, 97, Folder 1236, Turner/MGM Script Collection, Herrick Library, AMPAS; "Musical Numbers," From Stanley Donen, April 17, 1951, Box 56, Folder 1 of 6, Arthur Freed Collection, USC.

25. Playbacks, *Singin' in the Rain,* DVD, 2002; Behlmer, *America's Favorite Movies,* 268; Mariani, "Come On with the Rain," 11. Interestingly, Reynolds did not tell this story in her memoirs, although she briefly mentions it in *What a Glorious Feeling,* DVD, 2002. Yudkoff, *Gene Kelly,* 217, repeats the story of the onion used in the filming of "You Are My Lucky Star," but inserts inflammatory quotes by Kelly without giving the source of his information. Like so much of his book, this is highly unreliable.

26. Playbacks, *Singin' in the Rain,* DVD, 2002; *What a Glorious Feeling,* DVD, 2002.

27. Arthur Freed filmography, imdb.com.

28. *What a Glorious Feeling,* DVD, 2002; Behlmer, *America's Favorite Movies,* 267; *Singin' in the Rain* screenplay, October 14, 1950, 24, Folder 1235, Turner/ MGM Script Collection, Herrick Library, AMPAS.

29. Behlmer, *America's Favorite Movies*, 265; J. J. Cohen to Freed, June 18, 1951, Box 21, Folder 1 (1 of 2), Arthur Freed Collection, USC.

30. Drysdale, "Soundmatters," 67; Hay, *MGM*, 230; Astaire, *Steps in Time*, 201; Gene Kelly interview with John Russell Taylor, 1980, in Britton, ed., *Talking Films*, 197; Kelly, "Dialogue on Film," 40; Gene Kelly interview, 1973, in Knox, *Magic Factory*, 158.

31. Hay, *MGM*, 230; Gene Kelly quoted in Hay, *MGM*, 230; Donald O'Connor interview by Mindy Aloff, 1979, danceviewtimes.com; Behlmer, *America's Favorite Movies*, 267. IMDB incorrectly reports that Haney and Gwen Verdon dubbed Gene Kelly's taps for the "Singin'" number and that they "had to stand ankle-deep in a drum full of water." *Singin' in the Rain*, Trivia, imdb.com. Not only did Kelly dub all of his own taps for all his movies, it is not possible for anyone to record taps in ankle-deep water. It is possible that they recorded some extra sloshing sounds to be dubbed in after Kelly dubbed his taps, although no evidence of this was found in the archives or interviews with key players. IMDB also reports that Gene Kelly dubbed Debbie's taps "despite her hard work on the 'Good Morning' number," suggesting that she had earned the right to record her own taps as a reward. *Singin' in the Rain*, Trivia, imdb.com. First, no taps were recorded during the filming of dances, so *all* taps had to be dubbed later, no matter who the performer. Second, Debbie Reynolds was very new to dancing, and it would have been extremely difficult for her to dub her own taps at that point. Third, no one, even seasoned dancers, considered it a "reward" to do this tedious, precision-demanding chore, as Fred Astaire, Gene Kelly, and others have consistently reported.

32. Silverman, *Dancing on the Ceiling*, 156n; Music Clearance Request, September 18, 1951, and Lela Simone to George Schneider, September 25, 1951, Box 56, Folder 1 of 6, Arthur Freed Collection, USC.

33. "An Oral History with Lela Simone," Rudy Behlmer, 1990, 125–126, Oral History Program, Herrick Library, AMPAS.

34. "Dubbing Notes for 'Singin' in the Rain' Prod. 1546," Box 56, Folder 4, Arthur Freed Collection, USC.

35. Ibid.

36. Ibid.

37. Lela Simone, "Singin' in the Rain Music Notes," October 20, 1951, Folder 1238, Turner/MGM Scripts Collection, Herrick Library, AMPAS.

38. Ibid.

39. Silverman, *Dancing on the Ceiling*, 156n.

40. *Program*, 12, *Singin' in the Rain* Microfiche, Core Collection, Herrick Library, AMPAS. Partial copy also in Box 9, Scrapbook 8, Gene Kelly Collection, BU.

1. Wollen, *Singin' in the Rain*, 42; Hirschhorn, *Gene Kelly*, 184–185; *Singin' in the Rain* screenplay, August 10, 1950 (88, Folder 1230) and screenplay revision, May 23, 1951 (74, Folder 1236), Turner/MGM Script Collection, Herrick Library, AMPAS.

2. Behlmer, *America's Favorite Movies*, 265; Thomas, *Films of Gene Kelly*, 136; Gene Kelly inscription on cover of "Broadway Rhythm" song sheet #14, Box 27, Folder 1, Gene Kelly Collection, BU.

3. Arthur Freed filmography, imdb.com; Nacio Herb Brown filmography, imdb .com; *Program*, 10, *Singin' in the Rain* Microfiche, Core Collection, Herrick Library, AMPAS; Hemming, *Melody Lingers On*, 325–326; 328–332.

4. "Gene Kelly Interview," Marilyn Hunt, 1975, 250, Oral History Program, DD-NYPL; Hirschhorn, *Gene Kelly*, 187; Behlmer, *America's Favorite Movies*, 265; Donald O'Connor filmography, imdb.com.

5. Kelly, "Dialogue on Film," 37–38; Hanson, "An Interview with Gene Kelly," 24; Thomas, *Films of Gene Kelly*, 136.

6. Delamater, *Dance in the Hollywood Musical*, 103, 181.

7. Wollen, *Singin' in the Rain*, 34–35.

8. Ibid., 35, 38, 40; Hay, *MGM*, 219; Hirschhorn, *Gene Kelly*, 174; *Program*, 11, *Singin' in the Rain* Microfiche, Core Collection, Herrick Library, AMPAS.

9. Hirschhorn, *Gene Kelly*, 189; Program, 11, *Singin' in the Rain* Microfiche, Core Collection, Herrick Library, AMPAS.

10. Behlmer, *America's Favorite Movies*, 265; Cyd Charisse quoted in Mariani, "Come On with the Rain," 12; Cyd Charisse interview with David Fantle and Tom Johnson, 1996, in Fantle and Johnson, *Reel to Real*, 63; Martin and Charisse, *Two of Us*, 201–202.

11. Martin and Charisse, *Two of Us*, 30–31, 34, 39, 43–46, 82, 84, 89–91, 94–98, 117, 119–120, 128–129, 137; Cyd Charisse biography, imdb.com. Associated Press Report, June 17, 2008, mentions 1922 instead of 1921 as Charisse's birth year.

12. Martin and Charisse, *Two of Us*, 166–167, 195; Cyd Charisse quoted in Susan King, "50 Years Later, Still Singin' Praises of a Classic," *Los Angeles Times*, September 3, 2002; Gene Kelly, "The Women in My Dancing Life," *National Women's Weekly*, July 17, 1952. Charisse claimed in her memoirs that she had given birth to her second son, Tony Martin Jr., just before Freed offered her the role in *Singin' in the Rain*, and wanted her to take off eight pounds before filming. But in her memoirs, she correctly gave the date of her son's birth as August 28, 1950, which is confirmed on Cyd Charisse biography, imdb.com. Charisse obviously misremembered the timing of Freed's offer, which was a year later. Ironically, Kelly

repeated this story years later in an interview, as did Hirschhorn. See Martin and Charisse, *Two of Us*, 201; Gene Kelly interview with John Russell Taylor, 1980, in Britton, ed., *Talking Films*, 193; and Hirschhorn, *Gene Kelly*, 187. It is possible that the mix-up arose because Charisse wanted to lose some weight before filming, especially given her "vamp" role, and referred to it as the weight she had put on during the pregnancy.

13. Cyd Charisse interview with David Fantle and Tom Johnson, 1996, in Fantle and Johnson, *Reel to Real*, 63; Martin and Charisse, *Two of Us*, 205; Mariani, "Come On with the Rain," 12; Behlmer, *America's Favorite Movies*, 265–266; Hirschhorn, *Gene Kelly*, 188; "Gene Kelly Interview," Marilyn Hunt, 1975, 209, Oral History Program, DD-NYPL; "An Oral History with Lela Simone," Rudy Behlmer, 1990, 223–224, Oral History Program, Herrick Library, AMPAS; Cyd Charisse in *What a Glorious Feeling*, DVD, 2002.

14. Mariani, "Come On with the Rain," 12; Morley and Leon, *Gene Kelly*, 115; Louise Brooks biography and filmography, imdb.com.

15. Hirschhorn, *Gene Kelly*, 189; Assistant Director's Reports, August 20–25, 27–29, 31, September 1, 4–7, 10–11, 1951, Box 21, Folder 2, Arthur Freed Collection, USC.

16. Fordin, *M-G-M's Greatest Musicals*, 367, 369; clipping from *New York Herald Tribune*, January 18, 1951, Box 8, Scrapbook 6, Gene Kelly Collection, BU; Assistant Director's Reports, September 11–14, 1951, Box 21, Folder 2, Arthur Freed Collection, USC; Mariani, "Come On with the Rain," 12.

17. Assistant Director's Reports, September 15, 17–18, 20–22, 24–25, 28–29, October 1–6, 8–13, 1951, Box 21, Folder 2, Arthur Freed Collection, USC; playbacks, *Singin' in the Rain*, DVD, 2002.

18. Charness, "Hollywood Cine-Dance," 108–110; Debbie Reynolds in *What a Glorious Feeling*, DVD, 2002.

19. Randall Duell interview with Jerome Delamater, 1973, in Delamater, *Dance in the Hollywood Musical*, 249; Program, 14, *Singin' in the Rain* Microfiche, Core Collection, Herrick library, AMPAS.

20. Assistant Director's Reports, October 15–18, 20, 22–23, 1951, Box 21, Folder 2, Arthur Freed Collection, USC; Cyd Charisse interview with David Fantle and Tom Johnson, 1996, in Fantle and Johnson, *Reel to Real*, 63; Stanley Donen quoted in Silverman, *Dancing on the Ceiling*, 165.

21. Cyd Charisse in *What a Glorious Feeling*, DVD, 2002; Stanley Donen quoted in Silverman, *Dancing on the Ceiling*, 165; Cyd Charisse quoted in Susan King, "50 Years Later, Still Singin' Praises of a Classic," *Los Angeles Times*, September 3, 2002. In her interviews, Charisse says she never smoked again. But in her

memoirs, she writes that after this dance was filmed, she smoked three to four cigarettes a day for many years. Martin and Charisse, *Two of Us*, 202.

22. Debbie Reynolds in *What a Glorious Feeling*, DVD, 2002; Charness, "Hollywood Cine-Dance," 111–112; Hirschhorn, *Gene Kelly*, 189; Assistant Director's Report, October 24, 1950, Box 21, Folder 2, Arthur Freed Collection, USC.

23. Assistant Director's Reports, October 25–27, 29–30, November 8–10, 12–16, 1951, Box 21, Folder 2, Arthur Freed Collection, USC; Randall Duell interview with Jerome Delamater, 1973, in Delamater, *Dance in the Hollywood Musical*, 247.

24. Charness, "Hollywood Cine-Dance," 113; Gene Kelly quoted in Hirschhorn, *Gene Kelly*, 188; Martin and Charisse, *Two of Us*, 201; Fordin, *M-G-M's Greatest Musicals*, 360; Cyd Charisse quoted in Mariani, "Come On with the Rain," 12. China silk is a "soft, lightweight, lustrous silk" with a "slippery, smooth texture." www.denverfabrics.com. Voile is a "light, plain-weave, sheer fabric of cotton, rayon, silk, or wool, used especially for making dresses or curtains." thefreedictionary.com.

25. Gene Kelly quoted in Hirschhorn, *Gene Kelly*, 188; Mariani, "Come On with the Rain," 12; Gene Kelly interview with John Russell Taylor, 1980, in Britton, ed., *Talking Films*, 193.

26. Martin and Charisse, *Two of Us*, 201–202; Mariani, "Come On with the Rain," 12; Cyd Charisse in *What a Glorious Feeling*, DVD, 2002; Cyd Charisse interview with David Fantle and Tom Johnson, 1996, in Fantle and Johnson, *Reel to Real*, 63; Gene Kelly interview with John Russell Taylor, 1980, in Britton, ed., *Talking Films*, 193–194.

27. Assistant Director's Reports, October 24–25, 31, November 1–3, 5–6, 1951, Box 21, Folder 2, Arthur Freed Collection, USC.

28. Assistant Director's Report, November 5, 1951, Box 21, Folder 2, Arthur Freed Collection, USC.

29. Assistant Director's Report, November 6, 1951, Box 21, Folder 2, Arthur Freed Collection, USC; Mariani, "Come On with the Rain," 12; Stanley Donen quoted in Silverman, *Dancing on the Ceiling*, 165.

30. Assistant Director's Report, November 6, 1951, Box 21, Folder 2, Arthur Freed Collection, USC.

31. Stanley Donen quoted in Silverman, *Dancing on the Ceiling*, 166; Mariani, "Come On with the Rain," 12.

32. Assistant Director's Report, November 6, 1951, Box 21, Folder 2, Arthur Freed Collection, USC; Bradley, "Dali (Domenech), Salvador (Flip Jacint)," in Turner, ed., *Dictionary of Art*, vol. 8, 464–466, 468; Mast, *Can't Help Singin'*, 263; Charness, "Hollywood Cine-Dance," 113.

33. Charness, "Hollywood Cine-Dance," 113; Thomas, *Films of Gene Kelly*, 136. Note that the theme "Gotta Dance!" is similar to the lyrics, "I'll sing and dance whenever I will, no law on earth can keep me still," from *Anchors Aweigh*, and embodies Kelly's passion for dancing.

34. Charness, "Hollywood Cine-Dance," 114.

35. Ibid., 114; Gene Kelly interview with Gavin Millar, 1974, *An Evening with Gene Kelly*; Hirschhorn, *Gene Kelly*, 182; Stanley Donen quoted in Fordin, *M-G-M's Greatest Musicals*, 360–361.

36. Mast, *Can't Help Singin'*, 261; Mariani, "Come On with the Rain," 12; Behlmer, *America's Favorite Movies*, 266–267.

37. Behlmer, *America's Favorite Movies*, 266–267; Mast, *Can't Help Singin'*, 261; Hemming, *Melody Lingers On*, 327; Charness, "Hollywood Cine-Dance," 108.

38. Stanley Donen quoted in Casper, *Stanley Donen*, 34; Stanley Donen quoted in Silverman, *Dancing on the Ceiling*, 164; Stanley Donen interview with Ronald L. Davis, 1983, 25, SMU/Ronald L. Davis Oral History Collection, Herrick Library, AMPAS; "Gene Kelly Interview," Marilyn Hunt, 1975, 209, 251, Oral History Program, DD-NYPL; Kelly, "Dialogue on Film," 37; Gene Kelly quoted in Hirschhorn, *Gene Kelly*, 189.

39. "Gene Kelly Interview," Marilyn Hunt, 1975, 251, Oral History Program, DD-NYPL.

CHAPTER 8. BEST MUSICAL COMEDY I'VE SEEN

1. Randall Duell interview with Jerome Delamater, 1973, in Delamater, *Dance in the Hollywood Musical*, 251; Fordin, *M-G-M's Greatest Musicals*, 361; Wollen, *Singin' in the Rain*, 43; Mariani, "Come On with the Rain," 12.

2. Assistant Director's Reports, November 19–21, 23, 30, 1951, Box 21, Folder 2, Arthur Freed Collection, USC. The authors of this book checked the intersection of Sunset and Sepulveda and found that it is now at I-405, with no houses nearby because of exit ramp construction. No other houses in the vicinity seemed to be candidates for the exterior of Don Lockwood's house.

3. Behlmer, *America's Favorite Movies*, 267; Mariani, "Come On with the Rain," 12; Joe Finn to Walter Strohm, December 3, 1951, Box 21, Folder 1 (2 of 2), Arthur Freed Collection, USC; Hemming, *Melody Lingers On*, 327; Stanley Donen quoted in Silverman, *Dancing on the Ceiling*, 166.

4. *Advertising Billing*, October 8, 1951, *Singin' in the Rain* Folder, MPAA Production Code Administration Records, Herrick Library, AMPAS; Ralph Wheelwright to Arthur Freed and others, September 4, 1951, Box 21, Folder 1 (2 of 2), Arthur Freed Collection, USC.

5. *Advertising Billing,* January 7, 1952, *Singin' in the Rain* Folder, MPAA Production Code Administration Records, Herrick Library, AMPAS.

6. Arthur Freed to Ralph Wheelwright, July 30, 1951, Box 56, Folder 1, Arthur Freed Collection, USC; Fordin, *M-G-M's Greatest Musicals,* 361–362. Freed referred to Mervyn LeRoy, the experienced silent screen writer and director, and later a well-known actor in Warner Brothers movies of the 1930s. LeRoy became head of production at M-G-M after Thalberg's death, and also directed *Quo Vadis,* a lavish M-G-M picture set in ancient Rome that was released in November 1951. See Mervyn LeRoy biography and *Quo Vadis* information on imdb.com. Freed also had a personal and bumpy connection with LeRoy. Freed was associate producer of *The Wizard of Oz* (1939) with LeRoy as executive producer, and had to fight to get Judy Garland in the lead role. LeRoy wanted a star such as Shirley Temple or Deanna Durbin, but Freed had conceived the whole project with Judy in mind, even before LeRoy was brought on board. Fordin, *M-G-M's Greatest Musicals,* 8–9.

7. Basinger, *American Cinema,* 185; First Preview, First Report, *Singin' in the Rain,* December 21, 1951, Box 21, Folder 1 (2 of 2), Arthur Freed Collection, USC.

8. First Preview, First Report, *Singin' in the Rain,* December 21, 1951, Box 21, Folder 1 (2 of 2), Arthur Freed Collection, USC.

9. Second Preview, First Report, *Singin' in the Rain,* December 27, 1951, Box 21, Folder 1 (2 of 2), Arthur Freed Collection, USC.

10. First Preview, First Report, *Singin' in the Rain,* December 21, 1951, Box 21, Folder 1 (2 of 2), Arthur Freed Collection, USC; *Singin' in the Rain* screenplay, April 11, 1951, 5, 62, Folder 1236, Turner/MGM Script Collection, Herrick Library, AMPAS.

11. Gene Kelly quoted in Behlmer, *America's Favorite Movies,* 268; Behlmer, *America's Favorite Movies,* 268; Fordin, *M-G-M's Greatest Musicals,* 362; playbacks, *Singin' in the Rain,* DVD, 2002.

12. Rudy Behlmer in Commentary, *Singin' in the Rain,* DVD, 2002. Kelly's version of "All I Do Is Dream of You" is available on playbacks, *Singin' in the Rain,* DVD, 2002. Kelly sings it in stark contrast to the peppy version sung by Reynolds and the girls at Simpson's party—slow and dreamy, with some "English" applied to certain phrases such as "dreaming of you."

13. William LeVanway to E. J. Mannix et al., June 25, 1951, Box 21, Folder 1 (2 of 2), Arthur Freed Collection, USC; Assistant Director's Reports, December 11, 26, 1951, and January 2, 10, 1952, Box 21, Folder 2, Arthur Freed Collection, USC. The original release print of *Singin' in the Rain* apparently was lost due to a fire. It consisted of older nitrate film, which was highly combustible. Newer,

acetate-based film became available in 1951, but *Singin'* was photographed with the less stable variety. Rudy Behlmer in Commentary, *Singin' in the Rain,* DVD, 2002.

14. Silverman, *Dancing on the Ceiling,* 156n; Nicholas Schenck to Freed, March 16, 1952, Box 56, Folder 21, Arthur Freed Collection, USC. Schenck's comments show that he had a true appreciation for movies as well as musical numbers that were genuinely good, and paints a different portrait of him than the typical one-dimensional caricature reported about him. For example, Fordin, *M-G-M's Greatest Musicals,* 9, writes that Schenck's "ear was only receptive to the ringing of a cash register."

15. Theatrical trailer of *Singin' in the Rain,* DVD, 2002. Interestingly, M-G-M used a different take of the scene depicting the crowd of extras running toward Kelly in "The Broadway Ballet" for the trailer. The star ducks to avoid their hands as they approach him, which he does not do in the release print.

16. *Exhibitor's Campaign Book,* for *Singin' in the Rain,* not paginated, Ron Haver Papers, Special Collections, Herrick Library, AMPAS.

17. Ibid.

18. Ibid.

19. Ibid.

20. Ibid.

21. Clipping from *Independent Film Journal,* May 17, 1952, 20, Box 22, Folder 4, Arthur Freed Collection, USC.

22. *Exhibitor's Campaign Book,* for *Singin' in the Rain,* not paginated, Ron Haver Papers, Special Collections, Herrick Library, AMPAS; News release by Bakelite Company, n.d., and Norman Kuklin to Helen Went, May 3, 1951, Box 21, Folder 1 (2 of 2), Arthur Freed Collection, USC.

23. *Exhibitor's Campaign Book,* for *Singin' in the Rain,* not paginated, Ron Haver Papers, Special Collections, Herrick Library, AMPAS.

24. "Singin' in the Rain," *Variety* (weekly), March 12, 1952, *Variety* (daily), March 12, 1952, and clipping from *Hollywood Reporter,* March 12, 1952, all in *Singin' in the Rain* Microfiche, Core Collection, Herrick Library, AMPAS; Sherwin Kane review in *Motion Picture Daily,* March 12, 1952, and review in *The Independent Film Journal,* March 22, 1952, clippings of both newspapers in Box 9, Scrapbooks 7 and 8, Gene Kelly Collection, BU.

25. Sidney Phillips to Freed, March 19, 1952, and Jim Kason and Dick Fuselier to Hortense Morton, April 7, 1952, Box 22, Folder 4, Arthur Freed Collection, USC; Gale, "De Chirico, Giorgio," in Turner, ed., *Dictionary of Art,* vol. 8, 602.

26. Silverman, *Dancing on the Ceiling,* 156n; Irene Thirer, "'Singin' in the Rain'

Fine Fun," *New York Post*, March 28, 1952; Debbie Reynolds in *What a Glorious Feeling*, DVD, 2002.

27. Irene Thirer, "'Singin' in the Rain' Fine Fun," *New York Post*, March 28, 1952; Film Research Surveys report [March 27, 1952], 2, Box 21, Folder 1 (1 of 2), Arthur Freed Collection, USC. The survey was conducted at Loew's 72nd Street Theater in New York on March 27, 1952, the same day as the premiere at Radio City Music Hall. Apparently, the critics viewed the movie at the Music Hall and the public saw it on the same day at Loew's 72nd.

28. Film Research Surveys report [March 27, 1952], 2–3, Box 21, Folder 1 (1 of 2), Arthur Freed Collection, USC.

29. Betty Comden and Adolph Green quoted in Hirschhorn, *Gene Kelly*, 191.

30. Standard evaluation form for *Singin' in the Rain*, January 3, 1952, *Singin' in the Rain* Folder, MPAA Production Code Administration Records, Herrick Library, AMPAS; Joseph Breen to Dore Schary, January 3, 1952, MPAA Production Code Administration Records, Herrick Library, AMPAS.

31. Robert Vogel to Arthur Freed, Eddie Mannix, and Dore Schary, March 6, 1952, Box 56, Folder 3, Arthur Freed Collection, USC.

32. Report on Legion of Decency, Harrison's Reports, and Film Estimate Board of National Organizations, *Singin' in the Rain* Folder, MPAA Production Code Administration Records, Herrick Library, AMPAS.

33. Robert Vogel to Arthur Freed, Eddie Mannix, and Dore Schary, March 31, 1952, Box 56, Folder 3, Arthur Freed Collection, USC; Production Code Reports by Motion Picture Association, April 17, June 18, September 11, 1952, *Singin' in the Rain* Folder, MPAA Production Code Administration Records, Herrick Library, AMPAS.

34. "An Oral History with Robert M. W. Vogel," Barbara Hall, 1990, 53–54, 218, Oral History Program, Herrick Library, AMPAS.

35. Production Code Report, Motion Picture Association, April 15, 1953, August 10, 1953, *Singin' in the Rain* Folder, MPAA Production Code Administration Records, Herrick Library, AMPAS.

36. Gene Kelly interview with Jerome Delamater and Paddy Whannel, 1973, in Delamater, *Dance in the Hollywood Musical*, 225.

37. Bosley Crowther, "An April Shower," *New York Times*, March 28, 1952, clipping in Box 22, Folder 4, Arthur Freed Collection, USC, and in Box 9, Scrapbook 7, Gene Kelly Collection, BU.

38. Gene Kelly quoted in Hirschhorn, *Gene Kelly*, 182.

39. Irene Thirer, "'Singin' in the Rain' Fine Fun," *New York Post*, March 28, 1952; Wanda Hale, "'Singin' in Rain' at Music Hall," *Los Angeles News*, March 28,

1952, clippings of Thirer and Hale in Box 22, Folder 4, Arthur Freed Collection, USC.

40. Walter Terry, "Kelly's Exhilarating Dance Tonic for April: 'Singin' in the Rain,'" *New York Herald Tribune*, April 13, 1952, clipping in Box 9, Scrapbook 8, Gene Kelly Collection, BU.

41. Harrison Carroll, "Kelly, Freed Do It Again: 'Singin' in the Rain' New Musical Must," *Los Angeles Herald Express*, April 10, 1952; "'Singin' in the Rain' on Screen: Gene Kelly Starring in New Musical," *Christian Science Monitor*, April 11, 1952, clipping in Box 9, Scrapbook 8, Gene Kelly Collection, BU; "The New Pictures," *Time*, April 21, 1952, "'Singin' in the Rain,' at the Empire," *New Statesman and Nation*, April 26, 1952, and "Singin' in the Rain," *Cue*, March 29, 1952, in *Singin' in the Rain* Microfiche, Core Collection, Herrick Library, AMPAS.

42. Otis L. Guernsey Jr., "A Bright Easter Package," unidentified clipping, Box 9, Scrapbook 7, Gene Kelly Collection, BU; Harrison Carroll, "Kelly, Freed Do It Again: 'Singin' in the Rain' New Musical Must," *Los Angeles Herald Express*, April 10, 1952; Dick Williams, "Singin' in the Rain," *Los Angeles Mirror*, April 10, 1952, and Arthur P. Jacobs to Gene Kelly, n.d., attached to Williams's clipping, Box 9, Scrapbook 8, Gene Kelly Collection, BU.

43. "The New Pictures," *Time*, April 21, 1952, Arthur Knight in *Saturday Review*, April 12, 1952, "'Singin' in the Rain' at the Empire," *New Statesman and Nation*, April 26, 1952, all clippings in *Singin' in the Rain* Microfiche, Core Collection, Herrick Library, AMPAS; Otis L. Guernsey Jr., "A Bright Easter Package," unidentified clipping, Box 9, Scrapbook 7, Gene Kelly Collection, BU.

44. Arthur Knight in *Saturday Review*, April 12, 1952, "Singin' in the Rain," *Cue*, March 29, 1952, and Virginia Graham in *Spectator*, April 4, 1952, all clippings in *Singin' in the Rain* Microfiche, Core Collection, Herrick Library, AMPAS; clipping from *Film Bulletin*, April 7, 1952, and "'Singing in the Rain' Gets Top Mag Tribute," *Box Office*, May 17, 1952, both in Box 22, Folder 4, Arthur Freed Collection, USC; Otis L. Guernsey Jr., "A Bright Easter Package," unidentified clipping, Box 9, Scrapbook 7, Gene Kelly Collection, BU; "Singin' in the Rain: MGM—Grand Slam Musical," clipping in Box 9, Scrapbook 8, Gene Kelly Collection, BU.

45. Barbara Derix to Freed, no date, Box 22, Folder 4, Arthur Freed Collection, USC; Doyle L. McCuller to Freed, April 16, 1952, Emil F. Vacin to Freed, April 14, 1952, Harry Ruby to Freed, April 10, 1952, Marian Thompson to Freed, April 12, 1952, Leo Genn to Freed, April 12, 1952, and Michael Keller to Gene, Don, Debbie, and Hagen, April 13, 1952, all in Box 21, Folder 1 (1 of 2), Arthur Freed Collection, USC.

46. Fordin, *M-G-M's Greatest Musicals*, 331; Wollen, *Singin' in the Rain*, 9;

Yudkoff, *Gene Kelly*, 223; Hay, *MGM*, 287; Charles Brackett quoted in Knox, *Magic Factory*, 192; Hirschhorn, *Gene Kelly*, 174.

47. Silverman, *Dancing on the Ceiling*, 169; Mariani, "Come On with the Rain," 12; Wollen, *Singin' in the Rain*, 9.

48. Kurtii, *Movie Musical Trivia Book*, 18, 28–29; *Singin' in the Rain* Awards, imdb.com; Parish and Bowers, *MGM Stock Company*, 310; Jean Hagen biography, imdb.com; Reynolds, *Debbie*, 91; Betty Comden, Adolph Green, and Stanley Donen quoted in Silverman, *Dancing on the Ceiling*, 169–170; Adolph Green in Commentary, *Singin' in the Rain*, DVD, 2002.

49. *Singin' in the Rain* Awards, imdb.com.

50. *Singin' in the Rain* Release Dates, imdb.com; clipping from *The Times* of London, April 13, 1952, *Singin' in the Rain* Microfiche, Core Collection, Herrick Library, AMPAS; Max van Wesel to Freed, April 1, 1952, Box 21, Folder 1, Arthur Freed Collection, USC.

51. Behlmer, *America's Favorite Movies*, 268; Fordin, *M-G-M's Greatest Musicals*, 362; Debbie Reynolds in *What a Glorious Feeling*, DVD, 2002.

CHAPTER 9. YOU DANCE LOVE, AND YOU DANCE JOY, AND YOU DANCE DREAMS

1. Mast, *Can't Help Singin'*, 267–268, 287; Schatz, *Genius of the System*, 448; 459; Hirschhorn, *Gene Kelly*, 182; Hay, *MGM*, 318–319.

2. Fordin, *M-G-M's Greatest Musicals*, 524, 526; Arthur Freed biography, imdb .com; Nacio Herb Brown biography and filmography, imdb.com.

3. Comden and Green, *Singin' in the Rain*, 10.

4. Adolph Green filmography, imdb.com; Kurtti, *Movie Musical Trivia Book*, 26; Richard Severo, "Adolph Green, Broadway Playwright, Dies at 87," imdb.com.

5. Adolph Green filmography, imdb.com; Kurtti, *Movie Musical Trivia Book*, 26; Betty Comden biography, imdb.com.

6. "Reminiscences of Betty Comden and Adolph Green: Oral History, 1959," 35, Oral History Research Office, Popular Arts Project, CU; Comden and Green interview with Tina Daniell and Pat McGilligan, 1989, in McGilligan, ed., *Backstory 2*, 84–85; Comden and Green, *Singin' in the Rain*, 9; Comden, *Off Stage*, 259.

7. "Hollywood Reunion," *LA Weekly*, September 20, 2002; Adolph Green biography, imdb.com; Comden, *Off Stage*, 141, 227; Betty Comden biography, imdb .com.

8. Hagen, "Jean Hagen," 9–10; Parish and Bowers, *MGM Stock Company*, 310–311; Jean Hagen biography and filmography, imdb.com; Jean Hagen on msn .com.

9. Arthur Freed to Lela Simone, September 9, 1952, Box 55, Folder 2, Arthur Freed Collection, USC; Fordin, *M-G-M's Greatest Musicals*, 382–383; Gene Kelly quoted in Kilday, "Toeing the Lion," 41.

10. Kelly, "The Women in My Dancing Life," *National Women's Weekly*, July 17, 1952; Martin and Charisse, *Two of Us*, 202–203; Thomas, "Singin' in the Rain Dancer Charisse Dies," Associated Press, June 17, 2008.

11. Reynolds, *Debbie*, 92–94, 96.

12. Ibid., 96–97; Debbie Reynolds in *What a Glorious Feeling*, DVD, 2002; Debbie Reynolds interview with Robert Osborne, *Private Screenings*, 2002.

13. *I Love Melvin*, imdb.com.

14. Debbie Reynolds filmography, imdb.com.

15. Reynolds, *Debbie*, 149, 223, 429; Debbie Reynolds interview with Robert Osborne, *Private Screenings*, 2002; Fantle and Johnson, *Reel to Real*, 93–94.

16. Reynolds, *Debbie*, 92.

17. Debbie Reynolds quoted in Hirschhorn, *Gene Kelly*, 185; Reynolds, *Debbie*, 90.

18. "Gene Kelly Interview," Marilyn Hunt, 1975, 121, 124, 250, Oral History Program, DD-NYPL; Debbie Reynolds interview with Robert Osborne, *Private Screenings*, 2002.

19. Silverman, *Dancing on the Ceiling*, 152; Debbie Reynolds quoted in *Variety*, February 7, 1996, *Singin' in the Rain* Clippings, Core Collection, Herrick Library, AMPAS.

20. Donald O'Connor filmography, imdb.com; Kurtti, *Movie Musical Trivia Book*, 19.

21. Donald O'Connor interview with Mindy Aloff, 1979, danceviewtimes.com; Michael Blowen, "Donald O'Connor," *Boston Globe*, September 28, 2003.

22. Fordin, *M-G-M's Greatest Musicals*, 424; Donald O'Connor filmography, imdb.com. When asked why O'Connor did not make more movies for M-G-M, Lela Simone said she could not understand it as he and Gene got along so well. In trying to find a reason, she speculated that either Freed or Kelly, or both, did not want him to do so. However, there is no evidence to support her off-the-cuff speculation. "An Oral History with Lela Simone," Rudy Behlmer, 1990, 210–211, Oral History Program, Herrick Library, AMPAS.

23. Donald O'Connor quoted in Variety, February 17, 1996, *Singin' in the Rain* Clippings, Core Collection, Herrick Library, AMPAS; Donald O'Connor interview with Karen Idelson, 2002, dvdfile.com. O'Connor likely would have been hurt and insulted to read the IMDB report that he "did not enjoy working with Gene Kelly." *Singin' in the Rain*, Trivia, imdb.com.

24. Transcript of Hedda Hopper interview with Gene Kelly, June 3, 1954, File 1342, Hedda Hopper Collection, Special Collections, Herrick Library, AMPAS; Hedda Hopper, "Gene Kelly Prefers to Teach," *Los Angeles Times,* July 25, 1954, clipping in Scrapbook 9, Box 10, Gene Kelly Collection, BU; Gene Kelly interview, 1988, in Singer, *A Cut Above,* 149; Gene Kelly quoted in Michael Blowen, "Donald O'Connor," *Boston Globe,* September 28, 2003; Kelly, "Dialogue on Film," 43.

25. Donald O'Connor interview with Mindy Aloff, 1979, danceviewtimes.com. For examples of other commentators who thought that O'Connor danced better than Kelly, see Morley and Leon, *Gene Kelly,* 114–115, and "Interview with Joe Barbera," Betsy Baytos, 1996, 16, Oral History Program, DD-NYPL. Morley and Leon base their conclusion on their assessment that "Make 'Em Laugh" was "an act of virtuoso dancing almost unequaled even today," ignoring the fact that there is almost no dancing in that number. Barbera too says that he liked O'Connor best as a dancer, as no one else could have done the "Make 'Em Laugh" routine.

26. "The Gene Kelly Show," an episode of *Pontiac Star Parade,* November 21, 1959, Film and Television Archives, UCLA.

27. Donald O'Connor filmography, imdb.com; "Donald O'Connor," *A & E Biography,* December 29, 1999.

28. Debbie Reynolds and Donald O'Connor quoted in Michael Blowen, "Donald O'Connor," *Boston Globe,* September 28, 2003; Morley and Leon, *Gene Kelly,* 114; Donald O'Connor interview with Mindy Aloff, 1979, danceviewtimes.com; Donald O'Connor interview, 1988, in Frank, *Tap!,* 151; Donald O'Connor in *Anatomy of a Dancer,* DVD, 2002.

29. Donald O'Connor interview with Tony Bray, 2002, tv-now.com; Donald O'Connor interview with Karen Idelson, 2002, dvdfile.com; Donald O'Connor biography, imdb.com.

30. Stanley Donen interview with Ronald L. Davis, 1983, 26, SMU/Ronald L. Davis Oral History Collection, Herrick Library, AMPAS; Silverman, *Dancing on the Ceiling,* 176, 181–183; Stanley Donen quoted in Silverman, *Dancing on the Ceiling,* 157.

31. Debbie Reynolds quoted in Silverman, *Dancing on the Ceiling,* 153; Reynolds, *Debbie,* 91.

32. Casper, *Stanley Donen,* 45; Silverman, *Dancing on the Ceiling,* 169n; Stanley Donen, "Some Guys Are Never Satisfied," clipping from an unidentified magazine, Scrapbook 9, Box 10, Gene Kelly Collection, BU. In addition to Larry Parks, Elizabeth Taylor co-starred in *Love Is Better Than Ever,* about the time that she was having a relationship with Donen. At least eight actors and crew members on that

project would soon work on *Singin' in the Rain* as well. *Love Is Better Than Ever* filmography, imdb.com.

33. Hirschhorn, *Gene Kelly*, 208–211; Fordin, *M-G-M's Greatest Musicals*, 433–434, 436.

34. Silverman, *Dancing on the Ceiling*, 211–212; Fordin, *M-G-M's Greatest Musicals*, 436–437; Stanley Donen quoted in Fordin, *M-G-M's Greatest Musicals*, 436; Stanley Donen quoted in Silverman, *Dancing on the Ceiling*, 206, 211; Stanley Donen interview with Ronald L. Davis, 1983, 31–32, SMU/Ronald L. Davis Oral History Collection, Herrick Library, AMPAS; Silverman in *Anatomy of a Dancer*, DVD, 2002.

35. Fordin, *M-G-M's Greatest Musicals*, 434–435; Silverman, *Dancing on the Ceiling*, 211–212; Gene Kelly and Stanley Donen quoted in Fordin, *M-G-M's Greatest Musicals*, 435; Michael Kidd in Silverman, *Dancing on the Ceiling*, 210; "Jack and the Space Giants," by Michael Kidd, music by Andre Previn, 1–3, Folder 921, Turner/MGM Scripts Collection, Herrick Library, AMPAS.

36. *It's Always Fair Weather*, Special Features, DVD, 2006. Kelly's attempts to get his co-stars to look their best, as with Reynolds in "Good Morning" and "All I Do Is Dream of You," and arranging solos for them, as in "Make 'Em Laugh" for O'Connor, are well known. Moreover, in contrast to Kidd's interactions with the three kids, Kelly's performances with children work extremely well, in part because one can see the genuine excitement and joy on the kids' faces. Especially noteworthy in this regard are the construction site number from *Living in a Big Way*, "I Got Rhythm" from *An American in Paris*, and the sailor dance with the boy genie from *Invitation to the Dance*. Also, Donald O'Connor has commented that "Make 'Em Laugh" was so good that others would have cut it out due to jealousy, "but not Kelly." O'Connor said Kelly kept the number because "the better it is, the better it is for him," explaining that Gene was always focused on what was good for the ultimate product, a sentiment echoed by most film historians in discussing Kelly's approach to moviemaking. Donald O'Connor in Commentary, *Singin' in the Rain*, DVD, 2002.

37. Kelly, "Dialogue on Film," 37.

38. Silverman, *Dancing on the Ceiling*, 98, 347–364; Stanley Donen filmography, imdb.com.

39. Ann Miller in "Gene Kelly," *A & E Biography*, February 3, 1996; Gene Kelly interview with John Russell Taylor, 1980, in Britton, ed., *Talking Films*, 194; Stanley Donen interview with Ronald L. Davis, 1983, 26, SMU/Ronald L. Davis Oral History Collection, Herrick Library, AMPAS; Stanley Donen quoted in Silverman, *Dancing on the Ceiling*, 213.

40. Kelly, "Dialogue on Film," 37; Gene Kelly interview with John Russell Taylor, 1980, in Britton, ed., *Talking Films*, 194–195; Gene Kelly interview with Michael Singer, 1988, in Singer, *A Cut Above*, 144; Gene Kelly interview with Graham Fuller, 1994, in Boorman et al., eds., *Projections 4*, 281. Although their age difference was only twelve years, Kelly and Donen met when Gene was twenty-eight and Stanley only sixteen, and this explains Gene's fatherly view of the younger man he took under his wing. Also, recall Betsy Blair's comment that Stanley practically lived at the Kelly house in their early years of association.

41. Stanley Donen quoted in Silverman, *Dancing on the Ceiling*, 142; Stanley Donen quoted in Casper, *Stanley Donen*, 55; Stanley Donen interview with Ronald L. Davis, 1983, 25, SMU/Ronald L. Davis Oral History Collection, Herrick Library, AMPAS.

42. Silverman, *Dancing on the Ceiling*, 90, 333–334; Stanley Donen in "Gene Kelly," *A & E Biography*, February 3, 1996; *What a Glorious Feeling*, DVD, 2002; Stanley Donen interview with Robert Osborne, *Private Screenings*, 2006.

43. Betty Garrett interview with Ronald L. Davis, 1978, 29, SMU/Ronald L. Davis Oral History Collection, Herrick Library, AMPAS; Betty Garrett quoted in Delamater, *Dance in the Hollywood Musical*, 155; Delamater, *Dance in the Hollywood Musical*, 155; Chaplin, *Golden Age*, 59; Blair, *Memory of All That*, 116; Silverman, *Dancing on the Ceiling*, 106, 142.

44. Debbie Reynolds quoted in Silverman, *Dancing on the Ceiling*, 153; Debbie Reynolds in *What a Glorious Feeling*, DVD, 2002; Donald O'Connor in Commentary, *Singin' in the Rain*, DVD, 2002; Kathleen Freeman in *What a Glorious Feeling*, DVD, 2002.

45. Assistant Director's Reports, see, for example, July 18–19, 1951, Box 21, Folder 2, Arthur Freed Collection, USC; Leslie Caron in *Anatomy of a Dancer*, DVD, 2002; Stanley Donen interview, 1973, in Harvey, "Stanley Donen," 5; Kelly, "Dialogue on Film," 37.

46. Hirschhorn, *Gene Kelly*, 192–193; Billingsley, *Hollywood Party*, 233; "Gene Kelly's Six-Way Stretch," *New York Herald Tribune*, March 22, 1953.

47. Blair, *Memory of All That*, 167–168; Fordin, *M-G-M's Greatest Musicals*, 374.

48. Fordin, *M-G-M's Greatest Musicals*, 379–382; Hirschhorn, *Gene Kelly*, 204.

49. Transcript of Hedda Hopper interview with Gene Kelly, June 3, 1954, Hedda Hopper Collection, File 1342, Special Collections, Herrick Library, AMPAS; Blair, *Memory of All That*, 191; *Invitation to the Dance*, imdb.com; Fordin incorrectly reports that the movie was released in 1957, *M-G-M's Greatest Musicals*, 396.

50. Gene Kelly interview with Michael Singer, 1988, in Singer, *A Cut Above*, 146; Blair, *Memory of All That*, 191, 228, 231–233.

51. Wollen, *Singin' in the Rain*, 45, 47–48; Morley and Leon, *Gene Kelly*, 120; Billingsley, *Hollywood Party*, 233; "Reminiscences of Gene Curran Kelly: Oral History, 1958," 20, Popular Arts Project, Oral History Research Office, CU; Ceplair and Englund, *Inquisition*, 226–228, 273, 288–291; Caute, *Great Fear*, 490, 496; Cogley, *Report on Blacklisting*, 5–6; Billingsley, *Hollywood Party*, 191–192; Barrett, *Tenney Committee*, 11, 47, 75, 363; Gene Kelly to Edward L. Barrett Jr., July 30, 1949, *Tenney Committee*, 363.

52. Matthews, *Did the Movies Really Clean House?*, unpaginated copy at Herrick Library, AMPAS; Wollen, *Singin' in the Rain*, 51; Caute, *Great Fear*, 500–504. Yudkoff, *Gene Kelly*, 222, asserts that Matthews saw communist propaganda in *Singin' in the Rain*, "the rain as perhaps a symbol of a capitalist-induced Depression; the implication that the rich studio heads were incompetent buffoons." But in fact Matthews never wrote nor implied anything of the kind. He did not even see the movie before writing his article, for *Singin'* was not shown to any audience until several weeks *after* the article was published. Matthews did nothing more than list formerly suspected Hollywood figures and note which movie projects they were currently working on.

53. Cogley, *Report on Blacklisting*, 155–157, 159; Caute, *Great Fear*, 502.

54. "Reminiscences of Gene Curran Kelly: Oral History, 1958," 20, Popular Arts Project, Oral History Research Office, CU; Gene Kelly interview with Graham Fuller, 1994, in Boorman et al., eds., *Projections 4*, 288.

55. Hirschhorn, *Gene Kelly*, 135, 216–217, 234–236; Betsy Blair quoted in Hirschhorn, *Gene Kelly*, 213; Blair, *Memory of All That*, 218, 232–235.

56. Hirschhorn, *Gene Kelly*, 191; Yudkoff, *Gene Kelly*, 218; Morley and Leon, *Gene Kelly*, 116; Basinger, *Gene Kelly*, 91; Wollen, "Cine-dancer," 3, Gene Kelly filmography, imdb.com.

57. Transcript of Hedda Hopper interview with Gene Kelly, June 3, 1954, Hedda Hopper Collection, File 1342, Special Collections, Herrick Library, AMPAS; "Reminiscences of Gene Curran Kelly: Oral History, 1958," 8, Popular Arts Project, Oral History Research Office, CU; Hedda Hopper, "Gene Kelly Would Rather Teach," *Los Angeles Times*, July 25, 1954; Gene Kelly quoted in Thomas, *Films of Gene Kelly*, 22, 24; "Dancing, a Man's Game" script, 28, Box 1, Folder 5, Gene Kelly Collection, BU; McNeil, *Total Television*, 827; Hirschhorn, *Gene Kelly*, 246, 249, 257, 263, 270; Morley and Leon, *Gene Kelly*, 160–161, 164.

58. Hirschhorn, *Gene Kelly*, 177; Flatow, "Through a Lens Brightly," 11; Thomas, *Films of Gene Kelly*, 140. Kelly wrote in a letter, around 1970, that *Singin' in the Rain* was his favorite movie among those he had worked on, "but here again I hold sentimental thoughts for quite a few others." Burrows, *Gene Kelly*, 17.

59. Barnes, "Gene Kelly & Co.," 126. Lela Simone, who worked on postproduction of *Singin' in the Rain,* was one of the few people unmoved by the magic of that dance. She called it "idiotic" that people "think that it's a great piece of art to open a water main." "An Oral History with Lela Simone," Rudy Behlmer, 1990, 97, Oral History Program, Herrick Library, AMPAS.

60. Gene Kelly, "The Women in My Dancing Life," *National Women's Weekly,* July 17, 1952; "Reminiscences of Gene Curran Kelly: Oral History, 1958," 17, Popular Arts Project, Oral History Research Office, CU; Hanson, "Interview with Gene Kelly," 24; Gene Kelly to Selma Jeanne Cohen, February 1, 1967, Box 3, Folder 13, Gene Kelly Collection, BU; "Gene Kelly Interview," Marilyn Hunt, 1975, 10, Oral History Program, DD-NYPL; Gene Kelly interview with Ronald L. Davis, 1974, 53, SMU/Ronald L. Davis Oral History Collection, Herrick Library, AMPAS; Gene Kelly interview with John Russell Taylor, 1980, in Britton, ed., *Talking Films,* 194; Gene Kelly interview, 1994, in Fantle and Johnson, *Reel to Real,* 71.

61. "Gene Kelly Interview," Marilyn Hunt, 1975, 164–165, Oral History Program, DD-NYPL; Gene Kelly interview, 1992, in "Puddle Jumper," 86; Gene Kelly interview with Gavin Millar, 1974, *An Evening with Gene Kelly.*

62. Hirschhorn, *Gene Kelly,* 203–204.

63. *Dancing: A Man's Game,* December 21, 1958, Omnibus series, and "The Gene Kelly Show," *Pontiac Star Parade,* April 24, 1959, and November 21, 1959, Film and Television Archives, UCLA.

64. *The Julie Andrews Show,* November 28, 1965, and *The Tonight Show,* November 7, 1975, May 4, 1976, and January 24, 1985, The Paley Center for Media; *Gene Kelly: An American in Pasadena,* March 13, 1978, Film and Television Archives, UCLA; *The Muppet Show,* August 19, 1980.

65. Drysdale, "Soundmatters," 63; Jack Pittman, "Kelly in London Tribute," *Variety,* June 4, 1980.

66. *The American Film Institute Salute to Gene Kelly,* May 7, 1985, Film and Television Archives, UCLA.

67. Ibid.

68. Gene Kelly notations on "Gene Kelly—Favorite Film Hits," song sheet #40, Box 27, Folder 1, and "Singin' in the Rain," song sheet #143, Box 27, Folder 3, Gene Kelly Collection, BU; Morley and Leon, *Gene Kelly,* 164.

69. Robert Osborne, "For Kelly, Pittsburgh Has a Glorious Feeling," *Hollywood Reporter,* December 30, 1999; Tom Barnes, "Pittsburgh Council Approves Site for Gene Kelly Statue," *Pittsburgh Post Gazette,* December 5, 2001; Karen Dacko, "Kelly Tribute Withstands Stormy Disagreements," *Dance Magazine,* July 1, 2002,

17; Timothy McNulty, "A Statue of Mr. Rogers Will Adorn the North Shore," *Pittsburgh Post Gazette*, March 24, 2007.

70. Debbie Reynolds in *What a Glorious Feeling*, DVD, 2002; Debbie Reynolds interview with Robert Osborne, *Private Screenings*, 2002.

71. Cyd Charisse, Donald O'Connor, Stanley Donen in *What a Glorious Feeling*, DVD, 2002.

72. Kathleen Freeman in *What a Glorious Feeling*, DVD, 2002.

CHAPTER 10. LEGACY

1. Kurtti, *Movie Musical Trivia Book*, 18, 28; Silverman, *Dancing on the Ceiling*, 169.

2. Also in 1974, BBC-TV broadcast an interview with Gene Kelly by Gavin Millar which included excerpts from "Singin' in the Rain" and "The Broadway Ballet."

3. Clipping from *Los Angeles Times*, December 27, 1974, *Singin' in the Rain* Microfiche, Core Collection, Herrick Library, AMPAS; Casper, *Stanley Donen*, 55; Vincent Canby, "A Joyously Indestructible Movie Returns," *New York Times*, May 4, 1975.

4. In 1985, *That's Dancing*, hosted by Gene Kelly, included an excerpt from "Moses Supposes" which the segment host Ray Bolger called "one of the very best tap dance routines ever put on film." *That's Entertainment III*, released in 1994 to celebrate the seventieth anniversary of M-G-M, started the Overture with an orchestral rendition of "Good Morning" followed by "Singin' in the Rain." The Overture also included "Broadway Rhythm" after a medley of other tunes. Cyd Charisse hosted a segment on Gene Kelly that included an excerpt from "Fit as a Fiddle." An excerpt from Debbie's deleted number, "You Are My Lucky Star," introduced Reynolds as the host of a segment that did not include any other references to *Singin' in the Rain*. Gene Kelly hosted the start and the end of *That's Entertainment III*. At age eighty-two, it was his last screen appearance.

5. Rex Reed review, unidentified clipping dated September, 1983, *Singin' in the Rain* Microfiche, Core Collection, Herrick Library, AMPAS.

6. Susan King, "50 Years Later, Still Singin' Praises of a Classic," *Los Angeles Times*, September 3, 2002; Wendy Wasserstein, "After 50 Years, It's Still a Glorious Feeling," *New York Times*, November 3, 2002; clipping from *Hollywood Reporter*, December 19, 2002, *Singin' in the Rain* Production File, Core Collection, Herrick Library, AMPAS.

7. *Singin' in the Rain* release dates, imdb.com; French-language version in *Singin' in the Rain*, DVD, 2002.

8. Tina Daniell, "Five Yank Pix Going to China for 1st U.S. Fest in 30 Years," *Variety* (daily), April 30, 1981; Dale Pollock, "China Picks Bland Fare in Film Choices," *Los Angeles Times*, May 2, 1981.

9. Tina Daniell, "Five Yank Pix Going to China for 1st U.S. Fest in 30 Years," *Variety* (daily), April 30, 1981; Dale Pollock, "China Picks Bland Fare in Film Choices," *Los Angeles Times*, May 2, 1981; Michael Parks, "Gene Kelly Makes a Hit with 'Singin' in Rain' in Peking," *Los Angeles Times*, May 9, 1981.

10. Wollen, *Singin' in the Rain*, 9, 52; American Film Institute, afi.com; *Singin' in the Rain*, DVD, 2002. Wollen asserts that a film's availability counts for much in critical and popular rankings over time, believing that the more often a film is shown on television or in theaters the more likely people will rank it highly. He also believes films that "deal with the process of film-making" tend to be more popular among critics.

11. *Singin' in the Rain*, user ratings, June 25, 2007, imdb.com; "Mumbai Mirror" section of *The Times of India*, Mumbai, June 15, 2007.

12. Donald O'Connor and Betty Comden on *What a Glorious Feeling* (2002); Kathleen Freeman in Commentary, *Singin' in the Rain*, DVD, 2002.

13. Altman, *American Film Musical*, 272; Wollen, *Singin' in the Rain*, 55.

14. Scheurer, "Aesthetics of Form and Convention," 309–310; Wollen, *Singin' in the Rain*, 60.

15. Basinger, *Gene Kelly*, 73, 82–83, 88; Gerstel, "Singin' in the Rain (1952)," 264–266; Ames, *Movies about the Movies*, 70; Lawrence O'Toole, "The Happy Hoofer," *Entertainment Weekly*, no. 314, February 16, 1996, 15; Casper, *Stanley Donen*, 44; Silverman, *Dancing on the Ceiling*, 170; "The Raining Champion," *The Times* (London), July 26, 2004; Behlmer, *America's Favorite Movies*, 268; Hirschhorn, *Gene Kelly*, 289.

16. Wollen, *Singin' in the Rain*, 54–55; Morley and Leon, *Gene Kelly*, 163.

17. Gerstel, "Singin' in the Rain (1952)," 266; Casper, *Stanley Donen*, 48.

18. Ames, *Movies about the Movies*, 63, 66, 68–69. At least six movies prior to *Singin'* dealt in some way with dubbing but all were obscure adventure films. See dubbing link at *Singin' in the Rain*, on imdb.com.

19. Ames, *Movies about the Movies*, 68.

20. Wollen, *Singin' in the Rain*, 53, 55.

21. Ibid., 51.

22. Thomas, *Films of Gene Kelly*, 136; Morley and Leon, *Gene Kelly*, 113; Gerstel, "Singin' in the Rain (1952)," 266; Taylor and Jackson, *Hollywood Musical*, 87–88; Mariani, "Come On with the Rain," 7; Charness, "Hollywood Cine-Dance," 97–98.

23. Frank, *Tap!*, 146; Fehr and Vogel, *Lullabies of Hollywood*, 228; Hemming,

Melody Lingers On, 328; Kobal, *Gotta Sing, Gotta Dance,* 216; Gerstel, "Singin' in the Rain (1952)," 264–265. Ironically, "Make 'Em Laugh" is an incredibly energetic routine performed as a musical number, full of acrobatics and comedy, but it is not a dance.

24. Behlmer, *America's Favorite Movies,* 268; Wollen, *Singin' in the Rain,* 59; Basinger, *Gene Kelly,* 87.

25. Basinger, *Gene Kelly,* 87; Walter Terry, "Kelly's Exhilarating Dance Tonic for April: 'Singin' in the Rain,'" *New York Herald Tribune,* April 13, 1952, clipping in Box 9, Scrapbook 8, Gene Kelly Collection, BU; Taylor and Jackson, *Hollywood Musical,* 62; Charness, "Hollywood Cine-Dance," 112–113.

26. Charness, "Hollywood Cine-Dance," 114, 130.

27. Cutts, "Kelly," pt. 2, 35; Kobal, *Gotta Sing, Gotta Dance,* 216–217; Hirschhorn, *Gene Kelly,* 190; Adolph Green reports Leonard Bernstein's comment to him after Bernstein saw the "Singin' in the Rain" dance for the first time, *Anatomy of a Dancer,* DVD, 2002.

28. Ames, *Movies about the Movies,* 66; Basinger, *Gene Kelly,* 85; Thomas, *Films of Gene Kelly,* 138–139.

29. *Singin' in the Rain,* DVD, 2002.

30. Kurtti, *Movie Musical Trivia Book,* 23; Wollen, *Singin' in the Rain,* 9; Morley and Leon, *Gene Kelly,* 110; Basinger, *Gene Kelly,* 85; Fehr and Vogel, *Lullabies of Hollywood,* 228; Gerstel, "Singin' in the Rain (1952)," 264; Tom Charity review of *Singin' in the Rain, Time Out,* London, November 22, 2000, *Singin' in the Rain* Production File, Core Collection, Herrick Library, AMPAS.

31. Arthur Freed and Nacio Herb Brown filmography, imdb.com.

32. Silverman, *Stanley Donen,* 316n; Comden and Green, *Singin' in the Rain,* 9; Hay, *MGM,* 289.

33. Casper, *Stanley Donen,* 46; Thomas, *Films of Gene Kelly,* 138; Gerstel, "Singin' in the Rain (1952)," 265.

34. *Singin' in the Rain* goofs, imdb.com.

35. *Singin' in the Rain* trivia and goofs, imdb.com.

36. *Singin' in the Rain* goofs, imdb.com.

37. Ibid.

38. Hirschhorn, *Gene Kelly,* 191; Mariani, "Come On with the Rain," 7; Casper, *Stanley Donen,* 239; Feuer, *Hollywood Musical,* 105; *Singin' in the Rain* movie connections, imdb.com.

39. Tommy Nguyen, "Breakin' in the 'Rain,'" *Los Angeles Times,* March 7, 2005; John Harlow, "Hip-Hop Kelly is Rained Off in US," *The Times* (London), March 13, 2005.

40. Kurtti, *Movie Musical Trivia Book*, 35; "The Raining Champion," *The Times* (London), July 26, 2004; "Water Babies," *Los Angeles Herald-Examiner*, May 29, 1985; Clipping from *Hollywood Reporter*, June 18, 1985, *Singin' in the Rain* Microfiche, Core Collection, Herrick Library, AMPAS. Ironically, Gene Kelly had facetiously said in 1973 that the "Singin'" number could never have been performed on stage, "because we'd wash out the orchestra pit the first time through." Gene Kelly interview with Jerome Delamater and Paddy Whannel, 1973, in Delamater, *Dance in the Hollywood Musical*, 218.

41. Clipping from *Hollywood Reporter*, June 18, 1985, *Singin' in the Rain* Microfiche, Core Collection, Herrick Library, AMPAS; Dan Sullivan, "Another Way to Ruin a Great Movie," *Los Angeles Times*, January 11, 1987.

42. "The Raining Champion," *The Times* (London), July 26, 2004; Stanley Donen filmography, imdb.com.; Mast, *Can't Help Singin'*, 263; Dan Sullivan, "Another Way to Ruin a Great Movie," *Los Angeles Times*, January 11, 1987; Kurtti, *Movie Musical Trivia Book*, 35.

43. Frank Sinatra in Hirschhorn, *Gene Kelly*, 2.

44. Ball, *Tarzan, Gene Kelly, and Me*, 6, 64, 66, 69.

45. Fantle and Johnson, *Reel to Real*, 61.

46. Shawn Hubler, "Light's Out," *Los Angeles Times*, October 14, 1990.

47. Philip French, "This Movie Changed My Life," *The Observer*, London, November 26, 2000.

48. Ibid.

49. Ibid.

50. Wendy Wasserstein, "After 50 Years, It's Still a Glorious Feeling," *New York Times*, November 3, 2002.

51. Kael, *5001 Nights*, 535.

APPENDIX. CAST AND CREW LIST AND MINI-BIOGRAPHIES

1. *Singin' in the Rain* cast and crew list, imdb.com; "Call Bureau Cast Service, 'Singin' in the Rain,'" *Singin' in the Rain* Microfiche, Core Collection, Herrick Library, AMPAS; "Fashion Show #—12 girls," MGM Wardrobe Department Records, Folder 228, Herrick Library, AMPAS.

2. Luft, *Me and My Shadows*, 206.

3. Fordin, *M-G-M's Greatest Musicals*, 425.

\\\\\ Bibliography

ARCHIVES

Academy of Motion Picture Arts and Sciences Margaret Herrick Library,
      Beverly Hills, California (AMPAS)
    Core Collection
      Singin' in the Rain Clippings File
      Singin' in the Rain Microfiche
    Oral History Program
      "An Oral History with Lela Simone," by Rudy Behlmer
      "An Oral History with Robert M. W. Vogel," by Barbara Hall
    SMU/Ronald L. Davis Oral History Collection
      Stanley Donen Interview
      Betty Garrett Interview
      Gene Kelly Interview
      Charles Walters Interview
    Special Collections
      Ron Haver Papers
      Hedda Hopper Papers
      MGM Wardrobe Department Records
      MPAA Production Code Administration Records
      Turner/MGM Script Collection
Boston University, Howard Gottlieb Archival Research Center, Boston,
      Massachusetts (BU)
    Gene Kelly Collection
Columbia University Libraries, New York, New York (CU)
    Oral History Research Office, Popular Arts Project
      "Reminiscences of Betty Comden and Adolph Green: Oral History, 1959"
      "Reminiscences of Gene Curran Kelly: Oral History, 1958"
New York Public Library, Library for the Performing Arts, New York, New York
    Oral History Program, Dance Division (DD-NYPL)
      "Gene Kelly Interview," by Marilyn Hunt
      "Interview with Joe Barbera," by Betsy Baytos
University of Arizona Libraries, Tucson, Arizona (UAL)
    Hill Collection
      David Hume, "Old Man Moses"

University of Iowa Libraries, Special Collections Department, Iowa City, Iowa (UI)
   Marion Meade/Buster Keaton Research Files
University of California, Los Angeles, Archive Research and Study Center (UCLA)
   Film and Television Archives
University of Southern California, Archives of Performing Arts and Warner
      Bros. Archives, Los Angeles, California (USC)
   Arthur Freed Collection

NEWSPAPERS, MAGAZINES, AND PRESS REPORTS
Associated Press
Boston Globe
Box Office
Christian Science Monitor
Cue
Dance Magazine
Entertainment Weekly
Everyday Magazine
Film Bulletin
Hollywood Citizen-News
Hollywood Reporter
Independent Film Journal
LA Weekly
Los Angeles Daily News
Los Angeles Herald Express
Los Angeles Herald-Examiner
Los Angeles Mirror
Los Angeles Times
Motion Picture Daily
National Women's Weekly
New Statesman and Nation
New York Herald Tribune
New York Post
New York Times
The Observer (London)
Pittsburgh Post-Gazette
Saturday Review
Spectator
Time

Time Out (London)
The Times (London)
The Times of India
Variety

VIDEOS AND DVDS

A & E Biography. "Gene Kelly," February 3, 1996, and "Donald O'Connor,"
    December 29, 1999.
The American Film Institute Salute to Gene Kelly. 1985. CBS. Viewed at Film
    and Television Archives, Archives Research and Study Center, University of
    California at Los Angeles.
Anatomy of a Dancer. American Masters. 2002. PBS. DVD.
Dancing: A Man's Game. Omnibus series. December 21, 1958. ABC. Viewed
    at Film and Television Archives, Archives Research and Study Center,
    University of California at Los Angeles.
An Evening with Gene Kelly. Interview with Gavin Millar. 1974. BBC Television.
Gene Kelly: An American in Pasadena. March 13, 1978. CBS. Viewed at Film
    and Television Archives, Archives Research and Study Center, University of
    California at Los Angeles.
The Hollywood Revue of 1929. Viewed at Film and Television Archives, Archives
    Research and Study Center, University of California at Los Angeles.
It's Always Fair Weather. 2006. Turner Entertainment and Warner Home Video,
    DVD.
The Julie Andrews Show. Viewed at the Paley Center for Media, Beverly Hills,
    California.
The Muppet Show. August 19, 1980. ATV.
Pontiac Star Parade: "The Gene Kelly Show." April 24, 1959. CBS. "The Gene
    Kelly Show." November 21, 1959. NBC. Viewed at Film and Television
    Archives, Archives Research and Study Center, University of California at Los
    Angeles.
Private Screenings. Stanley Donen Interview with Robert Osborne, 2006, and
    Debbie Reynolds Interview with Robert Osborne, 2002. Turner Classic
    Movies.
Singin' in the Rain. 2002. Turner Entertainment and Warner Home Video, DVD.
The Tonight Show. November 7, 1975, May 4, 1976, and January 24, 1985. Viewed
    at The Paley Center for Media, Beverly Hills, California.
What a Glorious Feeling: The Making of 'Singin' in the Rain.' 2002. Fitzfilm and
    Turner Entertainment.

INTERNET SITES

afi.com

denverfabrics.com

classicimages.com

danceviewtimes.com

dvdfile.com

entertainment.msn.com

ibdb.com (Internet Broadway Database)

imdb.com (Internet Movie Database)

jitterbuzz.com

larryblyden.net

news.bbc.co.uk (British Broadcasting Corporation)

thefreedictionary.com

tv-now.com

wikipedia.com

ARTICLES, BOOKS, AND DISSERTATIONS

Altman, Rick. *The American Film Musical.* Bloomington: Indiana University Press, 1987.

Ames, Christopher. *Movies about the Movies: Hollywood Reflected.* Lexington: University Press of Kentucky, 1997.

Astaire, Fred. *Steps in Time.* New York: Harper and Brothers, 1959.

Ball, Murray. *Tarzan, Gene Kelly and Me.* Gisborne, New Zealand: Diogenes Designs, 2001.

Barnes, Clive. "Gene Kelly & Co." *Dance Magazine* 70, no. 4 (April 1996): 126.

Barnes, Tom. "Pittsburgh Council Approves Site for Gene Kelly Statue." *Pittsburgh Post-Gazette,* December 5, 2001.

Barrett, Edward L., Jr. *The Tenney Committee: Legislative Investigation of Subversive Activities in California.* Ithaca, NY: Cornell University Press, 1951.

Basinger, Jeanine. *American Cinema: One Hundred Years of Filmmaking.* New York: Rizzoli, 1994.

———. *Gene Kelly.* New York: Pyramid, 1976.

Behlmer, Rudy. *America's Favorite Movies: Behind the Scenes.* New York: Frederick Ungar, 1982.

Billingsley, Kenneth Lloyd. *Hollywood Party: How Communism Seduced the American Film Industry in the 1930s and 1940s.* Rocklin, CA: Prima Publishing, 1998.

Billman, Larry. *Film Choreographers and Dance Directors: An Illustrated Biographical Encyclopedia, with a History and Filmographies, 1893 through 1995.* Jefferson, NC: McFarland, 1997.

Blair, Betsy. *The Memory of All That: Love and Politics in New York, Hollywood, and Paris.* New York: Alfred A. Knopf, 2003.

Blowen, Michael. "Donald O'Connor." *Boston Globe,* September 28, 2003.

Bradley, Fiona. "Dali (Domenech), Salvador (Flip Jacint)." *The Dictionary of Art.* Vol. 8. Ed. Jane Turner. New York: Macmillan, 1996, 464–468.

Britton, Andrew, ed. *Talking Films: The Best of the Guardian Film Lectures.* London: Fourth Estate, 1991.

Burrows, Michael. *Gene Kelly—Versatility Personified.* N.p.: Primestyle, 1972.

Canby, Vincent. "A Joyously Indestructible Movie Returns." *New York Times,* May 4, 1975.

Carroll, Harrison. "Kelly, Freed Do It Again: 'Singin' in the Rain' New Musical Must." *Los Angeles Herald Express,* April 10, 1952.

Casper, Joseph Andrew. *Stanley Donen.* Metuchen, NJ: Scarecrow Press, 1983.

Caute, David. *The Great Fear: The Anti-Communist Purge under Truman and Eisenhower.* New York: Simon and Schuster, 1978.

Ceplair, Larry, and Steven Englund. *The Inquisition in Hollywood: Politics in the Film Community, 1930–1960.* Garden City, NY: Doubleday, 1980.

Chaplin, Saul. *The Golden Age of Movie Musicals and Me.* Norman: University of Oklahoma Press, 1994.

Charness, Casey. "Hollywood Cine-Dance: A Description of the Interrelationship of Camerawork and Choreography in Films by Stanley Donen and Gene Kelly." Ph.D. Diss., New York University, 1977.

Clarke, Gerald. *Get Happy: The Life of Judy Garland.* New York: Random House, 2000.

Cogley, John. *Report on Blacklisting.* Vol. 1, *Movies.* N.p.: Fund for the Republic, 1956.

Comden, Betty. *Off Stage.* New York: Simon and Schuster, 1995.

Comden, Betty, and Adolph Green. *Singin' in the Rain.* New York: Viking Press, 1972.

Crafton, Donald. *The Talkies: American Cinema's Transition to Sound, 1926–1931.* Vol. 4, *History of the American Cinema.* New York: Charles Scribner's Sons, 1997.

Crowther, Bosley. Review of *Singin' in the Rain. New York Times,* March 28, 1952.

Cutts, John. "Kelly: Dancer, Actor, Director." *Films and Filming,* pt. 1: 10, no. 11 (August 1964): 38–42; pt 2: 10, no. 12 (September 1964): 34–37.

Dacko, Karen. "Kelly Tribute Withstands Stormy Disagreements." *Dance Magazine* 76, no. 7 (July 2002): 17.

Daniell, Tina. "Five Yank Pix Going to China For 1st U.S. Fest in 30 Years." *Variety* (daily). April 30, 1981.

Delamater, Jerome. *Dance in the Hollywood Musical.* Ann Arbor, MI: UMI Research Press, 1981.

Drysdale, Bill. "Soundmatters." *Dancing Times* (November 2001): 63, 65, 67.

Fantle, David, and Tom Johnson. *Reel to Real: 25 Years of Celebrity Interviews from Vaudeville to Movies to TV.* Oregon, WI: Badger Books, 2004.

Fehr, Richard, and Frederick G. Vogel. *Lullabies of Hollywood: Movie Music and the Movie Musical, 1915–1992.* Jefferson, NC: McFarland, 1993.

Feuer, Jane. *The Hollywood Musical.* Bloomington: Indiana University Press, 1982.

Flatow, Sheryl. "Through a Lens Brightly." *Ballet News* 6, no. 10 (April 1985): 11–15, 38.

Fordin, Hugh. *M-G-M's Greatest Musicals: The Arthur Freed Unit.* New York: Da Capo Press, 1996.

Frank, Rusty E. *Tap! The Greatest Tap Dance Stars and Their Stories, 1900–1955.* New York: William Morrow, 1990.

French, Philip. "This Movie Changed My Life." *The Observer* (London), November 26, 2000.

Fuller, Graham. "An American in Paradise: Gene Kelly Interviewed by Graham Fuller." *Projections 4: Film-makers on Film-making.* Ed. John Boorman, Tom Luddy, David Thomson, and Walter Donohue. London: Faber and Faber, 1995, 277–289.

Gale, Matthew. "De Chirico, Giorgio." *The Dictionary of Art.* Vol. 8. Ed. Jane Turner. New York: Macmillan, 1996, 602–606.

Genné, Beth. "The Film Musicals of Vincente Minnelli and the Team of Gene Kelly and Stanley Donen: 1944–1958." Ph.D. Diss., University of Michigan, 1984.

———. "'Freedom Incarnate': Jerome Robbins, Gene Kelly, and the Dancing Sailor as an Icon of American Values in World War II." *Dance Chronicle* 24, no. 1 (2001): 83–103.

Gerstel, Judy. "Singin' in the Rain (1952)." *The A List: The National Society of Film Critics' 100 Essential Films.* Ed. Jay Carr. New York: Da Capo, 2002.

Goodwin, George, ed. *Song Dex Treasury of Humorous and Nostalgic Songs.* New York: Song Dex, 1956.

Hagen, Ray. "Jean Hagen." *Film Fan Monthly* 90 (December 1968): 7–11.

Hale, Wanda. "'Singin' in Rain' at Music Hall." *Los Angeles Daily News,* March 28, 1952.

Hanson, Curtis Lee. "An Interview with Gene Kelly." *Cinema* 3, no. 4 (December 1966): 24–29.

Harlow, John. "Hip-Hop Kelly Is Rained Off in US." *The Times* (London), March 13, 2005.

Harvey, Stephen. "Stanley Donen." *Film Comment* 9, no. 4 (July-August 1973): 4–9.

Haver, Ron. "Kelly." *Film Comment* 20, no. 6 (December 1984): 56–59.

———. "Pas de Deux with Saul Chaplin." *American Film* 10, no. 5 (March 1985): 23–26, 73.

Hay, Peter. *MGM: When the Lion Roars*. Atlanta: Turner Publishing, 1991.

Hemming, Roy. *The Melody Lingers On: The Great Songwriters and Their Movie Musicals*. New York: Newmarket Press, 1986.

Higham, Charles. *Merchant of Dreams: Louis B. Mayer, M.G.M., and the Secret Hollywood*. New York: Donald I. Fine, 1993.

Hill, Constance Valis. *Brotherhood in Rhythm: The Jazz Tap Dancing of the Nicholas Brothers*. New York: Oxford University Press, 2000.

Hirschhorn, Clive. *Gene Kelly: A Biography*. New York: St. Martin's Press, 1984.

Holtzman, Will. *Judy Holliday*. New York: G. P. Putnam's Sons, 1982.

Hopper, Hedda. "Gene Kelly Prefers to Teach." *Los Angeles Times,* July 25, 1954.

Hover, Helen. "Popping Questions at Gene Kelly." *Motion Picture* 68, no. 3. (October 1944): 40–41, 91–94.

Hubler, Shawn. "Light's Out." *Los Angeles Times,* October 14, 1990.

Jacobs, Jack, and Myron Braum. *The Films of Norma Shearer*. South Brunswick, NJ: A. S. Barnes, 1976.

Kael, Pauline. *5001 Nights at the Movies: A Guide from A to Z*. New York: Holt, Rinehart & Winston, 1982.

Kelly, Gene. "Dialogue on Film." *American Film* 4, no. 4 (February 1979): 33–44.

———. "The Women in My Dancing Life." *National Women's Weekly,* July 17, 1952.

Kilday, Gregg. "Toeing the Lion: Gene Kelly of 'That's Entertainment! III.'" *Entertainment Weekly* 222 (May 13, 1994): 41.

King, Susan. "50 Years Later, Still Singin' Praises of a Classic." *Los Angeles Times,* September 3, 2002.

Knox, Donald. *The Magic Factory: How MGM Made An American in Paris*. New York: Praeger, 1973.

Kobal, John. *Gotta Sing, Gotta Dance: A History of Movie Musicals*. London: Spring Books, 1988.

———. *Rita Hayworth: The Time, the Place and the Woman*. New York: W. W. Norton, 1978.

Kreuger, Miles. "The Birth of the American Film Musical." *High Fidelity and Musical America* 22, no. 7 (July 1972): 42–48.

———. "Dubbers to the Stars: Or, Whose Was That Voice I Heard You Singing With?" *High Fidelity Magazine* 22, no. 2 (July 1972): 49–54.

Kurtti, Jeff. *The Great Movie Musical Trivia Book.* New York: Applause Books, 1996.

Levant, Oscar. *The Memoirs of an Amnesiac.* Hollywood: Samuel French, 1989.

Luft, Lorna. *Me and My Shadows: A Family Memoir.* New York: Simon and Schuster, 1998.

Mariani, John. "Come On with the Rain." *Film Comment* 14, no. 3 (May-June 1978): 7–12.

Martin, Tony, and Cyd Charisse. *The Two of Us.* New York: Mason-Charter, 1976.

Mast, Gerald. *Can't Help Singin': The American Musical on Stage and Screen.* Woodstock, NY: Overlook Press, 1987.

Matthews, J. B. "Did the Movies Really Clean House?" *American Legion Magazine* (December 1951): 13, 49.

McCaffrey, Donald W., and Christopher P. Jacobs. *Guide to the Silent Years of American Cinema.* Westport, CT: Greenwood Press, 1999.

McGilligan, Pat. *Backstory 2: Interviews with Screenwriters of the 1940s and 1950s.* Berkeley: University of California Press, 1991.

McNeil, Alex. *Total Television: A Comprehensive Guide to Programming from 1948 to 1980.* New York: Penguin, 1980.

McNulty, Timothy. "A Statue of Mister Rogers Will Adorn the North Shore." *Pittsburgh Post-Gazette,* May 24, 2007.

Meade, Marion. *Buster Keaton: Cut to the Chase.* New York: Harper Collins, 1995.

Minnelli, Vincente. *I Remember It Well.* New York: Samuel French, 1990.

Morley, Sheridan, and Ruth Leon. *Gene Kelly: A Celebration.* London: Pavilion Books, 1996.

Mueller, John. *Astaire Dancing: The Musical Films.* New York: Knopf, 1985.

Nguyen, Tommy. "Breakin' in the 'Rain.'" *Los Angeles Times,* March 7, 2005.

Osborne, Robert. "For Kelly, Pittsburgh Had a Glorious Feeling." *Hollywood Reporter,* December 30, 1999.

O'Toole, Lawrence. "The Happy Hoofer." *Entertainment Weekly* 314 (February 16, 1996): 15.

Parish, James Robert, and Ronald L. Bowers. *The MGM Stock Company: The Golden Era.* New Rochelle, NY: Arlington House, 1973.

Parks, Michael. "Gene Kelly Makes a Hit with 'Singin' in Rain' in Peking." *Los Angeles Times,* May 9, 1981.

Pasternak, Joe. *Easy the Hard Way.* New York: G. P. Putnam's Sons, 1956.

Pittman, Jack. "Kelly in London Tribute." *Variety,* June 4, 1980.

Pollock, Dale. "China Picks Bland Fare in Film Choices." *Los Angeles Times,* May 2, 1981.

Previn, Andre. *No Minor Chords: My Days in Hollywood.* New York: Doubleday, 1991.

"Puddle Jumper." *People Weekly* 37, no. 23 (June 15, 1992): 86.

"The Raining Champion." *The Times* (London), July 26, 2004.

Reynolds, Debbie, with David Patrick Columbia. *Debbie, My Life.* New York: William Morrow, 1988.

Schatz, Thomas. *The Genius of the System: Hollywood Filmmaking in the Studio Era.* New York: Pantheon Books, 1988.

Scheurer, Timothy E. "The Aesthetics of Form and Convention in the Movie Musical." *Journal of Popular Film* 3, no. 4 (Fall 1974): 307–324.

Siegel, Joel. "The Pirate." *Film Heritage* 7, no. 1 (Fall 1971): 21–32.

Silverman, Stephen M. *Dancing on the Ceiling: Stanley Donen and His Movies.* New York: Alfred A. Knopf, 1996.

Singer, Michael. *A Cut Above: 50 Film Directors Talk about Their Craft.* Los Angeles, CA: Lone Eagle, 1998.

Sullivan, Dan. "Another Way to Ruin a Great Movie." *Los Angeles Times,* January 11, 1987.

Taylor, John Russell, and Arthur Jackson. *The Hollywood Musical.* New York: McGraw-Hill, 1971.

Terry, Walter. "Kelly's Exhilarating Dance Tonic for April: 'Singin' in the Rain.'" *New York Herald Tribune,* April 13, 1952.

Thirer, Irene. "'Singin' in the Rain' Fine Fun." *New York Post,* March 28, 1952.

Thomas, Bob. "Singin' in the Rain Dancer Charisse Dies." Associated Press, June 17, 2008.

Thomas, Tony. *The Films of Gene Kelly: Song and Dance Man.* Secaucus, NJ: Citadel Press, 1974.

Wasserstein, Wendy. "After 50 Years, It's Still a Glorious Feeling." *New York Times,* November 3, 2002.

Watts, Stephen. "On Arranging Terpsichore for the Camera Eye." *New York Times,* September 14, 1952.

Wayne, Jane Ellen. *The Leading Men of MGM.* New York: Carroll and Graf, 2005.

Williams, Dick. "Singin' in the Rain." *Los Angeles Mirror,* April 10, 1952.

Wollen, Peter. "Cine-dancer." *Sight and Sound* (London) 6, no. 3 (March 1996): 3.

———. *Singin' in the Rain.* London: British Film Institute, 1992.

Yudkoff, Alvin. *Gene Kelly: A Life of Dance and Dreams.* New York: Back Stage Books, 1999.

\\\\\ Index